The Impoverished Superpower

The Impoverished Superpower

Perestroika and the

Soviet Military Burden

Edited by
Henry S. Rowen
and Charles Wolf, Jr.

ICS PRESS

Institute for Contemporary Studies
San Francisco, California

This book developed from a conference held at the Hoover Institution on March 23–24, 1988, on the role of the defense sector in the Soviet economy. The conference was the first of the biennial symposia on this subject planned jointly by the RAND Corporation and the Hoover Institution. The editors, Henry S. Rowen and Charles Wolf, Jr., wish to acknowledge the generous support and encouragement for this effort received from the Pew Charitable Trusts, the Olin Foundation, and the Department of Defense.

Inquiries, book orders, and catalogue requests should be addressed to ICS Press, Institute for Contemporary Studies, 243 Kearny Street, San Francisco, CA 94108. (415) 981–5353. FAX: (415) 986–4878.

The analyses, conclusions, and opinions expressed in ICS Press publications are those of the authors and not necessarily those of the Institute for Contemporary Studies, or of the Institute's officers, directors, or others associated with, or funding, its work.

Distributed to the trade by National Book Network, Lanham, Maryland.

Library of Congress Cataloging-in-Publication Data

The Impoverished superpower: perestroika and the Soviet military burden / edited by Henry S. Rowen and Charles Wolf, Jr.
      p.   cm.
    Includes bibliographical references.
    ISBN 1-55815-066-8 (paper)
    ISBN 1-55815-070-6 (cloth)
    1. Soviet Union—Armed Forces—Appropriations and expenditures
—Economic aspects. 2. Soviet Union—Economic conditions—1976– 3. War
—Economic aspects—Soviet Union. 4. Perestroika. 5. Soviet Union—Politics
and government—1986– I. Rowen, Henry S.
II. Wolf, Charles, 1924–
    UA770.I55 1989
    338.4'3355'00947—dc20   89–29818
                                                      CIP

Contents

List of Tables

List of Figures

Foreword

HOW SMALL is Soviet national income, and what effect does its size have on Soviet military power? In this book thirteen of the most innovative and respected experts in the field examine the relationship between the Soviet economy and its military. Their conclusions put *perestroika* in an entirely different light.

For years we have known that the Soviet economy is in bad shape. But precisely how bad has been the subject of bitter controversy in the West. Soviet economic statistics are notoriously inaccurate; most consider them to be worse than fiction. *The Impoverished Superpower* confirms what a few iconoclast economists have long believed: Soviet national income, generally thought to be about half that of the United States, is in fact less than a third. That puts the Soviet military burden at as much as 25 percent of GNP, compared with the U.S. burden of around 7 percent. The implications are stunning. Gorbachev's efforts to overhaul Soviet society may be a desperate final battle to save a fundamentally unbalanced system. The West may finally be in a position to deal with the Soviets on its own terms.

Ten years ago, following the Soviet invasion of Afghanistan and the seizing of Americans in Iran, the Institute for Contemporary Studies commissioned a study by the nation's most distinguished strategic thinkers, including Richard R. Burt, Fred C. Iklé, Edward N. Luttwak, Paul H. Nitze, Sam Nunn, and Henry S. Rowen. *National Security in the 1980s*, edited by W. Scott Thompson, argued that the United States had allowed its defenses to decline even as the power of its principal adversary grew. The book made a strong case for actions that would move the nation from weakness to strength. These policies were the basis of the Reagan administration's military buildup during its first term. That buildup, we believe, made it impossible for the Soviet Union to hold its strategic advantage over the West: attempting to do so would surely have resulted in an economic burden unacceptable even by Soviet standards. *The Impoverished Superpower*, therefore, shows the indirect effects of policies of strength.

The question today, of course, is whether the Soviets will proceed with military reform as they restructure their economy. *The Impoverished Superpower* shows that the Soviets conceive of their military in an entirely different way than Western nations do, and it does not necessarily follow that Soviet economic crisis means Soviet disarmament. The West should look for hard evidence, not rhetoric, that confirms what we hope: that the firm resolve of the West has made the world a safer place.

Robert B. Hawkins, Jr., President
Institute for Contemporary Studies

San Francisco
October 1989

Henry S. Rowen &
Charles Wolf, Jr.

Introduction

I N THE YEARS since Mikhail Gorbachev took office, the West has come
to understand that the Soviet economy is in very poor shape. During
that period, Gorbachev began to speak of a "pre-crisis" condition existing
in his country. In the book *Perestroika*, Gorbachev noted that by the latter
half of the 1970s "the country began to lose momentum. Economic
failures became more frequent. . . . growth rates . . . by the beginning of
the eighties had fallen to a level close to economic stagnation."[1]

Soviet Economic Performance

In the new era of *glasnost*, many Soviet economists have published books
and articles describing and analyzing the crisis in Soviet economic
performance in detail. Even earlier, some were able to publish technical,
less broadly critical articles that were at variance with official positions,
including K. K. Val'tukh, G. Khanin, V. Krasovskii, and V. K. Fal'tsman.
Abel Aganbegyan, probably the most visible Soviet economist in the
West, asserts in his *Economic Challenge of Perestroika* that "in the period
1981–85 there was practically no economic growth," and that "during

Henry S. Rowen is assistant secretary of defense for international security affairs, on leave
from his position as professor of business policy at Stanford University's Graduate School
of Business. Charles Wolf, Jr., is dean of the RAND Graduate School and director of
RAND's economic policy research. They are the editors of *The Future of the Soviet Empire*,
published by ICS Press.

the period 1979–82 . . . production of 40 percent of all industrial goods actually fell" and "agriculture declined."[2] In 1987 the attack on official Soviet statistics was dramatically escalated by an article in the Soviet publication *Novy mir* by Vasilii Seliunin and Grigorii Khanin asserting that Soviet national income statistics from 1928 on had grossly overstated actual performance.[3] The authors instead offered their own estimates, which Richard Ericson analyzes in this volume. Seliunin and Khanin may have made the biggest public splash, but there have been many other critics, including Nikolai Shmelev, Leonid Abalkin, Oleg Bogomolov, and Alexander Zaichenko. These criticisms finally evoked a response from the Politburo, which decreed, according to the April 3, 1987, issue of *Pravda*, that there was a need for "an increase in the effectiveness and publicity of statistical information, of a rationalization of responsibility, of the necessity for absolute reliability and accuracy." This bureaucratic language can be construed as saying: "We have serious problems with our national statistics, which apparently have overstated our economic performance, that urgently need fixing."

We should pause a moment and ask, Is this gloom about the economy exaggerated, designed by Gorbachev to blacken the (already tarnished) reputations of his predecessors, intended to make his achievements look better and to soften up the West? This is a plausible interpretation of a politician's actions—especially one who holds Lenin to be the supreme model of a leader—but as several contributors to this book observe, we are not wholly dependent on sources under Soviet government control. For example, émigrés since the late 1970s have consistently reported that living conditions worsened after the mid-1970s. Western visitors and residents can see living conditions for themselves, which are about comparable to those of a relatively well off Third World country. Western engineers and businessmen have also been able to see something of the workings of Soviet industry, and they report very low levels of productivity.

We should also ask why the Soviet leadership has been behaving recently in ways that may reduce its military power, weaken its influence in Eastern Europe, stimulate latent desires for independence in many of its republics, cause its citizens to question the legitimacy of the system, and put its future in question. The answer, evidently, is that *not* to embark on such a risky path is considered even more dangerous. To be sure, one should not attribute all of the motivation for change to poor economic performance: The Afghan war, environmental degradation, rigidification of the social structure, and the awful dreariness of life in the Soviet Union doubtless all contributed. But these conditions would have been much less pressing had the economic welfare of the population been improving. The picture that emerges on the state of the economy is bleak:

- Official statistics are biased highly upward and generally unreliable.

- Inflation in the investment sector has been substantial, and much of the growth reported in capital investment in the 1970s and early 1980s did not occur.

- Inflation has been widespread throughout the economy, much of it hidden through the manipulation of fictitious quality improvements in products.

- Real growth has been much less than officially reported, and somewhat less than generally estimated in the West, with near-stagnation since the mid-1970s.

- The state now admits that it has a large budget deficit, around 10 percent of gross national product (GNP).

- Conditions in housing, health care, nutrition, and the environment are deplorable.

- Soviet officials now admit that previously reported military spending covered only a small portion of actual military spending.

These failings are not news to Western experts, although their scale and intensity have been widely underestimated. They are significant because the evidence comes increasingly from Soviet sources, and the performance portrayed is even worse than that previously described by Western experts. There have been controversies among these experts on many issues, including the level of capital investment and of consumption, rates of growth, and the cost of the military. But by and large, these new sources of information support those who have held a pessimistic view of Soviet performance.

A case in point is the controversy over the growth in Soviet investment, in which several British economists—Alec Nove, Philip Hanson, and Peter Wiles—have been pitted against, among others, Abram Berg-son. Boris Rumer's chapter concludes that for many years there has been little growth in capital investment—in effect, that the British experts have been right. As for the current situation, it is fundamentally different from that set for 1989 in the Twelfth Five-Year Plan, which intended an increased injection of funds into machine-tool building, automation technology, and other high-tech branches. The consumer sector of the economy had, according to tradition, been relegated to second place. But the crisis in consumer goods—the most serious in the postwar history of the country—is dangerous for Gorbachev, and has forced him to reallocate investment since 1988 toward housing construction and mod-ernization and the expansion of the capacity of light industry and the food-processing industry. Chaos is growing in the highly inert invest-ment sphere of the Soviet economy; the system cannot cope with such spasmodic changes in investment policy.

Anders Åslund's chapter reinforces the position, held by the émigré economist Igor Birman, that by the late 1980s Soviet personal consump-tion was in the range of 20 to 25 percent the U.S. level per capita, rather than the higher level of 28 to 43 percent (depending on the currency used as a measure) estimated by Imogene Edwards and Gertrude Schroeder for the late 1970s.[4]

Also at issue is the overall size of the Soviet economy. The relevant estimation method, pioneered by Irving Kravis and his co-workers and applied to countries at widely different levels of development, measures purchasing-power parity. Although this technique carries with it a wide range of uncertainty, especially when applied to nonmarket economies, it can nonetheless prove useful. A widely quoted Central Intelligence Agency (CIA) estimate puts Soviet GNP in 1985 at around 55 percent that of the United States, about 47 percent the U.S. level per capita.[5] Robert Campbell estimated a much lower ratio, around 37 percent per capita (with a large range of uncertainty), for 1980.[6] Åslund, in this volume, puts it still lower, at about 30 percent of U.S. GNP per capita for the late 1980s. Even this estimate might be too high.

One might ask what difference it makes if Soviet aggregate output grew little, if any, after the late 1970s, instead of at 2 to 3 percent annually; or whether it matters that Soviet GNP is, say, a third that of the United States or the European Community instead of a half. First of all, these are not trivial differences: A 2 percent difference in annual growth rates amounts to a 35 percent difference over fifteen years and 100 percent over thirty-six years. Second, no growth per capita over time—if that is indeed the case—together with no realistic prospect for future improvement, is a more plausible impetus for radical change than continued slow improvement. Third, given that we have independent evidence on the scale of the Soviet military effort, a substantially smaller Soviet economy implies that the share of resources taken by the military is larger than we had believed. This finding requires us to reassess the Soviet Union's ability to sustain its military competition with the West; it also provides evidence of strong motivation for reducing the Soviet military and changing its foreign policy.

The Soviet Military and the Cost of Empire

Analysis of the role of the defense sector in the Soviet economy entails both specific technical issues and broader security and policy questions relating to the structure of the system. At the narrower, technical level, analysis of the defense sector's role involves measurement of its size, including the militarily relevant activities usually left out of Western estimates, and also the cost of maintaining the Soviet empire. Here we are interested principally in the Soviet national security system broadly defined, the size of the Soviet economy as a whole, and the so-called defense burden ratio between them. As we have suggested, and as several of the chapters that follow report in detail (especially those of David F. Epstein, Norbert D. Michaud, and D. Derk Swain), estimating accurately both the numerator—the cost of the defense sector and the Soviet empire—and the denominator, or Soviet GNP, presents formidable problems. Our general, but tentative and admittedly controversial, conclusion is that the numerator has generally been underestimated and the denominator overestimated in most previous work. Consequently, we believe that the burden of the Soviet defense sector on the economy is appreciably higher than has been estimated by most Western analysts.

At the broader, policy level, the defense sector's huge share of the economy relates to the fundamental character of the Soviet system, to the extent that a large and highly developed military sector is an inherent characteristic of communist systems. For example, studies by Charles Wolf and Benjamin Zycher comparing communist and noncommunist systems show that there is much more military spending in the communist systems, many more people in the armed forces, and a higher level of military than of civil technology.[7] Several hypotheses can be advanced to account for this, but whatever the explanation, it seems quite clear that Marxist-Leninist systems generally show a marked tendency to accord their systems' military establishments relatively high priority and favored treatment in comparison with that granted by other political systems. (Some of these special characteristics are discussed in the chapters by Christopher M. Davis and by Arthur J. Alexander.) Consequently, a major decline in the priority of the military in the Soviet Union may translate into fundamental changes in the communist system itself; to put it another way, major changes in the Soviet system may be essential if there is to be markedly less emphasis on military power, and if that lower priority is to persist.

Spending on the military and on the Soviet empire abroad is the most important sector of the economy about which there has been little *glasnost*. Recently, Soviet officials have acknowledged that research and development (R&D) and procurement were excluded from the published military budget. Data released since June 1989 purport to include these large categories of outlays. But there is considerable evidence indicating that the new figures still substantially underestimate the real resources absorbed by the military.

There have also been public statements that military spending needs to be curtailed. Indirect evidence has been supplied by senior military officers' statements on the allegedly disastrous effects of Khrushchev's unilateral cuts in the late 1950s, which are clearly intended as warnings against any repetition of that policy by Gorbachev. Articles have also appeared expressing support for a professional and smaller military establishment. Clearly there has been an intense, mostly private, debate under way.

One outcome of this internal process has been the announcement by Gorbachev at the United Nations in December 1988 that the Soviet Union would reduce its existing military manpower by 10 percent (500,000 men), including ten tank divisions, half of which would be withdrawn from Eastern Europe. It is not clear from Gorbachev's announcement exactly how much of the manpower reduction would be in the form of active military servicemen, and how much would represent a reduction of authorized but unfilled manpower slots. Later he made it known that military spending and weapons production would be cut by 14.2 percent and 19.5 percent, respectively. In June 1989 Prime Minister Nikolai Ryzhkov announced that Soviet defense spending totaled 77.3 billion rubles, about 9 percent of GNP. This is about half the 15 to 17 percent level estimated by U.S. intelligence agencies (in 1982 rubles). Ryzhkov also said that the share spent on defense would be cut by a third to a half by the end of 1995. Too fine a parsing of these numbers seems unwarranted; the outcome might be a small shift in resources (say 1 to 3 percent of GNP) or a somewhat larger one.

To understand the economic benefits of such a reduction in defense spending or, retrospectively, the economic retardation caused by the long military buildup under Brezhnev, we need to consider to what extent the serious plight of the Soviet economy (which few have characterized in starker terms than Gorbachev himself) is due to the large defense share, and to what extent it is instead attributable to the shortcomings of the Soviet system itself. Clearly, both elements are responsible; the issue is determining their relative influence, a difficult task conceptually and empirically. The share directly attributable to the defense sector is more complex than is suggested by the familiar tradeoff between "guns and butter." At issue also is the relationship between "guns" and the structure of Soviet industry, infrastructure, and R&D, as well as the relationship among them over time. One does not need the explanation of a huge military burden to explain poor economic performance; the debilitating effect of the centrally planned command system on incentives, innovation, competition, and productivity is sufficient, as illustrated by the sorry condition of the Eastern European and Chinese economies despite their lower ratios of military spending.

More precisely, suppose the share of the Soviet military and empire were to be reduced from, say, 25 percent of GNP to 15 percent, with the saved resources reallocated equally between consumption and investment, but *with no other changes in the Soviet system*. What effect would such a major reduction in the size of the defense sector have on consumption and economic growth? One can assess such changes through the use of models of the kind described in Gregory G. Hildebrandt's chapter. Here we present some of the relevant magnitudes.

If we assume, as suggested earlier, that the Soviet GNP is about one-third that of the United States (or about US$1.7 trillion in 1989 dollars), that Soviet consumption is about 55 percent of GNP, and that the Soviet population is 280 million and growing at a rate of about 1 percent per year, the effect of this relatively large resource reallocation would be modest. Soviet consumption per capita is currently about $3,000, or about 25 percent of the U.S. level and about equal to that of Turkey or Mexico. Transferring, say, 5 percent of Soviet GNP to consumption would represent an increase in consumption of 9 percent. Assuming that the defense spending cuts and ensuing resource reallocations were spread over a four-year period, the resulting annual increase in aggregate consumption would be about 2.25 percent, and in per capita consumption about 1.25 percent. The annual increase in per capita consumption would be about $40 a year, accumulating to $165 over the four-year period. Moreover, this would represent a one-time boost in consumption, which would thereafter remain at the same level. Reallocating the remaining half of the 10 percent cut in military spending to investment and R&D—again assuming that the Soviet system otherwise remained unchanged—might add 1 percent to the annual rate of Soviet real economic growth. If this growth were sustained, further growth in consumer welfare would ensue as well.

While these are only rough approximations, they at least give an idea of the results of reallocating resources from military to nonmilitary uses without accompanying changes in the Soviet system itself. Altogether, they would give a boost to the economy, but would hardly transform it.

What would be the effects, on the other hand, of fundamental changes in Soviet economic institutions through genuine price reform, enterprise reform, property ownership, monetary reform, and currency convertibility, assuming only minor changes in the size of the defense sector? What would be the economic effects, apart from the possible political and social turbulence, that such drastic reform would set in motion? Would the burst of effort and energy released by the new environment propel the economy forward at a high and sustained rate, or would the still-massive size of the defense sector continue to exercise a severe braking effect on productivity and real economic growth?

Such systemic changes would transform the economy, but the maintenance of a huge military sector would clearly slow the process. Of course, the policy options open to the Soviet leadership are not this sharply drawn. Some military reductions might be seen as making an early and critical contribution toward motivating cynical workers, while most systemic changes would take many years to be felt. And there are other options, such as importing more goods from the West. It is likely that the Soviet leadership will pursue various combinations of reduced defense, increased imports, and gradual systemic reform rather than relying on any one of these options alone. The economic outcome as well as the political consequences are somewhere between uncertain and unfathomable.

A serious problem for Western leaders is that they do not know the base from which Soviet defense reductions will occur. There has been continued controversy, as noted earlier, over the magnitude of Soviet military spending, a controversy that we will not explore in detail here.

Suffice it to say that Western governments, especially the United States, can estimate the physical components of Soviet forces, presumably with fair reliability; the difficulty comes in estimating the cost of these forces. Various methods have been applied: the CIA's "direct costing" method; William Lee's attribution of the residual from the output of machinery ministries (after the deduction of known civilian goods) to weapons production; and Dmitri Steinberg's conclusion that value added in the defense production sector is excluded from Soviet national income accounts, and others. Some analysts (Lee, Steven Rosefielde) have concluded that Soviet military spending has been underestimated, and some (Franklyn Holzman) that it has been overestimated.

Epstein, in his chapter, does not enter this argument on the usual field of battle. Instead he addresses the scope of coverage of such estimates, and provides estimates of relevant categories omitted from the usual accounting. Over the past several years, the need for a broader scope of accounting has become evident, and has long been urged by Andrew Marshall, Director of Net Assessment of the Defense Department. Marshall argues that Soviet merchant ships also serve as naval auxiliaries, at additional costs in construction and operation; that Aeroflot is a branch of VTA, the Soviet military airlift fleet; that civil defense and the heavy costs of the "deep underground" program for leadership protection are omitted from the standard accounts; and much more. In general, the military gets preference in the Soviet shortage economy, while others go short, as discussed in Davis's chapter. There are, to be sure, offsetting influences in the form of military help with harvests and military work on dual-use projects (the Baikal-Amur Mainline railroad, for example), but the net effect is, as Epstein estimates, a heavy burden on the economy.

Another relevant category of defense spending is the cost of maintaining the Soviet empire abroad. The costs of supporting Cuba, Vietnam, Ethiopia, and Angola are borne principally to extend, and protect challenges to, Soviet power. So too are the costs of the overseas operation of the KGB. These costs have been estimated by Wolf and others at the RAND Corporation at about 3 percent of Soviet GNP in the mid-1980s. Epstein concludes that the share of Soviet GNP spent on security, using a broad definition, is 22 to 28 percent, a range that incorporates the 1987 CIA and the Defense Intelligence Agency (DIA) estimate of military spending, narrowly defined, of 15 to 17 percent of GNP. Such a high level is extraordinary, usually observable only in nations at war.

Which definition to use, broad or narrow, depends on the question at issue. If it concerns a comparison of the costs of fielding the American versus the Soviet military using some common metric—say, dollars—then the narrow definition is probably appropriate. If, in contrast, the question is the cost of maintaining the Soviet position of power in the world—that is, what resources are diverted from consumption, investment, education, health, housing, etc., to support the Red Army, the four other military services, Cuban troops in Angola, the communist states of Vietnam and Nicaragua, and what Gorbachev refers to as the "old thinking" in Soviet foreign policy—then a broad definition is more pertinent. Given the Soviet Union's economic crisis, the broad definition seems more relevant; the West's focus on the narrow definition has failed to convey the weight of the military-empire burden that the Soviet leadership must recognize and the public must feel.

How does this share of spending compare with that of the United States? In a democracy, such expenditures must be accounted for and approved by legislatures and be made public (although efforts are made to keep some details secret). For the United States, a broad definition that includes Department of Energy expenditures on nuclear weapons, security assistance, intelligence activities, the U.S. Information Agency, etc., in fiscal year 1989 comes to around $330 billion, about 6.5 percent of GNP. Similarly, our North Atlantic Treaty Organization allies and Japan spend between 1.5 and 5 percent of their GNPs on defense activities. The differences between these ratios and that of the USSR are huge.

Measuring the Soviet Military and Economy

Most of the basic empirical work that has been done to estimate the size and growth of the Soviet economy has made use of the adjusted factor-cost (AFC) methods developed by Bergson and his followers in the 1950s and 1960s and further refined since. Estimation of the size of the Soviet defense sector and its conversion into equivalent U.S. dollars has followed the building-block method described in Swain's chapter. While this method is meticulous and valuable as far as it goes, it suffers from serious shortcomings, beginning with the questionable assumption that official Soviet statistics on net material product reflect, in the aggregate, the cost of productive factors involved in generating a product. The AFC method proceeds by subtracting from each sector's product the sum of enterprise profits and "lump-sum taxes" paid to the state, and then redistributing this sum over all sectors of the economy in accordance with their estimated respective capital stocks. This "adjustment" does not affect the size of the product estimate, but rather its relative distribution across economic sectors. Thus, the AFC method does not account for the substantial differences between the reported costs of the factors of production and their "real" economic or opportunity costs. Nor does it account for the indirect and largely hidden costs imposed by the high priority accorded some sectors, notably the military (as described in the chapters by Stephen M. Meyer and by Davis), and the low priority accorded others, such as health care.

It is easier to criticize the AFC method than to design practical improvements. One possibility is to use several different, reasonably independent measures of the Soviet national product as cross-checks. For example, one might begin with physical production estimates from official Soviet sources, since these are presumably more trustworthy than ruble estimates, which involve the unreliability of ruble prices. The physical output of both defense and nondefense sectors might then be evaluated by relating them to the market prices for these goods—or similar categories of goods—on foreign markets. For example, Soviet cars are sold in Belgium and India; Soviet tractors and earth-moving equipment and machinery appear in other markets (especially in the developing countries); and Soviet military hardware trades on foreign markets at prices that can be ascertained by comparing the prices of Soviet and U.S. military equipment in various international arms-market journals. Independent estimates are made for some sectors such as the production of Soviet weapons and Soviet grain. Edwards and Schroeder have also compared consumption levels in the Soviet Union and the United States. We suggest that these types of comparison be extended.

One might use, along these lines, Gregory Grossman and Vladimir Treml's estimates, in their pioneering work on the Soviet underground economy, of what they call "legitimate state income" to arrive at estimates of real consumption.[8] Those estimates might then be supplemented by an independent estimate of grain production and other measures of per capita diet and caloric intake. Such preliminary measures of the consumption component of the Soviet national product would in turn need to be supplemented by estimates of producers' durable-goods output, which might be obtained from émigrés, Western businessmen, and information published in increasing amounts in the Soviet Union. Another approach is to take the existing AFC estimate made by the intelligence community and adjust it with information from published reports of losses and waste, hidden inflation, and quality deterioration, a course pursued by Vladimir Kontorovich in connection with the investment-goods sector of the Soviet economy.

By pursuing several independent methods for approximating the Soviet product—or at least substantial components of it—we may be better equipped to check our estimates against one another and against official figures. Furthermore, if *glasnost* proceeds in conjunction with *perestroika,* the availability of data for pursuing these various lines of inquiry and improving estimates of the role of the defense sector in the Soviet economy should expand significantly.

Finally, our knowledge of the Soviet economy and its defense sector, although it has improved modestly, remains inadequate, posing a substantial barrier to improved economic relations on the one hand and to confidence in arms-control agreements on the other. The Soviet government needs to make progress on both of these fronts, and it is thus in the leadership's own interest to be more forthcoming with information. Moreover, unless and until such information emerges, the United States and the West should be properly skeptical of high-powered Soviet rhetoric that stresses "new thinking," intended military cuts, and defensive reconfiguration of military forces without decisive actions and evidence that confirm these changes.

Anders Åslund

How Small Is Soviet National Income?

"If it is better than in 1913 then it is already good."

—The late Soviet comedian Arkadii Raikin,
quoted in *Izvestiia*, October 12, 1986.

IT IS A TIME of re-evaluation in the world of Soviet statistics. Since Mikhail Gorbachev became general secretary in 1985, ever more data and new assessments have appeared in Soviet print on a broad range of statistical issues. At all major institutes, economists pose serious objections to official figures; the most devastating criticism was presented by Vasilii Seliunin and Grigorii Khanin in the literary journal *Novy mir* in February 1987.[1] Official Soviet statements are increasingly acknowledging statistical shortcomings. In July 1987 the Central Committee of the Communist Party of the Soviet Union (CPSU) and the Council of Ministers adopted a decree with the terse title, "On Measures for a Fundamental Improvement of the State of Statistics in the Country."[2] A new quantitative perspective on the Soviet economy is emerging.

Extensive work has been undertaken in the West to reassess Soviet national accounts. The pathfinding studies by Abram Bergson, Abraham

Anders Åslund is associate professor at the Stockholm School of Economics and the author of *Gorbachev's Struggle for Economic Reform*.

Becker, the Central Intelligence Agency (CIA), and others deserve credit for developing systems of measurement that have made alternative assessments possible. CIA estimates are the natural Western point of reference, as they are calculated each year, but they have never been undisputed. Igor Birman, Alec Nove, Peter Wiles, Philip Hanson, and Michael Ellman have criticized the CIA for various exaggerations; others, notably Steven Rosefielde and Michael Boretsky, have argued that CIA estimates have been too low.[3] Another useful source is a recent World Bank study that generates somewhat lower estimates of Soviet income than does the CIA.[4] All Western calculations must be based on Soviet statistics, however, and it is not obvious which are best.

A Westerner intuitively expects the resource-rich Soviet Union to be relatively well off because it has the world's largest output of such products as oil, gas, steel, and cement. However, living in Moscow from 1984 until 1987 and traveling extensively in the country, I became ever more aware of its low level of economic development. The country's pattern of consumption corresponds to that of a reasonably well developed Third World country—what the World Bank calls "upper-middle-income economies." On the basis of 1976 Soviet statistics, Gertrude Schroeder and Imogene Edwards concluded that "the Soviet pattern [of consumption] . . . differs considerably from the composition of consumption in Hungary and most closely resembles that in Poland, Spain, and Portugal. The Soviet pattern in many respects conforms to that in the less developed countries, and remarkably little progress toward a more modern pattern has been made in recent decades."[5] Those decades were the 1950s and 1960s, the only period after the New Economic Policy that showed a substantial improvement in consumption. These observations are difficult to reconcile with the CIA assessment that Soviet gross national product (GNP) per capita, "converted at U.S. purchasing power equivalents," amounted to $8,370 in 1986, or 49 percent the U.S. level.[6]

Relative to the early 1970s, the contemporary Soviet economy appears stagnant or possibly even declining. The major Soviet complaint about the Brezhnev period is that the economy became stagnant soon after 1970. Academician Abel Aganbegyan has corroborated the situation in several statements:

> The statistical data concerning the increase in national income and the gross output do not sufficiently take into account the real increase in prices, particularly for consumer goods, equipment, and construction and installation work. Therefore, the [official] rates of increase in the

national income . . . for the Tenth and Eleventh Five-Year Plans [1976–1985] are too high. In reality, for a number of years, especially 1979–1982, the actual growth of the national economy came to a halt and there was stagnation.[7]

In *The Economic Challenge of Perestroika,* Aganbegyan has indicated that the national income did not grow from 1981 to 1985.[8] He has also hinted: "We have not simply marked time, but, I would say, in many ways fallen backwards."[9] A letter writer complains to *Ogonek* that

after the 27th Congress of the CPSU the period in our history linked with L. I. Brezhnev's activity began to be called the period of "stagnation." In my view, this term is absolutely incompatible with the situation in our country at that time. "Stagnation" can be applied to something immobile or, at least, that lacks movement forwards. The standard of living and the social and ideological spheres clearly slipped back in that period. This part of our history ought more appropriately to be described as "pre-crisis."[10]

In contrast, the CIA estimates average GNP growth of 2.4 percent a year from 1971 to 1985, and 1.9 percent a year even from 1981 to 1985.

What picture do the CIA figures actually offer? Harry G. Schaffer has used them as evidence of "truly impressive economic and social achievements," which he contrasts with Marshall Goldman's statement, "The Soviet Union in the post-Brezhnev era confronts an economic disaster on a vast scale. In virtually all sectors of the economy, evidence of stagnation, waste, and mismanagement proliferates."[11] It is Goldman who conveys the ordinary Soviet perception. Similarly, a reader of the *New York Times* comments on an article displaying CIA statistics, "There is a subtle inconsistency between the text of the . . . article . . . and its supporting statistical data . . . . The accompanying data for the Soviet Union . . . seems to indicate that, for the economy at least, things aren't quite so bad."[12]

If the CIA assessments had been reasonably accurate, the Soviet economy would be a maturing industrialized economy, as was stated in the American debate not long ago. There would be little need for a radical economic reform; Gorbachev's urgency would be incomprehensible; and most internal criticism in the Soviet Union would be unfounded. The high CIA estimates have been an important reason for the failure of most Western analysts to predict and understand the earnest craving for economic reform on the part of much of the current Soviet leadership.

This chapter provides a broad, critical examination of assessments of Soviet national income and its growth rate. The literature on this topic is immense; we shall focus on recent Soviet additions,[13] guided by Alec Nove's words, "Models need to be checked against the plausibility of their results and the (relevant) degree of realism of their assumptions."[14] Our ambition is to give a plausible indication of the magnitude of Soviet national income and its growth rate.

Methodological Pitfalls in Soviet Statistics

All assessments must be based on official Soviet statistics. The issues concern which ones to choose, how to process them, and how to assess the outcome. Fundamental questions arise over all statistics: What are their purposes? Who produces them? How are they controlled? We are not concerned with the distribution of blame for any flaws; our concern is the accumulated distortions.

Soviet statistics have two proclaimed uses: they are "not only an instrument for economists but also arms in the hands of propagandists and agitators."[15] The propaganda theme is taken very seriously by the statistical authorities (previously TsSU, the Central Statistical Administration, and since the summer of 1987, Goskomstat, the State Committee for Statistics).[16] Propaganda efforts are regularly emphasized in official statements on statistics.[17] Goskomstat's journal, *Vestnik statistiki*, even has a regular section entitled, "To Aid Agitators and Propagandists."

In spite of greater openness and poor economic results, Goskomstat continues its propaganda of Soviet success. The official NMPp (Net Material Product produced) in "comparable prices" grew by only 2.3 percent in 1987—a marked decline from an official increase of 4.1 percent in 1986. Yet Goskomstat's chairman, Mikhail A. Korolev, greeted the 1987 economic results with the statement that *perestroika* had "already begun to produce positive results," while belittling shortcomings and remarking that "there is a shortage of certain food products in a number of places."[18] His first deputy, Nikolai Belov, followed suit in a comment reported by TASS, the Soviet news agency, comparing an obviously inflated figure of 3.3 percent growth in GNP with Western growth rates, admitting simply, "It is not everywhere that the *perestroika* work was up to the spirit of the times."[19] Iurii Rytov, an economic journalist of insight and integrity, concluded more accurately that "the results cannot satisfy anyone," and posed the question: "What are the reasons for the failures?"[20] The Soviet press is hardly a beacon of truth, but in recent years it has seemed more interested in truth than has Goskomstat. Stephen Shenfield, analyzing Goskomstat's methodology, concludes: "Analytical work generally relies exclusively on very simple mathematical techniques."[21] Goskomstat's adversity to criticism and complexity is richly illustrated by the crude responses mobilized by *Vestnik statistiki* after Seliunin and Khanin's devastating criticism of Soviet statistics.[22]

Goskomstat's predecessor, TsSU, was a very weak authority. A frequent, faulty assumption has been that it was in charge of all statistics. On the basis of interviews with Soviet émigrés who had dealt with statistics, Shenfield concluded: "Particularly important enterprises (defense industry, some heavy industry) submit report data directly to the higher territorial level of TsSU (Republic, Union)."[23] This practice gave TsSU little control. For a long time, foreign-trade statistics have been the monopoly of the Ministry of Foreign Trade. One of Goskomstat's first demands was "the centralization of statistics on foreign economic relations to the statistical organs."[24] The construction industry is even more independent. The State Committee on Construction (Gosstroi) sets tariffs, estimates the value of construction, and elaborates construction statistics. Not surprisingly, no price index is calculated.[25]

Even where TsSU managed to acquire information directly, it was rarely able to control it. Contrary to common assumptions, planning was not based on TsSU's data: "Gosplan [the State Planning Committee] relies for its data requirement primarily on its own system for collecting and processing data. Data from TsSU are not considered very appropriate for planning purposes, and are used mainly when there is no other convenient source of data available."[26] A main reason for transforming the statistical office into a state committee was to improve its ability to control statistics.[27]

There is a conspicuous imbalance between the forces that want to boost results and the monitoring authorities. Soviet enterprise directors and ministers have been admonished to raise gross output at any price. Various tactics have been deployed, such as the manipulation of prices, production mix, quality, and classification.[28] Administrators at all levels are judged on their ability to reach output targets. It is of little importance whether targets are achieved through a real increase in production or through hidden inflation. G. A. Kulagin notes from his own experience that "there was no authority actually interested in opposing this tendency. Neither the producer, nor the consumer, nor even the Ministry of Finance showed interest in the stabilization and lowering of prices."[29] The Ministry of Finance benefits from price rises through larger revenues for the state budget. The State Price Committee (Goskomtsen) has limited authority to check prices, but the Soviet industrial nomenclature embraces about 24 million to 25 million different products, and Goskomtsen confirms about 200,000 prices every year, which means that three to four prices per Goskomtsen employee are set every day.[30] Academician Nikolai Fedorenko observes that "in the majority of cases [the price] that the producers propose is confirmed."[31]

The outspoken former chairman of Goskomtsen, Nikolai Glushkov, commented on the producers' practice of inflating price proposals that they "do not carry the responsibility for such an effect and calculations appear overstated by 30 to 50 percent . . . . As a result of controls undertaken and [consultations with] expertise, one-third of the proposed wholesale prices submitted for approval to Goskomtsen of the USSR is reduced by 20 to 30 percent, and for individual kinds considerably more."[32] A plausible interpretation of Glushkov's vague statement is that the approved wholesale price of a new commodity is inflated, on average, by about 28 percent.[33] The vast majority of prices are set by lower organs, which have minimal interest in limiting inflation.[34] The rest are controlled by few organs apart from the economic-crime branch of the police and the KGB, whose capacity appears very limited in this area. They cannot check inflation.[35] The decree on price formation adopted July 17, 1987, reinforces price controls through a unified price-control system, stricter checks, and economic sanctions against transgressors. This is not a cure, but it does represent a clear judgment on the insufficiency of current controls.[36]

Even when it is fully in charge, Goskomstat often prefers propaganda to information. Methodological notes are minimal, and there are a huge number of inconsistencies. As Bergson showed in his classic study, index-number tricks are exploited unscrupulously to raise national income figures.[37] Cases of double statistics do exist, contrary to conventional wisdom. According to three senior Soviet economists, no serious economist would use the published retail price index, because it is not based on prices actually paid. TsSU has calculated a second retail trade index, with average prices, which it uses for the deflation of retail sales.[38]

Soviet economic science as a whole is in a terrible state.[39] When propaganda became the main purpose of statistics, there was little request for sophistication. Contemporary price indexes are based on the listed prices of a certain group of commodities known to both producers and price authorities. No commodity baskets or sampling are used, and a proper consumer price index has not been attempted.[40] In short, producers firmly control Soviet statistics. Their aim is to boost recorded achievements so that output targets are attained with little endeavor. There is no serious control of delivered statistics. The central statistical authorities assist in exaggerating achievements, and their level of scientific sophistication is deplorable. It is difficult to say at what points they cheat and when they are cheated themselves. All major economic institutes in the USSR are involved in deflating statistics that are particularly important to them. Here, we shall discuss four major sources of statistical flaws: faulty reporting of physical data, material losses and extensive use of inputs, quality deterioration, and hidden price increases.

Western recalculations of Soviet statistics assume that Soviet physical output data, with the possible exception of agriculture, are reasonably accurate. But according to the Soviet scholar Aleksei Sergeev, the Soviet control organs estimate that 1.5 to 3.0 percent of production volume is fraud (*pripiski*) and is not produced, while he assumes that fraud accounts for a "considerably larger" share of the production volumes reported. In the raw material–producing sectors of the economy, "according to some calculations of economists, fraud accounts for 5 to 25 percent of the production a year."[41] Iurii Chernichenko describes how 20 percent of some of the wheat harvested consists of rubbish, weeds, and moisture.[42] Even a softer Western assumption that these aberrations remain constant over the years—"the law of equal cheating"[43]—appears doubtful. Michael Ellman has suggested that the degree of exaggeration rose in the period 1979–1982; similarly, Aganbegyan suggests that exaggeration of the official growth rate gradually increased after 1970.[44] Leonid Ivanov shows how the exaggeration of physical data on the production of meat and grain has grown since 1985.[45]

These conclusions can be generalized. First, this kind of fraud is likely to increase from year to year in line with the "ratchet principle." Boris Milner of the Institute of Economics writes: "To get accustomed to 'small' frauds is like economic narcotics. It quickly leads to the decay of management and deception on a large scale."[46] Second, revelations of fraud are likely to be more frequent when a national campaign is waged and personnel shaken out on an almost national scale, as is the case with *perestroika*. The state of Uzbekistan has won renown for its fraudulent reporting of the cotton harvest. During the six years from 1978 to 1983, the exaggeration of state procurement of cotton has been estimated officially at 4.5 million tons—12.7 percent of the officially reported state purchases of cotton during that period.[47] Milner cites the coal mining association Rostovugol', where "fraud reached 7 million to 8 million tons of coal—a fourth of the fuel it extracts."[48]

Material losses are extraordinary in production, transport, and storage. In Soviet national accounts, material losses, together with the foreign-trade balance, should be deducted from net material product produced (NMPp) in order to achieve net material product used (NMPu). Robert Campbell has investigated NMPu for 1970-1980 and arrived at deductions for material losses in the narrow interval of 2.9 billion to 5.7 billion rubles a year— slightly more than 1 percent of NMP on average.[49] This seems to be a plausible interpretation of Soviet statistics, but all other evidence suggests larger losses.

In agriculture particularly, material losses have attracted attention. Mikhail Lemeshev of the Central Economic-Mathematical Institute (TsEMI) has stated: "At present, losses in agriculture according to different estimates and different crops comprise from 20 to 50 percent of the harvest every year."[50] The new Soviet leaders have repeatedly discussed this problem. In June 1985, Gorbachev acknowledged that "almost a fifth of the grown harvest is lost."[51] According to Fyodor Kushnirsky, the actual waste of grain amounts to 30 percent, and the "waste and spoilage of fruits and vegetables are in excess of 60 percent."[52] Obviously, products are spoiled under any system, but the scale of Soviet spoilage is extraordinary. These problems afflict other branches of the economy as well, though probably to a lesser extent. For instance, the chairman of Goskomtsen, Valentin Pavlov, has noted that "a quarter of fertilizers produced simply doesn't reach the consumer."[53] Similarly,: "40 percent of the energy that is consumed in nonferrous metallurgy goes to waste," though it is unclear if this is a reference to sheer waste or inefficiency.[54]

A related problem is excessive hoarding of (primarily industrial) inputs. At the end of 1986, this amounted to 470 billion rubles, which corresponded to about 80 percent of the official NMPp.[55] About 40 percent is labeled "frozen assets" that are not likely to be used since they are located in the wrong place. Leonid Abalkin has pondered these stocks: "The warehouses are overloaded with unnecessary production, and [enterprises] continue to produce more and more of it: for the sake of the growth rate! If we take the growth rate in industry, there is an enormous intermediary product 'sitting' in it."[56]

Equipment decays outdoors or becomes obsolete before it is installed: "Equipment for nuclear power stations is installed *on average* three to four years after delivery to the site."[57] Fedorenko stated in 1981: "The construction periods for production projects reach ten to fourteen years, which exceeds by four or five times the installation time for analogous objects in industrialized countries of the West."[58] On October 1, 1986, TsSU estimated the share of unsalable goods in retail trade at 3.6 percent of total stocks in retail and wholesale trade.[59] "In Armenia, conclusions have been drawn, but peculiar ones—mountains of defective shoes were simply destroyed."[60] The amount of unsalable goods is likely to be heavily understated, for the authorities have little interest in sorting such commodities out.

An even worse problem is the excessive use of inputs in production. A steady complaint is that too much attention is given to intermediary production. On the one hand, gross output is exaggerated in fraudulent reports; on the other, material losses are large and inputs inefficiently used. Both reduce output, but it is difficult to distinguish between their effects. According to Fedorenko's 1981 article, "For one unit of final product in the USSR, 1.75 times more steel, 2.3 times more concrete, 1.6 times more mineral fertilizers, and 1.5 times more timber is utilized than in the USA."[61] Similarly, according to the Institute for World Economy and International Relations (IMEMO) calculations (presumably for 1986), the Soviet Union uses 1.8 times the working capital, 1.6 times the material inputs, 2.1 times the energy, and 2.0 times the transport the United States uses to produce one unit of final product. Yet these figures grossly overstate the efficiency of the Soviet economy. On the basis of official Soviet statistics, Seliunin has calculated that in 1983 the Soviet Union produced 2.2 times more oil, 3.7 times more pig iron, 3 times more steel, and 2.9 times more concrete than the United States per unit of national income.[62] These numbers give us only a vague sense of what is plausible. All of Seliunin's figures are much higher than Fedorenko's and IMEMO's, although they are based on exaggerated official assessments. Similarly, Gavriil Popov estimates: "For one worker, 2 to 2.5 times more industrial territory is used (all-inclusive) in this country than is the practice abroad."[63]

All these comparisons are understated because they use inflated Soviet assessments of national income in comparison with its U.S. counterpart. The political pressure in the Soviet Union to overstate economic achievement is great. A critical article in *Sotsialisticheskaia industriia*, castigating the new minister of Car Industry, Nikolai Pugin, illustrates prevailing practices: "The preparatory commission [of the Supreme Soviet] asserts in its report that the labor productivity in the branch is 4 to 6 times lower than in developed capitalist countries, but the minister says 1.5 to 2 times."[64]

The United Nations' Economic Commission for Europe (ECE) regularly calculates the energy intensity of production as the ratio of primary energy consumption to gross domestic product; it estimates that Soviet energy intensity was 3.3 times that of Western Europe in 1984, and that this disparity has increased steadily since the energy crisis.[65] Similarly, the steel intensity of the Soviet economy has been estimated at 3.2 times that of Western Europe in 1980.[66] When Western factories are reproduced in the Soviet Union as turnkey projects, the Soviet labor force tends to be three to four times as large as that of an identical factory in the West. *Pravda*'s economic editor Vasilii Parfenov notes: "The Mogilev factory produces electrical engines of one brand. An analogous Italian factory produces as many engines of eight different types. Nevertheless, at the factory in Mogilev 3,500 people work, but at the foreign enterprise—900."[67]

The famous chemical plant in Shchekino offers a similar example: "The [Western] consultants recommended a workforce of 278, but when the plant went into operation, the actual total staff was 806."[68] Capacity utilization is surprisingly low. Seliunin cites the use of electrical engines: "In the West, an engine is utilized on average more than 3,000 hours a year; here, 1,250 hours."[69] Aganbegyan notes, "Our park of machine tools is more than twice as large as the U.S. park of machine tools."[70] He has also pointed out that the USSR has 4.5 times as many tractors as does the United States. An odd official statistic is that in 1986 the Soviet Union got 27.5 tons of paper and carton out of 1,000 cubic meters of delivered timber, while Finland got 153 tons and Sweden 144—more than five times as much.[71]

Although the use of inputs is already inefficient, it is growing ever worse. Nikolai Fedorenko has depicted the following development for 1971–1980: "Every percent of growth in the national income . . . demanded an increase in productive funds of 1.4 percent, in material costs of 1.2 percent, and in labor of 0.2 percent."[72] Gavriil Popov and V. Novikov estimate that "the branch organization diminishes the efficiency of the economy by 1.5 to 2.5 times."[73] Their belief that a relatively minor change could boost efficiency so much is an indication of how inefficient they consider current Soviet production. It appears that the CIA gives the production of inputs great weight in its calculation of

Soviet GNP, even more so than does the TsSU. This is especially evident in estimates of performance for 1985 and 1986 (as discussed in Appendix Section 1).

A picture emerges of an enormously wasteful production process. There are no data that allow a precise overall assessment, but the Soviet production apparatus seems to need something like three times the basic inputs (raw materials, capital, and labor) that a modern Western economy uses to produce the same physical quantity of output—and that says nothing of quality comparisons.

Various Types of Inflation

Soviet and Western economists seem to agree that there is significant inflation in the Soviet economy—that official statistics understate it, that inflationary pressures have grown since the economic reforms of 1965, and that it has resulted in open as well as hidden inflation. Using Mario Nuti's definitions, we distinguish among three kinds of inflation: *open inflation*, officially recognized in national accounts; *hidden inflation*, which is a differential between official price indexes and actual inflation; and *repressed inflation*, the rise in excess demand (a flow variable).[74]

Khanin's view that wholesale prices rose significantly in the periods 1928–1940 and 1966–1980, but little in 1951–1960, is probably representative.[75] Repressed inflation has risen since 1971.[76] Gregory Grossman has shown that the financial flow did not abate when the growth rate fell drastically in 1979.[77] As a result, inflationary pressures soared both in the enterprise and cash sectors, as many indicators suggest. According to a Soviet estimate for 1988, the deficit in the state budget currently amounts to about 15 to 17 percent of budget revenues.[78] From 1970 to 1985, the official NMPp in actual prices doubled, while the amount of outstanding bank loans more than quadrupled.[79] (In the same period, total stocks rose by 184 percent in current prices.[80] Aganbegyan points out that stocks have grown twice as fast as production in recent years; equipment stocks in particular are estimated to have tripled between 1976 and 1984.)[81] On December 1, 1987, private bank deposits amounted to 257.4 billion rubles, compared with 46.6 billion rubles in 1970 and 156.5 billion rubles in 1980.[82] As Academy of Sciences member Nikolai Petrakov of TsEMI has put it: "As a result, a situation has been created that is well known to every manager: the least scarce resource is money."[83] The shortages are so great that the words *sell* and *buy* have largely been replaced by *give* and *take* in current spoken Russian, indicating a general perception of unequal exchange.

Since our interest is in the inflation of national accounts, we limit our observations to actual inflation, which has two components, open (official) inflation and hidden inflation. It must be remembered, however, that repressed inflation seeks outlets. Academician Stanislav Shatalin reasons:

> One of the difficult practical questions is the separation of the inflationary component from economic growth. It is composed of a [wide range] of factors: an increase in prices of new products exceeding the real improvement in quality; the deterioration of quality at unchanged prices; partial growth of the average price of a commodity; [and] an increase in the share of high [turnover] taxes, which is rather characteristic of a shortage economy.[84]

The problem with the pricing of new products is well known. Soviet price indexes are based on a fixed set of commodities. A new commodity is unlikely to be included in the price index group, which is rarely changed, or if it is included, it is not compared with commodities it replaces. Western recalculations of Soviet national accounts have focused on the effects of this phenomenon, which can be neatly estimated: "A slight change of a detail and a commodity receives the index 'N' [for "novelty"], and it becomes up to 20 percent more expensive. About a third of the whole production of light industry is marked by the index 'N'.[85] Gorbachev expressed his view of pricing practices at the Central Committee Plenum in June 1986: "Overstated prices based on the cost approach conceal shortcomings in the technology and organization of production and engender neglect for the search for rational ways of running the economy."[86] Aganbegyan gives an example: "A big robot costing 40,000 to 50,000 rubles replaces workers with an annual wage of less than 4,000 rubles. It works unreliably and demands certain costs for repairs and service."[87]

Some price increases are defended on the grounds of alleged, but not necessarily actual, improvements in quality. The prominent journalist Anatolii Rubinov expresses sound Soviet skepticism: "An increase in prices has never led to anything good."[88] An inevitable result is that the quality of these commodities, whose quality has not been officially improved, declines. A typical example was the introduction of a new, "better," and certainly more expensive bread in 1986, immediately followed by the deterioration of the quality of other breads.[89]

A characteristic phenomenon, frequently pinpointed in Soviet newspaper articles, is the disappearance of cheap products and the emergence of new, expensive ones. This is particularly common in light industry.[90] Kushnirsky notes: "Firms tend to discontinue production of inexpensive products with relatively low rate of profitability. Such inflation—through alterations of product mix—in terms of 'constant permanent prices' usually escapes both base-year and current-year weighted price indexes."[91] This inflation is in the interest of not only producing enterprises and their peers, but other authorities as well:

> At present the turnover tax is basically paid by industrial enterprises, or in the best case by wholesale trade. As a result, a completely intolerable situation has been created, as the financial organs, exploiting their enormous influence, try to achieve only production of "tax-intensive" commodities and their advancement to wholesale trade, without concern for their eventual sale to the population.[92]

Alec Nove has generalized: "In any system, when price control exists and the product mix can be varied, the price index will *always* understate price rises, and its use will lead to an overstatement of growth rates."[93]

Shatalin's second concern, the deterioration of quality at unchanged prices, has been essentially neglected in Western recalculations. Soviet economists Aleksandr Bim and Aleksandr Shokhin note that "at excessive demand (a result of low retail prices) the quality of commodities deteriorates and tendencies to a second turnover of foodstuffs appear."[94] Some Western economists who observe the actual state of affairs do pay attention to the deterioration of quality. Thus, Nuti writes: "The persistence of a seller's market depresses quality of goods and keeps producers out of touch with consumers' wishes . . . ."[95] Soviet émigrés are especially sensitive to this factor.[96]

V. Tolstov has investigated how Soviet branch authorities attempt to change state standards to justify lower quality.[97] The usual outcome is a gradual downgrading of quality until some major administrative intervention is undertaken. Tolstov conveys this picture in his almost weekly "commercial review" in *Izvestiia*.[98] "After having deteriorated its production, the enterprises in the vegetable oil industry did not lose anything but only gained an easier life, as the actual wholesale and retail prices remained unchanged, and there was markedly less trouble."[99] Producers slowly chip away at any quality that remains. It is striking to any traveler how much higher the quality of goods is in Eastern Europe than in the USSR— particularly in Hungary—although quality in East-ern Europe is much worse than in the West. The command system appears to aggravate quality ever more the longer it prevails, but the CIA assumes the opposite on the grounds of technological development, better education and training, and general development optimism. Technological development does occur, but according to Aganbegyan,

> We have in many cases a terrible [quality]. Year after year we lose our former advantages and positions here. We remember the fifties. Yes, our things were not so beautiful and not so fashionable as foreign ones, but instead, any of ours was more long-lasting .... But how is it now? It is a terrible matter: more than 2,000 times a year color television sets catch fire only in Moscow. Together with them the houses burn.[100]

According to I. I. Isaev, Deputy Chairman of the State Committee for Standards (Gosstandart), 14.2 percent of total (presumably industrial) production conforms with current world standards.[101] Nikolai Shmelev of the Institute of the USA and Canada writes that "according to the most cautious and pessimistic" estimates, only 7 to 8 percent of Soviet manu-facturing production corresponds to world standards.[102] There are few products outside the military-industrial complex (which includes space projects) that correspond to world standards. Appendix Section 2 pres-ents a fuller discussion of the low quality of Soviet products.

With few exceptions, Western calculations make the poor assump-tion of constant or improving quality.[103] The CIA assumes "the quality problem mainly affects our index of industrial production."[104] But the problem appears to be more pervasive. In agriculture, particularly, quality deterioration is considerable. A more realistic approach on the basis of conclusions by Benedykt Askanas and Kazimierz Laski, would be to assume about 2 percent overall quality deterioration each year.[105] This would give us a completely new perception of the Soviet economy. Gorbachev's constant focus on the damage caused by low quality ap-pears to be entirely merited.

Deception in Soviet Statistics

Any investigation into Soviet statistics uncovers a great deal of inconsis-tency, ambiguity, and outright fraud. According to the official statistical yearbook, 1,671,000 cars were sold to the population in 1986.[106] Yet the Soviet production of cars in 1986 amounted to 1,326,000, of which 306,000 cars were exported.[107] Imports of cars were almost infinitesimal. Thus, 651,000 more cars were sold than were available—64 percent more! Apparently, commission sales of second-hand cars are included in the number of cars sold, but the statistical yearbook offers no clarification.[108]

After several calculations based on Soviet foreign-trade statistics, Thomas A. Wolf and Ed A. Hewett concluded, "This analysis does create new doubts regarding the internal consistency and reliability of these statistics, and it also raises new questions about how Western analysts attempt to estimate the magnitude of Soviet arms deliveries to the Third World."[109]

One of the most confused branches of the economy is road transport, where inefficiency and fraud prevail. Aganbegyan described the situation: "Why are we producing so many lorries, while only two-thirds of them work? Yes, and only in one shift. Half of the lorries run empty. . . . And if they carry goods, then it is only within the limit of 75 percent of their capacity."[110] Seliunin and Khanin paint an even starker picture: "Checks by the control organs show that the actual volume of transports by the lorries comprises only 20 to 30 percent of what is shown in the accounts."[111]

Agricultural statistics engender similar confusion. In particular, data on meat production form a maze of inconsistent statistics that resists disentanglement (Appendix Section 3). On the basis of sales statistics at actual prices and state prices for state, cooperative, and *kolkhoz* (collective farm) market sales, one can calculate an implicit price index for the cooperative and private sectors in relation to the state sector. For foodstuffs, we find that *kolkhoz* market prices were supposed to have been 137 percent higher than state prices in 1985, which sounds quite possible. But cooperative prices of foodstuffs were allegedly only 5 percent higher than state prices, which is impossible.[112] A great many observations around the country show that they must in fact be about twice as high, given the observed price relations and the apparent dominance of meat sales in the cooperatives. It is all too obvious that statistics on agricultural produce, consumption, retail sales, and prices are utterly inconsistent and unreliable.[113]

The confusion grows even greater when we approach the most aggregated economic measurements. The national income, or NMPp, is defined as "the sum of net production of separate branches of material production. The net production of individual branches is calculated as the difference between gross production and material production costs."[114] Furthermore,

> The net production is evaluated at actual sale prices of individual enterprises and farms of their production in the given period; at sales through different channels, every part is evaluated at the sale price of the given channel. Thus, the production of agriculture that is delivered to the state as procurements is valued at state procurement prices; production sold to the state as [free] purchases at [state] purchasing prices; production sold at the *kolkhoz* market is valued at *kolkhoz* market prices.[115]

Notably, this means that the whole turnover tax is included in the NMP, so if turnover tax revenues rise, so does NMP; and if turnover taxes decline, NMP is reduced. However, these procedures were tacitly abandoned in 1985 and 1986, as Philip Hanson and Jan Vanous have shown.[116] The great puzzle in 1985 and 1986 was that NMPp in current prices grew by merely 1.6 and 1.5 percent, respectively, while NMPp in comparable prices purportedly rose by 3.5 and 4.1 percent, respectively (Table 1.1).[117] Thus, the "NMPp deflator" amounted to –1.9 percent in 1985 and –2.6 percent in 1986, which contradicts all observations: no price decreases worth mentioning took place, while there were a number of noticeable price increases. Hanson and Vanous located the source of the discrepancy in retail sales of alcohol, which fell drastically in both 1985 and 1986—by as much as 37 percent in 1986—but had been excluded from NMPp growth in "comparable prices."[118] Only NMPp in current prices was calculated in accordance with its definition in this regard. The reason for the strange values of the NMPp deflator since 1985 is that the NMPp in comparable prices has been redefined without notice, which amounts to intentional falsification. The calculation of the NMPp deflator reveals the trick. Appendix Section 4 details the problem with the 1985 and 1986 figures.

Soviet economist M. Siuniaev implicitly verified Hanson and Vanous's thesis and suggested a transition to factor prices in national income accounts in order to avoid influences from vacillating turnover tax revenues and prices on the world market. Others have concluded that hidden inflation caused by rising turnover tax revenues grew from the early 1970s until 1984. From 1970 until 1980, when NMP at current prices rose by 59 percent, turnover tax revenues increased by 90 percent, but they declined from 102.7 billion rubles in 1984 to 91.5 billion rubles

TABLE 1.1   Growth in Soviet NMPp in Current and "Comparable" Prices, 1980–1987 (percentage)

	NMPp		
	Current prices	Comparable prices	NMPp deflator
1980	4.9	3.9	1.0
1981	5.3	3.3	2.0
1982	7.5	4.0	3.5
1983	4.7	4.2	0.5
1984	3.9	2.9	1.0
1985	1.6	3.5	−1.9
1986	1.5	4.1	−2.6
1987	2.1[a]	2.3	−0.2[a]

a. Marked "calculated" in source.
SOURCES: *Narodnoe khoziaistvo SSSR 1980* (Moscow: Finansy i statistika, 1981), pp. 46, 379, abbreviated as *Narkhoz; Narkhoz 1982*, p. 378; *Narkhoz 1983*, pp. 41, 407; *Narkhoz 1984*, p. 52; *Narkhoz 1985*, pp. 40, 411; *Narkhoz 1987*, pp. 58, 122; *SSSR v tsifrakh v 1987 godu*, pp. 5, 9.

in 1986.[119] The attentive Western observer Abraham Becker suggested as early as 1972 that the "implicit price deflator of NMP may be downward biased."[120]

Another example of the degeneration of Soviet statistics is the already-mentioned static difference between the growth of NMPp and NMPu. Since the mid-1960s, this difference has vacillated around 0.5 percent per year. As the difference is supposed to be composed of the sum of net exports and material losses, one would have expected a decline in NMPp relative to NMPu from 1984 to 1985, when the foreign-trade surplus fell from 9 billion to 3.4 billion foreign-trade rubles.[121] However, NMPp minus NMPu fell by only 0.8 billion domestic rubles. Table 1.2 illustrates that there is little correlation between NMPp minus NMPu and net exports, for reasons explained by Vladimir G. Treml, Robert Campbell, Alec Nove, and Igor Birman.[122] They show that net imports measured in domestic rubles form a part of NMPp. Through impressive detective work, Treml established that the average "exchange rate" for exports has been on the order of 1 to 1.5 domestic rubles to a foreign-trade ruble, while for imports it has amounted to 2 to 2.4 domestic rubles to a foreign-trade ruble.[123] Because of the average

TABLE 1.2   Soviet NMPp, NMPu, and Net Exports, 1980–1986
               (billions of rubles in current prices)

	NMPp	NMPu	NMPp minus NMPu	Net exports[a]
1980	462.2	454.1	8.1	5.1
1981	486.7	477.9	8.8	4.5
1982	523.4	512.9	10.5	6.8
1983	548.1	536.4	11.7	8.3
1984	569.6	559.0	10.6	9.0
1985	578.5	568.7	9.8	3.4
1986	587.4	576.0	11.4	5.8

a. Measured in foreign-trade rubles that have no well-defined relation to domestic rubles.
SOURCES: *Narkhoz 1980*, pp. 379, 380; *Narkhoz 1982*, p. 378; *Narkhoz 1983*, p. 407; *Narkhoz 1985*, pp. 411, 572; *Narkhoz 1987*, pp. 122, 430, 640.

exchange rate, imports in domestic rubles are much larger than exports despite a positive trade balance in foreign-trade rubles. As foreign trade has soared, the foreign-trade component in NMPp has risen from 3 percent in 1965 to 10.9 percent in 1984.[124] The most positive interpretation is that the Soviet authorities incorporate gains in terms-of-trade.[125] In effect, the Soviets are boosting NMPp through customs and turnover taxes on imports, a practice which Siuniaev and General Secretary Gorbachev criticize.[126] None of this is clarified in ordinary Soviet statistical explanations, and the uncertainty about the evaluation of imports has led to widely differing views among Western experts on Soviet trade dependence.[127]

Another example of the insincerity of TsSU is its switching between NMPp and NMPu. In times past, emphasis was given to NMPp, which offered higher growth rates. During the Brezhnev period, NMPu became the leading official growth indicator, appearing in annual plans and plan fulfillment reports. In 1986 it was time to change again, and NMPp replaced NMPu in the quarterly plan fulfillment reports. The most recent statistical yearbook, published in 1987, does not even contain NMPu growth for 1986, presumably in order to obstruct comparisons and once again boost illusory results.[128] Furthermore, it was only toward the end of 1986 that a plan target of 3.9 percent for NMPp was published, while the result officially claimed was 4.1 percent. For NMPu, a target had been planned in advance (3.8 percent), but at 3.6 percent it was not reached even officially.[129] Typically, the Soviet authorities now turn their eyes to the concept of GNP when it indicates a higher growth rate than either of the NMP measures.[130]

I have chosen these examples for various reasons. Statistics on road transport and meat illustrate the extraordinary unreliability of Soviet statistics composed by a hierarchy of authorities, each of whom has an interest in taking advantage of methodological flaws. Most of the examples, in particular those concerning national income, illustrate how the central statistical authorities manipulate statistics for a variety of political purposes, but especially to boost fictive results. It is difficult to see any limits of decency in this world of deception.

Western Controversy over Soviet Investment

Since 1981, a debate has taken place in the journal *Soviet Studies* over the accuracy of Soviet investment statistics. It was opened by Nove, who brought to light an article by Viktor P. Krasovskii of the Institute of Economics in Moscow and another by Vladimir K. Fal'tsman of TsEMI.[131] Both presented figures indicating considerable hidden inflation in investment. Nove also pointed out that the official price index for machinery and metalworking implied a sizable deflation of 17 percent from 1970 to 1978, and concluded that "it must seem obvious that these indices are wrong."[132] Peter Wiles elaborated the implications of Krasovskii's and Fal'tsman's findings in a similar vein.[133] Philip Hanson pursued the analysis further on the basis of articles by Khanin, K. K. Val'tukh from the Institute of Economics and Organization of Industrial Production in Novosibirsk, and Fal'tsman and Aleksandr Kornev of TsEMI.[134] Extensive evidence pointed toward considerable inflation, but in the usual Soviet manner, statements contradicting major official statistics were not expressed unequivocally. The CIA had a special problem: its index of gross fixed investment virtually coincided with the TsSU index (Table 1.3).

The CIA investment estimates have been defended by Stanley H. Cohn and Abram Bergson.[135] A major issue is the nature of investment prices. Nove observed that increases in current investment expenditures were "very close indeed to claimed increases in investment volume in so-called unchanged prices."[136] Cohn retorted: "Soviet accounting practice refutes this argument because the valuation of investment, both in the budget document and in the plan, and the official investment index

are all in the same unit of measurement—estimate prices."[137] He reinforced his argument with the assertion that Stroibank and Gosbank use
estimate prices to control investment activities.

TABLE 1.3   Average Annual Growth in Soviet Gross Fixed
             Investment, 1951–1980 (percentage)

	TsSU	CIA
1951–1955	12.3	12.4
1956–1960	12.8	9.9
1961–1965	6.2	7.2
1966–1970	7.6	6.4
1971–1975	7.0	4.8
1976–1980	3.4	3.8

SOURCE: Abram Bergson, "On Soviet Real Investment Growth," *Soviet Studies*,
vol. 39, no. 3 (July 1987).

Examination of procedures for pricing construction statistics suggests a bias by Gosstroi to maximize the reported volume produced (see
Appendix Section 5). It appears that "comparable" prices are an approximation of current prices. "Estimate" prices have a similar inflationary
bias. It seems that they are input-determined, almost current prices.
Bergson has traced this phenomenon: "Indeed, one is led to wonder
whether TsSU may not itself be taking the volume of materials inputs as
an indicator of investment in construction."[138] This is what the CIA has
done.[139] Since the CIA and TsSU appear to calculate investment in
virtually the same manner, they should get approximately the same
results, so the similarity of their results does not validate either. It might
be objected that input costs are also used in parts of the GNP (notably,
public services) in the West; this is an unfortunate flaw, but its consequences are much greater in a command economy, which is input-maximizing. There seem to be no other principal objections to the
propositions by Nove, Wiles, and Hanson; Soviet as well as CIA investment statistics are greatly inflated.

A few related issues require further discussion. The interpretation
of Soviet sources poses an eternal problem. Bergson reviews the arguments of the Soviet economists in impressive detail, exposing caveats,
ambiguities, and unclarities.[140] However, apart from a comment in a
footnote acknowledging political realities ("Khanin is understandably
cryptic regarding his findings"), he appears to demand more explicit

statements from Soviet economists than the political context has allowed them.[141] Appendix Section 6, which profiles these economists, contends that they are likely to understate their cases. Cohn advances the argument of quality improvements in various contexts: "Technological change largely explains higher unit cost."[142] Bergson notes in a similar vein, "One must wonder also whether the acceleration of price increases per unit of design productivity that is reported . . . may not be largely, if not entirely, a reflection of increased outlays for design features other than machine output, especially labor economy."[143] Obviously, some technical development does take place, but not all that much, as I have argued. With its extraordinary shortages and power resting with the producers, the Soviet Union is an extreme case of a seller's market.

In the absence of hard evidence, assumptions are often drawn from methods used in the United States: "As the CIA recognizes, the underlying assumption that construction volume varies proportionately with materials employed is open to question. Such a simplification nevertheless has often been employed in the calculation of construction volume, and *in the light of U.S. experience it should not be wide off the mark*" (emphasis added).[144] Bergson's argument has been repudiated by Nove with the help of Krasovskii.[145] However, the very idea of drawing such an analogy between the U.S. and Soviet economies is questionable. Since the United States and the USSR have different economic systems, there are strong reasons to believe that no similarity exists between their production functions. I have suggested that the Soviet Union needs inputs roughly three times as large to generate the same physical output as a Western economy.

There seems to be sufficient reason to conduct a thorough re-examination of CIA investment statistics, given Bergson's suggestion: "Should the TsSU and CIA data on fixed investment growth be radically inflated, we surely would have to rethink our views on the Soviet growth process."[146]

Western Discussion of Soviet Consumption

One of the best and most conscientious studies published by the CIA on the Soviet economy is the international comparison of consumption carried out by Gertrude Schroeder and Imogene Edwards.[147] It is in line with the UN studies on international comparisons of real gross product carried out by Irving B. Kravis, Alan Heston, and Robert Summers.[148] Schroeder and Edwards studied a sample of 334 goods and services, pointed out the most essential caveats in Soviet statistics, and spelled out clearly what they were doing. Their lucidity and detailed tables facilitate a commentary.

The authors recognize that consumption statistics are a minefield. They try to compensate for quality differences, but only partially. In the case of meat production, they correct Soviet quantitative measures downward, but they do not doubt that in general their estimates are biased upward:

> On the less tangible aspect of quality, the bias is unmistakably in the USSR's favor. . . . The comparisons could not take these important aspects of consumer satisfaction into account. Similarly, allowance could not be made for the notoriously poor quality of retail prices in the USSR; only the added costs are reflected in product services. . . . Numerous products that are quite common in U.S. households could not be included in the sample, either because the USSR does not produce them at all or produces them in minuscule quantities.[149]

Birman has argued that it is "better even to give them an arbitrary quantitative assessment than to simply ignore" quality factors, a point long advocated by Wiles.[150] Given the state of Soviet statistics, which contain a multitude of upward biases, the difference between a conservative and a realistic estimate must be great. Any specialist is caught in a dilemma: whether to settle for a conservative assessment that can be defended by traditional arguments but is bound to be too high, or to attempt a realistic assessment based more on subjective evaluations and less on hard facts. Schroeder and Edwards chose the former option and Birman the latter.[151] Schroeder and Edwards did acknowledge that they estimated a ceiling of possible Soviet consumption:

> In 1976, real per capita consumption in the Soviet Union was 34.4 percent of that in the United States: this value is the geometric mean of comparisons in rubles (27.6 percent) and in dollars (42.8 percent). These comparisons, moreover, are believed to be biased in favor of the USSR because of the inability to allow fully for the notoriously poor quality and narrow assortment of Soviet consumer goods and services. The comparisons also cannot take into account the erratic, primitive distribution system and random shortages that make shopping difficult for Soviet consumers.[152]

Once a figure has been established, however, it easily becomes treated as more precise, and it is later compared in exact terms with GNP and consumption in other countries.[153] Schroeder and Edwards noticed that the structure of consumption did not match the assumed Soviet level of development and that it had not advanced in the preceding two decades. A natural inference would have been that Soviet consumption might not have increased all that much;[154] the authors are well aware of the material backwardness of Soviet society. However, they do not react to the relatively high figure for the Soviet level of consumption because two other statistical estimates support their results. One is the CIA growth rates and GNP estimates; the other is the UN international comparisons of real gross product (ICP), a very ambitious project which includes the Eastern European countries of Hungary, Poland, and Rumania.[155]

The ICP is an outstanding benchmark for international comparisons of national income. Generally, it produces a considerable flattening of income differentials between rich and poor countries, as one would expect when the quantity of each comparable good (including nontradable goods and services) is valued at the average international price. Still, the ICP figures for Eastern Europe seem particularly high, with Hungarian gross domestic product (GDP) per capita at 49.6 percent the U.S. level in 1975 and the Polish GDP at 50.1 percent.[156] The ICP suffers from several of the problems of the CIA estimation. Members of Paul Marer's project exposed several flaws in the ICP methodology as applied to centrally planned economies (CPEs): first, "The ICP did not sufficiently take into account the relatively poor quality and availability of CPE products and services. Second, the price inputs were based mainly on official price lists. . . ."[157] The ICP statistics were prepared in cooperation with the national statistical offices concerned, assuring a positive bias for dishonest dictatorships with poor-quality statistics.[158]

The most radical form of quality adjustment, one that Schroeder and Edwards attempt with a portion of their goods, is to assess Western market value. If this approach were maintained consistently, virtually all Soviet ready-made clothes and shoes (apart from furs, boots, and uniforms), Soviet canteen services, half of all Soviet cars (Volga, Moskvich, and Zaporozhets, but not Lada), and much else might be counted as close to worthless. This attitude is too radical, though, because these commodities still offer considerable consumer satisfaction and have some value on less-competitive markets.

Birman has written an extensive critical review of Schroeder and Edwards's study, discussing various biases. One example is that they essentially accept Soviet physical statistics that are, as we have seen, particularly exaggerated for food products. "In quantitative expressions, the Soviet-U.S. comparisons may be close to the mark."[159] Birman emphasizes quality differences and notices that, "according to the official literature and reports from eyewitnesses we know, the quality of foodstuffs has not improved, but rather deteriorated." In a somewhat arbitrary but probably realistic way, he adjusts the CIA estimates and offers alternative assessments of the actual level of Soviet consumption. His preferred alternative amounts to 22.4 percent, or one-quarter to one-fifth, the U.S. level.[160] It is difficult to find any point where Birman has reduced the CIA figures too much. The most dubious statement in his detailed study is that the consumption figures for health should be increased 15 to 40 percent. Given what *glasnost* has taught us about the current state of Soviet health services, as reflected in recent articles by Murray Feshbach and Christopher Davis, there can be little doubt that a considerable reduction had been required.[161] Birman reduces all other components of Soviet consumption apart from education.

Economist Alexander Zaichenko of the Institute of the USA and Canada in Moscow states (presumably on the basis of unpublished research), "Given the volume of goods and services consumed per capita, the Soviet Union ranks between fiftieth and sixtieth in the world (depending on the goods and services selected for comparison)."[162] To judge from his statement, Zaichenko has not considered quality differences. If his appraisal is substantiated, Birman would probably turn out to have been too optimistic in his assessment.

What Is a Plausible National Income?

Attempts in the current Soviet economic debate to establish the relative level of Soviet development acknowledge how poor Soviet statistics are. Soviet economists have lost interest in the immense production of industrial inputs. The indicators they choose tend to reflect final output and consumption rather than inputs and expenditures. Many of the measurements discussed are used in Western economic history. We shall pursue our inquiry in line with the current debate, using 1985 per capita figures to facilitate comparisons.

The large amounts of inputs used in Soviet production are an indication of economic inefficiency and backwardness. It is barely a cause for pride that in 1986 no other country in the world produced as much oil, gas, pig iron, steel, iron ore, cooking coal, mineral fertilizers, tractors, prefabricated reinforced concrete elements, timber, woolen

TABLE 1.4   Estimates of Soviet GNP, 1960–1985
             (billions of rubles in current prices)

	GNP	NMPp	NMPp as percentage of GNP
1960	177.7	145.0	81.6
1965	242.4	193.5	79.8
1970	370.5	289.9	78.2
1975	475.8	363.3	76.4
1980	614.5	462.2	75.2
1985	778.3	577.7	74.3

SOURCE: Genadii Zoteev, "Ob otsenke natsional'nogo produkta," *Ekonomicheskaia gazeta*, no. 42 (October 1987).

cloth, shoes, sugar beets, sunflowers, potatoes, milk, eggs, and sugar.[163] Most of these are industrial inputs that are used inefficiently; the shoes are of such terrible quality that a great excess needs to be produced; and the large production figures of several foodstuffs are due not only to the sheer size of the population but also to extraordinary rates of spoilage. Because command economies are input-maximizing, their per capita production of industrial inputs does not reflect their level of economic development in comparison with market economies.

A natural starting point for discussion is Soviet aggregate statistics. We have a Soviet estimate of NMPp in current prices. On the basis of these statistics and various additional information, Gennadii Zoteev of Gosplan has estimated Soviet GNP in current prices.[164] On the whole, his estimates are not far from the CIA's ruble estimates. However, the CIA estimated the part of GNP excluded from NMP at 29 percent in 1950, shrinking to 20 percent by 1970. Zoteev, on the contrary, sees growth in this area from 18.4 percent in 1960 to 25.7 percent in 1985 (Table 1.4), which he explains by way of increased amortizations.

One question concerns the appropriate exchange rate. As an initial reference, we can multiply Zoteev's assessment of GNP for 1985 by the official exchange rate at the time (US$1.196 per ruble), obtaining a Soviet GNP of $931 billion, or $3,340 per capita, 20 percent the U.S. level.[165] (The not-very-representative informal exchange rate was a constant one- fifth of this official exchange rate.)

Since one of the great Soviet aims has been to reach U.S. levels, TsSU has published figures on Soviet NMPp as a ratio of U.S. NMPp, without any explanations. The figures appear highly exaggerated, and even their

inconsistencies mean little. Probably the first semiserious figure, published in 1961, alleged that Soviet NMPp amounted to approximately 60
percent of U.S. NMPp in 1960.[166] A decade later, TsSU assessed the ratio
at 31 percent for 1950 and more than 66 percent for 1971.[167] However,
the accompanying growth rates published in the same statistical yearbook show that Soviet NMPp grew by 110.6 percent from 1960 to 1971,
whereas U.S. NMPp increased by only 50.4 percent.[168] These figures
suggest that Soviet NMPp should have grown to 84 percent the U.S.
level. Obviously, the ratios and growth rates are little more than wishful
thinking. The ratios currently published for Soviet to U.S. NMPp are 58
percent in 1958, more than 65 percent in 1970, 67 percent in 1980, and 66
percent in 1986.[169] The last three ratios suggest that Soviet national
income has not grown in relation to that of the United States in the last
sixteen years. As the average U.S. growth rate has been 3 percent a year,
average Soviet GNP growth can hardly have been more than 4.5 percent
a year, but that is already too high a figure.[170]

Boris Bolotin at IMEMO has published calculations of NMPp per
capita in U.S. dollars set at 1980 prices, based on purchasing-power-par-
ity (PPP) calculations. His estimate of Soviet NMPp per capita at 56
percent of U.S. NMPp in 1986 reduces the Goskomstat figures considerably, but without bringing them down to a realistic level.[171] It is quite
possible that Bolotin has used a combination of CIA and ICP figures. His
NMP comparison for 1986 matches the CIA estimate of Soviet GNP per
capita at 49 percent the U.S. level.[172]

Robert Campbell's work for the USSR in the World Bank project was
a significant improvement and stands out as the best estimate to date.
His estimate for 1980 was lower than the CIA figure—$4,190, or 37
percent the U.S. GNP per capita.[173] The essence of his methodology was
to complement domestic measurements of NMPp and relate them to U.S.
GNP, a process designed to avoid many of the pitfalls of the CIA
methodology. The key problem, however, was to find a reasonable
measurement of PPP. It appears as though this project, which was based
on the ICP methodology, incorporated some of its biases. Common
assumptions easily lead to shared biases: "It is striking that . . . the
Soviets' own PPP computations, adjusted for differences in coverage, are
very close to the U.S. results with Soviet quantity weights for the benchmark year 1976."[174] One of four methods of assessing the plausibility of
alternative estimates of GNP related "to the fact that, in per capita energy
consumption, centrally planned economies and market-type economies

establish rankings that can be used as reference points, because energy consumption per capita has been found to correlate highly with levels of economic development."[175] This is true only of market economies. Once again the high use of inputs has been turned into proof of a high level of net production. The estimate offered by the World Bank project was a considerable improvement, but it is still likely to be too high.

An obvious point of reference is communist countries with better statistics. The natural choice is Hungary, whose statistics are widely trusted. The ICP estimate of Hungarian GDP per capita (with real indexes based on international dollars) was 49.6 percent the U.S. level in 1975.[176] In contrast, the Marer project, with Ed Hewett as country expert, estimated Hungarian GNP per capita at 39 percent the U.S. level in 1980.[177] It seems obvious that Hungary has a more highly developed economy than the USSR, but according to the Marer project, Soviet GNP per capita was only 4.6 percent less than Hungarian GNP per capita. A rare Council for Mutual Economic Assistance (CMEA) study even concluded that Soviet NMP per capita was 8.8 percent higher than Hungary's in 1981.[178] The Institute of Economics and the Institute for the Economy of the World Socialist System in Moscow has carried out similar estimates, but according to reliable unofficial Soviet information, their figures indicated that Hungarian NMPp per capita was 30 to 40 percent higher (and East German NMPp per capita 70 percent higher) than Soviet NMPp per capita.[179] Still, without written evidence on such a technical statistic, we dare not draw any firm conclusions, and can go no further along this road than the Marer project has.

Next we shall turn to economic development indicators likely to possess intersystemic comparability. One is the basic structure of the economy— primary, secondary, and tertiary employment. Agricultural employment gives some indication of the development of an economy regardless of economic system. In Table 1.5, we have selected some countries that appear relevant.[180] Obviously, agriculture is a backward sector in some countries (Spain, Ireland, and Greece) and advanced in others (Argentina and Uruguay). Definitions vary, but matter less where the differences are great. Among Western European countries, only Portugal and Greece have a larger share of their labor force employed in agriculture than the USSR, and the agricultural share of employment is smaller in the wealthier Latin American countries. If allowances are made for foreign trade in agricultural produce and auxiliary labor, the relative Soviet position is even worse. In any case, it seems clear that the

TABLE 1.5   Employment Structure of Selected Countries, 1980
               (percentage of labor force)

	Agriculture	Industry	Services	1985 GNP per capita (US$)
USA	4	31	66	16,690
West Germany	6	44	50	10,940
East Germany	11	50	39	—
Italy	12	41	48	6,520
Argentina	13	34	53	2,130
Uruguay	16	29	55	1,650
Spain	17	37	46	4,290
Ireland	19	34	48	4,850
USSR	20	39	41	—
Portugal	26	37	38	1,970
Greece	31	29	40	3,550
Brazil	31	27	42	1,640

SOURCE: World Bank, *World Development Report 1987* (New York: Oxford University Press, 1987), pp. 203, 265.

USSR belongs to the group of so-called upper-middle-income countries, the richest of the three categories of developing countries in the World Bank classification.

A second development indicator is the structure of consumption, which Schroeder and Edwards compared with those of Poland, Spain, and Portugal to find that "remarkably little progress toward a more modern pattern has been made in recent decades."[181] Zaichenko appears even more pessimistic.[182]

A third indicator is health. In spite of varying cultural habits, there is a stronger correlation between economic level and health for less-developed countries than for the twenty most-developed countries. Consider two indicators: infant mortality and life expectancy. A cluster of representative countries have been selected in Table 1.6. Soviet citizens are far worse off in these respects than any Westerners. Among the twenty richest industrial market economies, infant mortality varies from 6 out of 1,000 to 12 out of 1,000 live births, while the Soviet infant mortality is three times larger. The Soviet Minister of Health, Evgenii Chazov, has stated that his country ranks fiftieth in the world in infant mortality and thirty-second in life expectancy.[183] The Soviet level of health indicators is similar to that of South Korea, Malaysia, Uruguay, and Argentina.

Unusual statistics and actual observations of the standard of living, increasingly reported in the Soviet press, also suggest that the USSR is a relatively advanced developing country. A Central Committee decree tells us: "80 percent of the population in towns live in separate flats with amenities," making clear that the remaining 20 percent live in shared flats and dormitories.[184] Aganbegyan has stated, "Approximately 17 percent of the families . . . about 40 to 50 million people, still live in communal flats or dormitories."[185] Shantytowns are typical of southern Soviet cities. In the city of Baku, which officially has a population of 1.7 million inhabitants, 200,000 people live in houses "built overnight," according to the city authorities.[186] Visiting Kirov *oblast'* (or province) in February 1987, Central Committee Secretary for Agriculture Viktor Nikonov complained that, of the houses in the countryside, 40 percent had tap water, 14 percent sewers, and only 4 percent hot tap water.[187]

TABLE: 1.6   Infant Mortality and Life Expectancy in Selected Countries, 1985

	Life expectancy[a]		Infant mortality[b]	GNP per capita (US$)
	Male	Female		
Japan	75	80	6	11,300
USA	72	80	11	16,690
West Germany	72	78	10	10,940
Spain	74	80	10	4,290
Italy	74	79	12	6,520
Portugal	71	77	19	1,970
South Korea	65	72	27	2,150
Malaysia	66	70	28	2,000
Uruguay	70	75	29	1,650
USSR	65	74	29	—
Argentina	67	74	34	2,130
Mexico	64	69	50	2,080
Brazil	62	67	67	1,640

a. At birth.

b. The number of infants who die before reaching one year of age per thousand live births.

SOURCE: World Bank, *World Development Report 1987* (New York: Oxford University Press, 1987), pp. 203, 259.

Surprisingly, the situation is not much better in provincial hospitals: "The USSR has 4,000 district hospitals, but more than 1,000 of them have no sewage system, 2,500 have no hot running water, 700 have neither hot nor cold running water."[188]

It is true that the Soviet population is reasonably well supplied with certain household appliances, namely television sets, refrigerators, stoves, and antiquated washing machines, but they have no freezers or video recorders, and dishwashers are virtually unknown. In 1985, there was one car for every 22.2 Soviet citizens.[189] At the end of 1985, there were only 31.1 million telephones in the country, of which only 17.1 million were private; in other words, one private telephone per sixteen people. The nadir of telephone density is the Tadzhik countryside, with six private phones per 1,000 people.[190] Statistics on computer stocks are hard to come by, but the number of microcomputers cannot have exceeded 200,000 at the end of 1987, when there were more than 25 million in the United States. Moreover, all the domestically produced microcomputers are of such poor quality that none can be compared with any U.S. brand still on sale. Many developing countries show more impressive records.

Foreign trade says much about a country's relative level of economic development, though a very large country tends to have less foreign trade in relation to its national income. Soviet foreign trade probably offers the most pessimistic perspective. Vladimir Treml has argued that the impact of foreign trade is much greater than previously perceived; in domestic prices, imports accounted for 16.7 percent of GNP in 1980, and this share has continued to grow.[191] Soviet dependence on foreign trade is particularly great in the field of machine-building. No less than a third of Soviet investment in equipment is covered by imports.[192] The share of machinery, equipment, and means of transportation in Soviet imports was 37.2 percent in 1985.[193] In the same year the Soviet grain harvest amounted to 191.7 million tons, while about 57 million tons of grain were imported—about 23 percent of total supplies, though this share later declined sharply.[194] The insignificance of the Soviet Union in world trade is brought out by the fact that it accounted for only 2 percent of Organization for Economic Cooperation and Development (OECD) trade in 1983, when oil income peaked, and ended up in twelfth place overall in terms of the size of its OECD trade.[195] The country's great dependence on foreign trade despite a small share of world trade is consistent with a GNP smaller than is usually assumed in the West.

The Soviet foreign-trade structure is also reminiscent of a relatively well developed Third World country. In its hard-currency trade, the Soviet Union is completely dependent on its exports of three commodities—oil, natural gas, and gold. The first two accounted for 73 percent of official Soviet exports to the OECD area in 1985.[196] When energy prices dropped, Soviet exports to the West fell by almost 40 percent from 1984 to 1986. The Soviet Union is slipping out of Western markets for manufactured goods. In 1955, 28 percent of Soviet exports to Western Europe consisted of manufactured goods, but in 1983 this share had fallen to 6 percent.[197] Admittedly, this development was caused primarily by an extraordinary expansion of Soviet energy exports. Still, in 1965 the USSR provided 0.82 percent of OECD imports of manufactured goods. By 1981, this share had shrunk to 0.51 percent, according to the UN ECE. In the same period, newly industrialized countries increased their share of Western imports of manufactured goods from 2.74 percent in 1965 to 6.95 percent in 1981,[198] far surpassing the Soviet Union.

So far, the Marer project offers the best assessment of Soviet GNP, although it should be seen as a ceiling. Given the substantial U.S. growth rate in the 1980s and presumed Soviet stagnation (Table 1.7), Soviet GNP per capita must have fallen to barely 33 percent the U.S. level in 1986, in sharp contrasts to the 49 percent figure suggested by the CIA.[199] How much lower the current level of Soviet GNP to U.S. GNP actually is remains an open question.

Although a discussion of Soviet investment and defense expenditures falls outside the scope of this paper, a few observations are in order. Both appear very high by international standards, but are difficult to evaluate. Upper-middle-income countries had an average investment ratio of 22 percent of GNP in 1985, while official Soviet investment accounted for 26.5 percent of NMPu.[200] Three adjustments to the Soviet figure are needed, one for prices, another for taxes, and a third for the notion of national income. Considering subsidies, uneven profit taxation, and the unequal distribution of turnover tax (97.5 billion rubles in 1985), Seliunin has suggested that "consumption accounts for about 60 percent of [national] income and accumulation correspondingly for 40 percent."[201] The same ratio of investment to GNP would account for an investment share of about 30 percent, but this can hardly be the whole truth.

The CIA estimate of defense expenditure is likely to be of a higher quality than CIA estimates of national income: since defense is the CIA's prime focus, its knowledge of physical numbers is probably more accu-

TABLE 1.7   Average Annual Growth of the Soviet Economy,
             1961–1985 (percentage)

	1961–65	1966–70	1971–75	1976–80	1981–85
NMPp					
Official	5.9	8.4	4.6	5.3	4.6
(current prices)					
Official	6.5	7.8	5.7	4.3	3.6
(fixed prices)					
Seliunin &	4.4	4.1	3.2	1.0	0.6
Khanin					
(fixed prices)					
GNP					
Zoteev	6.4	8.9	5.1	5.3	4.8
(current prices)					
CIA	5.1	5.0	3.0	2.3	2.0
(fixed prices)					
ECE	5.4	4.4	3.9[a]	—	—
(fixed prices)					

a. 1971–73.
SOURCES: *Narkhoz 1985*, pp. 38, 409; Genadii Zoteev, "Ob otsenke natsional'nogo produkta," *Ekonomicheskaia gazeta*, no. 42 (October 1987); Vasilii Seliunin and Grigorii Khanin, "Lukavaia tsifra," *Novy mir* 63, no. 2 (February 1987): 194–95; 1982, p. 25; U.S. CIA, *Handbook of Economic Statistics, 1986* (Washington, D.C.: GPO, 1986), p. 64; United Nations Economic Commission for Europe, no. 2 (1980): 26.

rate in the military field, and less compensation for lower quality is required, considering that Soviet arms are sold on the world market on a large scale. Thus, our deliberations suggest a greater reduction in the denominator (national income) than in the numerator (defense expenditure) of the CIA equation. Moreover, David Epstein's arguments for a broader definition of defense and defense expenditure appear rather convincing.[202] Both these considerations boost the CIA's current estimate of 15 to 17 percent defense share of GNP. I have heard from two Soviet specialists at a not-very-high level of government, but with some insight into defense-related statistics, that the defense sector absorbs 30 to 40 percent of NMP, that is, 22 to 28 percent of GNP.[203] Their assessments were based on parts of the economy that did not emerge in the civilian sector. Several colleagues have heard similar views from other knowledgeable Soviets.

Finally, a few words should be said about the second economy. Gur Ofer and Aaron Vinokur's Soviet émigré interview project in the early 1970s dealt with the urban second economy.[204] It concluded that 10 to 12 percent of total personal incomes were derived privately, but the addition to GNP would amount to only 3 to 4 percent. A later interview project, led by Gregory Grossman and Vladimir G. Treml, has not presented its final results, but partial figures indicate that 30 to 40 percent of total personal income is derived from private sources.[205] Much of private income is mere redistribution, and a considerable part is included in national income, as the public sector buys much private agricultural produce. If we assume, in line with Ofer and Vinokur's results, that the addition to GNP is about a third of private earnings, the increment would be a maximum of 10 to 13 percent—a moderate second economy by Western standards and a small one by Third World standards. It is not obvious, then, that the second economy is significant in an international comparison of national income.

An Assessment of Inflation

The old Soviet myth was that the country had no inflation. We have already criticized the statistical treatment of inflation. Many Western economists have long presented evidence of hidden inflation; however, their estimates are invariably lower than recent Soviet data, which are unfortunately incomplete. To offer some idea of the magnitude of inflation, a number of these Soviet estimates in various spheres are presented in Appendix Section 7. Recent figures are most interesting because they are both higher and more clearly defined than previous indications. This rise in estimates has been caused partly by more openness, a clearer realization of what has actually been happening in the economy, and an apparent recent rise in inflation. It is difficult to separate out the significance of these respective factors.

Several Soviet economists have estimated that retail inflation was in the range of 3 to 5 percent annually from the late 1950s on. Estimates for machinery and construction inflation tend to be higher after 1970, over 5 percent annually. Fal'tsman, interpreted by Wiles, shows investment of 2 percent a year in 1966–1970, 3 percent in 1971–1975, 3.5 percent in 1976–1977, and probably 5 percent a year in 1978–1980.[206]

Alternative Soviet figures on inflation can be gathered for different branches of the economy. The weights of each branch are public knowledge. Through a critical scrutiny, including checks with financial statistics, it should be possible to establish an inflation rate with reasonable accuracy (plus or minus 0.5 percent a year). Without any elaborate assessment, we may suggest that with regard to quality changes the inflation rate has been about 4 percent a year since 1978, when inflation appears to have begun substituting for production increases on a new scale. The only sectors that seem to fall below this level are raw-materials extraction, industrial production of intermediary goods, and most transport (notably railways and pipelines). Given the nature of the inflationary mechanism, the overwhelming priority awarded to the military-industrial complex, and the structure of that sector, one would assume that it accounts for higher inflation than any other sector.

Alternative Assessments of Growth Rates

The big event in Soviet statistics in 1987 was the publication of "Cunning Figures" in *Novy mir* by the senior economic journalist Vasilii Seliunin and Grigorii Khanin, an economist and specialist on national accounts.[207] Many of the arguments in their breathtaking revision of Soviet economic history have inspired our reasoning. Since it appeared in a literary journal, the article depicts their methodology only scantily, and their figures are largely approximate. But Khanin, who is primarily responsible for the calculations, has outlined his methodology elsewhere.[208] His approach is essentially to exploit as many alternative calculation methods as possible to deflate NMPp growth.[209] None of them is really satisfactory, but their results match. Seliunin and Khanin conclude that "the national income, calculated according to our methodology, grew six to seven times from 1928 to 1985."[210] This works out to between 3.2 and 3.5 percent growth a year. The fanciful official claim is eighty-seven times, or an average growth rate of 8.1 percent a year, notwithstanding war losses.[211]

One dutiful TsSU collaborator, V. E. Adamov, objects that if this were the case, "the relationship between the United States and the USSR with regard to this indicator would have stayed in 1985 at the level of 1928 (8 to 12 percent),"[212] which he claims is impossible, especially in view of the military parity between the two countries (without disclosing the source of his estimate for 1928). Whatever the exact level, it seems plausible that the USSR has not advanced economically in relation to the United States since 1928. Adamov failed to mention that, by his own low benchmark for 1928, extrapolating from the TsSU growth figure for that period would imply a Soviet NMPp more than 1.3 times that of the U.S. NMPp—twice as much as even Goskomstat claims. Bolotin has presented somewhat more reasonable figures: average NMPp growth of 6.6 percent a year in the periods 1921–1938 and 1951–1987.[213] The figure is a result primarily of his selection of 1920 as a starting point—an unfortunate choice, since the economy was then devastated by the civil war. However, his average annual NMP growth from 1950 to 1986 turns out to be just 3.5 percent a year (on the basis of his calculation of NMPp in dollars in 1980 prices), while Khanin stopped at 3.9 percent a year on average from 1950 to 1985.[214] Thus Bolotin implies that Khanin has overestimated Soviet economic growth in that period.

Seliunin and Khanin are not impressed with the growth rate under Stalin.[215] During its splendor in "1929–1941 the national income grew one-and-a-half times." The official rate for 1928–1940 is 14.6 percent a year (in 1926–27 prices).[216] Bergson's lowest growth rate, according to Soviet notions in 1950 prices, was 4.2 percent, which appears impressively accurate given the scarcity of information at the time. In his 1969 book, the late Albert Vainshtein commented that for Soviet statistics before 1950, "the disparity pointed out in the figures on the national income of the USSR gives a reason for our enemies to belittle the really high growth rates of the national income of the USSR, and at the same time sow great distrust about Soviet statistics."[217]

The revision of Soviet statistics has yet to be undertaken. Seliunin and Khanin see the 1950s as the only really positive period.[218] Their figures for the latest quarter century are recalculated into annual averages in Table 1.7, and presented with official growth rates of NMPp in current prices, Zoteev's GNP estimates in current prices, and CIA and ECE estimates of GNP in fixed prices.[219]

Seliunin and Khanin reckon that official growth figures have been exaggerated by an average of 3.1 percent a year during the last two decades, which corresponds to actual inflation of about 4 percent. The CIA deflation stops at 2.3 percent (disregarding the difference between NMP and GNP growth). Since the Soviet population has grown by almost 1 percent a year, the country has not enjoyed any per capita growth in national income during the last decade, and the economy has entered a state of stagnation turning into decline. Hidden inflation rose suddenly in 1966, when reform was introduced, and has not disappeared. Seliunin and Khanin even estimate that growth was slightly lower during the second half of the 1960s than during the first half. Toward the end of the 1970s, inflation was probably boosted, as Grossman has suggested, because of fulfillment of financial, but not production, plans.[220] In 1981–1982, the authorities appear to have raised prices both openly and tacitly in order to reduce the repressed inflation. If we accept as true Seliunin and Khanin's perception of the Soviet economy, the CIA growth estimates appear quite respectable on average, but seem to have overlooked the rise in hidden inflation during the second half of the 1970s and thus gradually have become more inflated.

In various conversations with leading Soviet economists in June 1987, I heard the standard opinion that Goskomstat's estimates were about one percent too high, but this view was so uniform that it sounded like a circular instruction, although it was not printed. This standard opinion has been overtaken by Aganbegyan's pronouncements that no growth occurred in 1979–1982 and 1981–1985. Actual inflation seems to have peaked in 1982, when there was no real growth, while the NMPp in current rubles rose 7.5 percent, which would equal the actual inflation rate.

The most obvious alternative method for assessing the Soviet growth rate, advocated by Wiles, is to assess actual inflation and deflate a measurement of national income in current rubles. One advantage of this method is that various types of information could be used to test and improve estimates; another is that it would deprive us of illusions of precision.

Seliunin and Khanin corroborate their argument with a sharp judgment on the development of consumption: "The standard of living fell during whole decades, and it was only in the '50s that it started to grow."[221] They illustrate the situation with food statistics. The grain harvest of 1913 was achieved again only in 1952 (disregarding dubious figures from the late 1930s).[222] The number of cattle held in 1916 was not reached again until 1956.[223] Other agricultural statistics are not much better. At the same time, the population increased 24.3 percent, from 159 million in 1913 to 198 million in 1956.[224] Considering the importance of meat and grain to the well-being of the population, we may conclude from these numbers alone that the average standard of living in the Russian Empire in 1913 cannot possibly have been duplicated in the Soviet Union before 1960. This has been demonstrated by J. G. Chapman, who calculated that Soviet real wages fell by about 40 percent from 1928 to 1937, reaching their 1928 level again only in 1958.[225] Vainshtein estimated that the 1916 level of national income was not reached again until 1929.[226]

In sum, during seventy years of Soviet rule the standard of living has risen above the prerevolution level only between 1960 and about 1975, and then not at a very high rate. Little wonder that this is reflected in poor development of the national income. The single economic achievement that appears remarkable by international standards is the buildup of the military might of a superpower.

Conclusion

Contrary to the conventional wisdom represented by CIA estimates, we have arrived at the conclusion that Soviet GNP per capita, measured in purchasing power parity, amounted to less than a third the U.S. level in 1985 and 1986. This boosts the defense share of GNP to possibly a quarter of GNP or more. Imports in domestic prices corresponded to as much as 17 percent of GNP in 1980. Inflation has been significant since 1966 and rose slightly beginning in the late 1970s. During the last decade it may have stood at around 4 percent a year, causing the Soviet economy to stagnate or decline slightly, as Aganbegyan has stated.

These findings cast new doubts on the precision of econometric models fed with Soviet physical data in general, and the CIA estimates in particular. Two methodological problems are of particular concern. The first is the accuracy of the input-output tables used by the CIA and others. I suspect that to some extent they measure output in gross value, which incorporates a large degree of inflation and does not fully reflect the inefficiency of the Soviet production process.

A second problem is the treatment of shaky statistics used in models as inputs. Economists traditionally approach dubious data "conservatively," that is, by making a minimal adjustment or none at all. Such an approach is acceptable if biases compensate for each other, or if the goal is to establish a ceiling. But in the case of Soviet statistics, in which all biases are upward (aside from parts of the second economy, which we can reasonably ignore in a comparative context), every "conservative" adjustment of Soviet data is bound to be exaggerated, and thus, in effect, not at all conservative. Economists must therefore make more daring—but more realistic—assumptions, or acknowledge that they are producing highly exaggerated ceiling estimates.

A complete reassessment of Western estimates of Soviet economic aggregates is urgently needed. There is, alas, no good way of assessing Soviet national income and its growth rate on the basis of information currently available. Any such construction must be based on an assumption of reliable data and good knowledge of the production function of the economy. Neither is currently possible in the Soviet case, so an eclectic method employing necessary adjustments of NMPp measurement plus deflation based on a variety of partial evidence appears to be the best way of assessing GNP growth. Not much precision can be achieved in this way, but at least the fiction of precision, when it cannot be supported, disappears. Whatever method is used, it must be accompanied by tests of plausibility. Various comparisons of the level of economic development offer a reasonable basis for assessment. Nevertheless, our best hope lies in the possibility that the Soviet leaders will realize it is in their interest to uncover the reality of the Soviet economy. Their poor statistics are misleading them, which is of far greater concern than confusion in the West.

Appendix

1. 1985–1986 Production Estimates

A comparison of estimates of Soviet GNP in 1985 and 1986 shows that in its calculations, the CIA gives the production of inputs more weight than does the TsSU. In 1985 the raw material–producing branches performed rather poorly, while they did very well in 1986 compared with the final stages of production.[227] In 1985 TsSU estimated NMPp growth at 3.5 percent, while the CIA estimated GNP growth at 1.2 percent. In 1986, however, the TsSU set NMPp growth at 4.1 percent, while the CIA exceeded it with a GNP increase of 4.2 percent.[228] The CIA/DIA report fails to analyze this radical shift of its estimate in relation to the Soviet one.

If we examine the CIA report, we find that agriculture is the most important component of the swing. In 1985, agriculture caused a deduction of 0.8 percent from the estimated GNP, while in 1986 it contributed 1.5 percent; the rest of the increase may be ascribed to industry at large.[229] The CIA's heavy reliance on Soviet statistics for gross agricultural output in physical terms appears ill-advised, since it did not account for spoilage and deducted only moisture. CIA estimates appear to be relatively high in relation to TsSU growth figures when the primary sector does well. While Soviets complain that Goskomstat pays too much attention to inputs and intermediary production, the CIA gives these factors even more weight.[230] The criticism is supported by an authoritative Soviet evaluation by Otto Lacis underlining the failure to achieve qualitative improvements in 1986.[231] If our suspicion is correct, flaws in the CIA's input-output tables are likely to lead to gross exaggerations in CIA estimates of the comparative level of Soviet national income, and need to be re-examined.[232]

2. The Low Quality of Soviet Products

Living in a well-supplied part of Moscow and carefully investigating state shops, we found that, of daily foodstuffs, only eggs, butter, a few cheeses, thin cream, kefir, bread, mineral water, salt, and sugar of satisfactory quality were available almost every day. Boris Yeltsin, then first party secretary of Moscow, stated in the spring of 1986 that 60 percent of the milk sold in Moscow as fresh was actually powdered. The fresh milk sold sours within a day of purchase, and its availability fluctuates. Of the few fruits and vegetables available, many are rotten or frozen, and all are extremely dirty. The official economic report for 1987 states that, of commodities received by the trade network, 10 to 17 percent of potatoes, fruits and berries, cabbages, melons, and onions; 26 percent of tomatoes; and 29 percent of grapes were of unsatisfactory quality (read: rotten).[233] In fact, edible fruits, berries, and tomatoes are hardly ever to be found in state shops as far north as Moscow. If they arrive, they are sold immediately in the street. Meat sold over the counter has always been frozen and looks inedible. A typical example is the decline in the quality of tea. The proportion of actual tea leaves has diminished gradually, replaced by tiny wooden branches and other leaves in order to make it easier to reach quantitative plan targets.[234]

The quality of Soviet clothing is terrible. Lacis reports that one-sixth to one-third of the clothes and shoes bought by the population in 1986 aroused complaints registered in family budget research.[235] The economic report for 1987 states that 7 to 9 percent of clothes and shoes delivered to trade were of insufficient quality.[236] Soviet consumers are not choosy, yet these figures are very high. Clothing may be one of the few areas in which there has been some check on quality deterioration, because many people sew their own clothes, giving rise to huge stocks of unsalable goods. Soviets usually distinguish between much-sought-after imported clothes and Soviet ones, while the difference between Western and Eastern European is less significant.

Before 1987, no new car model had been introduced on a mass scale for about fifteen years, so few improvements in quality could have taken place. Both the new Lada Sputnik and especially the new Moskvich are considered failures. Electronics have made a difference to radio equipment, but prices have probably increased. The quality of housing has risen since Khrushchev's construction drive, but a great deal of construction work is not properly completed. Soon after the official completion of a house, the workers return to extort sizable payments to finish their work. Therefore, the quality delivered by the public sector has probably not risen.

The more quality is scrutinized, the worse it appears. The very concept of value added is spurious in the Soviet context. I visited two fishing *kolkhozes* (collectives) in Estonia—one very rich, the other close to average. The major difference between them was that the rich one processed almost all its fish, primarily as conserves, while the average one sold its fish fresh. Under the state pricing policies, a fishery *kolkhoz* earns most from conserves, followed by smoked fish, frozen fish, and fresh fish, in that order. Consumer preferences, however, are of the opposite order, so low-quality fish conserves flood Soviet shops. They are one of the few commodities that are widely available, and many of them are considered inedible. Today fresh fish is rarely available in Moscow, while it was common in the 1950s.

The cotton industry illustrates the same point. Soviet and American cotton are of about the same quality. Soviet cotton fabrics, though not of a high standard, are quite exportable.[237] But ready-made Soviet clothes are of such deplorable quality and design that only exceptional products can be exported, at cut-rate prices. The relative quality of Soviet commodities diminishes with each step of processing. They can be sold domestically only because of extreme protectionism and insatiable demand. Much of Soviet processing is better understood as destruction rather than production. If Soviet goods at various stages of processing were sold in the West at whatever prices they might fetch, the market value of final outputs would probably be less than that of their original or semiprocessed inputs. Thus, raw materials overwhelmingly dominate Soviet exports to the West. How can we talk about value added in such circumstances? [238]

It is a startling experience to walk into Soviet stores, assess the Western values of Soviet-made commodities, and compare them with actual Soviet prices. In the vast majority of cases, the Western market value of a Soviet commodity—food as well as industrial goods—would be nil or close to nil, since their quality is so poor that they could not be sold in the West. None of these commodities are exportable to the West. The big Soviet car Volga, whose list price is 16,000 rubles and internal market price considerably higher, belongs to this class of goods. Aganbegyan says: "It is completely understandable why many states do not allow imports of it."[239] If we evaluated Soviet national income by such comparisons, it would include little more than armaments, unprocessed raw materials, numerous intermediary goods, certain basic manufactures, and a small quantity of handicrafts. Such an assessment would be too harsh, however. In several Third World countries, Soviet goods are sold, though at cut-rate prices.

Finally, I should note that there is a striking difference between the evaluation of Soviet quality by Soviet émigrés and by Western scholars, many of whom have seen little of the Soviet Union. The émigrés are likely to possess greater insight; furthermore, their views coincide with those of the Western community in Moscow and of Eastern European experts.[240]

3. The Confused Meat Statistics

The official production of meat in 1985 amounted to 17.1 million tons, measured in slaughter weight.[241] In the same year, meat consumption per capita (without any specification) is said to have been 61.4 kilograms.[242] If we multiply the per capita consumption of meat by the mid-year population (277.4 million), we end up with total meat consumption of 17.03 million tons. Calculations for other years indicate adjustments for net imports and changes in stocks. The untenable assumption has apparently been made that the whole slaughter weight is consumed, without any deduction for bones, gristle, other inedible parts, losses, or waste. The meat offered Soviet customers does consist to a large extent of bones and fat not included in similar Western statistics. One Soviet source recently stated that the annual per capita consumption of meat amounted to 57 kilograms in Estonia and 27 kilograms in Kazakhstan.[243] These two republics are likely to represent the extremes. Even if the national average were closer to the figure for Estonia than for Kazakhstan, it would still be relatively far below the official figure. Consumption and sales statistics do not match. In 1985, total sales of meat by state and cooperative trade amounted to only 12.7 million tons, of which 0.37 million tons was bought from the public by cooperative trade.[244] In addition, private sales through *kolkhoz* markets are estimated by the state at 2.2 percent of total sales of foodstuffs in volume, or 4.2 percent "of a comparative group of commodities" in volume.[245] If we simply assumed that the *kolkhoz* markets contributed an additional 4.2 percent of meat sales, total meat sales would amount to 13.3 million tons. However, state estimates of *kolkhoz* sales are, unlike nearly all the others, grossly underestimated.[246] Moreover, an unknown quantity of private production of meat for private consumption should be added.[247] Even so, the total supply of meat cannot possibly amount to the alleged level of consumption. Meat prices show similar distortions. With the help of official statistics on state and cooperative retail sales in current prices and volume, we can calculate the average price paid for 1 kilogram of meat at 2.04 rubles, which corresponds to the official list price in state shops.[248] However, "in Moscow and some other large cities people eat meat according to state prices: 2 rubles [per kilogram], the other according to 'commercial' [prices]: 4 [rubles] and higher."[249] Cooperative meat prices are never lower than 3.5 rubles per kilogram and usually 4 to 5 rubles per kilogram. I have seen cooperative prices of 8 rubles for mutton in Samarkand.[250] In recent years, the authorities have intentionally boosted sales of meat at cooperative prices while reducing sales at state prices in order to raise the average price of meat. The intention is to transform repressed inflation into hidden inflation and at the same time reduce subsidies. The trend does not appear, however, in official statistics.[251]

In *Izvestiia*, Nikolai Petrakov revealed average prices paid for meat according to (family) budget statistics provided by Goskomtsen.[252] The high-paid stratum of the population—with ample access to special shops—paid an average of 2.9 rubles per kilogram, while both the low- and average-paid strata paid 4.2 rubles. Without any knowledge of the size of these three groups, if we simply assume that equal amounts are sold at each average price, the average price overall would be no less than 3.77 rubles per kilogram. This includes private sales at *kolkhoz* markets, where prices are somewhat higher than the cooperative prices, and informal higher-price resales that are explicitly excluded from the official statistics.[253] Cooperative trade, which to a large extent specializes in the meat trade, allegedly accounted for 27.9 percent of retail sales of foodstuffs at state prices in 1985.[254] But Soviet family budget surveys are infamous for painting a rosy picture of Soviet consumption.[255]

For all these reasons, the average price of meat in state and cooperative trade can hardly be less than 3 rubles per kilogram—50 percent higher than what the statistical yearbook claims. The sales statistics must be wrong in value or volume, or both; the disparity is far too great to be explained by illegal resales and the like.

4. The Peculiar 1985–1986 National Income Figures

Jan Vanous calculated that "the growth in total NMP used in 1986 was around 0.8 percent, not the 3.6 percent claimed by the TsSU.[256] However, he assumed that Soviet growth data were correct until 1984, so his estimates are likely to still be too high.[257] But Vanous's judgment on Soviet statistics appears justified:

> In the last two years, the official statistics which Soviet leaders, and the world, use to measure Soviet economic performance have so obviously deteriorated in quality that they must be regarded only with the utmost

skepticism and care. . . . Published Soviet statistics . . . [suggest] a construction of a special "political" set of key aggregate economic statistics which were obtained using dubious methodology. This has the effect, intended or not, of exaggerating the improvement in performance. . . . At the very least, this reflects a fundamental breakdown in the Soviet statistical system.[258]

Soviet economist M. Siuniaev of the Institute of Economics and Forecasting of the Scientific–Technical Progress later confirmed that the low NMPp growth in current prices was caused by a decrease in alcohol sales, which "until recently accounted for one-sixth of the sales of commodities to the population."[259] He complains that "a false impression of a slower economic growth as a whole is created." In the 1970s, revenues from alcohol sales, most of which came from turnover tax, grew quickly. At the same time, the value of oil exports rose rapidly due to a more than sixteenfold increase in oil prices on the world market, and the resulting income was included in the NMPp in domestic rubles.[260] "As a consequence, the growth rate of the national income, measured in the prices of final consumption, was noticeably diverted from the real dynamics of social production." Soon afterward, General Secretary Gorbachev expressed the same ideas.[261] Siuniaev suggests that producer prices be used to calculate net material product (Table 1.8).

TABLE 1.8   Average Annual Growth in Soviet Net Material Product, 1966–1986 (percentage)

	Final consumption prices	Producer prices	Difference
1966–1970	7.8	7.8	0.0
1971–1975	5.7	5.3	0.4
1976–1980	4.3	3.4	0.9
1981–1984	3.7	3.0	0.7
1985–1986[a]	1.5	4.5	–3.0

NOTE: Growth measured in current prices
a. Marked "calculated" in the source.
SOURCE: M. Siuniaev, "Ekonomicheskomu rostu—novye izmeriteli," Ekonomicheskaia gazeta, no. 3 (January 1988).

5. The Controversy over Soviet Investment

Let us start with Soviet procedures for pricing and for gathering statistics in construction. Goskomtsen has no responsibility for, or influence over, construction tariffs. They are calculated by an economic institute that belongs to Gosstroi, which essentially set the tariffs.[262] More peculiar is the fact that Gosstroi also gathers and evaluates construction statistics. No Soviet body elaborates any price index for construction. A branch organization such as Gosstroi has an obvious interest in presenting construction volumes that are as large as possible. If it is allowed to put forward current prices as comparable, why shouldn't it do so? [263] Cohn appears to believe that Stroibank and Gosbank are effective controllers of investment. If so, would investment be spread over 350,000 objects, as is the case today?[264] Two conservative Soviet economists explain: "Unfortunately, rather often one encounters faulty ideas about the degree of centralization in the formation of prices. Sometimes the matter is perceived in such a way that almost all prices are set only by Goskomtsen of the USSR. But this has nothing in common with reality."[265]

"Estimate" (*smetnye*) prices are simply construction tariffs and do not appear to differ in principle from other Soviet prices. One distinguishes among six basic kinds of planned prices: wholesale prices of enterprises and industry, purchasing prices for agricultural production, tariffs for railway and other transports, planned estimate cost (*planovaia smetnaia stoimost'*) for construction objects, retail prices for commodities, and services for the population. All these prices include prime cost of production and net income (profit and, for a limited circle of products, turnover tax as well).[266]

Each branch has its practical peculiarities. Prices are estimated for the different elements that form parts of investment projects. These are revised every few years, most recently on January 1, 1984.[267] To these tariffs, special surcharges are added to represent increased wages and the like. Equipment and machinery are included at current wholesale prices. On the basis of all price elements, construction is valued on current account at what is called *smetnye raschety* (estimate calculation). Only when the tariffs are raised is a corresponding reduction made in investment costs in official statistics to maintain "comparable prices."[268] The latest statistical yearbook states quite frankly how these "comparable prices" are calculated: "All value indicators on investment are presented in comparable prices, that is, the estimate prices that were adopted on January 1, 1984."[269] In other words, the tariffs are fixed, and compensation is made in the investment index for their increases. Shmul B. Sverdlik seems to support this argument: "We determine the volume of investment in accordance with the statistical yearbooks for the corresponding years, assuming that the volumes shown here in comparable prices do not differ much from the volumes in actual prices."[270] Thus, Sverdlik uses "comparable prices" as an approximation of current prices. The essence of the much-acclaimed Belorussian construction experiment (which Gorbachev praised at the Central Committee Plenum in June 1986) is to establish a negotiated price for a construction project in advance in order to cut costs.[271] In other branches, negotiated prices are recommended when the authorities want to raise prices. Estimate calculations must therefore be perceived as even more inflationary. The decree on *perestroika* of the system of price formation spells out the problem with investment prices:

> Revise *estimate prices and valuation in investment* [emphasis in original] in the direction of reinforcing their role in order to increase the efficiency of investment and improve the work of designing and construction organizations. Reconstruct the mechanism of price formation in construction, *excluding unjustified influence of material intensity on the level of prices of finished construction* [emphasis added].[272]

6. Economists in the Soviet Investment Controversy

Victor P. Krasovskii is a cautious, elderly man of a pre-Stalinist cut. From the end of the 1930s he spent seventeen years in the camps, which he left slightly crippled. He is not likely to overexploit his material.

Vladimir K. Fal'tsman is in his fifties. He enjoyed the protection of the late academician Aleksandr Anchishkin and has a solid academic reputation as an outstanding expert on investment, particularly in machine-building. He is on a good career track, but has not reached a senior position and is not inclined to take significant risks.

Professor Delez Palterovich of TsEMI shares many similarities with Fal'tsman both personally and academically. He has taken almost the same stand on inflation in investment.[273]

K. K. Val'tukh is reminiscent of both Fal'tsman and Palterovich but is almost sixty, lives in Novosibirsk, and appears bolder in his thinking.

All three men are likely to be more cautious than they have academic reason to be.

Grigorii Khanin, who is approaching the age of fifty, is virtually an academic outcast. In 1987 he was given an academic job in the Tuva Autonomous Republic in a remote corner of Siberia. He lived a long time in Novosibirsk, but seems to have been considered too controversial and was barred from both the academic Institute of the Economy and Organization of Industrial Production, and its journal, *EKO*. For many years he was not allowed to defend his doctoral dissertation. A few individuals with good credentials have taken personal risks to enable him to publish: academician Tatiana Zaslavskaia, journalist Vasilii Seliunin, and the late Anchishkin, who was the leading Soviet expert on forecasting. Upon reading Khanin, one can hardly avoid noticing that he has been severely censored.[274]

All these economists are worth taking seriously. Considering the strong resistance they encounter from Goskomstat and the prevalence of censorship, we are well advised to read between the lines of their work rather than to demand complete lucidity.

7. Soviet Estimates of Inflation

Academician Oleg Bogomolov has stated: "The price index by Goskomstat unfortunately does not reflect the full reality.... The 'basket' of commodities consumed during a year by average town dwellers has grown more than twice as expensive as at the end of the fifties."[275]

His statement implies a retail trade inflation of about 3 percent a year. One of the most senior Soviet economists has privately said that retail inflation amounted to 3 to 5 percent a year since 1966. An economist from Goskomtsen's research institute, D. Shavishvili, is reported to have said that from 1970 to 1980, "the rise of average prices brought to nothing the efforts to increase the standard of living."[276] The natural interpretation of this statement is that real retail sales per capita did not expand. Considering that retail sales at current prices increased 5.7 percent a year from 1970 to 1980, and the population by 0.9 percent a year, inflation would then have been about 5 percent a year.[277] The general view among senior Moscow economists appears to be that retail inflation has been 3 to 4 percent a year since the start of the economic reforms of 1965. Since they do not consider quality deterioration, however, retail inflation must be slightly higher—at least 4 percent a year.

(One problem is that these figures refer to Moscow or other cities, not small towns or the countryside.)

Machine-building may be the branch with the highest inflation, since the introduction of new commodities and the design of special products render price control virtually impossible. "After many years of observation, the prominent specialist of the USSR State Committee for Material and Technical Supply (Gossnab), V. Doronin, [has concluded that] prices of technical equipment rise by about 10 percent a year; this increase is not always justified by the quality of production."[278] Dmitrii L'vov and Nikolai Petrakov have stated that "from 1970 to 1985 the average price of a metal-cutting machine tool increased from 5,200 to 14,300 rubles," while the productivity of such tools "did not increase more than 25 to 30 percent." This would imply excessive price increases of slightly more than 5 percent a year.[279] Fal'tsman has calculated the total energy capacity of Soviet production of machines and equipment as an expression of the actual value of production. He concluded that, from 1970 to 1983, prices increased 2.7 times more than real value,[280] implying an excessive price increase of 8 percent a year, though according to Fal'tsman a significant upward adjustment is required for technological development. Considering various calculations, Seliunin and Khanin draw the plausible conclusion that "in machine-building the fictive increase of production comprises at a minimum 5 percent a year."[281]

In raw-material-producing branches of industry, on the other hand, price inflation is difficult to attain, so average inflation in industry must be significantly smaller. Val'tukh and Lavrovskii have calculated an index of the physical output of industry based on the official published series, which covers 190 to 250 commodities.[282] Their results are presented in Table 1.9 together with the official statistics measured in allegedly fixed prices.

For numerous reasons, this compounded physical output series cannot be considered a serious assessment of undisclosed inflation. Such inflation is likely to grow faster with more extensive use of raw materials and when their processing is less developed; the weights are not specified; more-sophisticated machinery is not properly reflected in this kind of index; and the physical output data are unreliable. Still, the decline in the growth rate measured in physical terms is striking. The worst period for industry was 1977–1983, when the growth rate of physical production in machine-building averaged 1 percent a year.[283] Price increases in construction have been huge. As director of Gosplan's Economic Re-

TABLE 1.9   Average Annual Increase in Soviet Industrial Production, 1951–1980 (percentage)

	Physical output	Official value
1951–1955	16.8	13.1
1956–1960	13.8	10.4
1961–1965	9.9	8.6
1966–1970	6.8	8.5
1971–1975	4.6	7.4
1976–1980	1.4	4.4

SOURCES: K. K. Val'tukh and B. L. Lavrovskii, "Proizvodstvennyi apparat strany: ispol'zovanie i rekonstruktsiia," *EKO* 17, no. 2 (February 1986): 29; *Narkhoz 1922–1972*, p. 56; *Narkhoz 1985*, p. 38.

search Institute, Vadim Kirichenko stated that the cost of housing construction on average has increased by 5 to 7 percent a year, though he ascribes this to quality improvements, which we are prone to doubt.[284] According to S. Korneev and V. Loginov of Stroibank, the cost of housing construction in the period 1981–1985 was three times greater than in 1961–1965, while the number of completed apartments was 16 percent smaller, amounting to an average annual cost increase per apartment of 6.5 percent.[285]

Since both machinery and construction are especially affected by inflation, investment is especially susceptible to inflation. Wiles has further interpreted Val'tukh's investment deflator for 1975–1980 at 4 percent a year or more:[286] 2 percent a year in 1966–1970, 3 percent in 1971–1975, 3.5 percent in 1976–1977, and probably 5 percent a year in 1978–1980.[287] Thus, in the investment sector, Wiles estimates that the CIA "understatement of price rises in 1966–70 was about 2.2 percent per annum and in 1971–75 about 2.8 percent" per year.[288] Fal'tsman explains much of this inflation in terms of rising import costs, so that inflation is even higher in domestic import prices than in the engineering sector.[289] The inflation rate in agriculture is difficult to assess, since agricultural statistics are remarkably inconsistent and much of the actual inflation is due to quality deterioration, but it is not likely to be less than in retail trade.

The Soviet Statistical Debate:

Khanin versus TsSU

IN FEBRUARY 1987 the first of a series of articles attacking the founda-tions of Soviet economic beliefs appeared in the literary-political journal *Novy mir*.[1] Entitled "The Cunning Figure" ("Lukavaia tsifra") and written by the outcast academic economist Girsh (Grigorii) Itsikovich Khanin and the well-connected economic journalist Vasilii Seliunin, it offered a comprehensive challenge to the official statistics on Soviet macroeconomic performance that found immediate resonance among the Soviet intelligentsia and provoked a hostile response from the keepers of statistical orthodoxy.

The article claimed that the achievements of the Soviet era had been vastly overstated through the use of "cunning figures" having little or no relationship to the economic reality they purported to represent. Moreover, these figures were said to be an important cause of the steady deterioration of performance over the previous quarter century, because crucial economic decisions had been, and continued to be, based on the

Richard E. Ericson is professor of economics at Columbia University and the Harriman Institute for the Advanced Study of the Soviet Union.

unreliable information. The article argued that reliable (*dostovernaia*) information was now particularly crucial as the economy set out on a path of restructuring (*perestroika*) in the pursuit of the intensification and acceleration (*uskorenie*) of economic development. The authors called for a dramatic re-evaluation of statistical procedures and methodology, as well as a thorough recalculation of historical statistics, as the basis for proper analysis of the existing Soviet economic situation and as a foundation for successful *perestroika.*

The article combined and brought into sharp focus two intellectual trends that had been developing away from the public eye in the pre-*glasnost* period. The first, and deepest, was a growing feeling that not all was right with official statistics. People did not feel that they, or the economy, were as well off as officially claimed; despite impressive statistical gains in production and growth rates of income and consumption, after 1975 the impression became widespread that the economy and standard of living were no longer improving.[2] There was a growing, yet largely inchoate, feeling that the reported gains were fictitious (*lipovye*); this was supported by numerous critical articles in the economic press pointing to apparently massive falsification, fabrication, and distortion uncovered at every inspection and revision and propelled to the surface by the highest Party organs' critical evaluation of the economy begun in 1983 and accelerated after the April (1985) Plenum and the Twenty-Seventh Party Congress in February 1986. The heuristic arguments supporting the radical revisionism of "Lukavaia tsifra" drew heavily on this perception of stagnation in a "pre-crisis" period.

The second trend, economically more substantive, grew out of academic research into the return to investment and the productivity of capital. The work of only a handful of Soviet economists, it presented evidence of dramatic price and cost increases in the construction and machinery and equipment sectors. Generated in part by significant manipulation of price-setting rules and of production assortment by producers and builders, the inflation was not represented in official statistics due to the methodological inadequacy of Soviet calculation of "comparable" (*sopostavimye*) prices and statistical practice. The economists' significant revision of some of the investment, capital, and productive capacity statistics was published and subsequently noticed by Western observers such as Hanson and Nove.[3] The revision has major implications for the structure and productivity of capital and the nature of the economic policies that need to be pursued in order to bring about a qualitative improvement in the performance of the Soviet economy; it was to these implications that the Khanin-Seliunin article pointed. Their article also drew on decades of research that Khanin had carried out in the face of repeated rejection and ostracism by the central academic establishment. It was largely on the basis of that research that his conclusions on aggregate performance statistics were drawn.

Khanin and Seliunin's article became the first volley in an animated discussion about the quality and reliability of Soviet economic statistics, both in the Soviet Union and abroad, and about the nature and extent of the achievements of Soviet socialism. The discussion was both academic and journalistic. During the spring of 1987, Khanin presented his arguments in seminars at various institutes of the Academy of Sciences, addressing both the methodology outlined in earlier articles and his statistical results.[4] The seminars were highly controversial, generating tremendous emotion around the "achievements of socialism" issue as well as raising and discussing serious questions of methodology and data. Khanin and Seliunin also presented their results and arguments before various state and Party organizations, including the Central Statistical Administration (TsSU), to an apparently quite chilly reception.[5] The press also pursued the argument, focusing on the issue of reliability (*dostovernost' ekonomicheskoi informatsii*) rather than on the historical record. From that perspective, the coverage was almost uniformly positive. Indeed, the only significant negative voices came from TsSU and its research institute and appeared in the Central Committee newspaper, *Ekonomicheskaia gazeta*, and the TsSU organ *Vestnik statistiki*. TsSU officials went out of their way to attack Khanin personally in interviews in the other central newspapers, even on completely unrelated subjects, a sign of how deeply his critique had stung.[6]

This debate has coincided with—and been reinforced by—the other economic debates associated with economic restructuring and *glasnost,* especially three closely related discussions. First there has been the popular debate over the rate of inflation of consumer goods, in which the official figure of an 8 percent increase over twenty-five years has been widely ridiculed.[7] Indeed, the general opinion seems to be that the price of typical consumer goods is rising 3 to 5 percent per year, at least over the last decade. The fact that the methodology that allows TsSU to ignore these changes is the same as that concealing hidden inflation in wholesale prices lends plausibility to Khanin's analysis.

The second discussion revolves around the current nature of prices and price formation, especially their waste-stimulating and cost-expanding (*zatratnyi*) character. The persistent theme here—that price changes systematically and significantly overstate quality improvements, and indeed frequently hide a deterioration in quality[8]—again supports a hypothesis of significant hidden inflation exaggerating macroeconomic performance and distorting measures of effectiveness and efficiency on which rational planning decisions must be based.

Finally, a debate has arisen as to what the appropriate measures of aggregate economic performance are, implying that those in current use are inadequate. What is sought is some adequate measure of the real net sum of economic activity, the final result on which performance is to be judged and on which incentives, under the newly reformed economic mechanism, are to be based. The discussion has tended to revolve around the advantages of using international measures of net output such as gross national product (GNP), and how—in what prices—it should be measured.[9] These issues stand at the heart of the Khanin-Seliunin critique, though the discussion has so far avoided addressing them directly.

In this chapter I focus directly on that critique to clarify the discussion and explore its implications. In the next section I summarize the criticisms that have been made of Soviet economic statistics, both at home and in the West. Then I turn to the primary, and most complete, internal Soviet alternative, the statistics presented by Khanin in his explanatory seminars.[10] Unfortunately, even these figures reflect only the crudest summary of Khanin's extensive research effort, though they are more complete than any he has yet published. Next I briefly outline Khanin's methodology, to the extent that I understand it from his two papers published previously and his seminar discussions, and consider the various criticisms that have been made of it. Finally, I conclude with some discussion of the importance and implications of Khanin's results for Soviet economic performance and our attempts to understand it.

Soviet Statistics: A Critique

The consensus among Western observers of the Soviet economy has been that Soviet economic statistics, while misleading, do provide an adequate basis for reconstruction of a sufficiently accurate picture of the state of the Soviet economy and its rate of development and change. In particular, reported physical measures of inputs and output are generally believed to be accurate, as are the indexes of investment and capital stock, despite serious problems with value measures and indexes leading to systematic, significant exaggeration of both their levels and rates of growth. It is generally believed that the Soviet central authorities do not systematically fabricate data in order to mislead outside observers, though they are not beyond deliberate misrepresentation through the use of selective definition, partial revelation, and omission of key data and series. The statistics presented are still seriously distorted, however, based as they are on unreliable basic information and compiled using seriously flawed methodology.[11] Understanding these biases and problems allows a useful reconstruction of Soviet economic statistics.

Let us review the nature of the alleged biases, particularly at the aggregate level, as these are frequently raised in the discussion brought into the open by the Khanin-Seliunin article. One of the main problems is that the information base of these statistics is the aggregation of performance measures and reports of organizations that pursue plan targets stated mostly in value terms, and whose performance is judged on the basis of those measures and reports. This leads to direct exaggeration whenever it is unlikely to be detected, and indirect exaggeration through the manipulation of the details of operation and the means and methods of measurement—especially prices—whenever possible.

The opportunities for exaggeration—for "paper" (*bumazhnyi*) in place of real performance—depend strongly on the nature of the economic activity measured, and hence on the branch or sector of the economy. Where the complexity of the type of activity measured is low—that is, where the technologies are long established and well understood, the inputs standardized, and the variety of activities and assortment of output limited and changing only slowly—there will be little room for self-interested manipulation. Prices will be well established and subject to effective control, and hence the measures of aggregate activity levels and their changes should be relatively reliable. This is generally believed to be the case with the natural-resource base, the raw-materials and extraction sectors, agricultural procurement, electrical energy, basic metals, construction materials, and basic chemicals.[12]

On the other hand, where complex, multi-stage, frequently changing technologies using a vast and variable assortment of inputs are used to produce a large variety of increasingly complex and specialized goods and services, including many (purportedly) new items, the opportunities for exaggeration through fabrication, manipulation, and distortion of both physical and value measures of activity and performance are countless. In particular, fictitious output can be created through the pricing of "new" and "improved" products even though prices are set and approved by the central authorities, as those prices necessarily depend on information provided by the self-interested producer. This seems to be the situation in most processing, manufacturing, and engineering (machine-building) industries as well as in investment and construction, though there has been some debate in the West on the latter.[13]

Complementary to this data distortion is a series of problems created by the prevailing statistical methodology. Rather than attempting to correct for the inaccuracies and exaggerations introduced from below, the Soviet methodology seems to propagate and enhance them—in part, perhaps, intentionally. There are systematic biases in survey design, distortions through omission, the use of biased and inconsistent formulae, inconsistent calculation of components and chaining of aggregate measures, the use of inconsistent time periods and definitions in comparisons, and a general lack of proper documentation of definitions and methods.[14] There is also a systematic failure to take proper account of the distortions introduced from below by calculating appropriate indexes of changes in price and valuation, leading to a significant component of hidden inflation in the aggregate statistics, as the "comparable prices" used to aggregate reported or measured physical performance fail to reflect increases in actual prices, and hence exaggerate real performance. This effect is generally recognized to be important in those sectors with a heterogeneous and rapidly changing assortment of output, and effort is made to take account of it in Western (largely CIA) recalculations of Soviet national income statistics.

A major exception, however, was noted above: investment and capital-stock statistics. Until quite recently the Western consensus was that the Soviets' use of comparable "estimate" (construction) prices in investment and the periodic re-evaluation of the capital stock in "censuses" had largely insulated this sector from the effects of hidden inflation, so that reported investment was considered a real addition to a generally accurate index of real capital. This belief was reinforced by evidence that independent efforts to reconstruct the Soviet capital series had yielded numbers surprisingly close to the official Soviet statistics.[15] It has come under recent challenge, however, on the basis of both Soviet studies, including that of Khanin, and a deeper look at the Soviet methodological literature indicating that construction and investment statistics should suffer many of the same problems as machine-building output statistics.[16]

The internal Soviet critique brought out in the Khanin-Seliunin article touches on most of these points, while investigating further several areas either ignored or mentioned only in passing in the Western discussion. In particular, it accepts Western arguments on the problem of official Soviet index numbers arising out of aggregation in "comparable prices," and underlines the hidden inflation and ensuing distortion (unreliability) of aggregate value indexes of "real" economic activity. It is therefore widely recognized that the official methodology ignores the systematic overpricing of "new," "improved," or merely changed products; tends to absorb higher, temporary prices as basic—in practice if not principle—in indexes; and ignores frequent, dramatic shifts in the structure of production and output assortment.

Also emphasized—indeed, far more than in the Western discussion—is the strong self-interest of all actors in the economy, up to the highest levels, in the exaggeration (*zavyshenie*) of results through price changes. The incentives of all organizations and decision-makers below the level of the Central Committee, the Collegia of the Council of Ministers, and the State Planning Committee (Gosplan) are geared toward maximizing value measures of activity. Even where physical measures are important, at the enterprise and factory level, there are crucial associated measures of value—such as output and/or sales, profitability, expenditures per ruble output—that give the enterprise a vital interest in how its product is priced. This interest extends directly to the enterprise's immediate superiors: their strength increases as the level of aggregation rises and physical measures become increasingly meaningless, leaving only value aggregates as possible indexes of performance.[17]

The opportunity to introduce hidden inflation is recognized to be somewhat less universal than the motivation, with the same factors noted above determining where it is apt to be worse. In addition, the Soviet writing emphasizes that the problem of properly setting and controlling the price changes is insoluble; it is too vast to be dealt with even approximately. Thus we see visions of harried Goskomtsen (State Price Committee) employees, each reviewing three to four prices per day, with each price supported by thousands of pages of documentation. The system is able to review only 200,000 of 24 million to 25 million industrial prices alone, and it is doubtful that the resulting prices reflect appropriate changes in use characteristics and quality.[18] The argument is reinforced by the repeated observation that there is no natural tendency for quality to improve, as there is no direct consumer influence over producers, and changes are made only to satisfy arbitrary standards imposed from above or to get around inconvenient standards and constraints. The natural tendency under pressure from above has been to increase costs (*zatratnyi mekhanizm*) in order to generate, regardless of cost, the required observable outcomes.[19]

This does not mean, of course, that no quality improvements take place. It only implies that the changes in cost-justified prices that accompany these improvements are far greater than those commensurate with the quality change.[20] In fact, with regard to industrial consumer goods, there seems to be no systematic relation between price and quality changes, and there is some perception of deteriorating quality of existing goods with the steady disappearance of low-price basics and replacement with high-price substitutes.[21] It is not surprising that numerous Soviet authors, including Khanin and Seliunin, have found significant hidden inflation—that is, price changes far outstripping quality improvements—in industry, particularly machine-building, metalworking, and instrument making; in construction; and in transportation, particularly automobiles.

The area in which the Soviet internal critique departs furthest from that of Western observers is direct physical measures of output. As these are not subject to the vagaries of pricing in index formation, they have generally been accepted at face value by most Western observers. And indeed, the critical Soviet writings, such as those of Khanin and Seliunin, emphasize that they are significantly *more* reliable than value-based indexes. But even they should be subject to some suspicion, particularly during the 1970s and 1980s, as they too have become increasingly subject to manipulation and fabrication (*ochkovtiratel'stvo i pripiski*).

The problems with physical measures are said to be particularly bad in those sectors relatively unaffected by manipulation of value indexes due to stable nomenclature, relative homogeneity of product, and tight price control, such as raw-material production, construction materials, agricultural output, railroad transportation, energy, fuels, and basic chemicals.[22] A. Sergeev claims that even the central organs estimate 1.5 to 3.0 percent of reported physical output to be fictitious, though the author believes it to be much greater. Further, he claims that economists believe anywhere from 5 to 25 percent of the output of the extractive (raw materials) sectors to be fraudulent.[23] There is new evidence of massive fabrication (*pripiski*) with regard to ton-kilometers in railroad transport: losses of product during transport, much of which may not have initially been there, are thought to range from 8 to almost 50 percent, with construction materials and agricultural products in the upper range. There is also increasing evidence of physical measurements that include additives and impurities, thus exaggerating activity and output reports as well as lowering quality.[24] Even in construction, which deals with large, observable objects, there are numerous controversial reports of fictitious buildings and factories and of reported completions—which add to final output and capital stock—that will only occur well into the future, if at all.[25] All of these have helped to raise serious questions in the Soviet debate about the reliability of even the physical production statistics officially claimed.

There is a further issue raised by internal critics of Soviet economic statistics that deserves to be mentioned: much of the output of real economic activity in the Soviet Union should not be counted as "product" or as generating income, since it is absolutely useless, produced solely to fulfill production plans and hence devoid of any economic value.[26] The results of such economic activity are no more real output, an addition to social value, than results fabricated on paper in response to plan fulfillment pressures. Indeed, it is worse; such activity destroys social wealth by using up material, capital, and labor inputs, and hence should be accounted for as a natural disaster. Much of the explosive growth of material inventories and unfinished construction in the last twenty years can be attributed to this cause, as can the growing underutilization of capital stock in many sectors, particularly machine-building, and the inexorably rising materials intensity of all production and construction activity. Much of what Western economists would see as growing economic inefficiency is interpreted by these critics of Soviet economic statistics as fictitious output, producing no economic value.

Ultimately this critique of official Soviet economic statistics charges that, because they are formed though inappropriate aggregation of highly questionable numbers whose exaggeration is in everyone's interest, they are not to be trusted. A reliable substitute needs to be constructed, piece by piece, taking specific care to compensate for any expected bias in the underlying data. The challenge is to find as basic and physical a set of measures as possible—preferably measures unrelated to the economic interests or incentives of Soviet managers and their supervisors—and to aggregate them in an explicit, consistent, and economically meaningful way in order to learn the true structure and performance record of the Soviet economy. As Khanin explained it in his seminars, this was the task he first undertook more than fifteen years ago, one that *glasnost* is finally allowing to come to light. Below I present some of the results of this effort before turning to a brief discussion of his methodology and the official criticism that he, and his findings, have encountered.

Khanin's Statistics: An Alternative

Although criticism of official Soviet statistics is widespread and growing, and many Soviet economists are working on aspects of the problem, there has been no systematic effort aside from that of Khanin to reconstruct the entire edifice of Soviet economic statistics.[27] Due to the nature of his research and its findings, Khanin's access to publication outlets and the advancement of his academic career were largely blocked before 1985. His two methodological articles that appeared in an Academy of Sciences journal in 1981 and 1984 were narrowly focused and avoided drawing any broad macroeconomic conclusions, though they did propose some significant revisions of sectoral economic statistics.[28] The first indication of a grand revision came in an article entitled "Dust into the Eyes" ("Pyl' v glaza") in *Pravda* on December 30, 1985, written with Seliunin, with whom he had begun working in 1979.[29] In particular, problems with measuring investment, capital, and capital productivity were raised. Criticism of those statistics was again brought to light by Khanin in *Sotsialisticheskaia industriia* on August 27, 1986, in "Let's Count Capital Stocks . . ." ("Sochtem fondy . . ."), in which he questioned official capital-productivity (*fondootdacha*) figures and their apparent implications for the allocation of investment.

The first general indication that a comprehensive revision of Soviet national income accounts had been attempted came with the publication of the *Novy mir* piece. It presented an extremely sketchy picture of the results, however, providing no figures for the 1950s, for example, which was claimed to be the most successful decade. The picture has been only partially completed by the data Khanin presented at his academic seminars, and is further weakened by the lack of supporting computations and of any detailed description of the methodology and precise data sources used to arrive at the alternative statistics. However, because their work remains, to my knowledge, the only systematic Soviet effort to address the problems with Soviet official statistics, it deserves as wide dissemination as possible. Table 2.1 contains the most systematic compilation available of Khanin's results. They amount to a dramatic—almost shocking—devaluation of Soviet macroeconomic performance

TABLE 2.1   Soviet Economic Growth, 1928–1985: Khanin and TsSu Indexes

	National income		Capital (productive)		Capital productivity		Labor productivity (social)[a]		Materials intensity[b]		Investment (productive)	
	K	TsSu	K	TsSu	K	TsSU	K	TsSU	K	TsSu	K	TsSu
1928–41	1.50	5.46	1.95	2.97	0.77	1.84	1.36	4.33	1.25–1.30		—	
1942–50	1.15	1.60	1.24	1.24	0.93	1.32	1.10	1.55	1.10		—	
1951–60	2.00	2.65	1.70	2.50	1.17	1.03	1.62	2.15	0.95		—	
1961–65	1.24	1.37	1.33	1.56	0.93	0.88	1.19	1.32	1.02		1.29	1.53
1966–70	1.22	1.45	1.28	1.48	0.95	0.98	1.17	1.39	1.02		1.19	1.45
1971–75	1.17	1.32	1.21	1.52	0.97	0.87	1.08	1.23	1.05		1.05	1.44
1976–80	1.05	1.24	1.10	1.43	0.95	0.86	1.00	1.17	1.05		1.04	1.20
1981–85	1.03	1.18	1.03	1.37	1.00	0.86	1.00	1.17	1.05		0.95	1.15

NOTE: The figures represent the value of the index at the end of each period, where the value at the beginning of the period is 1.

a. In Soviet usage, "social" refers to all labor.

b. Khanin gives only his recomputation of materials intensity (materialoemkost), as the official numbers are absurd.

SOURCE: Khanin, presented here as written on the blackboard in seminars at Moscow State University on February 25, 1987, and at the Central Economic-Mathematical Institute of the USSR Academy of Sciences on May 7, 1987.

TABLE 2.2   Soviet Economic Growth, 1928–1985: Relative Size
             According to Three Indexes

	Index		
	Khanin	Western	TsSU
National income	6.60	10.96	88.83
Capital (productive)	9.59	51.06	63.30
Capital productivity	0.68	0.25	1.39
Labor productivity	3.64	3.93	44.60
Materials intensity	1.64	—	1.64
Investment (1961–1985)	1.59	3.76	4.41

NOTE: I do not know of any Western recalculations of materials intensity (*materialoemkost'*).

SOURCES: The Khanin and TsSU indexes are derived from chaining the period-by-period indexes in Table 2.1. The Western indexes are derived from exponential compounding of the growth rates presented in table 1 of Gur Ofer's excellent survey, "Soviet Economic Growth: 1928–1985," *JEL* 25, no. 4 (December 1987): 1767–1833. (They would be somewhat lower, and capital productivity somewhat higher, if geometric compounding had been used instead.)

over the history of the Stalinist planned economy. If accurate (reliable, or dostovernye, in Khanin's terms), they imply a need for a significant re-evaluation of the long-term systemic performance of detailed centralized planning and management of an economy.30 This is immediately apparent if we look at the overall scale of change, 1928–1985, implied by the indexes of Khanin, TsSU, and Western analysts (Bergson/CIA) in Table 2.2. Of particular interest is how close Khanin's recomputed labor productivity index is to the Western indexes and how much higher he finds capital productivity to be. This disparity is closely related to the general acceptance by Western economists of Soviet investment and capital construction statistics—that is, their belief that hidden inflation in these sectors has been quite moderate, as reflected in indicators 2 and 6.

More interesting than the overall long-term performance of the Stalinist system depicted in these numbers are their implications for the relative performance of the Soviet economy over various subperiods of its existence. Khanin explicitly argues that the results of the First Five-Year Plan (FYP) were largely fictitious, and that what development occurred before the war actually took place under the Second, far more sober, FYP. Unfortunately, he does not provide a detailed breakdown, neither in these statistics or elsewhere, to substantiate that claim. A claim that is substantiated by the statistics he provides is that the 1950s represented something of a golden age for the administrative economic mechanism.[31] It is only in that period that we see a true doubling of real national income and a strong increase in the real capital stock, coupled with strongly rising capital and labor productivity and the only drop in the materials intensity of production in Soviet history.

The 1950s was also the only period with truly stable prices for industrial output. Khanin notes that from 1928 to 1950 the true wholesale price index (including investment and construction) rose to over twelve times its initial level, while in the 1960s the hidden inflation in the machine-building sectors, including investment goods, rose from 18 percent for the first half to 33 percent over the Eighth FYP. This rate of real inflation (a Laspeyres index of wholesale price changes) for machinery and investment goods has remained between 27 and 34 percent for each succeeding five-year period—that is, from 5 to 6 percent per year. The real wholesale price index for all industrial products, Khanin and Seliunin argue, has been rising at a rate of 3 to 4 percent per year for the last fifteen to twenty years.[32]

This hidden inflation, they assert, is the primary consequence of the "reforms" of 1965–1967, and gave those reforms a false appearance of initial success in both the CIA and TsSU statistics. Indeed, Khanin's recomputations show the last twenty years as a period of growing rigidity of the system and unrelieved deterioration of economic performance in all spheres. The crisis of the early 1960s that prompted the reforms of 1965–1967 was merely aggravated by those reforms, though its consequences were hidden by the growing dishonesty and inflation they unleashed. Both Khanin and Seliunin assert that it is this crisis of the underlying economic system that the current reforms, *perestroika* à la Gorbachev, are beginning to address.[33]

The evidence for this negative assessment can best be seen by looking at the implied average annual rates of growth for various subperiods of the "command economy" era. Table 2.3 shows the same six indexes given in the first two tables for four versions of "long-run" (LR) performance for the system as well as for the initial period, the "golden age," the "reform" FYP, and the last two FYPs. We see immediately that the Eighth FYP (1966–1970) was in no way outstanding, though its performance was better than that of any period that followed. Indeed, in all areas but capital productivity, performance in the Eighth FYP was worse than in the preceding five-year period, as simple calculation

TABLE 2.3 Soviet Economic Growth, 1928–1985: Average Annual Rates for Five-Year Plan (FYP) and Long-Run (LR) Periods

	Index								
	LR1	LR2	LR3	LR4	1928–1941	1951–1960	8FYP	10FYP	11FYP
National income	3.33	3.64	3.84	2.60	2.90	6.90	3.98	0.98	0.59
Capital (productive)	3.97	4.21	3.94	3.40	4.80	5.30	4.94	1.90	0.59
Capital productivity	-0.70	-0.65	-0.20	-0.80	-1.90	1.60	-1.00	-1.00	0.00
Labor productivity	2.27	2.49	2.54	1.60	2.20	4.80	3.14	0.00	0.00
Materials intensity	0.87	0.83	0.38	0.74	1.60	-0.50	0.40	0.98	0.98
Investment (1961–1985)	—	—	—	1.86	—	—	3.48	0.78	-0.95

NOTES: LR1 = 1928–1985.
LR2 = LR1 without the 1940s period of war and recovery.
LR3 = 1951–1985, the "mature system."
LR4 = 1961–1985, the "great stagnation."
1928–1941 = the initial period.
1951–1960 = the "golden age."
8FYP = Eighth Five-Year Plan, 1966–1970; the "reform."
10FYP = Tenth Five-Year Plan, 1976–1980.
11FYP = Eleventh Five-Year Plan, 1981–1985.
SOURCE: Khanin's seminars (See Table 2.1).

shows with respect to each of the six indicators. The annual rates of growth for these indicators in the period 1961–1965 are: 4.3 percent, 5.7 percent, –1.45 percent, 3.47 percent, 0.39 percent, and 5.1 percent.

These results are all the more interesting when considered in light of the competing TsSU and Bergson/CIA statistics. Table 2.4 shows the relative rates of growth (percentage per year) for the first four indicators over the periods for which I have comparable data. The influence of the general Western acceptance of the Soviet physical series and invest-ment and capital data are clearly visible in the intermediate position of Western estimates of national income (GNP) growth and labor produc-tivity relative to the other two series, and the similarity of official Soviet and Western estimates of capital-related variables as opposed to

TABLE 2.4   Soviet Economic Growth, 1928–1985:
Estimates of Average Annual Rates (percentage)

	Khanin	Bergson/CIA	TsSU
National income (GNP)			
LR1	3.33	4.3	8.8
LR2	3.64	4.8	9.7
LR3	3.84	4.4	7.6
LR4	2.60	3.9	5.5
1950s	6.90	6.0	10.1
1970s	2.00	3.7	5.3
11FYP	0.59	2.0	3.2
Capital (productive)			
1928–1966	4.5	7.4	7.2
1950–1960	5.3	9.4	9.16
1960–1981	4.1	7.6	8.1
Capital productivity			
1928–1966	–0.66	–1.9	1.9
1950–1960	1.6	1.7	0.3
1960–1981	–1.03	–3.5	–2.2
Labor productivity			
1928–1966	2.8	3.3	8.2
1950–1960	4.8	4.6	7.65
1960–1981	2.04	2.7	4.85

NOTE: See Table 2.3 for periods covered by LR and FYP.
SOURCES: Derived from both Khanin's presentation and P. R. Gregory and R. C. Stuart, *Soviet Economic Structure and Performance*, 3rd ed. (New York: Harper & Row, 1983), chapter 11.

Khanin's estimates. But Western estimates of Soviet national income and labor productivity growth are generally much closer to Khanin's than to the official Soviet statistics. Only with the acceleration of hidden inflation in the 1970s do the Khanin and CIA national income growth estimates significantly depart.

These data highlight the impact of the significantly higher hidden inflation perceived by the Soviet critics of official statistics as a result of taking into account distortions in the physical data as well as illegitimate price changes. In particular, this perception follows from a much- reduced belief in the reality of quality changes in the assortment of goods actually available in the Soviet Union. Despite some Western and Soviet claims to the contrary, this belief is not based on ignoring quality changes, but rather on a deep skepticism arising out of analysis of that quality, its changes, and associated price/aggregating-weights changes.[34]

The claim behind this position is that, while there have been noticeable changes in quality and the continual introduction of new goods, the improvement in these products has been far less than the increase in costs and prices. For example, Khanin and Seliunin note that adding programming to a machine tool raises its price 7.3-fold, and making it a robot 12.3-fold, while its productivity rises barely 1.5-fold in either case. Fal'tsman has calculated that equipment productivity has risen only 37 percent of the increase in prices, and L'vov and Petrakov have estimated that the prices of metal-cutting equipment have almost tripled, while productivity has risen only 25 to 30 percent. These authors give estimates of hidden inflation of anywhere from 5 to 8 percent in machine-building, while Kirichenko claims there is 5 to 7 percent inflation in construction pricing.[35] Thus there are claims of less real Soviet output than even conservative Western reconstructions allow.

In addition to these aggregate results of his recomputations, Khanin also provides some scattered sectoral results, if only indirectly. Noting that hidden inflation has ranged from 27 to 34 percent every five years in machine-building and metalworking allows a reconstruction of Khanin's implicit output series for that sector. This calculation was carried out by F. Kushnirsky, and is presented in Table 2.5, together with the official series and another alternative series, compiled by Val'tukh and Lavrovskii and referred to by Seliunin and Khanin.[36] The numbers indicate that Khanin's calculations of hidden inflation may be on the conservative side since the 1965–1967 reforms. A similar exercise can be carried out for the construction industry using Khanin's estimate of

TABLE 2.5   Soviet Machine-Building and Metalworking:
            Average Annual Growth, 1961–1985 (percentage)

Five-Year Plan	Khanin-Seliunin	Val'tukh-Lavrovski	TsSu
1961–1965	7.7–8.7	10.7	12.3
1966–1970	7.8–8.0	5.9	11.7
1971–1975	6.8–7.9	4.7	11.6
1976–1980	2.7–3.9	1.2	8.2
1981–1985	0.2–1.6	0.3	6.2

SOURCE: Kushnirsky, "New Challenges to Soviet Official Statistics: A Methodological Survey," presented to a CIA conference December 11, 1987, table 9.

about 31 to 34 percent inflation in capital and construction costs every five years since 1970.[37]

It is interesting to note that these recomputed indexes seem to be having some impact on official thinking. An indication of this is the statistical series, always highly incomplete, used in the official discussions of the need for perestroika. For example, Abel Aganbegyan, writing in a recent issue of EKO, has stated that there was zero real growth during 1979–1982 due to hidden inflation.[38] This claim is expanded and elaborated in his recent book, prepared largely for Western audiences, *The Economic Challenge of Perestroika*, where he asserts that because of hidden inflation there was practically no growth (a zero growth rate) from 1980 to 1985.[39] Furthermore, there is much official discussion of the need to "restructure" statistics in the interests of "reliability" and greater realism and usefulness, even in the more recent issues of *Vestnik statistiki*, the organ of the State Committee for Statistics (Goskomstat). Though it refers to critics such as Khanin unfavorably, the publication does seem to show some concern for the substance of their critique.

Finally, at least indirectly related to these unorthodox estimates are the quasi-official recomputations of Soviet aggregate economic statistics by the Institute for World Economy and International Relations (IMEMO).[40] As a foundation for making direct international comparisons of economic rates of growth, researchers at that institute developed measures of Soviet national net material product and industrial and agricultural output in constant 1980 U.S. dollars for 1913, 1920, 1929, 1938, 1950, 1986, and 1987 (plan). These measures show growth of only a third to a fifth of that given in official statistics over a comparable period used by Khanin and Seliunin, 1929–1986. For example, Soviet national income is estimated to have grown only

17.27 times (versus 88.83 according to TsSU) and labor productivity 19 times (versus TsSU's 44.6), which is clearly significant despite limitations in comparability due to differing price weights and coverage of intrabranch turnover. Though the discrepancy is less after recovery from the war—for example, 5.2 times versus 10.2 times growth of national income from 1950 to 1986—these estimates are still much closer to those of Khanin and Seliunin. Going beyond even Khanin and Seliunin, however, the authors claim that capital productivity in the 1970s fell at a rate of 5 percent per year, though their estimates of average annual rates of growth still exceed those of both Khanin and the CIA.[41] This can be seen by comparing the national income and labor productivity growth in Table 2.6 with that of Table 2.4, despite the slightly different coverage.

The appearance of such quasi-official alternative estimates of Soviet aggregate economic performance highlights the growing dissatisfaction, even at the center, with the state of official statistics. It shows a willingness to countenance alternatives, albeit with hesitation and evident distaste, such as that provided by Khanin and Seliunin in their *Novy mir* piece. And it reinforces the atmosphere of skepticism about official economic claims that provided such fertile ground for "Lukavaia tsifra."

Khanin's Methodology

The methods used to generate these alternatives to official Soviet estimates have yet to be clearly explained by Khanin, largely due to constraints placed on him by his environment. Only a fairly general and somewhat cryptic discussion is presented in his two methodological pieces, and little was added to that in his seminar presentations.[42] In particular, his brief descriptions of various methods used to estimate national income and industrial, transportation, and construction output are unsupported by actual data, or even clarifying examples that would allow us to understand what was done. As a result, Khanin has left himself an easy target for both hostile criticism and simple misunderstanding. We see the former in the official responses to the Khanin-Seliunin critique, and may ourselves be guilty of the latter.

Khanin's methodology derives directly from his critique of official statistics. In particular, it aims for a reconstruction built, as far as possible, on those official statistical series that he feels are most reliable, and on data derived purely technologically, including those from other countries. In other words he ignores aggregate figures for the output of

TABLE 2.6   Soviet Economic Growth, 1929–1986: Average Annual
             Rates (percentage)

	National income	National income per capita	Labor productivity
1929–1938	7.7	6.2	6.1
1929–1950	5.7	5.25	5.28
1929–1986	5.0	4.1	4.1
1938–1950	4.2	4.5	4.6
1938–1986	4.5	4.5	3.76
1950–1986	4.5	3.7	3.46

SOURCE: Institute of World Economy and International Relations (IMEMO), "Sovetskii soiuz v mirovoi ekonomike (1917–1987gg)," *Mirovaia ekonomika i mezhdunarodnye otnosheniia*, nos. 11 and 12 (1987), tables 2, 3, 5, 20, 21.

the manufacturing, engineering, machine-building, transportation, and construction sectors and relies on reports of output in physical terms—on materials and energy inputs, on measurements of power capacity (such as electrical equipment and motors measured in terms of power or wattage), and on any other indicators (primarily technological and/or engineering) that are unrelated to the economic interests (according to the plan) or incentives of producers.

Unfortunately, only a few of these indicators are mentioned in his papers, and none is given any real content with data. Those that are used are manipulated independently in order to develop a number of different measures for each of the indexes being considered, such as industrial output and its growth. Khanin argues that each such measure, while addressing some significant aspect of the reality he is trying to measure, suffers from important shortcomings. Indeed, a substantial portion of each paper is spent outlining the problems with each of his alternative measures. To improve their reliability, he compares the different measures for each indicator, finds that they generally differ from one another by less than 10 percent while collectively differing from the similar official index by more than 30 percent, and then takes their simple arithmetic mean as a reasonable approximate alternative index.

The methodology thus stands on three principles: first, use natural, physical, or engineering indexes wherever aggregate statistics are unreliable; second, use multiple, independent methods to take advantage of all the reliable data available; and finally, average the measures to reduce the variance in error introduced by each individual method.[43]

Khanin implements this methodology by calculating six different, though not wholly independent, measures of industrial output; three measures of "prime cost" (*sebestoimost'*) of production; three measures of capital construction/investment output; two measures of productive capital stock (*osnovnye fondy*); three measures of automotive transportation output; three measures of national income produced (net material product); and several measures each of a number of other macroeconomic indicators (capital/labor ratios and profitability and profit growth for example). Each of the measures incorporates several assumptions and raises questions about the data used to calculate them. With respect to industrial output, these issues are addressed in a paper by Kushnirsky, who attempts (without success) to replicate some of Khanin's results; he concludes that Khanin must have had access to different data.[44] I will outline the different methods Khanin claims to have used to calculate his alternative indexes, and then turn to a brief discussion of some of the criticisms raised against him, particularly in the Soviet Union.

To get estimates of industrial output undistorted by hidden inflation and falsification, Khanin relies on six physical and indirect measures, the first four of which were applied to all subperiods of the Soviet era and discussed in his seminars. The first is a standard Laspeyres physical index based on a representative sample of about 100 products, weighted by official labor input coefficients for the base year. The base weights were updated for each FYP in order to take into account labor productivity and some quality changes. In his seminar Khanin claimed also to have calculated the index for samples of around 400 and 1,000 products, without significant change in the results. The second measure, in terms of reliability and importance, is based on the discrepancy between meeting plan targets in monetary terms and meeting them in physical terms.[45] Based on the assumption that initial value and physical plans are drawn up to be consistent, the measure deflates plan fulfillment in value terms by the percentage fulfillment in physical terms, thus revealing hidden inflation.[46] The third method of calculating real output growth is based on the growth of real materials consumption in industry. Noting that materials consumption per unit of output declined at a rate of 0.2 to 0.3 percent per year over long periods as a result of technological progress in the advanced capitalist economies, in particular the United States, Khanin made the assumption that it had remained constant in the Soviet Union. Hence he estimates an index of material expenditure as a proxy for an index of real production.[47] The fourth method is built on the assumption that there is a technologically determined relationship independent of the economic system, between the growth of labor productivity and the industrial consumption of electrical power per worker. The growth of labor productivity can then be determined from that (assumed reliable) of the United States at the same levels of electrical power consumption, that is, about twenty years earlier, allowing the construction of an index of physical output.

Khanin indicated in his seminar that he felt the last two measures to be less reliable than the first four. They are based on an assumed connection between the dynamics of "own cost of production" (*sebestoimost'*) of comparable output and that of labor productivity, and between the dynamics of *sebestoimost'* of exported production and that of export earnings in constant world prices. In the latter case, he uses the cost of producing a ruble of foreign earnings, assumed to reflect a unit of real output, to determine hidden inflation and hence "true" labor productivity. In both cases, indexes of *sebestoimost'*, wage changes, and the share of labor in total costs are used to construct an index of labor productivity and thus growth in real output.[48] Each of these methods was used to calculate the real output growth of several industrial sectors, such as machine-building, which was weighted by share in industry to give an index of overall industrial growth. The indexes were then averaged to give the industrial output component of Khanin's national income statistics.

The results achieved by these methods were claimed to be remarkably consistent, lending credibility to their claim of reliability. Khanin supports this with Table 2.7, which gives the relationship of the rates of growth of the machine-building sector over two five-year periods as calculated by each of the methods. (The last two methods were not used on the earlier period due to lack of data.) In his seminars, Khanin claimed that similar indexes for TsSU statistics on machine-building were between 1.28 and 1.34, indicating a significant divergence from each of his estimates reflecting hidden inflation. Apparently a similar consistency was found among his figures when applied to other branches of industry, giving Khanin and Seliunin a certain confidence in their reliability.

To support this index of industrial production, Khanin developed a number of derivative indexes: labor productivity, productive capital stock, capital productivity, materials intensity, "own cost" of industrial production, profit levels, and profitability (*rentabel'nost'*). Except for the "own cost" index, Khanin gave these calculations little discussion.[49] For example, the capital-stock index is split into two parts, machinery and equipment and construction work, and their increments deflated according to the computed index of (hidden) wholesale price inflation in the machine-building and metalworking sector and a price index for construction and investment activity. Where price data available were insufficient, real capital stock was estimated from the power of electrical motors and equipment in that branch of industry, on the basis of their (assumed) technological relationship to capital stock in the United States.

The *sebestoimost'* (own cost) index was calculated as the mean of three different methods. The first uses the unit cost of comparable products, where comparability is taken to mean in serial production for three or more years, excluding new products during their initial high-cost period of assimilation into routine production. The second method calculates the relationship between total production expenditures, excluding preliminary sorting and assembly (*komplektatsiia*), and the alternative index of final output derived by the six methods noted above; while the third is based on a weighted average of independently calculated movements in prime cost, including wages, materials costs, and profits. For example, profits are calculated as a residual from gross social product calculated in base-year prices after all expenditures are subtracted. Expenditures are determined by splitting base-year expenditures into variable and fixed-cost components, multiplying the variable costs by the alternative index of real output, and then adding base-year fixed costs.[50] That sum is divided by the index of changes in prime cost, and the result is divided by base-year costs to give the final index of profit growth. Profitability is the product of that index divided by the index of capital stock.

In his 1984 paper, Khanin discussed some of the methods he used to estimate growth indexes for components of national income other than industrial production. Indicating that he found official indexes of agricultural output and railroad transport to be reliable, since they were consistent with his alternative indexes of industrial production of related branches, Khanin turned to an estimation of growth in three trouble spots: construction and investment, automotive transport, and national income itself. For an alternative index of construction output, he found only three methods he could average. The first used an index of physical output—housing construction—divided by its share in total construction activity. The increase in cost of $1m^2$ of housing was assumed to reflect improvement in the quality of construction activity, allowing Khanin to determine the inflation component of overall construction

TABLE 2.7   Growth of Machine-Building Output, 1961–1970

Method	1961–1965	1966–1970
1	1.00	1.00
2	1.10	0.97
3	0.80	0.97
4	0.87	1.00
5	—	0.93
6	—	0.93

NOTE: Method 1 = 1.00.

SOURCES: Khanin, "Al'ternativnye otsenki rezul'tatov khoziaistvennoi deiatel'nosti proizvodstvennykh iacheek promyshlennosti," *Izvestiia akademii nauk*, Seriia ekonomicheskaia, no.6 (1981); "Puti sovershenstvovaniia informatsionnogo obespecheniia svodnykh planovykh narodnokhoziaistvennykh raschetov," *Izvestiia akademii nauk*, Seriia ekonomicheskaia, no.3 (1984).

expenditures. The second method to determine the dynamics of construction output is based on physical measures of capacity increases that were calculated for each branch of both the productive and unproductive spheres. These measures were then aggregated using the share of each branch in investment. The third method is based on the reported fulfillment of long-run (*perspektivnye*) plans for capacity expansion in each branch of the economy. Assuming those plans are consistent, these figures yield an accurate measure of the volume of construction activity carried out, revealing the degree of inflation in its value.

For the sectors of trade and public feeding, material-equipment supply, and food processing (*zagotovki*), alternative evaluations of dynamics were based on the number of workers and their productivity, assumed to increase by only 1 percent per year due to their slower-growing capital/labor ratios. For the final major trouble spot, automotive industrial transportation, the results of using three different methods were averaged. The first begins with branch-specific norms for required transportation per million rubles output (1970 prices), weighted by the share of each branch in overall output. Growth in the value of transportation services beyond that justified by the growth of output is considered fictitious. The second method, used only for the material-production sphere, compares the relationship between growth of truck transportation and U.S. national income over a given period of development to determine an index of transportation services based on Khanin's alternative index of Soviet national income. The third estimate assumes a stable relationship between railroad and automotive transportation. Each of these measures was much closer to the others for each period than to official indexes, although they were not as tightly related as those for industrial production growth.

Finally, Khanin used three methods to derive an alternative index of national income growth. The first aggregates his estimates of the dynamics of gross social product of different branches of the economy according to their shares in the social wage fund, and then subtracts from the resulting index his index of materials intensity. The second method uses TsSU figures for the ratio of Soviet to U.S. national income, 1956–1980; independent estimates of that ratio for 1928–55; and an index of the growth of U.S. national income over the whole period. Finally, an index of national income was calculated from changes in the physical volume of each of its components, calculated independently through the methods described. Again, all the results were much closer to each other than to the official Soviet indexes.

The Official Response

Khanin's results and their provocative presentation in the *Novy mir* article stimulated a hostile response that remained largely superficial in its critique of his work. It involved largely *ad hominem* attacks in the general press as well as analyses by hired guns of TsSU (now Goskomstat) that showed little or no acquaintance with Khanin's earlier methodological work.[51] The accusations ran from Korolev's charge that the authors were unqualified to discuss the issue to calls of incompetence (Belov, Adamov), ignorance and dishonesty (Adamov), trickery (Sheremet), lying to create a sensation, and "bourgeois subjectivism" (Kozlov). Though a number of points have been raised, the thrust of the critique is built on six main accusations.

First, the Khanin-Seliunin (K-S) results are said to be based on only a small set of unrepresentative physical indicators and chosen to impart an intentional bias to the results. Claiming that TsSU's coverage is exhaustive, the critics point to Khanin's use of 48 to 140 products as inadequate to measure accurately the dynamics of industrial output. Similarly, they assert that K-S's 56 to 60 "capacity" (*moshchnost'*) types are inadequate to determine capital-stock dynamics. This criticism shows an ignorance of Khanin's other, more or less independent, methods and runs counter to his seminar claim to have tried the wider, 400 and 1,000 assortments without significant impact on his results. Indeed, the problem is not in the use of samples, but in the methodology applied; TsSU's methodology applied to a representative sample would yield constant results, as would Khanin's applied comprehensively. This, as well as the other criticisms, shows that the critics have not bothered to study Khanin's earlier methodological pieces.

Second, all of the authors claim to find either profound ignorance of economic statistics, industrial technologies, and statistical methodology on the part of Khanin and Seliunin, or malicious intention in choosing just those branches and products that denigrate Soviet economic performance. By a selective choice of indicators, they argue, Khanin and Seliunin can get any results they want. Indeed, the critics claim, they chose to ignore progressive sectors and concentrate on those least touched by technological change, such as agriculture and the extractive, food-processing, and light industries. While there may be some truth to these charges, the critics ignore both the data problems of the "progressive" sectors and Khanin's careful, if incomplete, discussion of these issues in his earlier work, as well as the rather severe publishing constraints under which he was obliged to explain his results.[52]

Most of the critics are willing to attribute Khanin and Seliunin's results to ignorance rather than evil intention or "sensationalism," and each of them goes out of his way to claim that the authors don't really understand some aspect of official statistical methodology. Thus Adamov explains that in the construction of chain indexes, primary data are checked and "cleaned" many times, that "confirmed" (*utverzhdennye*) rather than "temporary" prices are used in computing indexes, and that any kind of index must rely on some form of prices.[53] The comprehensiveness of TsSU coverage and its purported incorporation of technological and quality change are stressed by all the authors, as if there were some simple misunderstanding on Khanin's part. Sheremet goes further, asserting that Khanin and Seliunin, as well as practicing "trickery" (*lukavstvo*), do not understand either railroad technology or the basic accounting categories for industry, although Korolev admitted the K-S figure on transportation, claiming that they lent plausibility to a "profoundly flawed" (*gluboko oshibochnyi*) analysis.

A fourth and related claim is that Khanin and Seliunin ignore quality change, either out of incompetence or intentional dishonesty. This is plainly stated by Sheremet, while Adamov, Korolev and Kniazevskii argue that the oversight is a necessary consequence of the kinds of physical indicators and types of products used by the authors in developing their alternative estimates. This criticism has also been raised in the West, though I do not believe it is wholly justified.[54]

Another criticism, more justified than any of the preceding, points to the lack of methodological detail and data sources in the *Novy mir* piece. The authors in *Vestnik statistiki* even accuse Khanin and Seliunin of failing to cite assertions for which footnotes were provided.[55] Once again, none of the published criticism shows any recognition of the existence of Khanin's earlier methodological pieces. Indeed, Khanin has attempted to explain his methodology, which is more than the defenders of official orthodoxy do. Rather than accusing him of hiding his methodology or engaging in "trickery," these critics could have raised real questions about the applicability and consequences of that methodology.[56]

The final argument raised is that the K-S implications are absurd: the Soviet Union could not have industrialized, won the war, or become a superpower competing "as an equal" with the United States if it had grown only six- or sevenfold, as Khanin and Seliunin claim. Both Korolev and Adamov state, for example, that if Khanin and Seliunin were correct, the Soviet Union would still be at its 1928 level relative to the United States in national income, that is, with only about 10 percent of U.S. national income, which is clearly absurd; that claim itself seems to be based on "trickery." Abram Bergson has calculated that Soviet real national income in 1929 was about 20 percent that of the United States; with the U.S. national income in 1985 about 4.3 times its 1928 level, the Soviet Union would have gained substantially even under the K-S rates of growth.[57] The actual implication of the K-S findings is that the Soviet economy is now about one-third the size of the U.S. economy, a quite plausible figure to anyone living in the Soviet Union.[58] Indeed, given the official estimate of growth by a factor of 90 starting from a base of national income 10 percent that of the United States, the Soviet national income should now be about double that of the United States.

Most of the other criticisms of the K-S work are also without substance. For example, Sheremet accuses them of using official statistics that they don't trust; Kozlov claims it is methodologically unsound to compare indexes based on different principles; and Kniazevskii and Adamov argue that simple averaging of alternative indexes is meaningless, implying that the indexes are sample products requiring appropriate value weights. The tone of the official response ranges from sarcasm to bitterness and expresses shock that anyone would dare belittle Soviet achievements. Indeed, in the Moscow State University (MGU) seminar a number of elderly economists who had apparently spent their lives working in Gosplan and other central organs came close to tears as they responded to Khanin's presentation. The official Soviet position seems to be that, as it is simply unacceptable to reach such conclusions, something must be wrong with either the methods used or the intentions and honesty of the researchers. Under current conditions of controlled access to publication, that attitude cannot be seriously challenged by Khanin, Seliunin, or other doubters of official aggregate economic indexes.

Conclusion

The past few years have seen the opening of a wide-ranging debate in the Soviet Union on the reliability and meaningfulness of the available economic statistical series. The dramatic, focal position staked out by Khanin and Seliunin in this debate in their article in *Novy mir* provided a comprehensive, if sketchy, reinterpretation of Soviet economic history through the calculation of several alternative series of macroeconomic indicators of economic performance. Those series purport to show that much of the claimed achievements of Soviet socialism are fictitious, the consequence of an exaggeration game played by subordinates and superiors, the outcomes of which are validated by the central statistical authorities' faulty methodology of aggregation and measurement. The level of exaggeration has varied over time, being particularly great in the 1930s and 1970s and quite moderate during the "golden age" of 1951–1960. It has grown steadily since 1965, in large part as a consequence of the treadmill of reforms beginning in that year.

Furthermore, the K-S series shows that not only the size but also the structure, of the economy are quite different from that indicated by the official statistics, containing hidden inflation, opportunities for exaggeration of physical output measures among sectors, and differing degrees of exaggeration in the reported capital stocks across sectors. The consumer goods, construction, and manufacturing sectors thus appear to be larger than they really are, while the extractive and basic-materials industries appear smaller. The result, Khanin and Seliunin argue, is that planners and the highest central authorities are systematically misled into making decisions that are wasteful and counterproductive. Indeed, such decisions, and even more so the statistics on which they are based, are a primary cause of the stagnation, the "pre-crisis" situation that has triggered Gorbachev's reforms.

The implications of the K-S results and the debate they have spurred
are dramatic, for they call on us to re-evaluate our understanding of the
nature and consequences of a Soviet-type economic system, as well as
of the strength and position of the Soviet Union. If Khanin and Seliunin
are anywhere near being correct, we can no longer believe in the "command economy" as an effective mobilizer of resources or instrument for
change over any but the shortest period of time.[59] Though resources can
be mobilized, the final results of that mobilization rapidly deteriorate.
Hence the "command economy" appears rather as an engine for the
dissipation of social energy and resources, and the propagation of waste,
inefficiency, indifference, and dishonesty in the social system. Moreover,
it is an instrument that is becoming increasingly ineffective over time,
even with respect to those tasks that it once did well, despite all efforts
to reform or improve its functioning. Past efforts have merely led to the
disabling of the statistical thermometer—through which the health of
the economy is measured—by opening the way to still greater exaggeration, manipulation, and falsification by subordinates using their greater
freedoms to create the perception of desirable performance. This, in turn,
has fostered deterioration in the effectiveness of planning, leading to a
series of faulty investment and development decisions that have culmi-
nated in the stagnation of 1979–1983. Both Khanin and Seliunin have
argued that, without the dramatic break in policy that has occurred
since, the economy would have reached a true crisis and broken down
by 1995.[60] This is a far cry from the dynamic Soviet development model
that threatened to bury us.

Khanin and Seliunin's alternative statistics also carry implications
for the nature of the problems facing the Soviet economy and the types
of solutions that should be applied. They indicate that part of the
Eleventh FYP slowdown can be attributed to a decline in the absolute
level of real investment, which for the first time since the 1950s prevented
a drop in the productivity of capital. They also indicate, at the sectoral
level, that investment is most needed in the basic-materials and extractive industries, not in machine-building and final manufacturing. Finally, they call for a revision of the standard view of the relative
efficiency of different sectors of the economy. In particular, the apparent
profitability of the machine-building, manufacturing, and construction
industries turns out, under the K-S estimates, to be a mirage created by
rampant hidden inflation. Khanin argues that it is precisely the loss-
making industries that are the most efficient and the source of greatest
potential social gain to investment,[61] which raises a number of questions

about the rationality of Gorbachev's investment policy for the restructuring of Soviet industry.

Seliunin has argued recently that, because past growth has been so much lower than believed, it is wholly unrealistic to expect that there is any real slack that would allow a dramatic increase in real rates of growth. There is no massive capacity waiting to be used efficiently; there is only fictitious capacity existing on paper that can never be mobilized. The only way that a significant boost in consumption can be achieved—so necessary for the success of *perestroika*—is through a dramatic cut in the share of national income going to investment, particularly in the engineering industries. Coupled with the rights and incentives granted in the new enterprise law, this should allow a significant increase in the rate of growth of consumption without further damage to overall industrial performance because of increased effort and efficiency of enterprises.[62] Such a result depends, of course, on the existence of reliable figures on which to base production, distribution, and investment decisions.

Another area for which the alternative estimates have significant implications is the share (burden) of the military and defense sectors in the Soviet economy. The K-S figures imply that the Soviet economy is about a third the size of the U.S. economy in terms of national income, and indeed may have been slipping even lower just before the death of Brezhnev. Assuming the accuracy of CIA estimates of the real level of defense effort, including research and development, military production and investment, and the maintenance of the defense establishment, the Soviet defense burden is far greater than the 15 to 17 percent of GNP estimated by the CIA. Given the K-S indexes implying that Soviet GNP is only about one-half to two-thirds what the CIA believes, the direct Soviet defense burden must be somewhere between 25 and 30 percent of GNP. Thus the military places a greater burden on the development of the economic system than is generally believed in the West, further aggravating the now widely acknowledged economic slowdown. Moreover, the slowdown must have a greater impact on the military, as there are fewer resources to shift in order to maintain its rate of growth. The demands of the military may be adding urgency to the drive toward radical reconstruction as it strives to maintain parity with the United States on a smaller economic base.

These are just a few of the consequences that might be inferred from the K-S alternatives to official Soviet economic statistics. Acceptance of those alternatives is, however, still a long way off, if it is ever to occur. In the Soviet Union, the debate over economic statistics has barely begun, and its continuation—much less its outcome—is far from certain. If allowed to continue, it should shed light on much of Soviet history as well as give us a clearer idea of just how economic data are turned into statistics.

Further development of the internal debate should follow two paths. First, there needs to be some public exploration of the competing methodologies, including the publication of heuristic examples by both sides. In particular, we might hope to see more technical details of Khanin's work published as the policy and practice of *glasnost* develop, together with scholarly criticism of his approach. Second, the debate should be expanded through the publication of other comprehensive alternative estimates of Soviet macroeconomic performance. For example, the IMEMO report might be expanded to address the issues raised by Khanin and Seliunin. These publications should be accompanied or preceded—indeed, driven—by the release of new historical and contemporary economic data by the statistical authorities. These sorts of developments would enrich the debate and enhance Soviet understanding of their economic system, which may be a prerequisite for successful *perestroika*.

Indeed, we are now beginning to see some movement, albeit very slow, in this direction. Khanin was recently allowed to publish revised figures from his seminars in the leading party theoretical journal *Kommunist*, and his results are beginning to be more widely discussed.[63] He was recently interviewed in the weekly Party paper of the Urals region, *Nauka urala*, which also published some of his alternative statistics,[64] and others have undertaken to use and extend his analysis.[65] Although the official economic and policy establishment has yet to recognize his effort, there is some hope that this work and the burgeoning statistical debate that has accompanied it has opened a new era for Soviet economics. Then the figures from Khanin's seminars will become more than the sole monument to his decades of effort.

3

D. Derk Swain

The Soviet Military Sector:

How It Is Defined and Measured

U.S. CENTRAL INTELLIGENCE AGENCY estimates of the dollar and ruble value of Soviet defense activities play a prominent, if often controversial role in Western assessments of the size of the Soviet defense effort and the Soviet Union's commitment of resources to defense. Public discussion of these estimates often reflects confusion over the activities covered and the proper uses to which dollar and ruble measures should be put. This chapter describes the different definitions of Soviet defense, the monetary measures that the CIA uses in its analysis, and the rationale for each. To illustrate the differences among various definitions and monetary measures, I present some rough estimates of the size of Soviet defense activities based on these definitions. The chapter concludes with a discussion of the confidence we have in the estimates and their constituent parts.

D. Derk Swain is deputy chief of the Defense and Economic Issues Group of the Central Intelligence Agency Office of Soviet Analysis.

How Defense Is Defined

We have three different definitions of *defense,* each developed for a particular purpose. First, there is defense as usually defined in the United States. One of the primary reasons for measuring Soviet defense activities is to compare them with similar activities in the United States. For such comparisons, we use a fairly traditional U.S. definition of defense activities:

- activities funded by the Department of Defense (DOD)

- defense-related nuclear programs funded by the Department of Energy

- Selective Service activities

- defense-related activities of the Coast Guard

For these activities, costs are allocated for research, development, testing, and evaluation (RDT&E); procurement; construction; operations and maintenance (O&M); and military pay and allowances (including retirement funds) according to DOD accounting rules.

A second reason for measuring Soviet defense activities is to assess them in the context of overall Soviet economic performance and to identify trends in the annual resource commitment to military forces. For this purpose, we use a Soviet definition of defense activities, which includes several additional elements not covered in the traditional U.S. definition:

- internal security troops of the Ministry of Internal Affairs

- railroad and construction troops of the Ministry of Defense

- military personnel in civil defense activities

- space programs operated by the Ministry of Defense whose U.S. counterparts are run by the National Aeronautics and Space Administration (NASA)

Soviet accounting rules, which assign capital-repair costs to procurement and current repair costs to O&M, are used under this definition.

The third definition of defense includes additional activities that support national security in a broad sense but are only loosely related to traditional concepts of defense. It can be used either for comparisons of U.S. and Soviet activities or for assessing Soviet resource decisions. This expanded definition adds to the Soviet definition activities related to mobilization and wartime preparedness, efforts to enhance a country's global position, and deferred payment for past defense activities. The opportunity costs of still other activities, such as giving priority access to supplies for defense plants, might be considered within this enlarged definition; but these costs cannot be quantified and are therefore not included.

Wartime preparedness and mobilization. This category covers activities that enhance national war-fighting capability or otherwise contribute to national security, and includes the following Soviet activities and their U.S. counterparts.

- *Civil defense.* Civil defense activities are much more extensive in the USSR than in the United States, and include a large civilian staff, urban and ex-urban blast shelters, and civil defense installations run by the military. Other programs include underground industrial plants, hospitals, power plants, food and fuel storage, individual protection gear, and equipment and material reserves.

- *Industrial reserves and surge capacity.* The Soviets plan reserves of industrial materials for mobilization and as a hedge against seasonal or temporary interruptions of supply. We believe they are intended to support military production for one to three months. The USSR also builds industrial surge capacity into its machine-building sector to increase military production during war time. Plants maintain contingency plans, production documentation, and in some cases tooling for military products.

- *Railroads and highways.* The USSR does not subsidize its railroads primarily for defense purposes. The Soviet rail system has struggled to meet economic needs for more than a decade, and ongoing improvements can be clearly linked to civilian needs. The Baikal-Amur Mainline (BAM) was probably intended for defense needs when work first began in the 1930s, but since 1974, before most of the line was laid, the BAM's economic value was the driving force for its completion. Defense needs, however, probably figured heavily in the building of a 30,000-mile highway network to provide all-weather supply routes from Moscow to the western borders.

- *Merchant shipping.* The cost of acquiring and maintaining the Soviet merchant fleet is greater than would be required to meet normal economic needs. The selection of ship types is influenced by the desire to have additional ships prepared for a variety of military contingencies, and wartime contingency features are added to new and existing ships.

- *Synthetic fuels.* Soviet development of synthetic fuels technology has both national security and commercial motives. The Soviet synfuel effort is defense oriented because of its emphasis on liquid synfuels (which can be used by existing military equipment) rather than on gas.

Enhancement of global position. This category covers activities that serve foreign policy goals:

- *Economic and military assistance.* The USSR extends economic and military assistance to support its allies and clients and to expand its presence and influence in less-developed countries. Much of the aid is in the form of price subsidies—particularly for oil—in trade with other communist countries.

- *Conduct of foreign affairs.* This category consists primarily of the activities of the Ministry of Foreign Affairs. Also included are several semi-official academic institutes that advise the government on foreign affairs, such as the Institute of the USA and Canada and the Institute of World Economic and International Relations (IMEMO).

- *Foreign information and exchange activities.* Foreign information and exchange activities are official attempts to project the nation's image abroad. For example, the USSR has long given support to foreign students to attend its universities as a way of enhancing its reputation abroad, and it has expanded this program rapidly.

Past defense activities. Some of the costs of defense activities are pushed into the future. When due, they represent payment for past goods and services and do not directly contribute to current capabilities, but are still payments that must be made.

- *Veterans' benefits and civilian pensions.* Veterans' benefits in the USSR differ considerably from those in the United States. Stricter Soviet eligibility rules and higher mortality rates limit the number of beneficiaries to well below the number in the United States. Civilian pensions consist of payments to former employees of the Ministry of Defense or the military services. Because the Soviets use military personnel to perform many tasks that would be performed by civilians in the United States, there are somewhat fewer Soviet defense civilians than in the United States despite the larger size of the Soviet military.

- *Legal action.* If the U.S. government loses a legal action brought against the Department of Defense, the award is paid from a "judgment fund" in general revenues administered by the General Accounting Office. We believe that the cost of judgments involving the Soviet Ministry of Defense is negligible.

- *Deficit financing.* Deficits raise the cost of government activities by the cost of borrowing, or the amount of interest paid. Government debt is not incurred specifically for any single identifiable activity; it is the result of financing the whole array of government activities. Nevertheless, were the pattern of past defense spending different, the level of current national debt, and the interest paid thereon, would also be different. The USSR has no concept of deficit financing comparable to that used in the United States. The Soviet system of central planning strives to balance resource inputs and outputs and to avoid borrowing. However, the government does own all the banks, and has access to the savings deposits of private citizens. In effect, interest payments on deposits represent a kind of national debt that assists the government in financing the budget.

How Defense Is Measured

The Soviet Union engages in a broad range of defense activities by any definition. Some of the activities add new weapons to military forces; others furnish and train military personnel; still others provide new technologies, keep equipment in good repair, and support Soviet policy objectives. The complexity of these activities makes it difficult to grasp the magnitude of the effort involved, to identify trends in the size of various categories of activity, or to compare Soviet activities with similar activities in the United States.

Summary measures are needed that are comprehensible, yet capture the important aspects of the underlying activities. This paper will concentrate on monetary measures, among the more useful of such measures and those we commonly use. A monetary measure is calculated by assigning a cost to each activity and then taking a sum of all the activities being considered. Different measures of the same set of activities can be obtained by choosing different kinds of prices to represent the costs. Monetary measures are not necessarily the best measures to use for all purposes, however. Other summary measures of Soviet defense activities range from total numbers of weapons to the results of elaborate war games.[1]

In general, monetary measures are most useful for:

- displaying trends and changing emphases in resource allocations

- evaluating economic costs and impacts

- sizing the overall magnitude of output of dissimilar goods and services for comparison with output of another period or country

Other measures are more appropriate and should be used for:

- assessing the capabilities of military forces

- estimating the relative efficiencies of U.S. and Soviet defense industries

- judging the wisdom of resource decisions

Dollar measures. The primary purpose of valuing Soviet defense activities in U.S. dollar terms is to compare them with corresponding U.S. defense activities. The dollar costs provide a measure of the physical size, quality, and trends of these activities. Constant prices are used to correct for the effects of inflation. Dollar valuations of Soviet programs in conjunction with U.S. defense-program data capture differences in the technical characteristics of military hardware, the number and mix of weapons procured, manpower strengths, and the operating and training levels of the forces being compared. They can be useful, therefore, in portraying the relative magnitudes of similar programs, general trends in the relative resources devoted to defense activities, and shifts in resources among those activities.

The dollar costs are calculated using prevailing U.S. wages and prices. For example, for weapons procurement they represent the cost to manufacture the weapons in the United States using the Soviet design and material specifications but U.S. manufacturing practices and efficiencies. Although such costs could be calculated in any currency, dollars are used because they are the frame of reference for U.S. policy-makers and planners who can conceptualize what a defense dollar will buy. Dollar costs are usually presented as annual outlays to show the intensity of new weapons systems additions and the rate of manning, maintaining, and operating the forces. Annual outlays do not, however, represent the dollar value of the equipment and supplies on hand.

To make costs in a given year comparable with those of another year, costs are standardized to a base year. Such standardization removes the effects of changes in price levels; in other words, it eliminates cost changes that are unrelated to quantity or quality of goods or services. These standardized costs are usually called "constant" costs. The constant dollar costs chosen for Soviet goods and services are based on the average prices and wages prevailing in the United States in the base year. If the Soviet good or service is identical to a U.S. good or service, the average price or wage for that good is used. For example, fuel consumed by Soviet forces is valued by applying the average prices of the same fuels in the United States; the valuation of a Soviet military person is taken as the average pay and allowances for a U.S. military person with the same job description or billet. If an identical good or service is not available in the United States, it is valued by estimating what the good or item would cost if it were available. Such estimates are usually based on a detailed analysis of the physical inputs that would be needed to produce the good or service and represented by the sum of the individual component prices plus an average profit. In all cases, prices and wages are assumed to be unaffected by the additional demands of actually procuring the foreign items in the United States. The fixing of a base year not only fixes the average price level for valuations, but also fixes the levels of manufacturing technology and productivity to those of the base year.

Dollar measures have the following important limitations:

- They do not measure actual foreign defense spending, the impact of defense on the economy, or the foreign perception of defense activities. The USSR does not spend U.S. dollars. The Soviet defense burden is more properly analyzed using estimates of defense expenditures in domestic currency.

- They do not reflect the Soviet view of the distribution of its defense effort. The costs for Soviet defense activities measured in dollars are distributed quite differently among the resource categories than when measured in rubles. For example, Soviet military investment in rubles accounts for about half of total defense costs, but accounts for only one-fourth when measured in dollars.

Ruble measures. Estimates in rubles are useful for gaining insights into how the Soviets might view their own spending. Moreover, because Soviet budgets are prepared and expressed in current prices, current rubles are probably the most appropriate measures to use in assessing the perceptions of Soviet leadership. Current ruble estimates also provide help in understanding changing economic conditions. Relative costs change as raw materials become more difficult to extract; capital and labor productivities change at different rates among sectors; and investment requirements vary. Estimates using current ruble prices partially capture these changing relationships. However, measures using current rubles do not provide reliable indicators of trends in the magnitude of goods and services being produced. General price levels have been rising in the Soviet Union as they have in most countries. Current ruble series reflect both changes in the volume of goods and services and changing price levels. When prices are generally rising, a current ruble series will exaggerate growth in the volume of goods and services produced.

Valuations of Soviet defense outlays in constant rubles provide measures of the level and real trend in the annual Soviet resource commitment to military forces. Constant ruble prices are chosen to reflect as accurately as possible the relative prices of military programs and activities within the Soviet economic system for a given base year. These estimates are also used to assess the impact of defense programs on the Soviet economy and, conversely, the impact of economic factors on Soviet defense activities.

Estimates of Soviet defense spending in current and constant rubles are calculated initially in "established" prices, which are set administratively rather than by market forces and are often inaccurate reflections of scarcity and value. These estimates are refined by the factor-cost adjustment, which adjusts the established prices to reflect the average costs of the factors (resources) in the economy as a whole used to produce the military goods and services. When the direct-costing estimate of annual defense expenditures have been adjusted to factor costs, the components can be integrated with the economic categories—consumption, investment, administration, research and development, and other outlays—of our estimate of Soviet GNP (also in factor-cost terms) to measure the share of resources devoted to military activities.

How these measures are derived. We develop the costs of all Soviet defense activities by first identifying and listing Soviet forces and their support organizations. Our data base contains a description of more than 1,500 distinct defense components—for example, individual classes of surface ships; ground forces divisions categorized on the basis of type and readiness level; and air regiments categorized by aircraft type for each service. It also contains the latest estimates of the order-of-battle, manning levels, and equipment purchases of each component.

To these detailed estimates of physical quantities and activities, we apply appropriate prices and wage rates in both rubles and dollars. The detailed estimates are then aggregated by military mission and resource category. The procedure is complex, but in general involves the following:

- For procurement, we estimate the dollar costs by calculating the cost of building the Soviet weapons and equipment in the United States at prevailing dollar prices for materials and labor (including overhead and profit) using U.S. production technology. We assume that the necessary manufacturing capacity, materials, and labor are available. Some ruble prices are applied directly; others are derived from the individual dollar prices by applying carefully constructed ruble/dollar ratios by product group.

- For operations and maintenance, we apply dollar prices to estimates of the labor, materials, spare parts, overhead, and utilities required to operate and maintain equipment and facilities the way the Soviets perform these functions. The ruble costs are based on Soviet prices and planning factors.

- For military personnel, we use Soviet pay and allowance rates in rubles. To obtain the dollar values, we first estimate the comparable military rank of the person in the United States and then assign the appropriate U.S. pay and allowance rates to that Soviet billet.

- For Soviet RDT&E our estimates are based on a "resource costs" method, which assigns ruble values to the resources used in Soviet military RDT&E activities. These include wages, materials, equipment, capital repair, capital construction, travel, training, and other operating costs. The ruble estimate is converted to dollars by using an average of our military-procurement dollar/ruble ratios. The use of a procurement dollar/ruble ratio gives a reflection of the different productivities of research and development resources in the two countries. In effect, we are assuming that the ratio of the dollar value to the ruble cost of research and development performed in the Soviet Union equals the ratio of the dollar value to the ruble cost of military hardware produced in Soviet defense plants.

Soviet Defense Activities

When viewed in the aggregate, the claim of defense on Soviet resources has been large by U.S. standards (Figure 3.1). Measured in constant 1982 ruble prices using the Soviet definition, defense consumed roughly 15 to 17 percent of Soviet GNP during the past two decades—more than twice as much as in the United States.[2] Military procurement accounted for almost half of the total, but its share of GNP declined in the late 1970s and early 1980s, when the economy grew at a modest pace but procurement remained flat. Each of the other categories of defense activities—RDT&E, construction, O&M, and personnel—accounted for much smaller shares of Soviet economic output.

When other national security activities are included in an expanded definition of defense, its share of GNP ranged from 1 to 3 percent higher. Most of the incremental cost consisted of economic and military aid, much of which took the form of deliveries of oil to allies and clients at subsidized prices. Because oil was the USSR's major currency export,

FIGURE 3.1   Soviet Defense Expenditures, 1970–1985

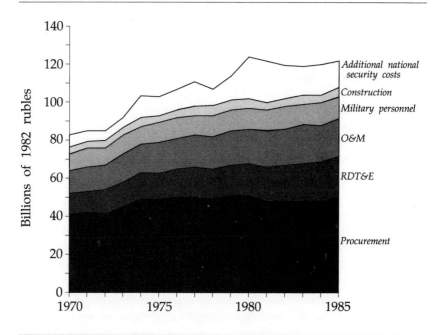

SOURCE: United States Central Intelligence Agency.

these oil deliveries were made at the cost of hard-currency earnings that could have been used to purchase needed Western agricultural and industrial products.

Measured in current prices, in which payments for defense goods and services would actually be made, defense appears to have consumed a rising share of GNP over time, regardless of the definition of defense used. In other words, there has been more inflation in the prices of defense goods and services than in the economy as a whole.

Although the share of defense in GNP is the simplest and most commonly used indicator of the economic impact of defense, this measure does not reflect the varying impact that defense spending has had on individual sectors of the economy. The large (more than 40 percent) claim of defense on machine-building and metalworking (MBMW) output is especially noteworthy because this sector also produces the investment machinery required to sustain economic growth and the consumer durables required to boost labor productivity through greater incentives. And the energy used to support the defense sector amounts to an estimated 20 percent of Soviet energy output.

The Soviets themselves do not compare their defense expenditures to GNP, although this year, for the first time, Moscow published data on economic growth using the GNP concept. The Soviets probably compare defense to national income, which is equal to GNP minus depreciation, and the nonmaterial component of "nonproductive" services. When comparing defense to national income, however, it is unclear whether the Soviets would include all their defense expenditures or exclude some outlays—such as pay and allowances for military personnel—on the grounds that they are not "productive." In either case, because GNP in current prices grew slightly faster than national income during 1970–1982, the Soviets may have perceived a slightly greater increase in the defense share of national resources than that suggested by our GNP measures.

Because the Soviets maintain larger military forces and procure larger numbers of weapons and support systems than the United States, the cumulative dollar value of Soviet defense activities has exceeded comparable U.S. defense outlays by more than 20 percent over the past fifteen years (Figure 3.2). Since 1976, however, the annual margin has been narrowing. In 1976 the Soviet dollar costs were 40 percent higher than U.S. defense outlays, but by 1987 they were roughly equal. Growth in the dollar value of Soviet defense activities averaged about 2 percent a year over the entire period. Military procurement was fairly level from 1974 to 1984, but began to increase somewhat in 1985 and 1986. RDT&E

FIGURE 3.2   Cost of U.S. and Soviet Defense Activities, 1965–1987

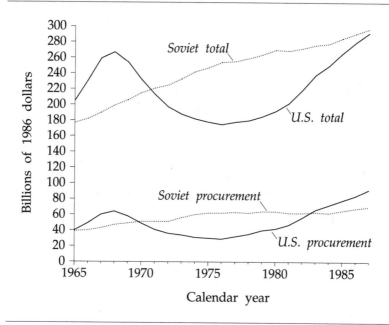

SOURCE: United States Central Intelligence Agency.

was the primary source of growth, although operating costs also increased. In military-mission aggregations, the costs (excluding RDT&E)
for general-purpose forces and support activities showed some growth
over the period, while the costs of strategic programs generally declined
but began to increase again in 1987.

In contrast, U.S. defense outlays, which had been steadily falling
after the Vietnam peak in 1968, began to increase in 1977, and by 1980
were growing about 6 percent a year. The rapid growth beginning in
1980 reflected large increases in operating costs and military investment:
growth more than tripled over the period, from an average of about 3
percent a year during 1973–1979 to more than 11 percent a year in 1980–
1987. Substantial growth occurred in each of the major missions. Growth
in spending for general-purpose forces doubled, from 3.5 percent a year
in 1973–1979 to 7 percent in 1980–1987. Spending on strategic forces
increased sharply, from an average annual growth of less than 1 percent
during 1973–1979 to more than 8 percent a year in 1980–1987. Support
costs—which declined during 1973–1979—grew more than 4 percent a
year during 1980–1987.

Looking at the expanded definition of defense activities for the year 1983, the total dollar value of Soviet activities exceeded that of the United States by about 15 percent. The dollar value of Soviet national security activities in 1983 (in 1985 dollars) exceeded comparable U.S. outlays in all categories except the costs of past defense activities, where U.S. outlays were almost twice as high as the dollar estimate for the Soviets.

Reliability of Estimates

Extensive data are used to estimate the physical numbers that constitute Soviet defense activities—order-of-battle, production quantities going to the military, manning levels, O&M practices, military construction, and RDT&E activities. Although there is general agreement on most of these data, they are still subject to errors, which are then reflected in the estimates based on them. This paper does not explicitly assess confidence in these physical data; that is best handled in the context of the individual estimates that generate them.

Estimates in dollars. A definitive assessment of the overall confidence one should have in dollar estimates is difficult. We are dealing with an analytical construct for which there can be no objective truth. A mole in the Kremlin could never reveal the dollar cost of Soviet defense activities because, as noted earlier, the Soviets do not spend dollars. So we must discuss confidence in terms of how well the estimates serve the stated purpose of providing a summary measure of the comparative size of U.S. and Soviet defense activities over time.

Several standards should be met for such comparisons:

- comparable coverage for both sides

- consistency of results

- quality control in the calculations and reproducibility of the measures

- robustness of the estimates to new information and methodologies

With one exception, the U.S. accounting scheme has been chosen as the standard for categorizing activities and costs. The exception is the use of calendar instead of fiscal years to present costs for both U.S. and Soviet defense activities. The cost estimates represent actual outlays, with total costs usually broken down by one of two schemes, by resource category or by military mission. The resource scheme follows the standard DOD definitions of RDT&E, procurement, construction, military personnel, and O&M; the mission breakouts use the definitions contained in the Defense Planning and Programming Categories (DPPC). Considerable care has been taken to ensure that Soviet military activities are placed in the appropriate categories.

The individual estimates have been reviewed repeatedly to ensure consistency of results. Many of these reviews are prompted by intuitive warnings that the estimated dollar costs of individual Soviet systems seem too low. Although the Soviets are able to procure many more weapons and pieces of equipment than the United States can, in total they have only a slightly greater dollar value, which leads to the conclusion that the individual dollar values must be too low. This apparent anomaly is termed the "procurement paradox." Repeated examinations have confirmed, however, that the individual costs are not understated when detailed characteristics of the Soviet items are considered. Detailed comparisons show that, in general, the large number of weapons procured by the USSR are simpler, less flexible, technologically less complex, and thus cheaper than their closest U.S. equivalents.

Every year we revise our previous estimates of the dollar and ruble values of Soviet defense activities using new information on costs, production quantities, operating practices, and order-of-battle. Presumably, our estimates for any one year improve as time passes because we know more about the quantities and characteristics of the weapon systems and facilities produced in that year. These annual revisions provide a method of assessing how well we estimate the dollar costs of major portions of Soviet defense activities. If estimates for a given year changed sharply with every review—indicating that new analysts, data, and methodologies produced very different results—we would have little confidence that we had an accurate estimate of military activities in that year. On the other hand, if the estimates fluctuated by only a small amount and no bias were detected, we would have greater confidence that the estimates were substantially correct.

Our experience makes us reasonably confident of the accuracy of our estimates. Indeed, the monitoring of our annual revisions, as well as other statistical techniques, lead us to believe that our dollar-cost estimate for total defense activities is unlikely to be off by more than 10 percent for any year from 1970 to 1985. The margin of error can be much wider for individual items and categories than for the total because of the tendency of errors at lower levels of aggregation to be partially offsetting.

Most improvements in costing methodologies and corrections of physical counts or weapon characteristics affect the estimates for several consecutive years. For example, a revised cost estimate for Backfire bombers would alter the estimates for more than a decade, and the changes would all be in the same direction. For this reason, we generally have more confidence in data that represent trends than in data for absolute levels, especially the levels for individual years.

Estimates in rubles. The reliability of the CIA's ruble-cost estimates again depends on the accurate identification and measurement of the physical characteristics of the Soviet armed forces over time, and on the application of appropriate cost factors. Our confidence in the estimates varies from one category to another:

- We have high confidence in our estimates of military manpower costs because of the information we have on manning levels, rank structure, and pay schedules for both uniformed and civilian personnel.

- We also have high confidence in our estimates of military procurement, especially for major weapons systems. We are somewhat less confident of our estimates of lower-visibility items of equipment and the support infrastructure—for example, base and airfield furnishings, field equipment for the ground forces, and portable shipboard items. These costs must often be measured in more aggregate terms by using Soviet cost-estimating relationships or U.S. analog relationships adjusted to known Soviet practices.

- We are less confident of our estimates of O&M costs and construction of military facilities. Nonetheless, present estimates are substantially more reliable than earlier methodologies, which drew heavily on U.S. analog experience, especially for POL consumption and aircraft and naval ship maintenance. Estimates of military construction also reflect improved methods and data.

- We are least certain of our estimates of the costs of Soviet military RDT&E. However, we have extensive evidence on the manpower and physical facilities on which our cost estimates are based.

We have checked our estimates by comparing them with intelligence reports, Soviet economic data, and estimates made by other intelligence analysts. Over the past twenty years, various foreign sources have provided independent information on Soviet defense spending. Comparison of our estimates with the values reported by foreign sources entails considerable uncertainty. There is no way to ensure that all of the figures refer to the same set of defense activities, because the sources do not define what is included in "defense." I can say, however, that our spending estimates are consistent with Soviet data, that they are consistent with credible intelligence reports, and that they are generally accepted by Western intelligence services. These checks reinforce our belief that our ruble estimates are sufficiently accurate to fulfill the purposes for which they are intended, and help confirm both our physical data base and our dollar valuations.

The Paradox of Current Soviet Military Spending

THE NEED TO KNOW what the Soviets are spending—or planning to spend—on their military is more critical today than ever. Mikhail Gorbachev's statements and the fervor for arms control in the West have led some to believe that the Soviets are now reducing their military outlays, or soon will, as a result of *perestroika*. Because the Soviet planning process is lengthy and cumbersome, some believe the new dialogue and certain token changes are signs of military reforms to come during the Thirteenth Five-Year Plan, 1991–1995. Fueling these expectations are Gorbachev's promises to be more forthcoming about the level of Soviet military outlays and to make the data more comparable to Western figures,[1] a reform that would please the United Nations, which criticized previous Soviet military budget–reduction proposals because the Soviets provided no basis for comparing their military outlays with those of the West.

The Gorbachev promises may serve only to exaggerate the Soviets' peaceful intentions, and outlays may continue to be understated. On the other hand, better Soviet information could provide greater knowledge and lessen misunderstanding, fear, and ultimately the threat of war, as

Norbert D. Michaud is an analyst at the Economic Affairs Branch of the Defense Intelligence Agency.

a recent *Kommunist* article maintains.[2] The impression is that of paradox. Soviet statements speak of disarmament, but their statistics suggest a robust military sector. Whether it is total military outlays or outlays for operations, procurement, or research and development (R&D), the data suggest the continued primacy of military spending. Therein lies an anomaly, however: Soviet outlays appear to be growing faster than the physical resources allocated to the military, thereby suggesting a degree of inflation in the Soviet statistics.

Despite their penchant for secrecy, the Soviets provide considerable information about their economy and about the industrial sectors that incorporate military production; in particular, they provide figures from their central government budget, or All-Union budget, which funds all national-level programs, including military and space activities. This budget has several accounts, one of which is the defense budget, the only declared military account. The All-Union budget is growing rapidly, and that itself can be taken as an indicator of rapid military and space-program growth, since those programs represent perhaps two-thirds of that budget. Some nonbudgetary information, such as data on the machinery-producing sector with its nine military and eight civil-industrial ministries, also provides some insight into Soviet military economics.

The Soviet data for the military sector tend to be general rather than specific, to lack precise definition, and to be ambiguous and misleading. The Soviets took a step in the right direction recently by providing an important definition confirming what was already known in the West: what is called the defense budget covers a very limited part of total military and space outlays. A recent statement by Deputy Foreign Minister Petrovskiy revealed that the "announced" defense budget covers only pay, pensions, material and technical supplies, military construction, and certain other military expenses; "financing for scientific-research and experimental design work and arms purchases and military technology come under different articles of the USSR state budget."[3]

For some time now the Western intelligence community has indicated that actual Soviet defense expenditures greatly exceeded those of the announced defense budget. Though the content of the announced defense budget had been fairly accurately described by William Lee and others even before tacit recognition by the intelligence community, Lee and most other observers dismissed the budget as an inaccurate representation of operating costs, since it went into a decline after 1970, suggesting a drop in operating costs, while Soviet military activities were by all other appearances growing.[4]

The recent Soviet revelations and promises to be more forthcoming in the future have some rather important implications: first, that the announced defense budget may hold some meaning as an operating-cost budget; second, that other budgetary accounts may have some validity as defense indicators; and finally, that the Soviets themselves may not have an accurate or full accounting of their national security expenditures despite their use of a variety of accounting or reporting formats.

The Defense Budget

There is reason to accept the general trend of the defense budget as a measure of the growth of operating expenses. A large percentage of operating expenses are driven by manpower costs for pay, food, energy, clothing, housing, medical, and recreation expenses. In the United States operating costs have risen only slightly more in constant terms than the level of total active-duty forces; for example, in the last ten years operating costs increased about 2 percent annually, with manpower increasing about 1 percent annually. In the Soviet Union the announced defense budget decreased by 4 percent in the period 1972–1977, but by only 1 percent during the period 1977–1982; during the entire period the number of seventeen- to twenty-one-year-old males increased 12 percent, peaking in 1977 and declining 7 percent by 1982 (Table 4.1). During the entire period 1972–1982, the announced budget decreased 4.5 percent, while the number of seventeen- to twenty-one-year-old males increased by 4.5 percent.

This difference is relatively small considering that there are other factors that figure in the operating costs; the small discrepancy could simply be attributable to a reduction in the number of career personnel during this period. Furthermore, efforts have been made to conserve energy within the military, reducing non-manpower operating costs and explaining the slight drop in operating expenses, or announced defense outlays. While the defense budget appears to be associated with most housekeeping costs, it is of course possible and probably likely that over the last twenty-five years some changes have occurred in definition or coverage of some accounts. Furthermore, some housekeeping expenses may now be situated in other accounts.

In 1985, however, an anomaly occurred. The number of eighteen-year-old males has continued to decline since 1982, and should have

TABLE 4.1   Soviet Defense Budget and Demographic Changes,
              1962–1987

	17- to 21-year-old males (millions)	Percentage change	Announced defense budget (billion rubles)	Percentage change
1962	7.1	—	12.6	—
1967	8.7	+23	14.5	+15
1972	11.3	+30	17.9	+24
1977	12.6	+12	17.2	–4
1982	11.8	–7	17.1	–1
1987	10.4	–12	20.1	+18

SOURCES: Frederick Leedy, "Demographic Trends in USSR," U.S. Congress, Joint Economic Committee Compendium (Washington, D.C.: GPO, 1973), p. 479; and W. W. Kingkade, *Estimates and Projections of the Population of the USSR, 1979 to 2025*, U.S. Department of Commerce (Washington, D.C.: GPO, December 1987), for number of 17- to 21-year-old males; *Narodnoe khoziaistvo* (Moscow: Finansy i statistika), various years, for announced defense budget (abbreviated *Narkhoz*).

been at its lowest in 1987. If true to form, the announced defense budget should have declined, or increased only slightly by 1987. The defense budget did decline until 1984, but in 1985 there was an announced increase of 12 percent. One possible explanation is the 1984 ruling requiring male students to serve in the military for two years before entering a higher educational institution.[5] It is unlikely that all male students would have been immediately affected by that order, since about 600,000 males enter college each year—about 30 percent of the available eighteen-year-old males. Deferring half and allowing them to attend college for two years would provide a more steady flow until full implementation.

If this is what actually happened, it would help explain the two boosts in the defense budget, one in 1985 and the other in 1987. I must stress the tentativeness of this conclusion, as there is no proof that such deferment was implemented. But the percentage of male students in higher educational institutions decreased gradually from 48 percent in the 1980–81 school year to 47 percent in 1983–84, and then moved rapidly to 46 percent in 1984–85, 45 percent in 1985–86, and 44 percent in 1986–87. Male enrollment between 1982 and 1987 dropped by 300,000, or more than 10 percent. In contrast, female enrollment increased by 4 percent, or 100,000.[6]

While there may have been gradual adoption of the new draft policy, its full implementation would better explain the 2 billion ruble increase in the defense budget. If the Soviets spend more than 3,000 rubles per man for housekeeping expenses (assuming 5.5 million personnel and a 17 billion ruble outlay for personnel) then the augmentation of about 600,000 men should have raised the corresponding expenses by about 2 billion rubles, the amount of the announced increase in 1985. The rise in the 1987 defense budget would still be unexplained however, and there would be a further anomaly: the defense budget might have been expected to show the impact of larger numbers of departures from the military in that year.

The Science Budget

If the defense budget is a meaningful indicator of operating costs, it is likely that the science budget is an indicator of the growth of military R&D and space operations. The science budget, like the defense budget, is part of the All-Union or central government budget that funds virtu-ally all military programs, as well as nonmilitary programs of All-Union institutions, including higher education, branch industrial institutes of All-Union ministries, the Academy of Sciences, and other institutes. Like the defense budget, the science budget would fund all the operating costs of military R&D and space programs, covering wages, operations, repairs, supplies and some equipment (but not capital facilities), and major equipment or prototypes. Another All-Union account, the one for financing the national economy, provides the funds for capital outlays.

There is no clear way of using the science budget as an indicator of the growth in military R&D and space operations, but comparing the growth of the science budget and the total number of scientific workers, we do see a fairly synchronous movement, especially between 1960 and 1975 (Table 4.2). After 1975, however, the science budget increased much more rapidly than the number of scientific workers. Outlays per science worker increased as a result of higher expenditures for materials and equipment rather than for wages. Nevertheless, productivity in Soviet science probably declined.[7]

It is also possible that since 1975 the rate of increase in the total number of scientific workers is not representative of the growth of those employed in military R&D and space programs. One reason to suspect an acceleration in military R&D and space programs relative to other R&D programs is that financing for science from sources other than the All-Union budget increased only 22 percent (without investment), while All-Union science financing increased 37 percent, thereby increasing the All-Union share of total science outlays. Even if all the new scientific workers were going into the military R&D and space programs, this increase would not have been sufficient to explain the rapid growth in the All-Union science budget. Military and space programs probably absorb 50 percent or more of the scientific workers now employed in R&D activities. If the entire 9 percent increase in scientific workers between 1980 and 1985 was placed in military R&D and space activities, the resulting increase in military R&D and space research workers would translate to only about 18 percent, compared with the 37 percent increase in the All-Union science budget.

In any event, the increased All-Union funding exceeded the growth in professional R&D personnel. Because productivity among science workers is not believed to have risen, the increase in outlay suggests both an effort to upgrade scientific equipment and the effect of inflation on research-sector costs. Because the Soviets do not publish a constant or comparable series for science prices, we have no idea how they would view that possibility officially. In light of the higher prices assigned to material and energy, especially with the major price adjustments in 1982 (Table 4.3) and the rising cost of high-technology equipment, it is not surprising that outlays should outpace manpower. Whether those outlays have been matched by productivity increases in military R&D and space programs would be difficult to determine, quite apart from data availability, because

TABLE 4.2   Changes in Soviet Science Budget and Number of
             Scientific Workers, 1960–1985

	Scientific workers	All-Union science budget
1960–1965	188	200
1965–1970	140	161
1970–1975	131	121
1975–1980	112	130
1980–1985	109	137

NOTE: Indexed to the base year of each period.

SOURCES: *Narkhoz,* various years, for number of scientific workers; *Gosudarstvennyi biudzhet SSSR i biudzhety soiuznykh respublik,* various five-year periods, for All-Union science budget.

TABLE 4.3   Change in Soviet Prices, 1981–1982 (percentage)

Fuels	+62
Electric power	+24
Ferrous metals	+23
Light industry	+11
Food industry	+5
Chemical industry	0
Wood, paper	–1
Machinery industry	–11
Military-machinery ministries	–23

SOURCE: Iu. V. Iakovets, *Planovoe tsenoobrazovanie* (Moscow: Ekonomika, 1986), pp. 86, 136–40. Military-machinery ministries figure was derived from analysis of price changes in the civil ministries.

military R&D lacks an evident output standard as might be devised for commercial R&D—for example, patents and cost savings.

Planned growth in total science expenditures in the period 1986–1990 exceeds growth in the previous ten years (6.7 percent versus 5.1 percent annually) and especially in the investment account (11.2 percent versus 6.0 percent annually during 1971–1985).[8] The All-Union budget probably represents a disproportionate share of the planned increase because of growth in military R&D and space activities. The particularly large planned increase in investment certainly portends considerable equipment purchases and prototype construction. These outlays represent procurement of equipment from the machinery sector, which has expanded rapidly, especially the nine military ministries responsible for producing military and space equipment.

Industry and Construction Budget

An All-Union budget account referred to as the account for financing the national economy (FNE) is the most likely source of funding for procurement of military equipment; construction of military research, space, and industrial facilities; prototype development; and possibly military base construction and repair. Within this account is the subcategory industry and construction (I&C), which has grown even more rapidly than the All-Union budget as a whole, and now makes up a large part of that budget, 37.6 percent in 1985 (Table 4.4). Its large share implies that military R&D and space is not the only military sector well endowed with facilities and equipment. The growth of the I&C account speaks to the large size of the military industries, extensive military bases at home and abroad, and the high level of procurement.

The I&C account and possibly the FNE residual (or unaccounted) funds are probably the source of financing of output by the military and civil ministries producing military and space equipment. Consequently, the growth of output of the military ministries is likely to be similar to the growth of the I&C account. With the exception of the period 1965–1970, the growth patterns are indeed similar (Table 4.5).

The discrepancy in growth for 1965–1970 may be explained by the price adjustments that took place then. The larger growth in budget funding suggests that significant subsidization occurred to offset lowered prices on final goods, while the cost of inputs was raised. If that were the case, the same process should have occurred in the period 1980–1985, when another major price reduction apparently took place in the military ministries. In that period, however, it is the FNE residual that shows a considerable increase—about 40 percent between 1980 and 1982. The growth rate of the combined I&C and residual accounts in that period was 10.8 percent annually, greater than the recorded growth rate of the military ministries without the residual. It is highly probable that the FNE residual is used for special programs, for reserves or contingency funding, and for subsidies.

TABLE 4.4   Industry and Construction Component of the All-Union Financing National Economy Account, 1960–1985

	Billions of rubles	Percentage of All-Union budget
1960	4.0	13.2
1965	7.9	18.3
1970	22.7	28.2
1975	36.3	33.1
1980	54.2	34.3
1985	76.2	37.6

SOURCE: *Gosudarstvennyi biudzhet SSSR i biudzhety soiuznykh respublik*, various five-year periods, for All-Union budget and the industry and construction account.

TABLE 4.5   Average Annual Growth of Military Ministries Output Compared with Average Annual Growth of the Industry and Construction Budget, 1965–1985 (percentage)

	Growth of output, military ministries[a]	Growth of All-Union budget, industry and construction
1965–1970	11.1	23.5
1971–1975	8.1	9.8
1976–1980	7.9	8.3
1981–1985	7.5	7.1

a. Growth of output in gross value.
SOURCES: Methodologies and sources of military-ministry figures described in N. Michaud, *Soviet Defense Industry: The Fastest Growing Sector, 1965–79*, U.S. DIA DDB–1960–1–82 (Washington, D.C.: GPO, 1982). *Gosudarstvennyi biudzhet SSSR i biudzhety soiuznykh respublik*, various five-year periods, for All-Union budget.

Total Outlays

I believe that total direct defense outlays are fairly well accounted for by the combination of the defense, science, I&C, and FNE residual accounts. That would be expected, since the All-Union budget is the source of all defense outlays, with the possible exception of civil defense and paramilitary activities.[9]

Direct military outlays that are not accounted for by the above are situated in other All-Union accounts. These probably fund activities that would be included in the broader definitions of defense, such as military aid, higher education for military personnel, health or medical facilities, and transport for military personnel. The level and growth of these four major accounts are interesting in the context of what has been revealed regarding total Soviet defense outlays. A Chinese report revealed precise figures for their share of national income in 1970, 1974, and 1975 that in retrospect coincide quite well with data from other sources for those years (Table 4.6). Consequently, actual outlays reconcile quite closely with the four major All-Union budget accounts most directly associated with military funding. During that period the defense-related accounts

TABLE 4.6   Soviet Defense Outlays and Defense-Related
               All-Union Accounts, Selected Years

	Defense-related All-Union accounts (billion rubles)	Defense outlays (billion rubles)	Percentage difference
1970	52.1	49.6	5.0
1974	66.5	69.3	4.2
1975	70.9	72.4	2.1

SOURCES: *Gosudarstvennyi biudzhet SSSR i biudzhety soiuznykh respublik*, various five-year periods for All-Union accounts; defense outlays based on *Peking Review*, Nov. 7, 1975, and Nov. 27, 1975.

represented about 65 percent of the All-Union budget. If they have continued to fund total defense and space programs to the same extent as in the past, extrapolation generates total account estimates of 98 billion to 107 billion rubles for 1980 and 125 billion to 136 billion rubles for 1985. These figures correspond to about two-thirds of the All-Union budget.

The growth rates indicated by these values are surprisingly high, considering what we now know about the Soviet economy during this period. They indicate a defense-sector growth rate of 3 to 7 percent in current rubles for 1980–1985, which is much higher than the real growth of the economy, probably less than 2 percent. Growth of national income in current or nominal rubles was about 4.6 percent in this period. These estimates suggest that the share of defense did not continue to climb in the past five years. With regard to Western estimates of current GNP, however, the military share rose to an estimated 15 to 17 percent of GNP in 1985 from 12 to 14 percent in 1970.

All-Union budget figures for the period 1986–1990 are not yet available, but we can expect the defense and space sector to continue growing: total science outlays are planned to increase by 37 percent and the military ministries by 43 percent. The defense budget will probably increase slightly as well, based on the number of eighteen-year-old males eligible for service. This growth is already indicated in the Soviet accounts. In 1986, for instance, the All-Union budget and presumably the defense-related accounts increased almost 10 percent following increases in the defense budget of 12 percent in 1985, and almost 6 percent in 1987.

These high growth rates in current outlays do not necessarily translate into real growth rates, however. As indicated earlier, there is reason to believe that considerable overpricing, particularly of new equipment, has occurred in the machinery sector. The major source of overpricing appears to be for new products, for which managers are able to apply higher costs and excessive resource utilization. If the Soviets are forthcoming in revealing the real increases in military-output values, more accurate estimates of real growth will be feasible.

Inflation in the military accounts is implied by Western estimates. The intelligence community has publicly estimated the real increase in total Soviet military outlays and procurement from 1985 to 1986 at about 3 percent.[10] This rate, based on direct costing of Soviet programs, is lower than the estimate based on defense-related accounts or military-ministry output. In light of the priorities and pressures on military producers, it seems likely that the defense sector has been able to commit abundant resources to their aims, resulting, perhaps, in relatively low productivity and considerable waste.

The growing exception to the surfeit of defense resources is labor, which has become especially scarce in recent years. Industrial labor has increased by only about 5 percent between 1980 and 1987, and decreases are expected through 1990. Though neither the civil- nor military-machinery sector can expect any labor increases, plans for both sectors call for rapid output growth (Table 4.7). If the Soviets are to realize any significant real growth, it will have to be through higher productivity resulting from improved use of resources. Otherwise, meeting the plans will be accomplished only by an overvaluation of output, especially in the machinery sector, where new-product introductions allow for greater use of higher-price materials as well as higher prices and profits.

The quantity of labor that is assigned to the various sectors in the future will probably be a good indicator of priorities. Moreover, labor growth in the past is probably a fairly accurate measure of real growth that has occurred in the economy and defense sector, given the assumption that there has been little change in labor productivity in recent years.

A similar relationship exists in the United States. When U.S. defense procurement figures are deflated to allow for price increases, the resulting real growth is similar to the growth in the defense-related industrial labor force. The relationship between military R&D outlays and employment shows a similar trend. Total U.S. defense outlays increased rapidly, but real growth was only 3.6 percent annually between 1975 and 1985, while defense-related employment increased 2.4 percent annually, implying an average productivity increase of 1.2 percent.

If the labor force of the Soviet military-machinery ministry is a reasonable proxy for defense-related employment, and if labor produc-

TABLE 4.7   Growth of Output in Military and Civil Ministries,
             1975–1990 (percentage)

	Military ministries	Civil ministries
1975–1980	61	35
1981–1985	41	26
1986–1990 (plan)	43	43

NOTE: Based on growth of output in gross value.
SOURCE: Michaud, Maddalena, Barry, "Commentary" in U.S. Congress, Joint
Economic Committee, *Gorbachev's Economic Plans*, vol. 1 (Washington, D.C.:
GPO, November 1987), pp. 485–90.

tivity did not increase, then defense growth diminished substantially in
the last ten years compared with the previous ten years due to low
growth in the labor force. Similarly, the growth of scientific workers
declined dramatically, as did the growth in the number of seventeen- to
twenty-one-year-old males (Table 4.8).

Based on the labor data, it may be reasonable to conclude that the
military sector increased 4 to 5 percent in real terms in the period 1965–
1975 and 2 to 3 percent in the period 1975–1985, and will grow 1 to 2
percent annually in the period 1985–1990 in the absence of any unusual
events that change the current trends. It is clear, then, why the Soviets are
so concerned about the future: they can no longer afford to commit huge
labor pools and must instead seek improvements in efficiency through
systemic change and better equipment quality. If this happens, manpower numbers will become a less-accurate indicator of real growth.

Will *Pravda* Prevail?

Will the Soviets reveal what their military commitment has truly cost? I
doubt that they will reveal all of their most direct military outlays or
admit to the indirect costs of support from their entire economic and
societal infrastructure. And they will certainly not admit to those immea-
surable costs resulting from the high priority accorded the military in its
access to quality inputs, or to the costs imposed on individuals inside
and outside the Soviet Union.

The Soviets now admit that the military is burdensome, and to make
that point they may be willing to identify certain outlays beyond the
narrowly defined defense budget. They may simply follow the format

of their revelations about World War II expenditures (Table 4.9), which show only a portion of the total defense outlays. Some direct costs are obviously omitted: R&D, repairs, construction, industrial investment, training, and medical expenses. If the Soviets publish additional information on current military outlays, it is likely to reflect different terminology and a different allocation of outlays between maintenance and procurement than used previously.

We should not expect a full accounting of direct outlays, among other reasons because there is no single stage of the accounting process in which all military expenses are covered. The Soviets have several series to choose from: the Smeta, or estimate, of the Ministry of Defense; the military accounts of the All-Union budget; the military accounts in Gosbank; and the reporting of the State Committee for Statistics. Each provides different accounting information and methods, yet the data are referred to as though there was only a single source. Sometimes the Soviets refer to shares of the budget, while at others they refer to shares of national income, and it is not clear whether they are basing their statements on the same military outlays. When the military speak of defense outlays, they probably have a much more limited impression of military outlays than does the political leadership.

The Ministry of Defense Smeta does not include military R&D or the cost of developing new industries. Military R&D and space are apparently the prerogatives of the Military Industrial Commission, which undoubtedly controls the All-Union science budget, including military

TABLE 4.8   Changes in Soviet Labor Supply, 1965–1990 (percentage)

	17- to 21-year-old males	Scientific workers	Military ministry employment
1965–1975	+50	+84	+43
1976–1985	+7	+22	+21
1986–1990	+2	+4	—

SOURCES: Frederick Leedy, "Demographic Trends in USSR," U.S. Congress Joint Economic Committee Compendium (Washington, D.C.: GPO, 1973), p.479; and W. W. Kingkade, *Estimates and Projections of the Population of the USSR, 1979 to 2025*, U.S. Department of Commerce (Washington, D.C.: GPO, December 1987), for number of 17- to 21-year-old males; *Narkhoz*, various years, for number of scientific workers; Michaud, Maddalena, Barry, "Commentary" in U.S. Congress, Joint Economic Committee, *Gorbachev's Economic Plans*, vol. 1 (Washington, D.C.: GPO, 1987), pp. 485–90, for military ministries' employment.

TABLE 4.9   Soviet Military Outlays, 1941–1945

	Billions of rubles	Percentage of total
People's Commissariat of Defense	535.5	92
Armaments and combat matériel	173.7	30
Artillery and ammunition	74.7	13
Air armament	52.1	9
Armor, vehicles, tractors	38.0	7
Other	8.9	1
Pay and allowances	145.8	25
Other wages	7.8	1
Clothing, food, and fuel	138.2	24
Military transport	18.8	3
Other	51.2	9
People's Commissariat of the Navy	46.9	8
Total military outlays	582.4	100

SOURCE: F. Doe, *Understanding the Soviet View of Military Expenditures*, U.S. DIA submission to U.S. Congress, Joint Economic Committee (Washington, D.C.: GPO, July 1982).

R&D and space outlays. The source of information on World War II expenditures was probably the Smeta of the Ministry of Defense (or its Narkom Oborony/Voenno-Morskoi Flot predecessor), which may very well be the source of any information revealed in the future.

Even though the All-Union budget is said to cover all defense outlays, paramilitary activities such as civil defense are probably not included. Furthermore, the military units have many sources of revenue, such as agriculture and construction, which provide funds for food, recreation, and miscellaneous expenses. Such other costs as depreciation or amortization of facilities, equipment and prepaid expenses, as well as the cost of the social and industrial infrastructure that pertain to the support of national security, are also unlikely to be revealed.

Another source of information on military expenditures are the Gosbank accounts through which budgetary funds flow. These accounts categorize outlays differently than do the budget accounts, although the respective totals generally equate. Discrepancies do occur, however, between what has been budgeted and what has been expended, and credit extensions may allow outlays to surpass the budgets on a short-term basis.

The State Committee for Statistics collects information from military units, research institutes, and enterprises. Their reporting includes military R&D and space estimates as well as operations and maintenance expenses. With regard to investment and procurement, however, their accounting departs from the budgetary accounts in reporting final values that include depreciation and amortization. In this case, there is a risk of double-counting and not being able to distinguish final products and end-users—that is, to discriminate between the military and other uses.

Publication of the Soviet military accounts would be of value to the Soviets as well as to the West, since few of the Soviet leadership are knowledgeable about the full extent of the Soviet commitment of resources to national security or have a clear understanding of the real cost of their military effort. Without this knowledge the Soviet decision-making process is warped, and collective decision-making about external, as well as internal, affairs impaired. Because of the counterthreat that it provokes, the secrecy surrounding Soviet defense spending has not served the Soviets well. Full disclosure might serve not only to lessen this threat, but also reveal the full and true cost of Soviet overcommitment to the military. My hope is that the Soviet military paradox that we see today reflects a transition from a militant society to one in which greater emphasis is placed on citizens' welfare.

David F. Epstein

The Economic Cost of Soviet Security and Empire

T HE SUBJECT of this chapter is usually referred to as the Soviet Union's "defense burden"—that is, the share of Soviet economic output that goes to the defense budget. I have avoided that term in my title because the range of activities I examine extends considerably beyond the bounds of a "defense budget" as understood in the West, and because those activities partly support a Soviet empire that may not be understood simply as a means to national defense. My question is not the purpose of Soviet military, security, and imperial activities, but rather their cost to the Soviet economy. Soviet secrecy regarding the country's military programs has led Western intelligence analysts to make their own estimates of Soviet military costs. The best known is the CIA's building-block approach, which attempts to make an exhaustive inventory of Soviet military activities and apply appropriate prices to them; using this approach, the CIA estimates that the Soviet defense burden is 15 percent of gross national product (GNP).[1]

Or perhaps one should say that this estimate represents a judgment of only the *quantifiable* Soviet defense burden, and that "the true burden of defense includes many intangibles associated with defense activity

David F. Epstein is deputy director of net assessment, Office of the Secretary of Defense. The views in this chapter are his own.

that cannot be easily measured in quantitative terms."[2] Such caveats are sometimes, but not always, appended to the quantitative estimate.[3] But some analysts concerned with the Soviet defense burden, and particularly with the economic effects of increasing or reducing Soviet defense spending, have concluded that the intangible burden must be considered. Econometric studies that simulate a shift of resources to or from defense show "not . . . much effect on output growth."[4] So to "take account of the qualitative impact of diverting resources to or from the defense sector" econometricians have resorted to making separate adjustments in the projected rate of productivity growth. While the "results . . . indicate that the rate of growth of defense expenditures will have a significant impact on the growth of GNP over the next decade . . . most of the growth impact . . . is a result of the assumed rates of productivity growth," that is, of ad hoc adjustments intended to reflect the qualitative defense burden.[5] The use of this procedure amounts to a judgment that the standard quantitative estimate of the Soviet defense burden does not correspond to the real opportunity cost of the activities it covers.

Moreover, the quantitative estimate does not refer to the full range of security-related activities. It excludes some activities either because they have no close analogues in the U.S. defense budget or because measurements have been thought too difficult or uncertain. Among such excluded activities are "subsidized weapons sales, support for surrogates such as Vietnam and Cuba, civil defense programs, the dispersal and hardening of industrial sites, intelligence activities, some communications facilities, and joint purpose projects, such as the BAM [Baikal-Amur Mainline] railroad and city subway systems."[6]

In this chapter I attempt to think through how those missing elements of the standard quantitative estimate might change our view of the Soviet defense burden. First I describe some of the main military activities not included in the standard estimate. Then I discuss possible disparities between the ruble prices that compose the standard estimate and actual economic costs in the Soviet Union. Finally I consider how alternative views of the absolute size and growth rate of Soviet GNP may affect the estimate. In discussing these matters, I will resort to numbers, none of which should be taken literally.[7] I aim only to indicate what might be the broad magnitude of the adjustments that might be appropriate. A very precise treatment is probably impossible, and a reasonably precise treatment is possible only with information not readily available. My intention is to provide a kind of catalogue of the relevant issues in the hope that others can improve on my rough treatment of them.

The starting point for these excursions is the CIA's estimate that Soviet spending for "about the same" activities funded by the Department of Defense in the United States totaled about 106 billion rubles in 1982 (in 1982 rubles), subdivided roughly as shown in Table 5.1. This figure amounts to 14.7 percent of a 1982 Soviet GNP estimated by the CIA at 719.7 billion rubles.[8] The CIA's own estimate of the defense share of GNP appears to be slightly higher, and reflects a conversion to "factor-cost" prices, which are intended to eliminate distortions introduced by Soviet taxes and subsidies. This factor-cost adjustment appears to add about 4.4 billion rubles to the defense cost, making defense about 15.3 percent of Soviet GNP in 1982.[9]

TABLE 5.1   CIA Estimate of Soviet Defense Spending, 1982

	Billions of 1982 rubles
Procurement	49
Construction	5
Research, development, testing, and evaluation (RDT&E)	20
Personnel	13
Operating and maintenance (O&M)	18

SOURCES: Total is read from a graph in U.S. CIA, *A Guide to Monetary Measures of Soviet Defense Activities: A Reference Aid* (Washington, D.C.: GPO, November 1987), p. 13. Procurement and nonprocurement totals are read from graphs, ibid., pp. 11, 13. Construction is assumed to remain at roughly the <10 percent share of the sum of procurement and construction that it was in 1970 rubles for the period 1967–1977, according to U.S. CIA, *Estimated Soviet Defense Spending: Trends and Prospects* (Washington, D.C.: National Foreign Assessment Center, June 1978), p. 2. RDT&E is read from the graph in U.S. Congress, Joint Economic Committee, *Allocation of Resources in the Soviet Union and China, 1985*, hearings before the Subcommittee on Economic Resources, Competitiveness, and Security Economics (Washington, D.C.: GPO, 1986), part 11, p. 109. Personnel is calculated at 1.8 percent of GNP, from U.S. CIA and DIA, *The Soviet Economy under a New Leader* (Washington, D.C.: GPO, July 1986), p. 19. O&M is the residual.

Missing Pieces

In this section I catalogue a range of military and related activities that impose costs on the Soviet economy but are not included in the CIA estimate. Some of these have the character of dual-use goods. The most difficult cases to judge are those in which the activity is in itself indivisible, but is carried on for a mixture of military and nonmilitary motives (for example, the construction of the BAM railroad). In other cases it is clear that incremental costs are incurred when military considerations impinge on nominally civilian activities (even if those costs are hard to estimate). The "planned" or "command" character of the Soviet economy makes it well suited to the imposition of military requirements on a whole range of economic decisions. Resources for military purposes need not be extracted by taxation as a kind of afterthought to an economy with a logic of its own; rather, "The unified leadership of the Communist Party ensures agreement between the aims and actions of military strategy and the economy. . . ."[10]

Transportation assets. The assortment and design of all means of transportation is a clear case in which military considerations raise costs. "Most of the Soviet merchant fleet has been designed to be able to perform military tasks. All the Soviet dry-cargo ships are roll-on roll-off ships, which means that they are military ships first. By contrast, Western shipowners prefer to build container ships because they have greater commercial practicality. . . . Soviet airliners are adapted for use as military transport planes. The same holds true for Soviet-designed buses, railway cars, and so on."[11] In addition to the cost of designing and building assets to meet military specifications, two other types of costs must be considered. Soviet civilian transportation performs some military missions in peacetime—for example, troop transport services by Aeroflot and support provided to the Navy by the merchant and fishing fleets. Moreover, the number of vehicles procured and operated is determined partly by their usefulness as wartime reserves. Thus we should, in principle, try to attribute to the military not only the additional costs of militarily useful designs, but the cost of providing peacetime services and the costs of building a wartime reserve in excess of civilian needs.[12]

Aeroflot. Aeroflot manifests all these types of costs. The "military exerts its influence" on the design and construction of all Aeroflot aircraft. . . . The responsibility for both military and civil aircraft and engine designs belongs to the Ministry of Aircraft Production, an agency closely tied to the Ministry of Defense. . . . The overriding military requirements for a continually utilized, readily available reserve military transport fleet results in Aeroflot's use of aircraft which are far from optimal for the commercial roles they perform.[13]

Soviet planes have excess power, have more landing wheels, and are heavier than Western aircraft. "Most Aeroflot aircraft consume more fuel than equivalent commercially-designed aircraft," have limited ranges and payloads, and spend more time in maintenance.[14] Some of these flaws may simply reflect inferior design, or normal operating conditions. For example, rugged planes are useful for more primitive runways. But the decision to strengthen planes rather than improve runways may make more military than economic sense.[15]

Peacetime security-related uses of Aeroflot include troop lift (including the semi-annual troop rotation in Eastern Europe), intelligence collection, clandestine transport, and maintaining a presence abroad for diplomatic purposes.

It is a common sight to see Aeroflot aircraft in many African cities empty except for debarking/embarking Soviet diplomatic and other government personnel. . . . Most Aeroflot routes are economically infeasible, and would be abandoned by profit-motivated commercial air couriers (as indeed they have been). . . . [Aeroflot's] excess of unprofitable routes, and aircraft flying them which are marginally cost-effective . . . should not be surprising, for Aeroflot is essentially a military air transport adjunct dressed in respectable civil air finery.[16]

Merchant and fishing fleets. The fact that the merchant fleet earns hard currency argues against attributing its economic inefficiency entirely to its wartime reserve (or peacetime "presence") role, but the Soviets' ability to earn hard currency by this means (and apparent inability to earn it by, for example, producing consumer goods) manifests a basic political choice to emphasize an economic sector that is conspicuously suited to military purposes.

Soviet merchant ships are designed and equipped to meet military requirements. In peacetime, merchant tankers serve the navy while merchant and fishing fleets perform intelligence missions. "In contrast to the U.S. Navy, which buys and paints gray the support ships that it needs for current operations, the Soviet Navy makes extensive use of the merchant marine. Some of the ships in the merchant marine are designed for transport of troops and have a number of special features that allow this."[17] Indeed, it appears that some "civilian" ships are built at the navy's behest. In one case, the fishing industry's plan for tanker production was reviewed by the navy, "which proposed that three ship designs of varying tonnage and fueling capacity be included and that the total capacity of the tanker fleet be doubled. . . . The Navy gets to use these tankers for its current operations and has them available in future crises or war, but the expenditures show up in the fishing industry's budget."[18]

The size of the Soviet merchant and fishing fleets is probably excessive from the standpoint of economic efficiency. The weight of fish caught compared to fishing fleet capacity is far lower for the Soviet Union than for the United States, Europe, or Japan.[19] According to a knowledgeable source, many merchant vessels sail with loads nowhere near their capacity.

Trucks. As for Soviet trucks, Abel Agenbegyan has complained that "80 percent of the trucks that are produced have a capacity of 4–5 tons. . . . The world output of trucks with this capacity totals only 3 percent. It is not surprising that ZIL trucks drive around half empty and operate during one shift only. Or they stand around in garages. Some 40 percent of them are not used at all."[20] In this case, as in others, apparent economic irrationality (which can often be traced simply to the Soviet economic system) appears to have a rational military root. Light trucks and very large trucks are efficient for the civilian economy, but medium-size trucks form the best military reserve. It is also probable that the military determines or influences the design of Soviet trucks.

Railroads and internal waterways. Michael Checinski's assertion that railroad cars are designed to perform military tasks suggests that some procurement cost should be attributed to the military. Peacetime military use of Soviet railroads no doubt exacerbates the general shortage of rail capacity, but that shortage suggests there is no specific increment of stock procured as a wartime reserve. The fleet of Soviet ships for use on internal waterways also forms a useful military reserve,[21] but I have found no assertions that its quality or quantity exceeds peacetime needs. The BAM railroad should probably be treated as a special case, since one of its main purposes appears to be to improve and better protect logistic support for Soviet forces in the Far East. According to one estimate, BAM cost 3 million rubles per kilometer; if we divide the 4,300 kilometers over ten years, we get a figure of roughly 1.3 billion rubles per year.[22] If we attribute half of that to the military, the total is 0.09 percent of GNP.

Costs. It ought to be possible to estimate the additional costs of the items catalogued above. We would need to know the cost of producing Soviet civilian trucks, airplanes, ships, and rail stock; roughly what share of that cost could be attributed to design features that suited military purposes; roughly what share of total production was used in peacetime for military purposes, or is surplus to peacetime needs and forms a wartime reserve; and the incremental operating costs associated with the design peculiarities of the vehicles, their military use, and the maintenance or manning of surplus vehicles.[23] In the absence of such information, I can only offer a straw target for the bayonets of those more knowledgeable. Of the total operating and production costs of Soviet aircraft, ships, and trucks, is it unreasonable to attribute, say, 20 percent to the military (that is, 1.25 percent of GNP)? Or 10 percent (0.62 percent of GNP)? [24]

Hardening, protection, and civil defense. It is clear that the Soviet Union has undertaken extensive measures to protect its industrial capacity and leadership from wartime damage, even damage from a nuclear attack. The category "civil defense" is too narrow to capture this effort, as it usually refers to shelters for the population and the operating costs of officials who organize sheltering and evacuation programs; the Soviet approach to protection is more comprehensive.[25] Checinski notes that, while the Soviet regime had previously favored locating key industrial facilities far behind the borders to make them less vulnerable to invasion, in the early 1960s a new policy designed to reduce vulnerability to nuclear attack favored dispersing "industrial concentrations as much as possible in small units throughout the nation. Underground construction of at least parts of new factories was recommended as well. This magnified costs enormously. . . ."[26] He provides examples of specific factories built partly or entirely underground.[27]

Besides measures to protect industry, the Soviets have invested heavily in facilities to protect rulers and workers. "The Soviets provide their Party and government leaders with hardened alternate command posts located well away from urban centers—in addition to many deep underground bunkers and blast shelters in Soviet cities."[28] The "deep underground facilities today are, in some cases, hundreds of meters deep and can accommodate thousands of people."[29] It has also been suggested that some Soviet city subway system costs are incurred for military purposes.[30] Public participation in civil defense exercises exacts some opportunity cost. "Literally thousands of civil defense exercises are held each year, with city districts quite commonly stopping all activity for training exercises that last a full day. Factories, plants, schools, and other such institutions hold still more frequent exercises."[31] The direct costs of some civil defense activities have been estimated as follows:

> The annual military and civilian cost of four elements of the program—pay and allowances for full-time Civil Defense personnel; operation of specialized military Civil Defense units; construction and maintenance of facilities for these units; and shelter construction—is less than 1 percent of the estimated Soviet defense budget. . . . The cost of construction and equipment for leadership relocation sites over the past 25 years is between 8 and 16 billion rubles. . . .[32]

These statements imply costs of roughly 1.5 billion rubles annually (0.2 percent of GNP), but clearly do not include all of the Soviet activities that belong in this category. "The deep underground program . . . rivals Soviet offensive strategic weapons programs both in scale and level of commitment," according to the U.S. Department of Defense, while one commentator, noting that "official estimates are not yet available," offers a "guess" that the forty-year effort would cost "several hundred billion dollars"—implying that this program cost perhaps 0.25 to 0.5 percent of Soviet GNP annually.[33] One interesting point of comparison is an estimate that close to 0.5 percent of Israel's GNP is devoted to sheltering programs.[34] While the size of the country and the immediacy of the threat in the Israeli case might suggest that the Soviet proportion would be lower, the Soviet aspiration to limit the effects of nuclear and not merely conventional attack points the other way.

Industrial capacity. Another Soviet military cost is incurred in building and maintaining the industrial capacity to produce military goods. One part of this cost is implicit in the standard estimates of defense spending: the figure for weapons procurement is supposed to include a cost for capital services included in the price of each weapon system. But this figure may not capture the cost of investment in production capacity that is underutilized, not yet producing weapons, or not used at all. For example, there has been a "doubling of defense production capacity since 1965";[35] but procurement since 1965 has gone up by only 55 percent.[36] And if "production capacity" is measured quantitatively, any qualitative improvements in the defense industrial base will only add to the disparity. This comparison suggests that the Soviet commitment of resources to the defense industrial base may be understated by calculations derived from observed procurement totals.

One reason to maintain excess capacity is to be prepared for a future surge in production, or for mobilization in crisis or wartime. The "defense production capacity" referred to above presumably includes only factories whose primary product is military goods, but Soviet investment in defense production capacity extends more broadly. "Almost all non-defense industry is required to maintain a stock of wartime industrial mobilization raw materials and tools. . . . The capital tied up in these mobilization kits cannot be trivial."[37] According to Checinski, beginning in the 1930s the

> idea of a kind of permanent state of mobilization was accepted, whereby all newly built factories and enterprises were designed so that they could immediately begin mass-production of military goods should the need arise. The obvious advantage of this concept was that it greatly accelerated the process of economic mobilization, neglecting as a matter of principle the price which would have to be paid for this to occur.

Even the government was thereafter unable to calculate the cost of this mobilization capacity.[38] "Transportation facilities, metal-processing factories, dairies, and even school buildings are being built so that they can easily be converted to military or wartime use. . . . Soviet dairy factories are equipped with special centrifuges that can be used to produce plasma."[39] Soviet factories making military-type goods (airplanes, for example) use general-purpose equipment more easily convertible for wartime use rather than special-purpose equipment that would be more efficient for ordinary civilian production.[40] "Mobilization kits" include not only machinery but raw materials. In the absence of information on Soviet stockpiles, it is worth noting that such mobilization stockpiles in Israel have been estimated to cost about 0.5 percent of GNP,[41] although the prominence of oil in that calculation may limit its relevance to the Soviet Union.

Arranging nondefense production capacity to be suitable for mobilization involves not only choosing convertible tools, even at the price of efficiency; it also affects the very assortment of products that the Soviet economy plans to produce, and thereby imposes an additional burden to the extent that those products do not represent the mix desired by consumers. "Production of consumer goods in the USSR is organized so that it favors the production of consumer goods employing technology that can be easily switched to the production of military goods. . . . The least convertible are capacities involved in production of food and clothing (i.e., nondurables). . . . The most convertible are capacities of production of durable goods such as cars and radio-electronics." As a result, the Soviet Union historically shows relative and absolute decreases in production of some nondurable goods.[42] The same phenomenon has affected the choice of capital goods; Aron Katsenelinboigen cites the controversy in choosing between tractor and fertilizer production in the 1930s, in which the solution that contributed more to military potential was chosen. He says there has been a gradual shift in policy since then, but still wonders "how sensible these policies are for the development of Soviet agriculture in light of how much they are determined by the preferences of the Soviet military-industrial complex."[43]

Such preferences may even affect the specific design and quality of nondefense goods. For example, while agricultural purposes are most efficiently served by durable tractors on wheels, "from the military point of view it is necessary to give priority to tractors whose production can be easily converted into production of tanks. These tractors should have tracks, a lot of power, and need not last very long." In 1973, more than a third of Soviet tractors had tracks.[44] Moreover, the shortage of spare parts for tractors as well as for automobiles and other equipment is due in part to "military objectives":

> In wartime the service life of tanks, motor vehicles, mortars, and other types of weapons and equipment is quite short. Hence there is no need for machines with a long service life; spare parts for these machines are also needed in comparatively limited quantities. This suggests that the capacities of Soviet machine-building plants and the proportions between assembly and machine shops are set up to maximize military production if it is needed. However, since the production of peacetime products requires different proportions between the production of machines and spare parts, a conflict arises. It is resolved in favor of military objectives.[45]

All these examples suggest that the costs that belong in the category of defense industrial capacity are substantial, but they do not give much basis for an estimate. Let us nevertheless incautiously append the following prices to three items in our catalogue:

- excess weapons production capacity: 2.2 billion rubles[46]

- additional investment costs for civilian production to make facilities useful for military mobilization: 0.9 billion to 1.8 billion rubles[47]

- mobilization stockpiles: 1.8 billion rubles[48]

Costs of empire. Another category of military-related expenditures has been catalogued in the RAND Corporation reports on the "costs of Soviet empire." This category includes a variety of activities designed to maintain or increase control in countries under Soviet domination and increase the likelihood of additions to that empire. For 1982, RAND tabulates the following costs:

(1) trade subsidies, calculated as the reduction in prices charged for Soviet fuel exports to Eastern Europe and other parts of the empire, compared with then-prevailing world-market prices, as well as the premium prices paid by the Soviet Union for imports from these countries, compared with prevailing world-market prices for similar products [18.93 billion to 24.76 billion rubles];

(2) export credits, construed as the Soviet Union's trade surpluses with communist and Third World countries, where these net surpluses exceeded $10 million in any one year [4.84 billion rubles];

(3) Soviet economic aid, net of aid repayments [0.95 billion rubles];

(4) military aid, calculated as total military deliveries minus hard-currency military sales [7.87 billion rubles];

(5) incremental costs incurred by Soviet military forces in Afghanistan, above what these forces would cost if their normal basing and operational modes were maintained [0.49 billion to 1.18 billion rubles]; and finally,

(6) a part of total Soviet covert and related activities that, by a series of plausible as well as arguable assumptions, can be assigned to the Soviet imperial enterprise, as distinct from maintenance of the system's control within the Soviet Union itself [2.66 billion rubles].

[Total: 35.74 to 42.26 billion rubles][49]

For our purposes, one or two adjustments to these numbers seem appropriate. First I will delete the costs of the war in Afghanistan, since all of these should show up in the CIA's accounting of Soviet defense activities.[50] Second, a large share of the figure for trade subsidies reflects the Soviet practice of setting a price for oil sales to Eastern Europe that lags behind and dampens world price fluctuations. This implicit subsidy has been declining since the world price of oil fell from its peak in 1979. Although it is true, strictly speaking, that delivery of oil to its clients deprives the Soviet Union of the hard currency it could earn by selling that oil on the world market—and therefore of the domestic ruble equivalent of that hard currency—such a calculation has the effect of valuing oil exported to clients much more highly than oil used by the Soviet military or civilian economy. If one wanted to approximate the greatest payoff from Soviet relinquishment of military and imperial programs, one could say that the oil used by both is worth the domestic ruble equivalent of its world market price.[51] On the other hand, oil reallocated from military and imperial purposes could simply be used in the civilian economy (whose requirement for oil is not fixed, and whose inefficiency in using oil reflects the Soviet policy of sheltering it from the world market).[52] As a low estimate, then, I will reduce the trade subsidy figure by 10 billion rubles to try to eliminate this oil pricing effect.[53]

Miscellaneous. The bulk of Soviet military training takes place prior to induction, in schools or at places of employment, and amounts to billions of man-hours each year. Advanced specialty training is provided by a massive voluntary organization (DOSAAF) whose 80 million members contribute time and money. Training for officer candidates takes place not only in Ministry of Defense schools but in all college-level civil schools.[54] And when reservists are called to active duty for training, their salaries are paid by their industrial enterprises, not by the military.[55] The CIA announced in 1976 that it had begun including "explicit estimates for Soviet preinduction military training," but these do not appear to include all the activities just described, or their opportunity—as opposed to budget—cost.[56]

"Intelligence activities" and "some communications facilities" were among the excluded activities noted by Robert Gates.[57] Some intelligence costs are included in RAND's cost-of-empire estimate. The communications sector may have many of the same characteristics of the transportation sector in that civil installations are planned to meet military requirements (particularly for wartime mobilization) without charge to the military.[58]

When Soviet personnel are needed in certain locations for military purposes, the cost of maintaining or attracting them may not take the form of military allowances, but simply appear among the subsidies provided by the state. A *New York Times* article on Murmansk, a city in the far north of the USSR that is the site of key Soviet military facilities, described wage supplements and other amenities intended to make life there more agreeable, noting that "the cost to the Kremlin is considerable. Western diplomats said the annual subsidy totals billions of rubles."[59] This seems like a considerable exaggeration, but presumably Murmansk is not the only site where such expenses are incurred.[60]

A full accounting should not only consider these additions, but also make appropriate deductions where the military is paying for goods and services that would otherwise have to be paid for by the civilian sector. William Odom notes several such examples: "Much military training . . . benefits the civil economy. Drivers, mechanics, and many other specialists for the civil economy are trained in the military programs. Military construction troops build civilian buildings. Military trucks are used for the grain harvest."[61] I will assume that these practices offset the civilian contribution to military training.[62]

Missing Prices

I turn now to consider whether the prices attached to Soviet military activities in the standard estimate are appropriate. That these prices fall short of the economist's concept of opportunity cost is quite clear, but it is less clear how short they fall. We must consider both the accuracy with which Western intelligence is able to estimate Soviet prices and the degree to which the prices themselves depart from the opportunity cost standard.

The CIA has said that its "confidence is greatest in our estimates of the production rates and costs of major weapon systems and equipment. ... We base this confidence, in part, on the substantial increase over the past 5 years in the number of available ruble prices for Soviet weapons and equipment."[63] Even though "for many Soviet weapons we have an actual ruble price, ... For others we must derive a ruble price either by applying ruble-dollar ratios created for weapons groups or by using cost estimating relations (CERs) that make the price a function of certain performance parameters."[64] It appears that ruble/dollar ratios are derived at least primarily on the basis of ruble/dollar ratios for weapons whose actual ruble price is known, rather than on the basis of ruble/dollar ratios estimated for analogous civilian products.[65] According to Donald Burton, "Contrary to the impression created by some critics, the sample of prices of Soviet military goods used in developing these ratios is large, with prices available for numerous weapons in virtually all categories."[66]

According to Abram Bergson, the CIA "has to operate with a relatively limited sample of ruble/dollar ratios. Although the sample has grown in time, the ratios themselves must often be inferred from indirect evidence. The calculations in ruble terms therefore must be especially crude."[67] Abraham Becker in 1980 called ruble/dollar ratios the "most vulnerable" point of the CIA's costing procedure, "as was demonstrated by the doubling of the CIA ruble estimates in 1976. In the intervening years considerably more attention has been paid to expanding and refining the ruble-dollar data base."[68] Becker expressed particular concern that the 1970 ruble price base that by then had been expanded and refined was growing too old to reflect current costs. The CIA has since remedied that difficulty by switching to a 1982 price base, but in order to make this improvement it might have been forced to rely on a less expansive list of prices. Much appears to depend on the accuracy and representativeness of the sample of actual ruble prices. One important question is whether those prices are clearly defined; for example, is it possible that the producer receives other payments, not reflected in the unit price, for overhead or capital investment? Another issue, discussed below, is whether all payments received by the producer fully cover the economic cost of what he produces.

The CIA's estimates are adjusted "to a factor-cost valuation" to correct for the fact that "Soviet prices are established administratively rather than by market forces, and thus do not reflect the true relative scarcities of goods and services in the Soviet economy. The factor-cost valuation is obtained by adjusting price values to reflect the average costs of factors used up in production."[69] This adjustment removes the effects of subsidies and taxes, and adjusts profit to correspond with the amount of capital used for production.[70] Unless full information is somehow available on profits, subsidies, and capital used in the production of military goods, the factor-cost adjustment can only be made very generally and by analogy with data on civilian production. For whatever reason, the factor-cost adjustment "has little practical effect on total procurement."[71]

Profit. Various suggestions have been made about ways in which the prices of Soviet military goods may be explicitly or implicitly subsidized. The simplest of these is the view that Soviet weapons production differs from civilian production in that no profit is earned on the former. In the CIA's view, such a policy is no longer in effect:

> We believe that in 1967, when the Soviets undertook a major price reform, one of the things that they did was remove substantial subsidies on military procurement. It is acknowledged in several places in Soviet literature that military production was heavily subsidized prior to 1967. ... Precisely what they did was to eliminate subsidies on materials that were being purchased by the defense industrial [ministries], and to change the profit rates that they charged on defense products to better reflect real resource cost.[72]

This view has been challenged by Dmitri Steinberg, who suggests that Soviet-source statements about defense producers' profits in fact refer to profits on their production of nondefense goods. "Since planners treat production of weapons as a non-productive activity performed for the Defense Ministry, enterprises making these weapons are themselves budget-supported. Hence, prices on weapons exclude profit. With this accounting trick, planners are able to reduce significantly the total value of produced weapons that appears in their own version of Soviet national accounts."[73] If Steinberg is right, putting weapons prices in line with the prices of civilian goods would require increasing them (and total GNP) by 4.7 billion rubles.[74]

Overhead and capital charges. A more subtle form of subsidy suggested by several sources is the policy of allocating capital costs and overhead away from military production and charging them to civilian production lines in factories that produce both types of goods, or diverting those costs to the civilian economy more generally. According to Becker, the general policy of "low capital charges and the continued reluctance to allow such charges to affect resource allocation make for particular understatement of costs in a capital-intensive branch of the economy such as production of military hardware."[75] While Paul Cockle mentions Soviet claims that the Ministry of Defense "settles its accounts with full coverage of costs to the national economy," he cites a possible exception to that policy: in the machine-building and metalworking sector the "Fund for Mastering New Technology is supplied from deductions which are 'charged to the cost of the civilian output of the enterprise.' . . . Could these funds be redistributed to defence establishments, or are they scrupulously returned to civilian enterprises within the group?"[76]

According to Igor Birman, "defense branches . . . receive exceedingly cheap capital investments. . . . The overwhelming part of budgetary capital investments goes for so-called heavy industry, and the capital investments of light industry are covered mainly by their own profits (and depreciation)." Defense production is very capital intensive, and "the so-called payments for the [capital investment] funds are very low," resulting in "significant reduction in the official indicators of" Soviet military spending.[77]

Checinski thinks that such opportunities for creative bookkeeping are exploited extensively in the Soviet Union and Eastern Europe. He says overhead costs are systematically allocated away from military goods, and describes procedures in Poland whereby budget subsidies made up for military prices that were set unrealistically low.[78] Military-industrial factories are in no way "self-financing":

> All financial operations needed for the permanent changes of the production programs, and frequent changes of the production processes are paid from a special fund controlled by the military department of the Ministry of Finance and the military department of the Gosbank. The official financial controls act only formally in the military-industrial factories and operate without strong interference. Presumably, only in such a way is Gosplan able to force the military-industrial ministries, and their plants, to fulfill the demands of the Soviet armed forces.[79]

More generally,

> On the macro-scale, the essential starting point is the thesis that there is no direct link between costs and prices for armament products in the

Comecon countries; so that all calculations . . . made on the basis of formally stated Soviet armament prices reflect neither the degree to which the supply of these arms to the Army or to other countries burdens the Soviet budget nor what part they actually constitute in the gross national product.[80]

Checinski's apparently extreme position has recently gained support from Soviet statements promising future disclosure of defense budgets but justifying delay on the grounds that price reform must come first. According to the *Washington Post*, General Vitalii Shabanov, principal deputy minister of defense for armaments, "said current figures 'would not be objective' because the cost of weapons and other military goods is often fixed arbitrarily, without regard to economic measures commonly used in the West."[81]

If Checinski and Shabanov are correct, "actual ruble prices" give utterly no insight into the Soviet defense burden. Checinski's practical suggestion is to derive the burden of weapons production by assuming that the ratio of the price of a tank to that of a bus, for example, is the same in the Soviet Union as in Western countries, and that Soviet bus prices roughly represent real economic costs (see the section "GNP and military goods in dollars" in this chapter). For the moment, however, I will guess that the subsidy to military production from shifting overhead and capital investment charges to civilian goods is 0 to 2.2 billion rubles.[82]

If subsidies flow freely to defense industrial producers, those producers need not object to whatever low prices the military wishes to set on individual products. But the more common view assumes that prices do have some practical effect on their operations, so that plant managers have an incentive to be somewhat harder bargainers. According to the CIA, "the price of the military good can be changed each year. . . . The incentive for the plant manager to obtain a high initial price for a new military product is greater than for a civilian product. Unlike the civilian case, the price of a military product can be forced down."[83]

Quality advantages. Several other types of subsidy for military production consist, not in deliberately suppressing prices (which the producer would presumably protest, unless he were funded otherwise, as Checinski suggests), but in deliberately suppressing the price of the producer's inputs (which the producer would be happy to accept in any case). The Soviet Union has followed this policy by providing the timely and highest-quality supply of materials and labor for defense production lines without charging a premium. There is broad agreement that this kind of implicit price subsidy is practiced and that it is unquantifiable.

"The defense industries receive priority access to raw materials and are given preferential access to the transportation and distribution networks for delivering materials. They also have access to the highest quality machinery and labor."[84] In factories that produce both civilian and military goods, "the best quality resources go into the military product line," leading to "a large siphoning effect from the civilian production line to the military one which is not noted in any accountant's books."[85] A study by Gur Ofer describes the "nonmonetary advantages" of the Soviet military research and development (R&D) sector.[86] His general argument is supported by a recent study based on a survey of émigrés:

> The military is in fact the first claimant on all research and production no matter where it is carried out. The ability to extract resources from the civilian sector means that Soviet military spending does not have to be increased for them to conduct more military R&D.... The Soviet military achieves its relatively successful performance by extensive exploitation of the entire economic system. This exploitation occurs in two major ways. First, at tremendous expense the military maintains high-level R&D institutions that perform work at a level of sophistication much greater than the prevailing norm. Second, at a multitude of "ordinary" facilities some portion of the work or share of the best quality output is claimed by the military. Our interviews suggest that the extent of the costs imposed on the rest of Soviet society by these military needs might exceed even the highest estimates in Western literature.[87]

Any attempt to quantify this phenomenon runs into the following question. How much better are the military's grade A items (tools, steel, scientists, trucks) than the civilian grade B items? It depends on the overall distribution of relevant qualities and on the share of the universe of items that the military will be taking. Since the military takes virtually all eighteen-year-old males, its average quality will be equal to that of the population; if it takes half the transistors, or steel, or scientists, it can be more selective. It is unlikely that the military is uniformly successful in exerting its prerogative; it is also possible that not all measurable differences in quality make a significant difference in value or output. In the case of human resources, at least some of the difference in quality will be reflected in wages or other costs incurred for the equipment, working conditions, or perquisites that attract the best talent; however, many very attractive perquisites are not paid for with money, but consist of official permissions—for example, to shop in certain stores, visit certain vacation spots, or (most important) to obtain an apartment.

To quantify roughly the "quality effect" as a whole, I assume that for most goods the military can claim a share that, on the average, ranks at the seventieth or seventy-fifth percentile of all such goods, and estimate the relative quality of those selected goods on the basis of studies of the distribution of human abilities.[88] The result is that the military gets a 10 percent quality edge; assuming the military already pays for half of that (in wage and equipment costs), I increase most defense prices by 5 percent.[89] This adds 4.4 billion rubles (0.6 percent of GNP) to the defense burden.

Supply advantages. Quite apart from this access to superior-quality inputs, the Soviet military production sector also has a considerable advantage over civilian production in its access to a timely supply of raw and intermediate materials:

> Military branches work under much better conditions than all others, and these better conditions are reflected little, if at all, in the level of expenditure. So defense branches receive all the items they need—imported equipment, any materials—ahead of all the others: often what is not available to other branches. Insofar as supplies are a cardinal problem, such a particular system gives to defense branches an enormous advantage, and provides the conditions for the colossal difference in the results of their work. But defense branches obtain everything needed at the same prices as other branches, and their exceedingly substantial advantages are in no way reflected in the level of expenditures.[90]

Birman notes Soviet statements indicating that production equipment in the civilian sector is idle about 20 percent of the time due to inadequate supply; this may be a considerable understatement (due to enterprises' reluctance to report their own inefficiency).[91] Supply of the military sector need not be perfect, nor its priority enjoyed without exception, to make its overall priority in obtaining supplies a major advantage in the "taut" Soviet economy.

The general problem with supply is caused by the Soviet economic system rather than by the existence of a privileged military sector, and it is difficult to say how much more efficient the civilian sector could become if the military's privilege were eliminated. But the military's supply privilege is a form of price subsidy. Soviet prices that accurately represent the factor cost of production will reflect the labor and capital services employed, but if that labor and capital is idled for a period of time by supply shortages, the price will also include the cost of hiring or having those factors for the idle period. If the military, on the other hand, always (or more often) receives the supplies it needs, the prices applied to its labor and capital services will include no (or a smaller) charge for the time that those factors are idle. This means that military goods priced at their factor cost will be less expensive than they would be if they were produced under civilian supply conditions. If this were simply due to the military sector's superior internal organization, it would be no "burden" on the resources of society as a whole. But since it is due to the military's ability to command more timely access to the resources it needs (without paying a premium), it seems appropriate to try to state what the cost of the military's output would be if it were produced under the average conditions prevailing in the economy as a whole. To put the point another way, we wish to estimate not the share of the nation's productive resources formally assigned to the military, but the share of those productive resources that are actually given the wherewithal to produce.[92]

Manpower and pension costs. It is well known that Soviet conscripts are paid low wages, although Soviet officers are paid quite well. A 1973 study by Earl Brubaker found that Soviet wages considerably understate the opportunity cost of Soviet military personnel, and estimated that pay and subsistence for conscripts would need to be raised 34 percent to reflect their opportunity cost. Brubaker also concluded that the "implicit taxes on Soviet conscripts" were growing rapidly.[93] Although the CIA's factor-cost adjustment may account for some of this, the nature of that adjustment is unclear.[94] The CIA's factor-cost estimate of military personnel is 1.8 percent of GNP (13 billion rubles);[95] it is possible that an opportunity-cost figure would be, say, 4.4 billion rubles higher.[96] Military pensions are another part of personnel costs apparently not included in the standard estimate of the defense burden, although they represent a deferred cost of past military activities. Steinberg estimates pensions at 3.6 billion rubles in 1982.[97]

Gross National Product

I have not yet paid much attention to the denominator in the calculation of the Soviet defense burden, Soviet GNP. How do the uncertainty and controversy concerning both the size and rate of growth of the Soviet economy affect our view of that burden?

Growth rate. Some Soviet economists have suggested new estimates of Soviet growth far below official Soviet claims and somewhat below the CIA's estimates.[98] Juxtaposing a correct estimate of Soviet military growth with an overestimate of Soviet economic growth would, over a period of years, lead to a progressive understatement of the military share of GNP. But this problem does not apply to the CIA's estimate for 1982 in 1982 prices. If the prices for that year are accurate (or, more precisely, if the prices reflect relative resource costs as of that year), then the estimate for 1982 would be accurate. As the price base year grows more distant, some distortion may be introduced if inflation in defense goods differs from inflation in the entire economy, or if the growth rate of either is misstated. When the CIA changed from a 1970 to a 1982 price base, it found a small increase in the defense burden. Table 5.2 offers a crude approximation of the CIA's results. The defense sector appears to have grown in real terms at about the same rate as GNP, and to have experienced a slightly greater rate of price increases than the nondefense sector. For procurement, inflation was estimated to be much faster, and real growth slower, than for the whole economy.

Khanin and Seliunin estimate Soviet growth for the period 1970–1982 at roughly 1.6 percent per year.[99] That figure, if applied to GNP and

TABLE 5.2	Real Growth and Price Change in Soviet Defense and GNP, 1970–1982 (average annual increase)		
	Nominal	Real	Price change
GNP	5.4	2.6	2.8
Total defense	5.5	2.5	3.0
Procurement	6.6	1.4	5.2

SOURCES: Defense and procurement in current and 1982 prices are taken from graphs in U.S. CIA, *A Guide to Monetary Measures of Soviet Defense Activities: A Reference Aid* (Washington, D.C.: GPO, November 1987), pp. 11, 13; GNP figures in 1982 prices are from U.S. Congress, Joint Economic Committee, *Allocation of Resources in the Soviet Union and China, 1985*, hearings before the Subcommittee on Economic Resources, Competitiveness, and Security Economics (Washington, D.C.: GPO, 1986), p. 77; 1970 GNP in 1970 prices is from idem, *USSR: Measures of Economic Growth and Development, 1950–80* (Washington, D.C.: GPO, December 1982). Real growth is calculated in 1982 prices.

compared with the CIA's nominal GNP figures, implies inflation of 3.8 percent per year, which (using the CIA's defense estimates) would make inflation in procurement appear less extreme, and imply that defense prices on average grew less rapidly than prices in the whole economy. Since this finding—although it conflicts with the CIA's calculation—is not inexplicable, Khanin and Seliunin's growth rate does not necessarily contradict the CIA's view of the defense burden as of 1982.

1982 GNP in rubles. Several possible adjustments to the CIA's estimate of Soviet GNP would apply directly to its estimate for 1982 in 1982 ruble prices. The activities of the Soviet "second economy" add something to Soviet GNP. While some second-economy activities are simply redistributive in nature, value is added by labor creating goods and services. Anders Åslund (in this volume) suggests that the increment to GNP might be "10 to 13 percent—a moderate second economy by Western standards and a small one by Third World standards." Such an addition would shave several percentage points off the military-imperial share of GNP.[100] It should be noted, however, that second-economy production is not readily available for Soviet rulers to reallocate to military purposes. Another adjustment is suggested by Steinberg, who believes that Soviet statistics—and therefore, CIA figures—exclude the wages and social security payments to weapons industry workers.[101]

Adjustments in the opposite direction are suggested by observations that some portion of Soviet output is fictitious or worthless. Richard Ericson (in this volume) reports "serious questions in the Soviet debate about the reliability of even the physical production statistics officially claimed," as well as an argument that some of what counts as Soviet economic "product" is in fact "absolutely useless, . . . devoid of any economic value." Waste appears in various forms; for example, production of goods for which there is no demand, construction projects left unfinished, and the careless transportation or storage of goods such that production as measured by the factory's output substantially exceeds the value actually delivered to customers.

Calculations of Soviet GNP focus on what the Soviet economy supplies, not on the extent to which those supplies correspond to demand. Accordingly, estimates of the Soviet defense burden do not assess the value of the military and nonmilitary product; they are rather estimates of the quantity of resources being devoted to that production. The factor-cost estimate of Soviet GNP might better be titled "gross national inputs." While worthless and wasted goods included in GNP would appear to be correctly accounted for from this point of view (since Soviet factors of production were indeed at work in making them), the treatment of fictitious goods should depend on whether the labor and capital services attributed to their production are in fact employed or are themselves fictitious.

But if, as the lack of markets seems to require, we describe the structure of the Soviet economy only on the basis of the allocation of inputs, and ignore the value of outputs, we are in fact giving an incomplete description of the inputs. Fictitious or worthless goods in civilian production directly correspond to the absence of a key factor of production that has been allocated elsewhere. Military production appears to be more carefully planned and inspected than civilian production. For example, military representatives in factories are not joined by representatives of other customers for finished or intermediate goods. The planning system, faced with the impossible task of specifying the huge array of goods to be produced and allocated, does not devote the care to shoes that it does to military aircraft. The military sector enjoys not only the supply and quality advantages discussed earlier, but the privilege of being an attentive and demanding customer; a resource that I will call "managerial care" is therefore devoted to the satisfaction of the military customer. This may be an extremely limited resource in command economies—markets may provide the equivalent of such care more routinely and universally—but since this managerial resource is allocated to the military more than to other sectors, it burdens the ability of those other sectors to produce economic value. It is therefore appropriate, although difficult, to place a shadow price on managerial attention proportioned to the quantity of fictitious, wasted, and worthless goods produced by sectors that lack it.[102]

GNP and military goods in dollars. Estimates of Soviet military and nonmilitary product in dollars offer an alternative to rubles as a standard of measurement, and may help in the calculation of appropriate ruble prices. These estimates are themselves controversial, however. The valuation of Soviet GNP in dollars has little or no direct implication for the CIA's estimate of the Soviet defense burden in rubles. While the CIA derives ruble prices for some Soviet weapons by applying a ruble/dollar ratio to an estimate of what it would cost to produce the weapon in dollars, that ratio is itself derived from ruble price information and dollar estimates for other Soviet weapons.[103] In principle, the question of how many dollars it would cost to produce Soviet weapons or buy Soviet

TABLE 5.3   Implicit Estimates of What a Ruble Can Buy

Goods	1985 dollars, per 1982 ruble
a. Weapons, using apparent CIA prices	1.63
b. Weapons, using adjusted prices	1.30
c. Transportation equipment, 1976	4.18
d. Average 1978 import or export	1.33
e. Average 1980 import	0.91
f. Average economic good (CIA)	2.88
g. Average economic good (Birman)	1.45–1.94

SOURCES: a. The figure for 1982 procurement in 1985 dollars is read from the graph in U.S. CIA, *A Guide to Monetary Measures of Soviet Defense Activities: A Reference Aid* (Washington, D.C.: GPO, November 1987), p. 14. I have made a further adjustment to account for the fact that the CIA's dollar figure reflects the "definition of procurement . . . used by the United States, which differs slightly from the definition used by the Soviets" (ibid). To make the ruble and dollar figures for procurement properly comparable, I have multiplied the ruble figure by .78 in order to approximate the narrower definition of procurement used in the dollar figure. The factor .78 is derived from a comparison of the 36 percent procurement share of defense spending indicated in the CIA publication, *Estimated Soviet Defense Spending in Rubles, 1970–75*, in May 1976, and the 46 percent share indicated in the CIA publication, *Estimated Soviet Defense Spending: Trends and Prospects* in June 1978. While these figures are approximations based on less precise statements in the reports themselves, and refer to somewhat different sets of years (1970–75 and 1967–77), the larger share appears to reflect the CIA's adoption in the later report of "a wider definition of investment, and a narrower definition of operating than [is] employed in U.S. defense accounts," based on Soviet assignment of more costs for spare parts and repair to the investment account (ibid, p. 2n). I am grateful to Gregory Hildebrandt for suggesting this line of reasoning and calling my attention to the sources upon which it is based.
b. The CIA ruble procurement figure has been adjusted in the ways suggested in this chapter to account for profit, overhead, quality advantages, and supply advantages.
c. This figure is the geometric mean ratio reported in Imogene Edwards, Margaret Hughes, James Noren, "U.S. and U.S.S.R.: Comparisons of GNP," in *Soviet Economy in a Time of Change*, vol. 1, a compendium of papers submitted to the Joint Economic Committee (Washington, D.C.: GPO, October 10, 1979), p. 380, roughly adjusted to approximate a 1985 dollar per 1982 ruble instead of a 1976 dollar per 1976 ruble. Adjustments were made using the U.S. GNP deflator and

continued next page

TABLE 5.3 *continued*

the average rate of inflation implicit in CIA estimates of Soviet GNP (see the section "Growth rate" in text).

d. The ruble/dollar ratio for total foreign trade turnover in 1978 is reported in Vladimir G. Treml and Barry L. Kostinsky, *Domestic Value of Soviet Foreign Trade: Exports and Imports in the 1972 Input-Output Table,* Foreign Economic Report No. 20, U.S. Department of Commerce (Washington, D.C.: GPO, October 1982), p.16. I have modified it to reflect 1985 dollars and 1982 rubles.

e. Vladimir G. Treml, "Soviet Dependence on Foreign Trade," in *External Economic Relations of CMEA Countries: Their Significance and Impact in a Global Perspective* (Brussels: NATO, 1983), p. 37. His figure for 1980 imports in foreign trade rubles was converted to dollars using the exchange rate in U.S. CIA, *Handbook of Economic Statistics, 1987: A Reference Aid* (Washington, D.C.: GPO, September 1987), p. 59, and that dollar figure compared with Treml's figure for imports in domestic ruble prices; the ratio was then adjusted to reflect 1985 dollars and 1982 rubles.

f. The CIA's dollar valuation of Soviet GNP in its *Handbook of Economic Statistics,* p. 35, has been adjusted to 1985 prices using the U.S. GNP deflator, p. 36.

g. According to Igor Birman, "Soviet GNP . . . is closer to 30–40 percent" of American GNP. Overview of the CIA Study, "Consumption in the USSR: An International Comparison," Report no. 13 (Foundation for Soviet Studies, May 1983), p. 353.

consumer goods in the United States is entirely distinct from the question of what resources the Soviets devote to those activities. Underlying the judgment that defense burdens must be calculated in internal prices is the assumption that different economies are more or less efficient in producing various goods.

Still, dollar estimates may cast some light on a ruble burden estimate, particularly if we are uncertain as to the accuracy or meaning of the ruble figures. Checinski's view that Soviet weapons prices are arbitrary, and that more meaningful ruble figures could be derived from the ruble/dollar ratios of nonmilitary goods, suggests the question, How does the CIA's implicit ruble/dollar ratio for weapons procurement compare with ruble/dollar ratios for other goods? Because the CIA estimates Soviet defense spending in dollars as well as in rubles, those estimates contain an implicit assessment of how many "dollars' worth" of military goods and services a ruble will buy.[104] Checinski suggests that we may have more accurate information about how many "dollars' worth" of civilian goods and services a ruble will buy, and could use that information to improve upon Soviet military prices. But in addition to the difficulty of finding analogous products—since the "dollar value" of a ruble is bound to vary considerably across different goods—disagreements about the comparative size of the Soviet economy result in a wide range of opinion even about the average value of a ruble for the economy as a whole. Table 5.3 shows several rough, implicit estimates of what a ruble can buy.

In the CIA's estimate, weapons production appears to be an area of comparative disadvantage for the Soviet Union. For defense activities other than procurement, a ruble will buy $2.99 worth of goods and services, but for procurement the Soviets get only $1.63 worth of weapons for their ruble. If the adjustments I have suggested for weapons pricing result in a "fairer" ruble price, Soviet weapons production appears even less efficient. The closest I can come to Checinski's suggested comparison of ruble and dollar prices for "lorries" is a 1976 study of price parities for "transportation equipment," but the ratio reported there found that production of that sort comes relatively easy for the Soviets.[105] By analogy, it would seem, Soviet weapons are overpriced, unless (as is plausible) the somewhat more limited scale of production and the technological sophistication of weapons makes the comparison inappropriate.

Another benchmark for the value of a ruble can be derived from studies of the domestic value of Soviet foreign trade (although there is controversy about whether Soviet pricing policies for imported goods reflect their true economic value to the economy, as opposed to providing a convenient mode of raising revenue). Imported machinery may serve as a fair analogy for some of the more sophisticated Soviet weapons, as the technological challenge of producing that machinery is presumably the reason for importing it and attaching a high domestic price to it. When buying such machinery, Soviet domestic customers appear to have gotten only 91 cents' worth for their ruble.

While the CIA's estimates indicate that Soviet weapons prices are quite a bit higher than the price of an "average" good (relative to that comparison in dollars), Birman's much lower valuation of the Soviet economy would imply either that the efficiency of Soviet weapons production is close to the average for the economy as a whole, or that the relative difficulty of producing weapons is not reflected in the weapons prices the CIA uses.

TABLE 5.4   Estimated Economic Cost of Soviet Security and Empire

	Security and empire (billions of 1982 rubles)	GNP (billions of 1982 rubles)	Share[a] (percentage)
CIA narrow definition	106	719.7	14.73
CIA factor cost adjustment	4.4	0	0.62
Coverage adjustments:			
Transportation	5.1 to 9.6	0	0.71 to 1.34
Hardening, protection	3.2 to 4.9	0	0.44 to 0.68
Industrial capacity	4.9 to 5.8	0	0.68 to 0.81
Costs of empire	25.2 to 41.1	8.9 to 24.8	3.47 to 5.52
Miscellaneous	1.2 to 2.2	0	0.17 to 0.31
Subtotal (incl. coverage adj.)	150 to 174	729 to 744	21 to 23
Price adjustments:			
Profits	0.0 to 4.7	0.0 to 4.7	0.00 to 0.65
Overhead and capital charges	0.0 to 2.2	0	0.00 to 0.31
Quality advantages	4.35	0	0.60
Supply advantages	3.7	0	0.51
Manpower and pensions	8.0	4.4	1.10
Subtotal (incl. coverage and price adj.)	166 to 197	733 to 754	23 to 26
GNP adjustments:			
Adjusted GNP growth	0	0	0.00
Second economy	0	93.6 to 72.0	−1.69 to −1.34
Missing wages	0	20.4 to 0	−0.41 to 0.00
Fictitious or worthless output	0	−21.6 to −43.2	0.46 to 0.94
Total (including second economy)	166 to 197	825 to 782	20 to 25
Total (excluding second economy)	166 to 197	732 to 710	23 to 28
Variant total (based on alternative ruble/dollar ratios)[b]	183 to 209	733 to 749	25 to 28

a. Each line's figure reflects the net effect of numerator and denominator adjustments in that line only. Totals are higher because of combined effects of adjustments in different lines.
b. See "GNP and Military Goods in Dollars" in text. Higher ruble/dollar ratios are applied to procurement, RDT&E, and sheltering programs; coverage adjustments are included; but of price and GNP adjustments only the manpower and pension adjustment is retained.
SOURCE: Author. See text of this chapter.

Alternative estimates of the size of the Soviet economy in dollars are logically compatible with a variety of estimates of the military-imperial share of that economy measured at internal opportunity costs. The compatibility depends, however, on complementary assumptions about the relative efficiency of different economic sectors. If the value of Soviet nonmilitary output is lower than we have thought, then (holding constant our estimate of the value of Soviet military output) we must raise our estimate of the relative efficiency of the Soviet military production sector or else raise our estimate of the military burden.[106]

Conclusion

It may be useful to summarize the numbers that have been ventured in this paper, bearing in mind their status as very rough guesses. Table 5.4 shows how my suggested adjustments would alter the CIA estimates of Soviet defense and GNP. The categories in Table 5.4 form a guide to further research; the numbers in the table should provoke, and be substantially improved by, such research.

The High-Priority Military Sector in a Shortage Economy

THE SUBSTANTIAL INCREASE in Soviet military power over the past two decades has been accompanied by growth in the supporting institutions of the defense industry, military research and development (R&D), and military foreign trade, increasing the already large burden imposed by the defense sector on the Soviet economy. This occurred despite declining growth rates of national income and factor productivity, sectoral imbalances, shortages of goods and services, and recurrent poor harvests. In order to evaluate the Soviet defense burden, the prospects for economic reforms, and the impact of resource transfers from defense to civilian sectors, it is necessary to understand the priority of the defense sector, its relationships with civilian branches, and its efficiency, technological level, and political influence.

According to the "dual economy" view, the defense sector is insulated from the civilian economy and receives uniformly high priority treatment in obtaining resources. The authorities intervene to ensure that the defense industry provides weapons that are as competitive as possible with Western products. As a result, military-industrial enterprises are considerably more efficient and technologically sophisticated

Christopher M. Davis is a lecturer in Soviet studies at the Centre for Russian and East European Studies at the University of Birmingham in England.

than their civilian counterparts. In other words, if resources were transferred from the defense sector to civilian branches, they would be used less efficiently.

Another school of thought holds that the defense sector is not more efficient than the civilian sector, but simply more effective in producing military goods because of its access to virtually unlimited quantities of superior-quality inputs and high-priority protection. The defense sector receives many inputs from the civilian sector and supplies it with numerous outputs. Because of this interdependence, defense institutions suffer from the many problems of the civilian economy. This interpretation suggests that civilian branches would use resources as productively as the defense sector if they had equal priority.

Although the balance of opinion is shifting in favor of the latter view, there is no sufficient explanation of why the defense sector performs as it does. There has been too little research on the theory and measurement of priority in the socialist economy.[1] Most existing models are too abstract or aggregated to portray the microeconomic behavior of defense institutions[2] and do not take adequately into account the disequilibrium and shortage phenomena characteristic of socialist economies.[3] In this paper I attempt to remedy some of these problems by analyzing the impact of priority protection on the performance of defense industry enterprises in the Soviet shortage economy.

The Defense Sector

The production process. Soviet military capabilities are determined by both economic power and the performance of the defense sector.[4] Economic power at the sectoral level determines the productive capabilities of civilian branches relevant to the armed forces, such as machine-building, fuels, and computers.[5] A. I. Pozharov describes this relationship:

> In order for economic power to be converted into military strength, it is necessary to provide for the production of armaments, combat technology and other items of a military nature, the correct distribution and timely delivery of them to the troops, and the creation of all the conditions for their effective utilization. A special social organism serves these goals—the military economy. The scale and effectiveness of the military economy characterizes the military-economic power of the state, that is, its actual capability to provide its armed forces and to support the necessary defensive capacity of the country.[6]

The defense sector has been examined using a variety of models: descriptive, institutional, defense spending, national accounts, input-output, and econometric. Most do not define the sector in enough detail to make microeconomic analysis possible. Here it is defined by the usual accounting procedure of identifying a unique economic activity or output and then assigning to the related branch all institutions engaged in producing it. The appropriate final sectoral outputs are military services. These can be subdivided into potential services, such as those that deter attacks or threaten potential opponents, and actual combat services, which use force to attain desired goals.

Military services are an output of a complex production chain that involves many civilian and defense organizations. For analytical convenience it is best to define the defense sector (or military economy) narrowly as comprised of institutions that produce military services, commodities, or technology; distribute military or civilian commodities to the armed forces; or administer defense activities. On this basis, the defense sector contains six main institutions: the armed forces, domestic military-supply network, defense industry, military R&D, military foreign trade, and central defense bureaucracy.[7] Each uses inputs of labor, capital, and intermediate goods, which are (with the exception of military services) sold and purchased in a variety of "markets."[8] They are all financed through the state budget and self-financing, with the exception of the central defense bureaucracy, which is financed entirely through the state budget. Table 6.1 provides information about their type and outputs.[9] Figure 6.1 shows that military services are the final outputs of the activities of the six main defense-sector institutions.[10] This production process is controlled by the central defense bureaucracy, which determines the levels of activity and budget allocations for these institutions.[11]

Central defense bureaucracy. The dominant economic institution of the defense sector is the central bureaucracy, which includes the agencies above the ministerial level that allocate resources, develop plans and budgets, and manage defense programs.[12] The top decision-making bodies are the Politburo and Defense Council, which determine national security objectives, approve external threat assessments and military doctrine, decide on civilian and defense shares of national income, establish performance targets for the other five defense-sector institutions, and allocate resources to military-related programs. They are supported by the Central Committee Secretariat of the Communist

TABLE 6.1   Economic Institutions of the Soviet Defense Sector

Institution	Type	Primary outputs
Armed forces	Service-producing	Potential or actual military services
Domestic military supply	Internal trade	Sales of consumer and producer commodities to the armed forces
Defense industry	Industrial enterprise	Military commodities: armaments, munitions
Military R&D	Service-producing	Military-related scientific results, designs, and technology
Military foreign trade	Foreign trade	Export and import of military goods
Central defense bureaucracy	Service-producing	Administration of the defense sector

SOURCE: Author.

Party of the Soviet Union (CPSU). The party staff work is supervised by the Secretary for Defense and Heavy Industry and carried out by the Department of Defense Industry, Department of Administrative Organs, and the main political administration of the army and navy.

The central bureaucracy is also assisted by numerous state bodies, including the Ministry of Finance, State Planning Committee (Gosplan), State Committee for Material Reserves, State Committee for Material and Technical Supply (Gossnab), and State Committee for Standards (Gosstandart). In addition, the Military Industrial Commission of the Council of Ministers USSR (VPK) has special responsibility for coordinating the activities and managing the main programs of the defense sector, including military R&D and foreign technology acquisition.

The central defense bureaucracy provides crucial administrative services, allocating resources as shown in Figure 6.1. Various inputs, such as labor, capital (buildings and office equipment), and intermediate goods, are obtained in the defense bureaucracy labor market (DBLM), capital market (DBCM), and intermediate-goods market (DBIM). These operations are financed entirely by the state budget.

Armed forces. The armed forces generate military services and other commodities used for military purposes or provided to the civilian economy.[13] The outputs of the armed forces are produced in military units (regiments, ships, aviation squadrons) using inputs of labor (military officers and enlisted men), capital (arms, military and civilian equipment, and buildings), and intermediate goods (munitions, food, fuel, medicine).

In this paper, the *armed forces* refer to the Ministry of Defense units minus those engaged in defense industry production, military R&D, domestic and foreign military trade, and central administration. (The latter have been reallocated to the other five defense-sector institutions.) They include the five main military services (strategic rocket forces, ground forces, air defense troops, air forces, and navy), most special troops (for example, chemical and engineer), and some of the rear services (for example, railroad troops). The KGB border guards and Ministry of Internal Affairs troops are also included.

The armed forces labor input is obtained from the national labor market (AFLM) using both economic incentives (wages and benefits) and administrative means (conscription). Military and civilian capital and intermediate goods are acquired in the armed forces producer-commodity market (AFWM) from the domestic military-supply network. Consumer goods and services are bought in the special military retail market (AFRM) run by the rear services (Tyl). The state budget is the primary source of finance, but supplemental funds are obtained from payments made by the civilian economy for goods and services provided by the military.

Domestic military-supply network. This institution, otherwise known as the military logistics system, buys goods from the civilian economy and other defense-sector institutions and supplies them to the armed forces and the civilian population.[14] It has been developed in response to the special needs of the military. A. I. Pozharov points out that "the civilian infrastructure cannot ensure the fulfillment of a whole series of specific tasks related to the distribution of final military products."[15] For this reason a special section of the military economy (*osoboe zveno voennoi ekonomiki*) exists to handle the distribution of goods to the military.

The domestic military-supply network is made up of all the Ministry of Defense units that buy and distribute goods to the armed forces, including organizations responsible for supplies other than weapons,

FIGURE 6.1   Production Process of the Soviet Defense Sector

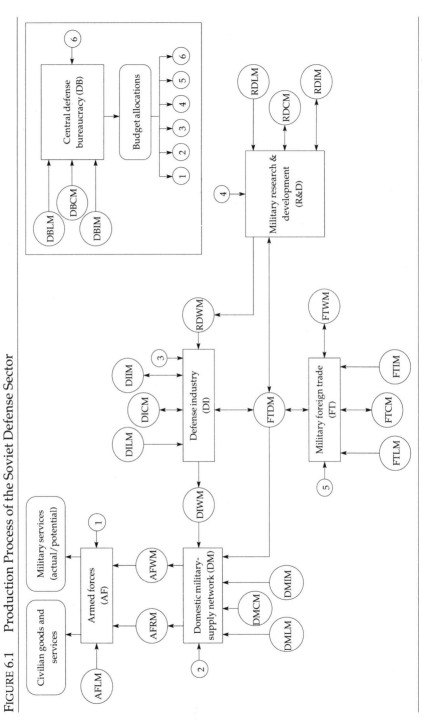

continued next page

FIGURE 6.1 *continued*

NOTES: Soviet Defense Sector Markets.

The defense-sector markets are used to show the main flows of goods and services into or out of the defense sector and between institutions. They do not show payments for supplies. The return flows of tax or profits from institutions to the state are not shown. Abbreviations:

AFLM	Armed forces labor market
AFRM	Armed forces retail market
AFWM	Armed forces producer-commodity market
DMLM	Military supply labor market
DMCM	Military supply capital market
DMIM	Military supply intermediate-goods market
DIWM	Defense industry producer-commodity market
DILM	Defense industry labor market
DICM	Defense industry capital market
DIIM	Defense industry intermediate-goods market
RDWM	Military R&D producer-commodity market
RDLM	Military R&D labor market
RDCM	Military R&D capital market
RDIM	Military R&D intermediate-goods market
FTDM	Military foreign-trade domestic market
FTLM	Military foreign-trade labor market
FTCM	Military foreign-trade capital market
FTIM	Military foreign-trade intermediate-goods market
FTWM	Military foreign-trade world market
DBLM	Central defense bureaucracy labor market
DBCM	Central defense bureaucracy capital market
DBIM	Central defense bureaucracy intermediate-goods market

SOURCE: Author.

such as the Main Administration for Trade, Fuel Supply Administration, Central Food Supply Administration, and Central Clothing Supply Administration. The network also contains the staff of the First Deputy Minister for Armaments, the armament directorates of the five services, and the General Staff Armaments Section.

The outputs of this supply network are sales of military and civilian producer commodities to armed forces units in AFWM and retail sales to military personnel and civilians in AFRM (through the Voentorg stores, for example). The capital, intermediate, and consumer goods sold in these markets are bought from both defense-sector and civilian organizations, largely in accordance with Gosplan and Gossnab supply plans. Military commodities, such as weapons or ammunition, are acquired in either the defense industry producer-commodity market (DIWM) or the military foreign-trade domestic market (FTDM). Civilian goods for the armed forces come from the domestic military-supply capital market (DMCM) and intermediate-goods market (DMIM). The capital stock of this network includes warehouses, storerooms, administrative equipment, transport vehicles, and inventories. Investment goods are purchased in DMCM. The supply network is staffed by military and civilian sales, administrative, custodial, and transportation personnel. The labor inputs come from the domestic military-supply labor market (DMLM). The system also acquires intermediate goods and services from the civilian economy in DMIM.

The domestic military-supply network seems to operate on a self-financing basis, in a manner similar to that of pharmacies in the health sector.[16] If this is indeed the case, commodities sold to military units in the producer-commodity market (AFWM) are priced to cover purchase and distribution costs and are funded by bank transfers of state budget funds. Goods sold through retail outlets (such as Voentorg stores) are priced to generate a profit after costs are taken into account. Part of the network's resulting profits are retained for bonuses and investment, with the remainder transferred to the state budget.

Defense industry. The defense industry's core is formed by the industrial enterprises and staffs of the nine ministries under the Military Industrial Commission of the Council of Ministers that produce mainly military commodities.[17] These include aviation (aircraft and helicopters), communications equipment (electronic-warfare equipment), defense (conventional armaments), electronics (computers), general machine-building (rockets and space equipment), machine-building (munitions), medium machine-building (nuclear warheads), radio (radar), and shipbuilding (naval ships). Some enterprises of the ministries of the electrical equipment industry, chemical industry, and petroleum-refining and petrochemical industry also belong to the defense industry and operate under the supervision of the Military Industrial Commission. The defense industry includes as well the factories of the Ministry of Defense and military-related production units of many civilian ministries (the chemical industry, for example).

Military commodities are sold either to the domestic military-supply network through DIWM or to the foreign-trade system for export through FTDM. Civilian goods produced by the defense industry are distributed through the capital and intermediate-goods markets (DICM and DIIM). Its inputs of labor (workers, supervisors, managers), capital (factory buildings, inventory, machinery, and equipment), and intermediate goods (metals, fuel, chemicals) are supplied for the most part by the civilian economy through the labor market (DILM), capital goods market (DICM), and intermediate-goods market (DIIM). It also obtains inputs of domestic military technology from the military R&D producer-commodity market (RDWM), and foreign technology and intermediate goods from the military foreign-trade system through FTDM.

Soviet defense enterprises are primarily self-financing, which means that sales revenue should cover the cost of current production and some investment. It may be that strict controls make it difficult to earn substantial profits from military commodities, whereas production of civilian consumer goods is more profitable and an important source of bonus funds for managers and workers. Revenue from sales is supplemented by grants from the state budget.

Military research and development. The military R&D system's institutions include scientific research institutes, laboratories, and design bureaus.[18] Military R&D establishments are scattered among a large number of ministries and authorities. Many of the most important are administratively subordinate to the nine defense industry ministries and have close connections with production enterprises. The armed forces have scientific institutions under the control of the central ministerial apparatus, General Staff, armaments directorates, and individual military services. Furthermore, many scientists and institutes of the Academy of Sciences, the republican academies, and the higher-education system perform contract research on military-related projects. The

Military Industrial Commission attempts to direct and coordinate the military R&D activities of these institutions.

The outputs of the military R&D network include military-related scientific theories, experimental results, designs, models, and prototypes. They are sold either to the defense industry in RDWM or to the foreign-trade system in FTDM. Military R&D uses inputs of military and civilian scientific labor, capital (machinery, scientific equipment, buildings), and intermediate goods appropriate to scientific institutions. In addition, the R&D sector obtains foreign military-related technology and goods from the military foreign-trade system through FTDM.

The financing of these institutions varies with their ministerial affiliation. Ministry of Defense establishments are financed almost entirely through the state budget; on the other hand, if a facility is part of a defense industry, self-financing plays a larger role. In the case of civilian university and Academy of Science institutes, revenues come from the defense organizations via project-related contract research.

Military foreign trade. The Soviet defense sector's foreign-trade institution includes elements of the Ministry of Defense, Gosplan, the Military Industrial Commission, the nine defense ministries, and the new Ministry of Foreign Economic Relations (made up of the old Ministry of Foreign Trade and the State Committee for Foreign Economic Relations). The trade system is organized differently for socialist and nonsocialist countries.

The Soviet Union has well-developed bilateral and multilateral military R&D, production specialization, and commodity-trade programs with Warsaw Pact nations.[19] These are developed by Soviet institutions, discussed with other socialist countries, coordinated through the Military Industrial Commission of the Council for Mutual Economic Assistance (CMEA) and the Warsaw Pact technical committees, and then put into legally binding medium- and short-term plans. Intra-CMEA trade in military goods is usually conducted in transferable rubles by the Ministry of Foreign Economic Relations on behalf of domestic organizations. It buys commodities for export from defense industries and R&D institutes using domestic rubles in FTDM, and sells them in the military foreign-trade world market (FTWM). Imports are bought in the socialist countries' component of FTWM and sold in FTDM for domestic rubles to various defense-sector users.

The Soviet Union exports large quantities of equipment to nonsocialist countries, primarily in the Third World.[20] If these transactions are carried out on a commercial basis, they are paid for in domestic rubles in FTDM and sold for hard currency in FTWM. If the sales are part of a military-economic aid package, the Ministry of Foreign Economic Relations and the Foreign Military Assistance Main Directorate of the General Staff play important roles. To support its weapons exports, the armed forces provide training for military personnel of client nations in the USSR and overseas advisory and technical-support services.

Soviet imports of weapons and related supplies from nonsocialist countries are conducted covertly, due to the trade controls of Western governments. To overcome such obstacles, the USSR has developed both trade-diversion and "special information" (*spetsinformatsiia*) collection programs.[21] The former involves the Ministry of Foreign Economic Relations and the KGB; the latter is managed by the Military Industrial Commission. The VPK receives orders for information or samples from its constituent defense industries, prepares an acquisition plan and budget, and assigns collection tasks to five agencies: the KGB (Directorate T), Soviet Military Intelligence (GRU), Ministry of Foreign Economic Relations, State Committee for Science and Technology, and Academy of Sciences. These bodies obtain as many of the military-related documents and samples as possible in FTWM and send them to the VPK. The VPK also forwards accounts of its hard-currency expenditures, expressed in foreign-trade rubles. It then distributes the acquisitions to users through the FTDM, charging them appropriate domestic ruble prices.

The military foreign-trade system operates on a profit-making basis. Over the past two decades the revenue from its exports has considerably exceeded the costs of its imports.

Defense-sector relationships with the civilian economy. Figure 6.1 shows numerous interconnections between the defense sector and the civilian economy.[22] Some outputs flow into the civilian sector, and the six defense-sector organizations receive many inputs from civilian markets. The burden imposed on the civilian economy is influenced by both the defense sector's activity level and its efficiency in production.

The central defense bureaucracy exerts the greatest influence because it allocates the national income among consumption, investment, and defense. It also determines the intensity of operation of the other components of the defense sector and provides finance and supply plans to them. Finally, the central bureaucracy sets priorities among defense and civilian institutions that govern the allocation of resources.

The armed forces routinely provides goods and services to the civilian economy, and on special occasions, such as harvest failure or disaster, release some of the stocks of food, clothing, equipment, and medicine that are held in military reserves.[23] More important, the defense industry produces substantial quantities of many civilian goods.[24] In 1971 Brezhnev stated that 42 percent of defense industry output (by which he may have meant Ministry of Defense Industry output) was civilian in nature. Cooper has estimated defense industry shares of various consumer goods in 1985 as follows: bicycles, 40 percent; motorcycles, 63 percent; washing machines, 27 percent; and televisions, 100 percent.[25] It also supplies civilian industry with capital equipment (passenger aircraft, railway wagons, tractors) through DICM, and intermediate goods (alloyed steel, chemicals, and electronic components) through DIIM. The Gorbachev regime has ordered an expansion of defense industry production for the civilian economy.

The military R&D sector also generates spin-offs for the rest of the economy.[26] These are distributed through the military R&D capital market (RDCM) and intermediate-goods market (RDIM) and help raise the productivity and accelerate the technological progress of civilian sectors. Finally, the military foreign-trade system brings in hard currency, which helps finance imports of food, machinery and equipment, and industrial consumer goods from countries of the Organization for Economic Cooperation and Development. The military-oriented *spetsinformatsiia* system gathers documents and samples in the West that are supplied to civilian industries and research programs through the military foreign-trade capital market (FTCM).[27]

The defense sector obtains inputs from the civilian economy through sixteen markets (Figure 6.1). Each of its six institutions uses labor and consumes capital and intermediate goods. (The armed forces receive these commodities through the military-supply network rather than directly from civilian organizations.) For example, Agursky and Adomeit report that "Soviet economists with access to secret statistics estimate that 60 percent of Soviet enterprises are to a greater or lesser degree engaged in production for the armed forces."[28] Furthermore, there is evidence that the defense sector is guaranteed supplies of better-quality inputs from Gosplan and Gossnab.

Intersectoral Priority of the Defense Industry

Leaders of centrally planned economies have many objectives and severely limited resources. In order to ensure attainment of their most important goals, they develop priority rankings of sectors and use rationing procedures and enforcement mechanisms that protect privileged activities and penalize less-important ones. The priority system is used to control developments in a socialist economy that is characterized by considerable complexity in its structure and activities. It follows, therefore, that Soviet policy-makers use a variety of priority-linked instruments at different stages of economic processes (during plan formulation and implementation, for example) that influence allocations of resources to a sector, as well as wages, investment, inventories, and supplies of intermediate goods.[29]

Scholars have used a variety of measures to assess priority rankings of sectors.[30] This section identifies ten indicators of priority. Four relate to priorities expressed during plan formulation. The first measures the weight given to sectoral output in a planner's welfare function or in national income. The second reflects Kornai's idea of control by norms; it evaluates the planner's response, expressed in the allocation of resources to a sector, if a performance indicator exceeds an established "tolerance limit."[31] Priority is also reflected in the ranking of wage rates and work conditions established for a sector relative to the economy average or to measures of labor quality. The fourth indicator evaluates whether the financial norms of a sector are adequate relative to the prevailing actual prices of planned inputs.

Additional indicators refer to the plan-implementation period. One simple measure is the degree to which output plans are fulfilled; a condition that should be almost guaranteed for a high-priority sector.[32] The sixth indicator reflects the idea that the "hardness" of budgets, as defined by Kornai,[33] varies by sector in accordance with priorities. The more important a sector, the softer the budget, and vice versa. The next two indicators assess whether the authorities have ensured that a sector obtains planned amounts of inputs and investment in the face of the supply disruptions and deficits characteristic of a shortage economy. Another indicator expresses the idea that the authorities will have different tolerances of input inventories according to priorities: the more favored the sector, the greater the allowed stocks. Finally, priority could, in principle, be evaluated using the shortage-intensity function defined by Kornai, which measures shortage intensity relative to the average for the whole economy or to the norm in the sector.[34]

Weight in planners' preference functions. One traditional opinion is that priority is expressed in the utility weight given to sectoral output—or some other measure of sectoral performance determined by central planners—during the solution of the overall allocation problem. Such an indicator poses numerous difficulties. If the authorities determined that the achievement of a certain level of output in some sector was of highest priority, it is unlikely they would be content with receiving as a substitute a large volume of output from a different, low-priority sector such that there was equivalence in utility values. In reality, planners probably have discontinuous preferences that can be represented by a lexicographic ordering.[35] In other words, they may have a ranking of sectors and distribute resources so that the most important one receives the inputs needed to achieve its output targets before the other sectors are provided for, in sequence. If lexicographic orderings do exist, utility weights would be inappropriate in a social-welfare function.

Another difficulty with the use of utility analysis is determining the structure and weights of the social-welfare function. For example, it is not clear whether planners really include indicators of national security, military capabilities, or defense industry output in the objective function, or view defense allocations as input costs. If the defense industry is represented in the objective function, then the task becomes one of making explicit the implicit preferences of central decision-makers, which is problematic in both theory and practice.

If a welfare approach to priority definition were to be used, one could gain insights into decision-makers' relative values, even though the utility weights were unobservable, by comparing a centrally planned economy's shares of national income for various activities to an international standard. An end-use significantly higher than the average for other nations would imply that the activity had high priority, and vice versa. The defense burden of the USSR could then be compared with that of both socialist and Western countries. K. Crane estimated defense expenditures (excluding R&D) and shares of national income used for four Eastern European nations;[36] the defense sector in the USSR in 1980 clearly had a high priority relative to other socialist countries. Comparisons of the defense share of reconstructed Soviet GNP with Western standards also support the high priority of defense: the defense share of current-price Soviet GNP in 1981 was far above that of the major NATO countries.

Over time, there have been some shifts in the Soviet defense burden.[37] During World War II the defense share of national income was probably more than 40 percent.[38] This fell drastically during the postwar years (1945–1948), but rose during the period of the Korean War and Cold War. The defense share then dropped to about 10 percent in 1960. From the early 1960s to the mid-1970s, defense spending grew more rapidly than national income, so the GNP share rose to about 13 percent. According to the CIA, the growth rate of defense expenditure decelerated to about 2 percent over the next decade, and that of procurement to around zero.[39] Since the average annual growth of Soviet GNP was estimated to be 2.3 percent in 1976–1980 and 1.9 percent in 1981–1985,[40] the defense share stabilized over this period. The Gorbachev regime may have lowered defense-sector priority even further in the Twelfth Five-Year Plan.[41] If so, the result would have been a decline in the defense share of GNP during the late 1980s. There is no evidence yet, however, to confirm a downward trend.

Responsiveness to tolerance-limit violations. Kornai believes that one reason for the shortage and investment tension in a socialist economy is that planners' allocations follow a cyclical pattern of postponement release that is governed by responses to performance indicators —such as "social costs"—exceeding predetermined tolerance limits.[42] This policy of "putting out fires" entails neglecting a sector while conditions remain within tolerance limits, even if they are deteriorating, and then allocating sufficient resources to it when those limits are violated to bring the performance indicator back into an acceptable range. Although Kornai suggests that this rule is universal, its validity should vary among sectors according to their priority. In high-priority sectors there should be an immediate, if not anticipatory, response, while in a low-priority area no such reaction would be likely, and social costs could remain above tolerance limits for extended periods. For example, in another work I argue that the Soviet government delayed responding to serious health problems, such as rising mortality rates, because the health sector had low priority.[43]

In order to evaluate priority responsiveness, one needs appropriate social-cost indicators. These could range from the abstract and hard to measure, such as the correlation of forces or measures of national security status, to the particular, such as a defense-industry supply bottleneck. Establishment of tolerance limits is feasible conceptually (as in the case of a lower limit on the national security index), but the definition of stable, measurable boundaries is complicated. Resource-responsiveness indicators could include the size of the defense budget, its proportional change, defense shares of the total state budget, shares of GNP (or net material product), and allocations of specific commodities to institutions.

It is difficult to determine unambiguously the priority of the Soviet defense sector. Some analysts have argued that the Soviet military buildup is the long-term consequence of the trauma of the Cuban missile crisis and the U.S. strategic-missile expansion and defense-budget increases during the Kennedy era; in other words, that the perceived national security index dropped below tolerable limits and generated an energetic response. There are several problems with this argument, however. B. Parrott has argued that in the late 1960s there were conflicts among Soviet leaders over resource allocations to defense, with Kosygin and Podgorny arguing for stable funding, while Brezhnev, Suslov, and Shelepin called for an acceleration.[44] Even early in the period, then, there may have been differences over assessments, tolerance limits, and suitable responses. Furthermore, one would have expected to observe a deceleration of defense spending in 1971–1975, since strategic parity had been achieved and the correlation of forces appeared to be moving in a direction favorable to the USSR.

Over the past decade the environment of external threat to the Soviet Union has increased economically, politically, and militarily.[45] One would assume that various Soviet security tolerance limits would have been violated by the increases in the U.S. defense budget, the Strategic Defense Initiative (SDI), deployments of intermediate-range missiles, the stalemate in Afghanistan, and the enhancement of NATO's conventional capabilities, producing an acceleration of Soviet defense spending. Instead, the CIA estimates that the rates of growth of real defense spending and procurement declined, at least through 1984. This may reflect general economic stringencies or the impact of "new thinking" on national security policy-making. The Soviet leadership may now be attempting to reduce threats by working diplomatically rather than by expanding military power.[46]

On the other hand, the CIA's interpretation of defense spending trends over the past decade may be more reflective of the view from Langley than from the Kremlin. The CIA may be doing a good job of measuring expenditure according to U.S. definitions (subject to substantial estimation errors associated with its methodology) in constant 1970 (now 1982) prices that have some in-house rationale, such as the fact that reconstructed GNP accounts are maintained in those prices. But Soviet policy-makers probably think in terms of current rubles. According to U.S. Defense Intelligence Agency (DIA) testimony: "Current ruble defense spending estimates are important because it is likely that Soviet leaders use cost estimates and budgetary data reflecting current prices in making key resource allocation decisions. Constant ruble estimates are of little use in replicating the economic environment in which the Soviet leaders operate."[47] The DIA's estimate that current defense spending increased at an annual rate of 6 to 7 percent and that the defense burden from a Soviet perspective rose represents the type of resource-allocation responsiveness expected in a high-priority sector.

Labor conditions. The defense industry elite (higher ministry officials, plant managers, top designers, and scientists) receive high wages and substantial perks. Much has been written about their rewards and lifestyles.[48] These people are included by Voslensky in the "military *nomenklatura*" and by Willis in the "rising class."[49] Since this group is small, it is not considered here.

If the defense industry has a high priority, one would expect its average wages to be greater than those of the whole economy. In general, industry as a whole is relatively privileged and has higher-than-average monthly wages. In 1985 the average monthly wage of an industrial worker was 210.6 rubles, whereas the average for the whole economy was 190.1 rubles.[50] In order to assess priority, more-detailed comparisons should be made of the labor conditions of comparable groups in the civilian and defense industries. Agursky and Adomeit claim that the wages of scientific personnel in the defense industry are higher than those of their civilian counterparts, and that "differentials are in the range of 20 to 25 percent and can be even higher, although they never exceed 40 to 50 percent."[51] Such differentials are reduced by the extra earnings civilian scientists can make through writing, consulting, and tutoring. For security reasons, defense scientists are more restricted in such outside activities. Furthermore, the bonuses of managerial, scientific, and design personnel in the defense industry are held down by the rigorous production quality-control system and restraints on price increases for weapons systems.

In the case of workers, Agursky and Adomeit claim that wage levels are close to those of competitive civilian branches, and that past differentials have been eroded.[52] Perhaps more serious is the fact that security at defense plants (gate inspections, passes, close supervision, and the like) makes it more difficult for workers to steal tools, materials, and time for second economy activities. As a result, skilled workers in the defense industry may actually earn less than their colleagues in the lax civilian sector.

Moreover, according to Agursky and Adomeit, scientists in the defense industry are less qualified than those in civilian branches.[53] The defense industry does not recruit many graduates of the top higher-education establishments, but relies instead on less-prestigious, special institutes linked with the defense sector, such as the Moscow Aircraft Institute. Peter Almquist reports that a manager of the Dmitrov plant in Tbilisi complained of inadequate continuing education of engineers and specialists resulting in degradation of skills over time.[54] Due to security restrictions on publications, and even on circulation of postgraduate or postdoctoral works, it is easier for defense scientists to obtain *kandidat* and *doktor* degrees. All this results in defense industry educational standards that are lower than those in similar civilian institutions. Moreover, defense industry employees cannot move among institutions or travel abroad as easily as their civilian counterparts.

Because money plays a limited role in the Soviet economy, perks and work conditions are often of greater importance than wage differentials. In the past, the defense industry provided its workers with more or better benefits, such as housing, access to closed shops, theater tickets, medical care, vacation homes, and domestic tourism opportunities.[55] Over the past two decades, however, the housing supply and general standard of living have increased, social benefits and medical services have improved, and profitable civilian enterprises have used their discretionary bonus funds to create and develop benefit packages similar to those of the defense industry. This has narrowed the defense-civilian differential in nonwage benefits.

Adequacy of financial norms. Judging from the scarce available data, the financial norms governing the calculation of defense industry enterprise budgets for new construction, capital repairs, and supply acquisition have been sufficient relative to their needs and the prices of inputs. In this sense, the Soviet defense industry is a high-priority sector. However, Almquist observes that considerable stress is placed in the defense industry on producibility of weapons systems, unification of design, and standardization of components.[56] Pressure for unification and standardization may be accompanied by financial norms based on input prices of the targeted, and presumably cheapest, components or materials. In a shortage economy, however, planned inputs are often in short supply. If better-quality inputs are substituted for the deficit planned ones, then the initial budget could be less than final costs.

Fulfillment of output plans. Conceptual and measurement problems make assessment of priority on the basis of fulfillment of initial output plans difficult. If performance is measured relative to physical targets, and a quantity drive exists in the defense industry that involves quantity-for-quality substitution, then the quantity of weapons supplied could exceed targets while their quality was below planned standards. A second problem is that Soviet data on weapons output objectives and plan fulfillment do not exist, and Western intelligence agencies' estimates are subject to considerable uncertainty. For example, U.S. Defense Department estimates of the number of tanks produced in the USSR during 1983 (minus exports) varied in the period 1984–1986 from 2,400 to 2,700 to 3,000. It is risky to make conclusions about output trends, especially for the most recent years.

Western studies show that the Soviet leadership is strongly committed to meeting military goals. For example, under Stalin, the atomic bomb program was characterized by disregard for costs, willingness to employ tough sanctions for failure, and generous rewards for success.[57] This high-priority treatment was supposedly continued at least through the 1970s. According to a 1978 CIA assessment,

> There is no indication that economic problems are causing major changes in defense policy. The atmosphere in Moscow with regard to the economy, however, is one of concern, and the Soviet leaders could be contemplating modest alterations in military force goals. But even if such alterations were undertaken, the rate of growth of defense spending over the next five years or so would probably slow only marginally [from the historical trend of 4 to 5 percent].[58]

Other evidence comes from institutional arrangements made to guarantee high-quality output. Defense enterprises have the departments of quality control (*otdel tekhnicheskogo kontrolia*) common to all branches of Soviet industry.[59] In addition, the defense industry has been a source of several innovative quality-control procedures, such as the Saratov system for the "defectless manufacturing of products," the Lvov "system of defectless labor," and the Gorky Aircraft Plant's KANARSPI quality and reliability program.[60] Finally, the armed forces assign military representatives (*voenpredy*) to all defense plants to monitor production schedules and inspect independently the quality of output.[61]

Despite special treatment, numerous weapons systems have been deployed or put into mass production behind schedule. One, originally described by Agursky and often cited, is that of delay in SS-18 deployment due to a production bottleneck caused by a shortage of appropriate machine tools.[62] In the period 1977–1985, the production of many major weapons declined, including intercontinental ballistic missiles (ICBMs), submarine-launched ballistic missiles (SLBMs), tanks, major surface combatants, and submarines.[63] Furthermore, the CIA believes that the slowdown in weapons output—which was caused by a variety of factors, including downturns in procurement cycles—was to a large extent unintentional. The CIA has repeatedly revised its estimates of aggregate procurement costs downward because weapons systems were deployed in smaller numbers than anticipated due to problems with the economy and technology.[64] According to R. F. Kaufman, "the CIA believes that for a number of weapons, technical delays pushed back serial production for several years, lowering annual production rates and delaying deployments for some new systems."[65] In the past, such an outcome probably would not have been tolerated. But after analyzing the situation in the late 1970s, the CIA concluded that the leadership, although aware of the difficulties of the defense industries, did not try to overcome obstacles by allocating supplemental resources or adopting remedial administrative measures. Kaufman correctly observes that this behavior raises questions about the invariant high priority of the defense sector.[66]

It does appear, however, that control programs ensure the attainment of at least the minimum specified standards. According to the CIA, Soviet quality control is "a 'brute force' system consisting mainly of high levels of production and high rejection rates."[67] Such an approach indicates that priority arrangements are insufficient to create a defense industry that efficiently and consistently produces commodities of top quality.

Hardness of budget constraints. In *Economics of Shortage,* Kornai creates the impression that the budget constraints of all institutions producing goods and services in a socialist economy are relatively soft.[68] In a later work, however, he acknowledges that priority influences the degree of budget hardness: "In sectors enjoying priority in central plans, the constraint is softer. In sectors permanently neglected, it is hard."[69] I have argued that, as a general rule, actual spending is greater than planned in a high-priority sector, and routinely less than planned in a low-priority sector (the hard budget-constraint condition).[70]

Because censorship in the USSR makes it difficult to obtain detailed budget data for even low-priority branches of the civilian economy, it would be sensible to concentrate not only on budgetary statistics, but also on the extent of competition, penalties for failure (such as bankruptcy), and the nature of paternalism (strict or indulgent).[71] The conventional view is that the defense industry has generous, soft budgets. It receives large initial allocations of resources, and central authorities tolerate cost overruns and quickly provide supplemental funds and real resources if constraints become binding. According to Almquist, the famous missile designer S. P. Korolev had an "open budget."[72] Almquist also claims the military usually pressures designers and managers to produce weapon systems that satisfy the demands for mission capabilities "regardless of cost."[73] The CIA claims that when new weapons programs are introduced, the planning bodies tend to allocate resources "in a 'spasm' in which more resources are allocated at one time than can be fruitfully absorbed."[74] Finally, there has been an escalation in production costs of weapons systems, such as the 2.8-fold increase in the cost index of comparable fighter aircraft from the 1961 Fishbed C/E to the 1983 Fulcrum.[75] In some programs, substantial cost overruns have been tolerated in order to ensure attainment of targets.

Andrew Cockburn also claims there was less competition among design bureaus after Stalin's death and "everybody's plane got built."[76] Gradually, defense industry institutions acquired a permanence that was reinforced by incremental resource-allocation policies. Almquist believes that "one of the legacies of the Brezhnev era may have been the establishment of permanent design bureaus whose leaders serve until their death and are then replaced by their deputies."[77] Second, higher authorities appeared to have a benevolent attitude toward their subordinates, and clear-cut patronage networks developed. Much has been written about the domination of the defense industry in the 1970s by the men associated during their careers with D. F. Ustinov, especially at the Ministry of Defense Industry (or its precursor, the Ministry of Armaments), men such as L. V. Smirnov, I. F. Dmitriev, I. S. Silaev, Y. D. Masliukov, A. A. Reut, S. A. Afanas'ev, and V. V. Bakhirov.[78] Other examples of patronage and nepotism affecting designers in the defense industry include Stalin and Yakovlev, Khrushchev and Sukhoi, Khrushchev and Cholomei (who married the leader's daughter),

Ustinov and Kovalev, Mikoyan and Mikoyan, and the inheritances of the design bureaus of Yakovlev and Tupolev by their sons.[79]

As a result, there was a gradual weakening of sanctions for failure. In Stalin's time, managers and designers who did not deliver the goods faced labor camps or execution. Cockburn cites the reminiscence of a chief scientist in the atom bomb project, V. Emel'ianov: "What would have happened if we hadn't made it then? They would have shot us."[80] In later periods, severe punishment for failure was rare. Design bureaus and enterprises were allowed to churn out one mediocre weapon after another without being forced into bankruptcy or closed down. Among the eminent failures were Sukhoi and his inferior fighters; Yakovlev and the Yak-25; Simonov, who had three out of one-hundred gun designs accepted; Nadiradze and his ineffectual solid-fuel missiles (the SS-13, SS-15, and SS-16); and Yangel's inadequate SS-17.[81]

Some indications of budget hardness also exist. Almquist reports that a request by leading defense scientists for a pay raise for their lab staff was turned down by Kosygin, who informed them that the funds were not available, and that after Korolev's death, funds for his design bureau dried up.[82] He also claims that defense ministry officials manipulate budgets of subordinate enterprises and design bureaus, hardening and softening them in order to maintain their control.[83] Finally, U.S. government sources argue that constraints on the defense industry hardened in the late 1970s, as shown by the zero growth in procurement from 1977 to 1983.[84] Kaufman observes:

> The CIA explanation represents a fundamental revision of the conventional view of the relationship between defense and the economy. If the CIA is correct about the defense slowdown, it would be incorrect to continue asserting that the Kremlin fails to consider costs as a major factor in its decisions or that the defense sector is impervious to problems in the economy.[85]

Fulfillment of intermediate-goods supply plans. Priorities also protect important sectors from disruptions caused by endogenous and exogenous factors.[86] The prevailing assessment of the defense industry's supply situation in the USSR is summarized by the CIA: "The defense industries receive the highest quality raw materials and are given preferential access to the transportation and distribution networks for delivering materials."[87] Agursky and Adomeit make the same point.[88] Other indications of the sector's high priority are the large VPK *spetsinformatsiia* technology-acquisition program and the willingness to make hard-currency purchases of foreign machinery, equipment, and materials that support military production programs to compensate for domestic shortages.

Western authors and Soviet émigrés suggest that supplies are routinely diverted from civilian to defense programs when bottlenecks and shortages develop.[89] The CIA asserts, however, that "resources devoted to the military are shielded from diversion to other claimants by the mechanics of the planning system," and that "the extreme secrecy accorded national security planning helps prevent other sectors from laying claim to defense production resources."[90] Available evidence suggests that the Gorbachev regime continued this preferential treatment at least through 1988. A defense industry official, L. A. Voronin, was appointed chairman of Gossnab in November 1985, and the June 1987 Plenum reform measures indicated that state orders (*goszakazy*) that govern production of defense industry goods would be backed up by centrally rationed inputs.[91]

Despite efforts to protect the defense industries, there is evidence of deficiencies in input planning, attempts by central authorities to minimize enterprises' requests for supplies, shortages, managers' complaints, vertical integration, use of *tolkachi* (or "expediters"), and supply-linked disruptions in production. Evidently, supply disruptions and shortage phenomena in the civilian economy spill over into the protected defense sector.

Fulfillment of investment plans. A state of investment tension usually exists in the socialist economy due to planners' errors and firms' behavior.[92] One compensatory method used by central planners is to apply priorities in the investment reallocation process during plan implementation. The original investment budget and planned supplies of the high-priority sector's capital goods are protected, if not augmented, so that it is usually able to attain its objectives. However, to protect investment plans of important institutions, it is necessary to siphon off capital goods and services from low-priority sectors. As a result, the investment plans of a less-important sector, such as health, are chronically underfulfilled, and its ratio of actual to planned investment remains below the average for the whole economy.[93]

The empirical evidence on the investment priority of the Soviet defense industry is mixed. On the one hand, efforts clearly are made to ensure that it receives the funds and allocations of capital goods and services needed to carry out planned investment programs. The CIA reports that "capital investment in the defense industries has continued at high levels" despite the numerous problems in the Soviet economy, and that "they also have access to the best machinery."[94] According to Agursky and Adomeit, defense industry enterprises are given more funds than their civilian counterparts to obtain new capital equipment.[95] The industry is also served by the *spetsinformatsiia* network, which acquires advanced Western technology that is unavailable or in short supply within the USSR.

On the other hand, the priority system cannot fully protect the defense industry from systemic deficiencies in construction work, technological innovation, and the quality of machinery; production plans for military commodities are sometimes underfulfilled due to shortages. Furthermore, certain civilian programs may have higher priority than some defense programs, and may siphon away investment goods. In sum, the Soviet government wants to ensure fulfillment of the defense industry's investment plans and assigns it high priority, but is unable fully to protect it from disruptions in the supply of capital goods and services.

Inventories and spare production capacity. In a centrally planned economy, institutions attempt to acquire inputs in excess of production requirements and build up substantial inventories of intermediate goods, labor, and capital. These reserves provide them with protection against supply disruptions and enable them to respond successfully to demands from their superiors for above-plan output. The central authorities attempt to control this tendency to hoard, but their rigor varies by sector in accordance with priority. One would expect to observe a greater tolerance of large inventories and reserve production capacity in more important sectors.

According to this criteria, the defense industry appears to have a high priority. Its factories are designed to accommodate substantial extra production capacities and to maintain reserves of labor and intermediate goods that are greater than normal for the civilian economy. In peacetime the spare labor and capital are used to produce civilian commodities or military goods for export. As demonstrated during World War II, these resources could be shifted rapidly to the production of weapons. The large inventories of defense-related intermediate commodities such as fuel, metals, and spare parts are not regularly drawn down to support peacetime production, however, but rather maintained at predetermined high levels. As a result, the defense industry is well protected against supply disruptions in the event of war, with a surge capability that would enable it to boost output significantly on short notice.

Intensity of shortages. Kornai argues that aggregate indexes of shortage intensity can be formulated that are an increasing functions of observable shortage-related indicators, such as length of queues, forced saving, hardness of budget constraint, fulfillment of supply plans, quantity drive, production bottlenecks, and forced substitution.[96] At the sectoral level, one would expect the high-priority defense industry to have low shortage intensity, whereas the inverse would be true for the low-priority medical system.[97]

The defense industry apparently does have relatively low shortage intensity, but its enterprises are still afflicted by shortage-related problems.[98] On the input side, defense firms experience difficulties—although less acute than those of civilian institutions—in obtaining planned goods and services from suppliers. A similar situation prevails with respect to production. Because of the protection of their supplies, above-average inventories, and reserve productive capacity, defense firms engage in less "storming" and forced substitutions than their civilian counterparts. Finally, defense firms produce for a customer— the armed forces—that has much greater-than-normal market power. Given all these factors, defense firms have a weaker quantity drive, and carry out less quantity-for-quality substitution, than the average firm.

Intrasectoral Priority of Defense Institutions

Although the defense sector has a relatively high overall priority, there are considerable intrasectoral differences in rankings and privileges. These variations occur not only among different types of institutions in the sector (such as between military units and defense firms) but also among those of the same type.

Institutions of different types. Because these institutions are integrated components of a production process, it is difficult to assign relative rankings within the defense sector itself. Nevertheless, available evidence suggests the following ranking of importance of defense-sector institutions, in descending order: the central defense bureaucracy, defense industry, armed forces, military R&D, military foreign trade, and domestic military supply.

The central defense bureaucracy has remained dominant by acting decisively against any challenges by the elites of other defense institutions, especially the armed forces, or by their representatives within the central apparatus. Among the examples are the retirement of Zhukov in 1957, the promotion of D. F. Ustinov instead of Marshal Kulikov to Minister of Defense in 1976, the reassignment of Ogarkov in 1984, and the retirement of Romanov in 1985. At the bottom of the defense-sector priority scale is the domestic military-supply network, which carries out a service-sector function, trade. Its highest leaders are deputy ministers (for example, V. M. Shabanov for armaments and S. K. Kurkotkin for rear services), and it can assert only modest independent influence on the other institutions.

In the 1960s military foreign trade was also a low-prestige institution. Most of its dealings were with Warsaw Pact nations, destitute Third World socialist countries, and revolutionary movements. Its priority was radically upgraded in the 1970s, first, by a substantial expansion of the *spetsinformatsiia* system.[99] Its bureaucracy and budget grew, as did its influence on the defense industry and military R&D. Second, in the mid-seventies, arms exports were greatly expanded to take advantage of hard-currency earnings possibilities in Third World countries that had benefited from oil price rises.[100] By the early 1980s, arms were the top Soviet export commodity after oil and gold. In a number of cases, modern weapons were diverted from scheduled deployments with Soviet or East European military units in order to satisfy hard-currency customers.

Some priority shifts have affected the remaining three institutions, as reflected in changes in their shares of defense expenditure: operations and maintenance (armed forces), procurement (defense industry), and military R&D. To some extent this reflects variation in the leadership's perception of the time horizon of the most crucial challenges. If a war is being fought or is impending, highest priority probably would be given to the armed forces. If a crisis is anticipated in the medium term, priority might be shifted in favor of the defense industry to enable it to produce the most weapons using existing technology. If serious challenges are perceived in the distant future, such as those posed by SDI or smart conventional weapons, then military R&D might receive preferential treatment to enable it to develop new technology for the long-term benefit of the defense industry and the military.

As a general rule, military R&D ranks below the defense industry and armed forces in terms of power and priority.[101] This is to be expected, since top scientists and designers do not, for the most part, occupy high-level decision-making positions in the defense bureaucracies, and their organizations are administratively subordinate to the Ministry of Defense and the defense industry ministries, which are dominated, respectively, by military officers and managers of enterprises.

A more difficult issue to resolve is the relative standing of the armed forces and defense industry. Although the power balance can shift over time, the defense industry is usually dominant in a political sense and receives higher-priority treatment. For example, Almquist interprets the selection of Ustinov as Minister of Defense in 1976 as evidence of an ascendance of defense industry power at the expense of the military.[102] In the Gorbachev period, the leadership is treating the defense industry as a source of ideas (such as quality control), organizational forms (such as superministries), and competent managerial personnel (for example, Lev Voronin, first deputy chairman of Gosplan) for the civilian economy,[103] while the armed forces are being severely criticized and subjected to increasingly energetic *perestroika*.[104]

Institutions of the same type. Priority fluctuations are caused by changes in the perception of threat, military doctrine, strategic objectives, and requirements.[105] These result in changes in emphasis on specific types of military activities. For example, the CIA identifies three major potential missions of the Soviet armed forces: intercontinental attack, conventional combat with NATO forces, and conventional combat with Chinese forces.[106] In connection with these, it shows that mission-related priorities and defense expenditure changed significantly in the period 1967–1977. Spending on intercontinental attack grew more slowly than average so that its share of the total defense budget declined. Significantly higher than average growth rates of expenditure on forces devoted to the other two missions during this period resulted in a doubling of spending on Soviet forces in the NATO area and a tripling in the case of military units on the Soviet-Chinese border. Such changes have ripple effects through related production chains and cause priority variations in the armed forces, defense industry, and military R&D.

There have been fluctuations over the past three decades in the priority of individual military services. In the late 1950s Khrushchev decided to reorient the missions of the armed forces away from conventional combat toward nuclear war. The strategic rocket forces were established as an independent service and given highest-priority support, whereas the ground forces suffered cuts in personnel and budgets.[107] Khrushchev also tried to reduce the size of the air forces, but this was resisted, according to Almquist, by a coalition of air force officers and aircraft designers.[108] In the period 1967–1977 the air forces received preferential treatment; their share of defense spending rose from 17 percent in 1967 to a peak of 26 percent in 1973.[109] Expenditure shares of the navy, strategic rocket forces, and air defense forces declined, but since total spending increased significantly, all were able to expand and upgrade their capabilities. For example, the number of ICBMs and SLBMs rose from about 300 in 1965 to 2,400 in 1975.[110] Individual services also altered their priorities; the navy clearly expressed a preference for ballistic missile and attack submarines over surface ships and aircraft. In the decade 1975–1985 there were some additional marginal shifts in priorities and procurement.[111] More radical changes appear likely under Gorbachev. Due to progress in arms-control negotiations, recent combat experience in Afghanistan, and developments in doctrine, it appears that the priority accorded to the strategic rocket forces will be reduced, and that of the ground forces raised.

Shifting priorities have affected the domestic military-supply network, especially the armament directorates. In his assessment of the Deputy Minister of Defense for Armaments, Almquist concluded: "The changing background of the post's occupants is indicative of Soviet objectives and priorities, as the men have changed from specialists in missiles (when this was a high priority item) to specialists in electronics (an increasingly important area in contemporary weapons research)."[112] Because of the attention being paid to "human factor" issues in the perestroika of the armed forces, it is likely that Voentorg, the trade component of the rear services, will benefit from a higher priority in the late 1980s.[113]

The status and resources of defense industry ministries also have changed in response to shifts in the priorities of branches of the armed forces. The Ministry of General Machine Building benefited from the creation of the strategic rocket forces, whereas the Ministry of the Aviation Industry and the Ministry of the Defense Industry suffered in the 1950s. According to the CIA, "Defense production capacity has doubled since 1965. The industries that produce missiles and aircraft expanded most rapidly."[114] In the late 1980s there will be further changes in priorities affecting the defense industry. Factories producing missiles affected by arms-control treaties, such as the Volgograd Barrikady Factory, will be forced to close down or convert production lines.[115] Enterprises that make smart conventional weapons, on the other hand, should do quite well.

Two other features of defense industry priorities should be mentioned. First, there can be variations between enterprises engaged in final weapons assembly (a tank factory, for example) and those involved in production of high-technology subsystems and components (such as radio electronics and specialty materials): the CIA believes priority has shifted in favor of the latter group in the 1980s.[116] Second, there are differences within an enterprise in priority treatment of assembly lines producing goods for the Soviet armed forces, export, and the domestic civilian sector.[117] As a general rule, the departments of a defense firm producing civilian consumer goods have had a relatively low priority status and have encountered more problems in fulfilling plans, meeting quality standards, and receiving allocated supplies than have their counterparts involved in weapons production.

The final defense-sector institution is military R&D. Almquist argues that the considerable variation in the priority accorded to particular projects, institutes, and design bureaus reflects both production chain developments and the personal and professional relationships of designers and scientists with central defense bureaucracy decision-makers.[118] Similar points about priority differentials in the R&D sector are made by Holloway, Cockburn, and the CIA.[119]

Conclusion

In this chapter I have described the main institutions of the Soviet defense sector, the relationships among them and between it and the civilian sector, and the workings of the priority system. According to the ten measures described, the defense industry has a relatively high priority ranking. However, I have also shown that the existing priority arrangements are insufficient wholly to protect defense firms from production disruptions and shortages of inputs. It appears that forces in the Soviet economy have been undermining the mechanisms and overwhelming the barriers used in the past to guarantee the defense industry's privileged operating conditions. My findings on intrasectoral variations in priorities conflict with assertions that the defense sector has a uniformly high priority and that all its institutions have higher priority than equivalent civilian ones.

Arthur J. Alexander

Soviet Weapons Acquisition in the Era of *Perestroika*

IN THIS CHAPTER I consider the future performance of the Soviet weapons acquisition sector under the conditions of Mikhail Gorbachev's policies as they have been revealed thus far and as they may develop in the future. I focus on the systemic influences operating throughout the weapons acquisition process and the technological change in the weapons research and development (R&D) sector. I review the principal impediments to Soviet innovation, how the military sector has avoided or mitigated the effects of many of these impediments, and finally, the ways that current and future policies may change civilian and defense industries' capabilities in promoting technological change.

The main elements that influence innovative behavior in the Soviet Union (as elsewhere) include values, policies, and the four properties of economic systems described by Joseph S. Berliner: prices, decision-making rules, incentives, and organizational arrangements.[1] Berliner focuses on economic elements, but since it is the differences between the civil and military sectors that generate their sharply divergent success with innovation, we look to values and policies for the sources of those differences.

Arthur J. Alexander is a senior economist at the RAND Corporation.

Innovation in the Civil Sector

The standard litany describing the problems of Soviet civil innovation is that decision-making rules that the Soviet elite would like managers to use are inconsistent with the incentives these managers face. In particular, the leaders would prefer to see more innovation, new and better products, reduced costs, better use of internally generated R&D, better cooperation among research, design, and production organizations—in short, greater adherence to growth on the so-called intensive path rather than on the customary extensive route based on ever-greater use of resources. However, enterprise managers, the final implementers of innovation, face high risks with innovation, and small and uncertain returns; little penalty for failure to innovate; and generally a guaranteed return from following a conservative, no-change strategy. These conditions produce powerful incentives to eschew technological change despite official rhetoric and formal decision-making rules that insist on innovation. In order to understand the difference between these conditions and those faced by the defense industry manager, and to predict future trends, it is necessary first to establish the reasons behind the forces that are brought to bear on the civil-sector manager.

Supply uncertainties. R&D and the implementation of innovation always entail risks of future uncertainties. But for the Soviet innovator, the economic system produces additional risks. Probably the most important of these arises from the supply of inputs. Weakness of the interenterprise supply system has been a fundamental shortcoming of the Soviet economy since the 1930s. Uncertainty about supply is the primary problem managers face, and it is magnified for innovating managers or directors of research institutes. A great deal of management effort is devoted to developing reliable relationships with suppliers, tracking down late or missing supplies, sending dispatchers to problem enterprises, and attempting to obtain support for these activities from local party and government organs. Once a manager has identified and incorporated a set of suppliers, components, and materials into the plans and operations of an enterprise, he is reluctant to disrupt these arrangements.

Supply problems arise from many sources—faulty planning procedures, overcentralization of planning and allocation, complexity of the economy (with its tens of thousands of enterprises and millions of commodities)—but primarily from the tautness of the planning system.[2]

Tautness is another name for excess demand that arises from planners' attempts to motivate workers and managers to produce more by stimulating effort throughout the hierarchical management system. When tautness is combined with an incentive system that primarily rewards the meeting of output targets, the result is a permanent seller's market with constant shortages.

Despite repeated attempts since the 1960s to replace output targets with more complex indexes of plan fulfillment—including profitlike measures—short-term output continues to dominate the reward structure for one simple and powerful reason: the outputs of one organization are the inputs of others; in a Soviet-type planned economy, the authorities cannot tolerate schemes that could disrupt the vast number of bureaucratically contrived connections among organizations without contemplating a chaotic breakdown of the production system.[3] Thus, supply uncertainties have been an abiding feature of the Soviet economy, produced by a control system that abhors organizational autonomy and flexibility and penalizes managers who dare to follow the official decision-making rules and attempt to innovate.

One of the enterprise's responses to supply uncertainty has been to strive to produce as much as possible of needed inputs within the enterprise; if this is not possible, an industrial ministry will try to have it produced within the ministry. One consequence of such behavior is widespread small-scale, unspecialized, and inefficient production of countless items by multitudes of plants, leading to high costs, low quality, low rates of technical progress, and—where innovations do occur—low rates of diffusion.

While the risks of innovation are magnified for the Soviet manager, the rewards for successful implementation of technological change are stunted due to a reward structure that continues to be based predominantly on gross output. Despite several attempts to make new-product prices favor innovation and to create output indexes based on the number or value of innovations, such modifications have been relatively minor and ineffective. Moreover, as Berliner noted, the Soviet system of central planning protects producers from the positive pressures to innovate generated by competition and the potential entry of new enterprises in a market economy. As a result, enterprises face only administrative pressures to innovate, not economic incentives. In sum, the Soviet economy is characterized by a set of strong disincentives for innovation, an absence of large rewards for innovation, and the absence of the risks of lost markets, profits, and enterprise existence for failure to innovate.

Organizational structure. In addition to the supply uncertainties and other disincentives retarding technological change, Soviet organizational structure also acts to discourage innovation. Economic organizations in the Soviet Union are marked by large-scale bureaucratization, complexity, hierarchical rigidity, and horizontal boundaries that are often more difficult to bridge than international boundaries between unfriendly states. Where technology is fluid and change rapid, successful innovating organizations require flexibility, lateral interactions, and organic, nonhierarchical structures. Soviet economic organizations generally violate all of these norms.

For example, Soviet enterprises are large and lumbering. Twenty years ago, only 15 percent of Soviet enterprises employed fewer than fifty people, compared with 85 percent in the United States and 95 percent in Japan. On the other hand, 24 percent of Soviet enterprises had more than five hundred employees, compared with 1.4 percent in the United States, and 0.3 percent in Japan.[4] Since then, Soviet organizations have grown even larger with enterprise mergers and the creation of production associations, in which many enterprises have been joined under a single management. Ironically, the amalgamation of enterprises and research institutes into enormous complexes was intended to correct the organizational boundary problem epidemic in the Soviet economy.

Despite the large scale of individual research and production organizations, Soviet industrial structure has been characterized by functional specialization. Production enterprises perform little R&D; research institutes have little capacity for prototype construction and testing or for pilot-plant production. Design and project organizations produce blueprints for products they will never produce and factories they will never manage. Market economies can, for some products and technologies, coordinate these different functions through arms-length market transactions, but for the majority of products these functions are integrated within individual companies in which intense personal communication and movement of people with technical knowledge and know-how are facilitated. Even under such conditions, however, research-intensive companies in market economies find that developing effective links among research, design, development, production, and marketing is difficult and time-consuming; in the Soviet system it is nearly impossible.

Not only are the functions associated with developing new technologies and products located in separate organizations, but in the Soviet Union they are often in totally different sectors of the economy. The research institutes of the Academy of Sciences—the country's major scientific organizations—lie entirely outside the production sphere managed by the industrial ministries. Even when a research institute and a production plant are within the same ministry, the mangers' differing incentives produce only weak forces for the interactions and personal commitment required to innovate and to transfer innovation to a production organization. Moreover, the forces of demand are so blunted that there is little incentive to produce even a successfully transferred innovation.

Contracts for R&D. The Soviet government has put forward several policies intended to reduce the deleterious effects of organizational boundaries. Contracts were introduced and promoted in the late 1960s as vital links between researchers and research users. Research institutes in industrial ministries and in the Academy of Sciences were informed that their support budget was to be reduced or held steady, and that growth would have to be sought through contracts with industry. Incentives were thus provided to the research community to attend to the needs of users.

The success of this approach has been mixed, often depending (as in market economies) on the branch of industry and type of production or product. Also important is the entrepreneurial spirit of the research directors, the encouragement given by higher-level authorities, and the availability of research-contract funds in production enterprises. The Ukrainian Academy of Sciences and the Siberian branch of the Soviet Academy of Sciences have gone the farthest in industrial participation— so far, in fact, that by the mid-1970s complaints arose that scientific institutes were being diverted from the basic goal of advancing science.

In sum, the policy of promoting contractual relationships can be considered a success in improving links across functionally differentiated organizations, although the endemic problems of weak producer incentives for innovation remain. Moreover, the difficulty of writing and enforcing contracts for R&D is even more severe than the problems of contractual relations wholly within the sphere of production.

Production associations. A different approach was taken to the fragmentation problem with the creation of science-production associations (NPOs) beginning in the late 1960s. A September 1968 decree called for several types of research, development, and production associations throughout industry, agriculture, transport, construction, and other branches. The NPO was only one of several new types of organizations intended to bring together under a single management the various functions required to improve production, products, work organization, product development, and R&D. The greatest interest in forming NPOs was in the research-intensive industrial ministries.[5]

These NPOs, with a research institute (or design bureau) as the lead organization and its director acting as manager of the entire complex, are intended to serve as technical centers for an entire branch of industry. The other, ordinary types of production associations also include R&D establishments, but they are more inwardly focused, with the research institutes acting as subordinate organizations serving only the needs of the association. The operations of the various industrial associations have had substantial problems. For example, the question of whether NPOs should have their own production facilities was vigorously debated. Most had at least pilot-plant capabilities, and many had considerable production capacity as well, but ministries planned the production sections as though NPOs were ordinary enterprises, creating the usual impediments to innovation. When production capabilities were eliminated from the association, the usual difficulties of transferring technology across organizational boundaries remained, although they were somewhat attenuated. The ordinary production associations appear to have gone further toward integrating the different functions, although they are even more subject to the usual web of disincentives than are NPOs.

Furthermore, the formal organizational structure of the associations masks some serious boundary problems that continue to plague association managers. Elimination of organizational boundaries has often not been accomplished by consolidating several kinds of organizations into a presumably unified association. In many instances, after ten or fifteen years of operation, full integration of operations has not prevailed over the jealously guarded prerogatives of the original managers. The original organizations often have continued to act as individual enterprises, maintaining their traditional links to superior organs and even continuing to be issued separate plans by the planning agencies. Nevertheless, despite the imperfections, some progress has been made toward reducing one kind of barrier to innovation by obscuring the boundaries among functionally separate organizations.

Goal-oriented planning and program management. One other policy development in the civil sphere deserves mention, due to both its growing prominence and its links to military-sector practices: the use of program planning and management.[6] This approach emphasizes a set of goals or technical achievements, such as the development of a specific new product or the creation of some production capability. Planning is centered on the achievement of the goals rather than on creating an organizational unit, such as an enterprise. Many of these programs in the civil sector appear to be related to high-level party or government objectives and are managed outside the usual organizational frameworks. In some cases, time schedules, resources, and participants are designated in the formal documents authorizing the project. For important interministry problems, a lead organization may be assigned authority over resources and the other participating organizations. For the most important projects, high-level political backing is used to solve the ever-present problems of bottlenecks, unreliable supplies, uncooperative partners, and general disinterest in results. Such approaches have been used for such major campaigns as exploitation of Western Siberian oil and gas reserves and for more narrowly defined goals, such as a shipbuilding development program.[7]

While often effective, program management can not be generalized. Its effectiveness depends on the ability to isolate a high-priority goal from the general economic structure. Indeed, high priority and privileged access to supplies and organizational talents can disrupt the plans of others and impose an additional burden on the already-taxed capabilities of ordinary managers. As Berliner notes, when the source of problems is systemic, the creation of remedies by exceptions only adds complexity and arbitrariness to resource use and decision-making.[8] To the extent that program planning is effective, it contributes additional barriers to innovation by the unfavored residual claimants of resources.

Innovation in Military Industry

Soviet military industry avoids many of the impediments to innovation faced by the civilian production sector through a variety of organizational devices and politically supported management policies. I will focus on the two chief impediments to innovation by civilian industry: supply problems, and functional fragmentation caused by organizational boundaries. But first it is necessary to comment on the issue of incentives in military industry.

Military incentives. Unlike most civil production, the Soviet military faces true competition as it considers its real and imagined adversaries circling the country's borders. The highly skilled and experienced military professionals of the Soviet General Staff formulate weapons acquisition requirements and policies in light of the ever-changing capabilities of the forces opposing them. Although the Soviet military maintains large forces and receives a commensurately large budget, in the development and acquisition of new weapons it must act within overall budget constraints. The combination of real international competition and budget constraints generates a phenomenon that is rather rare in the Soviet Union: a buyer with incentives to make optimizing choices that appear rational to an outside observer.

Rational incentives combined with political authority transform the defense industrial sector into a buyer's market, dominated by consumers. The incentives transmitted to defense industry are therefore consistent with the decision-making rules mandated by the political leadership. Unlike most other actors in Soviet economic affairs, defense leaders and defense industrial managers, in general, actually choose what they *ought* to choose. They are astute buyers. This is not to deny that price distortions and other disequilibria introduce many deviations from strictly optimal behavior; however, the military has been given something that other producers do not have: authority to undertake uncertainty and risk, and the ability to escape the customary Soviet preoccupation with the narrowly defined efficiency of producers at the expense of the utility of users. It must be emphasized, however, that competition and constrained choice do not automatically confer special rights; rather, political values and policies have transformed these objective conditions into a favorable environment for procurement. We will return to this point later.

Access to supplies. Beginning with planning at the highest level, military allocation—as determined by the interplay of politics, economics, and military demands—is satisfied first, with the rest of the economy treated as a residual.[9] In production plans, military orders must be completed before the demands of other customers. Capital equipment in short supply goes first to military plants, with the remainder allocated to lower-priority enterprises. Advanced, high-productivity foreign equipment, both bought and stolen, flows in large volume to military producers, and high-quality workers and managers have been channeled to the military-industrial sector and rewarded with high salaries, bonuses, and such perquisites as better housing.

In order to guarantee the quality of its inputs, the military itself manages a network of representatives at plants producing final goods or inputs for the military customer. These representatives have the responsibility and authority to reject products that do not meet contractual specifications and to work out corrective procedures with local managers. Even more than in civilian industry, the military-industrial ministries and factories try to assure as far as possible that their supplies and inputs are produced under their own control. The Ministry of Aviation Industry, for example, has aluminum production capabilities and rubber plants for tire production. In short, military producers escape many of the effects of a seller's market. They insist on inputs that meet agreed-upon quantities, qualities, and schedules. And they have the advantage of planning priority, delivery authority, and independent, on-the-scene inspection to implement their demands.

Party and government organs contribute to the reduction of supply uncertainties facing the military industry. As part of their general responsibility to obtain supplies for enterprises under their jurisdictions, local party secretaries pay special attention to military production. They can divert needed supplies from civilian plants to military plants, comb the local area for reserves, and call on their comrades in other areas to do the same in exchange for commodity trades or future favors. Local party leaders can use political pressure on producers to speed up production to meet deadlines, find transport equipment to move available goods, and solve the thousands of bottleneck problems that afflict Soviet industry. Some analysts claim that these functions legitimize the existence of local party leaders, impeding reforms that would eliminate those functions and with them, the local party's *raison d'être*.

When supply problems cannot be solved at the local level, party secretaries can seek resolution at higher levels of the party hierarchy. At the top, the Party Secretary for Defense Industry can presumably call on the entire national economy to solve a critical military-industrial supply problem, mobilizing the planning and supply agencies, industrial capabilities, and stocks and reserves. The party therefore establishes the priority of the military sector and, in its deployed capacity throughout the country, stands ready to help implement its own policy.

It is aided in this task by an agency nominally attached to the Council of Ministers, but closely supervised by the Party Secretary for Defense Industry: the Military Industrial Commission (VPK). The VPK primarily implements military-industrial policy rather than creating it; one of its main jobs is to coordinate and police military priorities throughout the economy and to see that decisions are carried out. The VPK participates in planning weapons R&D and procurement at the national level in the State Planning Committee (Gosplan), the Academy of Sciences, and the State Committee for Science and Technology (GKNT). With a supra-ministerial role and commensurate authority, its instructors have the knowledge, skill, and power to enforce compliance with contracts and program plans; apparently they are not reluctant to use these powers, even if fulfilling military demands has adverse consequences for lower-priority users.

Two modifications are needed to bring this rather bald description of priority closer in line with reality. First, although the military has high priority, which is recognized and acted upon throughout the system, actors at all levels are not unaware of the harm done to other sectors of society by slavish and unreasonable attention to military demands. Dramatic changes in military requirements will be fought by decision-makers and party leaders if they drastically disrupt established plans and relations. From the top budget and planning agencies to the low-level supply organizations, there is evidence that "reasonable" and "customary" military demands will be satisfied more or less automatically, but that unreasonable requests will be opposed or compromises sought. Over the long run, however, the military industry has been successful in obtaining what it needs.

A second modification to the top priority of military industry has to do with the proliferation—or "blizzard"—of priorities. As with many other units of exchange not backed by real resources, it is all too easy for the authorities to demand more than the available production capacity can support, leading to inflation. We have seen just such inflation of priority in military production. Enterprises overbooked with priority orders end up fulfilling those that are easiest to produce. We thus see orders possessing highest party-government priority, Council of Ministers priority, Ministry of Defense priority, VPK priority, industrial ministry priority, and so on down the list. As priorities proliferate, the military industry becomes more like the civil sector, with all the attendant problems of tautness and a seller's market.

Organizational structure and the chief designer. The military industry deals with problems resulting from the functional separation of organizations in two principal ways: through the integrative role of the chief designer, and through the VPK decision. The chief designer stands between the research institute and the production plant, and between the industrial sector and the military user, often in a separate organization within an industrial ministry. He is responsible for the development of new systems and the integration of technologies into a useful and acceptable product. He negotiates with the military customer over the characteristics of the product and, sensitive to the ability of the economy to support his designs, he is usually extremely conservative in agreeing to highly advanced capabilities that would require sharp departures from previous practices. Although the military industry can be buffered and isolated from the supply uncertainties and disincentives of the rest of the economy, it cannot be totally independent. The chief designer, knowing the deficiencies of the Soviet production sphere and the penalties for not fulfilling agreed-upon military demands, attempts to reduce the demands to manageable size—with a good margin of safety.

Once these demands have been agreed to, the designer has the incentive and authority to develop a product with the cooperation of subsystem developers and producers and the support of the research establishment. Prototype construction and pilot-plant production can be accomplished either in the design bureau or at designated factories. The design bureau formally and informally develops close relations with the production facilities to guarantee the feasibility of the design and its successful transfer into production. Production specialists move from the plant to the design bureau in the later stages of design, and design personnel travel with the design to the factory for the life of the product.

Over the past fifty years, the military design process has taken many steps to minimize the negative effects of risks and functional specialization in the Soviet economy. Design handbooks closely control the choice of technologies, components, and manufacturing techniques, reducing interorganizational requirements for coordination and minimizing the degree of risk in a new product, including the necessity of seeking new sources of supply. Organizations setting standards at all levels ensure that standardized parts and techniques are used to the greatest extent possible. Each project proceeds according to a formal set of precisely laid-out steps that specify the tasks to be carried out and the review and acceptance procedures.

Despite the advantages given to the military sector, the forces of conservatism are pervasive and powerful. Designers, customers, and producers prefer strategies that ensure steady progress over radical solutions that may ultimately pay off but would do no good if failure cut short a promising approach—and the participants with it.

Organizational structure and the VPK. The goal-oriented, program planning approach to managing complex problems in the civil economy mirrors the role of the VPK in military industry. The VPK decision is equivalent to a project plan: it sets forth the overall project goals, establishes a lead organization, names the other participants and their tasks, allocates budgets, and sets up the timetables. It is legally binding on all concerned parties, and its implementation is subsequently reviewed by the VPK and party organs. Failure to abide by the terms of the decision can lead to severe reprimands for noncomplying organizations, which can affect the careers of the responsible managers and the fortunes of the offending organizations.

The VPK decision thus integrates complex, multi-branch projects largely by ignoring the boundaries among organizations and functions. The VPK does this by assigning an overall manager, usually a chief designer, whose authority cuts across ministries, academies, research institutes, and production plants. For the life of the project, the designer possesses the kind of authority found in similar projects in a U.S. corporation. Since it is generally the chief designer who has produced the draft VPK decision in the first place, the project plan is congenial to his desires. It must be recognized, however, that it is neither the decision nor the work plan it embodies that allows organizational and functional boundaries to be ignored in this way, but rather the supraministerial authority of the VPK, which is delegated to the lead organization.[10] It is instructive to note that the several commissions established with nominally similar roles in the civilian economy over the past ten years have not been able to duplicate the VPK's performance, largely, I suspect, because they have not had the political authority granted to the VPK. It must be questioned whether even a politically supported civilian commission could achieve similar results without the other powers accorded the military industry: priority and the ability to say no to deficient suppliers.

The Future of Weapons Acquisition

It should be clear by now that I believe the military industry's success in the design, development, and production of advanced weaponry depends upon political values and policies. Gur Ofer delineates a Soviet leadership utility function that differs significantly from the social-welfare functions usually attributed to modern industrial countries whose goals are to maximize consumption and the long-term welfare of the population.[11] Inferring the Soviet leadership's goals from its choices over the past sixty years, Ofer develops a so-called extreme view for analytical purposes that "the maximand is internal and external power building, and that its translation into economic terms is the maximization of the growth rate of heavy industry and defense production capacity."[12] Ofer notes that the inferred preferences of the Soviet leadership as it has evolved since Stalin's death suggest a softening of the extreme view to include greater scope for social welfare. At a minimum, in the absence of the terror and naked compulsion of Stalinism, higher consumption levels are a necessary social cost to encourage the labor force to produce the things the leadership desires. However, political developments suggest that social welfare also enters the leadership utility function directly, if only weakly. The key question, therefore, is whether social welfare has been assigned a higher value by the leadership, either as an intermediate good or as a final objective, and whether such a reassignment would have effects on weapons acquisition in general, and on the technological capabilities of the Soviet military industry in particular.

Political-economic "new thinking" could affect the military industry in three ways: budget shares could be shifted to favor the civil sector; military priorities could be reduced or shifted toward civil uses; and civilian industry could be reformed to make it more efficient. A decrease in the proportion of resources going to weapons acquisition would certainly have a visible effect. However, if other things remained unchanged, such a policy would not improve weapon innovation and technology much. In the civilian sector, plans would remain just as taut, supplies would still be uncertain, organizational boundaries would still impede technical progress, and priorities and other existing mechanisms would still favor military industry. Quantity, but not quality, would be affected. Of course, in other areas things might not remain the same. Additional resources for civilian users might induce planners to reduce plan tautness for civil industry and raise it for military producers. Such changes in supply uncertainty would increase the innovative tendencies among civilian managers and make the weapons developer more cautious and conservative than he is now.

The reduction of military priority, were it to occur, could have significant effects on both military and civilian innovation. The major effect would be to reduce supply risks to the civil enterprise manager and increase them on the military side. Such a policy would require rooting out decades of practice and habit, beginning at the top planning levels and extending down through party cadres and the government to the lowest-level economic managers. It would mean, for example, that were sheet aluminum in short supply, it would more probably end up at a toaster factory instead of an MiG aircraft plant. It would require that countless daily decisions guided by powerful institutional incentives and reinforced by decades of habit and experience be reshaped according to new priorities. Soviet experience suggests that, in order to be effective, such a change in values and policies would require a massive mobilization campaign, wholesale removal of old cadres and appointment of replacements, and visible punishments and rewards to emphasize that the desired performance on which incentives were based had indeed changed.

If priority were shifted to the civilian sector, much of the clout of the VPK would also vanish. The delegated authority of a chief designer would no longer be effective as he sought the cooperation of an electronics laboratory that was now designing components for color television sets or compact disc players. The VPK would still provide useful coordination, but implementation of its decisions would become less effective.

Considering the effects of successful economic reforms is more complex, partly because it depends on just what shape such reforms could take. A reform along the lines of those taking place in contemporary China would mean giving enterprises greater autonomy, more freedom to enter or exit a product line or industry, incentives based on a profitlike measure, and greater reliance on interenterprise contracts and wholesale trade rather than on central plans and supply allocations.

We will assume, to begin with, that such changes may occur in the civilian sector but would be less likely in the military, where traditional Soviet planning and management practices would continue to prevail (as they apparently do in China). To the extent that military industry is isolated from, and independent of, the rest of the economy, civilian-sector reforms would have little effect on military productivity. But such isolation is not the case in the Soviet Union: military industry does depend on its ability to divert resources from the civilian economy through its higher priority in order to relieve the tautness of its plans and to assure its enterprises the inputs they require. This interdependence is almost certainly increasing as military producers use a broadening array of materials, components, and other inputs from advanced industrial producers throughout the economy. If a reform such as we are assuming were to take place, the military enterprises would have to join the queue with other customers and compete for its inputs. Even if nominal priorities were preserved, it would become harder to enforce them in the face of profit-making incentives influencing enterprise managers: priorities are more enforceable when the alternatives are less compelling. If the profitability of nonmilitary production greatly outweighed that from directed production for military uses, managers throughout the economy would find methods to evade the imposed demands, and greater autonomy and freer access to resources would weaken the levers used to enforce priority. We are witnessing a similar situation in China today.

If the military industry were included in the reform, the possibilities would be still greater: innovation in civilian industry could flourish, and the resulting technological progress could benefit the military as well, if it had the flexibility and resources to take advantage of new developments. The net effect could leave the relative position of military industry unchanged, while it would gain the benefits of a more innovative and flexible civilian sector. It would lose some of its customary advantages, but also benefit from its own reform and have to adapt to a different style of management. In the long run, the growth of national economic and innovative capacities would almost certainly put military industry in a stronger position.

How, then, do we evaluate current Soviet policies? It is uncertain whether there has been a shift in allocation to or from the military. Growth trends have not shown sharp change in either consumption or weapons acquisition. We have seen high-level military-industry managers shifted to management positions in civilian industry and the central government agencies, which could signify a slight shift in priority as these highly competent managers redirect their skills to new tasks.[13] Unfortunately for the Soviet economy, these transfers have not produced any evidence of progress, for the main reason that nothing else has been transferred: not priority, political power, managerial authority, nor command over scarce resources.

Another recent policy shift has been the transfer to military industry of enterprises formerly belonging to light industry, and of new plans for military industry to produce civilian goods. Although such moves may be indications of high-level preferences, unless these enterprises and products are given the benefit of the full panoply of military advantages, they are unlikely to demonstrate the kind of advances that the leadership would like to see. That this may be the case is apparent in a Central Committee reprimand of four military-industry ministers for allowing the manufacture of poor-quality television sets, radios, and tape recorders.[14]

When we examine the range of economic reforms that are now being implemented, there is little to suggest the kind of radical reform that would speed up innovation or the rate of technical change, or that would change the balance between civilian and military industry. As Gertrude Schroeder has noted, the reforms "display the traditional conviction that economic development—the composition of output and the direction of investment—as well as the broad content and direction for scientific and technological progress must be managed by the center."[15] She adds that, "since all of this does not create a competitive market environment, enterprise strategy likely will continue to emphasize risk avoidance and center orientation."[16]

Any real change in the ability of military-industrial managers and designers to carry on as they have since the 1930s will be clear enough to outside observers. Such changes will be accompanied by new priorities, wholesale movements of cadres, complaints from the military-industrial sector about supply problems, and an overall transformation of relative capabilities. Although I see no changes of this magnitude on the horizon, these are the things to look for.

Economic Constraints in Soviet Military Decision-Making

ESTIMATES OF SOVIET military spending and its corresponding burden on the Soviet economy have been controversial in the West for almost two decades.[1] It is widely held that these estimates represent important guideposts for assessing the adequacy of U.S. defense spending and priorities, and many Western analysts and policy-makers use estimates of Soviet military spending as a surrogate for "the threat." If Soviet military spending is comparable to U.S. spending in absolute terms, to many this implies that the Soviet military threat is manageable at current (or perhaps reduced) levels of U.S. defense spending. Conversely, others argue that if the Soviet Union is significantly outspending the United States, there is a clear need for greater U.S. defense resource commitments.

A related issue is the relative defense burden. Some people feel that if the overall Soviet military burden—measured in terms of military spending as a share of gross national product (GNP)—is in the moderate range of 10 to 15 percent, then it can be assumed that the Soviets have considerable room to expand their military programs. The implication is that, under such circumstances, a major increase in U.S. defense

Stephen M. Meyer is a professor in the Department of Political Science and the Center for International Studies at the Massachusetts Institute of Technology.

spending would only provoke a corresponding increase in Soviet defense spending, and that the increase in U.S. military spending would not only fail to produce a net increase in U.S. security, but could actually result in a net decline. On the other hand, if Soviet military spending imposes a tremendous burden on an already strained economy (on the order of 20 to 30 percent of GNP), then little room remains for increased military efforts. In this case, it is asserted, increases in U.S. defense spending could not be readily countered, and might result in a genuine increase in U.S. security.

Central to these arguments are questions about the Soviet defense decision-making process: Do Soviet leaders ever think about defense and economic issues in these terms? If so, how and where do economic considerations enter the defense decision-making process, and how do they affect defense planning and policy? Do Soviet leaders even know how much they spend on defense? Do they care?

Amazingly, such questions have, for the most part, been ignored.[2] Perhaps this oversight is due to the lingering effects of the totalitarian model of the Soviet state, according to which the Soviet government, driven by ideological and historical imperatives, acts with singular purpose to expand its empire at all costs. Influenced by this model, Western academic and policy discussions often resort, either explicitly or implicitly, to a "blank check" hypothesis of Soviet military spending. In its crudest form, this model assumes that the Soviet defense constituency has virtually limitless authority to withdraw resources from the economy, leaving the civilian sectors to rummage through the leftovers. More sophisticated subscribers to this view acknowledge that economic constraints do affect Soviet defense policy, but only in a very general way: Soviet military planning and policy, they believe, are based on considerations of doctrine, strategy, threat assessments, and force requirements. Only at the very end of the process is defense demand compared with available economic resources. These analysts believe that, while macroeconomic constraints may force a scaling back of defense plans to more reasonable dimensions, economic considerations rarely, if ever, interact directly with the substance of defense policy.

In this paper I argue that economic considerations have played a more intrusive role in Soviet defense policy-making than is commonly assumed, and that economic factors have had—and continue to have—macro and micro effects on Soviet defense policy, including military doctrine and strategy. Explicit resource constraints interact with implicit ones, such as scarcity-based limitations on technology, industrial development, innovation, and productivity, to affect policy and programs.

Who Decides What?

Information from the Soviet Union suggests that there are three decision-making levels involved in the formulation and execution of Soviet military-economic policy.[3] Level 1 is occupied by the top political leadership of the Soviet Union, the Politburo and Defense Council.[4] In the context of Soviet defense budgeting, Level 1 decision-making is primarily concerned with answering the question, How much is enough?[5] It does this principally by approving or rejecting major weapons programs and force-structure changes, and ultimately by approving a specific correlation between expected economic output and defense demand.

Level 2 is occupied by intermediate institutions involved in middle-level policy-making, intended to support and implement Level 1 decisions. The Ministry of Defense is the locus of Level 2 military decision-making; its basic task is to construct the draft five-year defense plan and then implement it. Its component institutions and actors—the minister of defense, the General Staff and its chief, and the Collegium of the Ministry—each have special roles to play. Gosplan (the State Planning Committee) is the corresponding economic center of Level 2 decision-making. Its job is to plan and balance Soviet economic development for the years ahead. It also has the task of ensuring, through its military department, that defense-sector demand is met.

Level 3 is occupied, on the defense side, by the armed services—the strategic rocket forces, ground forces, air defense forces, air forces, and navy—and other combat and support commands. On the economic-industrial side, Level 3 is composed of the various industrial ministries. These organizations convert Level 2 decisions on how to utilize defense resources into concrete programs.

Given the tight interconnection between the defense industrial and supply sector and the national economic base, it is inconceivable that any national economic plan could be devised without a parallel process for projecting defense demand.[6] Specifically, Gosplan's draft economic plans must include a coherent body of assumptions about defense manpower, procurement, construction, and supply requirements.[7] Authority for setting this correlation between projected economic-industrial performance and expected defense demand rests with Level 1, the top Soviet political leadership.

But this setup only begs a more basic question: Do Soviet political leaders impose resource constraints on defense "demand" *a priori*, or is military planning allowed to proceed according to its own agenda and scaled back only if economic realities are grossly violated? From a decision-making perspective we might ask: Where is the Soviet defense-budget agenda formulated: at Level 1 or Level 2? If the Soviet leadership promulgates its own view of the appropriate level of defense demand and the corresponding availability of national economic resources *a priori*, Level 2 agendas and policy options would represent responses to the priorities and constraints set forth by Level 1 decisions, and Level 1 constraints would be explicit. If, on the other hand, the political leadership waits to react to Level 2 agendas and policy options, it would be Level 2 institutions that, *de facto*, set the defense agenda and provided the political leadership with policy option menus—primarily in the form of weapons programs and force structures from which to choose. The ways in which Level 2 institutions framed the issues and policy options could be used to manipulate Level 1 decisions. At this stage any Level 1 constraints would be only implicit.

Historical evidence suggests that both these situations have occurred, and that neither can be considered the dominant mode of interaction between Level 1 and 2. Some of the best-known episodes of policy disputes among Soviet leadership have been played out around the issue of the defense-budget agenda: the Khrushchev-Malenkov rivalry, Khrushchev's efforts to cut military spending and manpower in the early 1960s, Brezhnev's address to the military in 1982, and most certainly the ongoing doctrinal discussions and decisions surrounding Gorbachev's new political thinking on security. All are examples of involvement by the political leadership in attempting to articulate levels of military sufficiency *a priori*. In the last three cases, macroeconomic exigencies placed explicit constraints on the Soviet defense-budget agenda in terms of how much would be available and how it should be apportioned.[8] Defense policy choices on force levels, readiness, programs, and even strategy were thus directly affected by Level 1 preferences concerning the defense-budget agenda and options. In particular, weapons programs were cut from the defense plan.

It may be more than coincidence that the most innovative departures from traditional Soviet military thinking, doctrinal and strategic, have occurred during periods when the political leadership attempted to constrain the defense agenda on economic grounds. Khrushchev, for example, decided that a force structure based on nuclear weapons and missiles would be far less expensive in the long run than the tremendous conventional-force posture advocated by military professionals. He instituted cuts in military manpower, readiness levels, and salaries in those areas he declared not essential to defense—most notably the ground and air forces. Gorbachev, in contrast, chose to begin by reducing nuclear forces. Although they represent only a small part of the Soviet defense burden, nuclear-force reductions will free precious resources and production capability. It is also calculated that this reduction will set the stage for much more difficult, but potentially much more rewarding, conventional-force reductions via Gorbachev's agenda of "reasonable sufficiency" and "defensive defense."[9]

At other times, Level 2 institutions have dominated the Soviet defense-budget agenda process. This was especially true during much of the early Khrushchev period, most of the Brezhnev era, the Andropov and Chernenko interregnums, and the initial Gorbachev years. During these times, macroeconomic requirements implicitly constrained agenda-setting activities of the Ministry of Defense. While the Ministry of Defense certainly had a fuzzy impression of what the reasonable limits on its resource requirements might be, it would not have felt explicitly constrained from pushing its own agenda. Indeed, it is likely that both the Ministry of Defense and Gosplan found it convenient to present bureaucratically negotiated plans to the political leadership.[10] Not surprisingly, at these times agenda-setting was dominated by traditional Soviet military notions of threats and requirements. These were the periods of across-the-board surges in Soviet forces and capabilities.

Of course, in the situation just described, Level 1 decision-makers may not be happy with the options that Level 2 institutions offer for consideration. For example, the Twelfth Five-Year Plan (FYP) was a creature of Gosplan, composed in the shadows of Andropov and Chernenko. At the eleventh hour, Gorbachev reportedly rejected several times what Gosplan considered to be its final version of the plan, ordering a number of changes.

The bureaucratic manipulations of Level 2 institutions may also be all too transparent to the Soviet political leadership. One might reflect on the firing of former General Staff Chief Ogarkov in September 1984. At precisely the time that Level 1 decisions on the defense allocation should have been taking place, he was relieved of his post for "unpartylike" behavior. Might he have used his position as Defense Council secretary to continue to contest the Politburo's decision regarding defense allocation in the Twelfth FYP? Soviet sources have floated rumors to that effect.

In other words, even when Level 2 institutions do have nominal control of defense-budget agenda-setting and option-formulation tasks, Level 1 decision-makers still retain decision authority and can impose constraints from above. Indeed, much Level 2 activity is designed to anticipate those constraints and provide plans that fall *a priori* within reasonable bounds.

How Much Is Enough, and How Is It Imposed?

The ways in which Level 1 decisions regarding "how much is enough?" are specified would also affect how they constrain defense planning. Much of the Western debate over Soviet defense spending takes for granted that the level of defense burden is specified in rubles, as a share of national income or of government spending. This form of fiscal budgetary authorization would be a loose constraint, affecting defense planning only in the aggregate. Within the mandated fiscal cap, the Ministry of Defense would be free to use its financial resources as it deemed appropriate, shifting priorities via fiscal reallocation.

But given the characteristics of the Soviet Union's centrally planned and administered economy, a material balance correlation—a Level 1 cap imposed in terms of physical units—is also a possibility (and could be discussed and implemented on a program-by-program basis). This form of allocation would constrain military planning more than a fiscal allocation would, especially in the areas of weapons procurement, operations and maintenance (O&M), and construction. It would mean that the military establishment could not pursue its own priorities by shifting resources from one account to another. Unexpected increases in the resource demands of a weapons procurement program could not be compensated by shifting resources from O&M accounts. Once Gosplan's draft economic plan was approved by the political leadership, the Ministry of Defense would not be able to respond rapidly to changing priorities or program requirements outside the industrial and production framework worked out with Gosplan.

A growing body of evidence now suggests that the Soviet defense burden is not *initially* formulated in fiscal terms as either a ruble sum or share of GNP. In other words, rubles are not used as an overall allocative mechanism;[11] rather, a mixture of fiscal authorizations and material correlations is established, with total ruble "value" assigned at the end as an accounting mechanism. Authoritative Soviet sources, including former General Staff Chief Akhromeev and Deputy Minister of Foreign Affairs Petrovskii, have pointedly asserted that Soviet leaders do not have figures for defense resource allocation in units comparable to the general economy—that is, in rubles.[12] While ruble prices are used in both the civilian and defense sectors, those prices do not reflect true values, nor are they comparable across sectors. Consequently, knowledge of defense "spending" as a share of national income would have little utility for Soviet Level 1 decision-makers.[13] It may be that CIA estimates are the Soviet leadership's best data on the aggregate level of their military burden.

Given the structural and functional peculiarities of the Soviet central planning and supply system, a single budgetary authority could not be granted as an allocative mechanism to the Ministry of Defense. If the Ministry of Defense were merely handed a satchel of rubles and instructed to go out and purchase its needs, the industrial production system could never be sure what the final mix of demand might be. CIA reconstructions of the Soviet defense burden place it between 15 and 18 percent of total economic product, a demand too large to leave unspecified in the five-year economic plan. In fact, the defense sector actually uses a much higher proportion of precious economic resources, such as microelectronics, special materials, optics, and trained labor. The Soviet economic system would have to operate under an intolerable threat of uncertainty and disruption if the Ministry of Defense were constrained solely by a fiscal budget.

Given the artificial pricing system used in the Soviet Union, fiscal budgetary authority would also have limited utility. Rubles, even defense rubles, are not a guarantee of access to a given quantity or quality of resources in a system where such resources are rationed by fiat, not price. Moreover, a purely fiscal budgetary allocation to the Ministry of Defense would produce chaos in the defense sector once those rubles were distributed among the armed services. Bidding wars over precious resources in limited supply (such as microprocessors, special-grade lubricants, and food) would create enormous inflation, bring the planning and supply system to a crashing halt, or both.

This argument implies that the initial correlation between economic capacity and military demand must be set, at least in part, via a collection of material indexes that are not combined into a single measure.[14]

Gosplan, working with the Ministry of Defense, could estimate the major components of defense industrial demand and set an initial roster of allocation caps covering a variety of key resources. Establishing resource demands within the Ministry of Defense would certainly seem straightforward for needs related to the operation and maintenance of forces in the field (for example, liters of gasoline or cubic meters of cement). It would also be convenient—and almost certainly required—for major aspects of weapons procurement and construction. Production of titanium, for instance, is something that cannot be started and stopped, nor can demand be altered, very quickly.

Of course, some parts of defense demand are almost certainly specified in fiscal units. This is possible where the value of the ruble used in the defense sector equals the value of the ruble used in the economy as a whole. Salaries, pensions, and other personnel-related costs are good examples. Research and development (R&D) activities are labor intensive—Soviet military R&D projects allegedly are initially costed and indexed in manpower units.[15] Many low-level O&M requirements are fulfilled by contracting with local civil-service providers.[16]

It is reasonable to assume, then, that the initial effort to decide how much is enough for Soviet defense demand is accomplished using a disaggregated combination of material balance and fiscal correlations. The former is probably most influential in weapons acquisition, while the latter is particularly relevant to R&D. Under this system, Gosplan could develop a notion of the defense burden by using the defense-related material demand estimates to determine direct impact on the economic plan. By presenting several variants of the draft five-year plan that include some parametric variations in defense demand—produced by including or excluding specific weapons programs flagged in previous Level 1 decisions—Gosplan could allow the Politburo/Defense Council to select the integrated combination of national economic and defense plans that seemed appropriate. Stated in these terms, the Soviet political leadership would understand the tradeoffs and opportunity costs of their defense efforts, but not in terms of rubles. Such a system would seem to correspond with what is known about Level 1 decisions to reduce the Soviet defense burden. In those cases where cuts were specified, they were determined either in terms of personnel, salaries, program eliminations, and direct force reductions, or by "economizing" on physical resources used in O&M. The "cost savings" reported were a consequence of these cuts, not of the mode of implementation.

Only after Level 1 approval of the economic and defense plans had been granted would the Ministry of Defense be given a ruble budget. This budget, a consequence of the defense allocation process, is an accounting tool that facilitates resource transfers among the Ministry of Defense, its prime contractors, and their subcontractors, and is not an allocative tool.

How Are Resources Distributed in the Ministry of Defense?

Irrespective of whether Level 1 interjects itself into the process to impose explicit constraints on defense planning, or Level 2 constrains the defense plan implicitly by trying to second-guess Level 1, the defense plan itself represents a huge resource demand. The primary "spenders" in the Ministry of Defense are the five armed services. They implement and administer the R&D programs, buy and operate the weapons, and train and maintain the forces in the field. Thus, in pursuing the issue of economic constraints on Soviet defense decision-making, we turn next to how the defense pie is divided within the Ministry of Defense, specifically, Do the various Level 3 agendas of the armed services prevail, or are they constrained by Level 2 (Ministry of Defense level) decisions?

In fact, the cutting of the defense resource pie is very tightly controlled by Level 2 decisions. Curiously, this is not carried out by the Ministry of Defense's own administrative organs, but rather by the General Staff. The institutional responsibilities and power of the Soviet General Staff have increased markedly since the mid-1960s.[17] It exercises its control over service "spending" at three basic stages: by exercising substantive control over the development and promulgation of Soviet military strategy (as well as aspects of its military doctrine), by controlling the development of the ministry's five-year defense plan, and by setting the resource priorities assigned to individual programs. We are interested in the last two control mechanisms.

Continuity across defense plans. Preparation of a draft defense plan involves a wide range of preliminary activities: forecasting threats, reviewing current programs, evaluating baseline requirements, and assessing mission priorities. While this may sound like an enormous undertaking, it is not a "zero-based" activity. Strategic concepts evolve slowly; the emergence of genuinely new threats is quite rare; and the Soviet General Staff looks more toward continuity than innovation in strategic planning.[18] The large number of programs that span past, present, and forthcoming five-year defense plans impart great continuity in planning. R&D programs from previous plans continue to mature, some of them moving into experimental design. Most of these will develop into proved systems and make the transition to production. While some older production programs may end, others, in modernized form, will continue serial output.

The vast scale and scope of Soviet forces in the field imply continuity in O&M requirements: all those people need to be fed, all those machines need to be fueled and lubricated, and all those worn tires need to be replaced. Thus, significant changes in requirements are unlikely from one five-year defense plan to the next. Similarly, military construction programs are long-term projects that carry over from one planning period to the next. Only during times of major doctrinal revision (for example, 1958–1961, 1966–1970, and perhaps the current period) is a full-scope review of the defense effort initiated.

Changing priorities. Of course, new issues do appear on the Ministry of Defense agenda, and important decisions need to be made regarding the distribution of expected defense resources among missions and services. For example, R&D priorities change as emerging technologies and processes such as lasers, composite materials, microelectronics, and improved high-explosive chemistry raise the possibility of new weaponry. Older systems need to be modernized, or replaced by follow-on weapons (for example, the SS-20 intermediate-range ballistic missile replaced the aging SS-4 and SS-5 missiles), so the procurement agenda evolves. Force structures change as prevailing views of the nature of a future war change. The early 1970s, for example, saw a major resurgence of tactical aviation in the Soviet force structure, and helicopters appeared in great quantities in the late 1970s and early 1980s.

Perhaps the most important part of the General Staff's preparatory work for the defense plan is the review of mission priorities — the concrete manifestation of military strategy. Mission priorities are reviewed and adjusted in accordance with changing estimates of threat, changing technology, changing Soviet capabilities, and evolving notions of doctrine and strategy. Examples of possible missions include strategic nuclear operations involving prompt destruction of hard targets (for example, the silos of intercontinental ballistic missiles), strategic nuclear operations for retaliation (which in turn could be subdivided into launch-on-warning, second strike ride-out, and so on), interdiction of NATO surface shipping, and strategic defense against aircraft and cruise missiles.

The setting of mission priorities has a cascading effect, establishing priorities among all the service programs. Past experience and a host of estimating norms allows the General Staff to attach some preliminary resource ceilings on the various missions.[19] This distribution of resources by mission is the first step in determining how the defense pie will be divided. Within each mission category the General Staff then reviews current and alternative programs for accomplishing its goals. Alternative military technical solutions (weapons systems and organizational structure) and military operational solutions (strategy, tactics, deployments) are studied, and force mix options are evaluated. These studies and analyses are conducted by the General Staff; the armed services merely provide data and support. Among the information provided by the armed services are evaluations of candidate programs to support General Staff missions and attendant resource demands, including first-order costs of the program options.[20] "Costs" are determined by books of norms and prices set within the defense sector based on past and current experience.[21] A number of estimating rules of thumb are employed to derive approximate figures for new R&D, procurement, O&M and construction programs.

The General Staff compiles data from the armed services—an unrealistic wish list even from the General Staff's point of view—and then proceeds to impose its own priorities and preferences, approving some programs, scaling some down, and rejecting others.[22] Cuts in program resource "costs" may be required before they are approved for inclusion in the defense plan.[23] Naturally, there are opportunities for feedback to the General Staff when Level 2 resource caps on particular programs are perceived by a branch of the armed services to be unduly constraining. The General Staff, in turn, may re-examine the distribution of resources pertaining to a particular mission category.[24]

In sum, the General Staff establishes mission priorities that bind all the armed services. It then sets a resource cap for a given mission, and provides a rough resource-cost target for each of the major weapons systems under that mission. The armed service (or armaments directorate) is then authorized to proceed with detailed technical and cost specification.

Interesting exceptions. Not surprisingly, the armed-service commands may not be pleased with specific General Staff decisions. Such situations are said to be rare and almost always ironed out quietly with the General Staff.[25] However, service chiefs have the right to appeal to the Collegium of the Ministry of Defense. This collegium, composed of the minister of defense and the deputy defense ministers (which includes the chief of the General Staff and of all the armed services), is a ministerial review body that assists the minister in administration. Appeal to the collegium is one of the few ways in which the armed services can affect resource distribution decisions within the Ministry of Defense.[26]

An even more exceptional procedure is a direct appeal by an armed-service chief to Level 1. Such a procedure may explain how Admiral Gorshkov was able to fund the expansion of the Soviet Navy into a blue-water surface fleet despite what seems have been strong General Staff objection. Gorshkov must have been able to convince Brezhnev to insert this mission priority into the defense plan above other General Staff priorities.[27] To be sure, this would not be the first time the Soviet political leadership injected its preferences into Level 2. Khrushchev's imposition of his nuclear strategy is perhaps the best-studied case. Interestingly, there is some evidence that Gorbachev's "new thinkers" hope to do the same, but by persuasion rather than fiat.

Level 3: Developing Programs

Do economic factors explicitly constrain R&D projects, weapons system design, force readiness (O&M), and military construction? The evidence here is overwhelmingly affirmative. The resource ceilings set by the General Staff have a cascading effect, so the research institutes, armed services, and other Level 3 commands of the Ministry of Defense formalize their R&D, procurement, O&M, and construction programs under the substantive and resource constraints set by the General Staff.

Research and development. The armed services devise and implement their own R&D agendas, but their programs are fiscally constrained: specific amounts are earmarked for a given program. Resources are not fungible across the R&D, weapons procurement, O&M, and construction categories.[28] Consequently, should an R&D program require more support than was originally planned, the best that a Level 3 actor can do is to take resources from one of its other R&D efforts.[29] Requests for additional funds from the ministry force the same tradeoff at Level 2—though across a larger resource base—through a shift in R&D support from other armed-service programs. R&D programs are also heavily constrained by facilities, instrumentation, and manpower shortages. A decision to expand laser research, for example, means slowing research in other areas, as laboratories, equipment, and research teams are pulled off some projects and assigned to others.

From time to time a few very high priority programs may be given what approaches unlimited access to resources. This was reportedly true for the Soviet space program in the 1960s.[30] But this merely forces cutbacks in R&D efforts elsewhere in the defense sector.

Weapons procurement. Weapons acquisition is likewise constrained. Here the armed-service (or armament directorate) acts as the military customer, drawing up the basic technical requirements for prospective weapons systems. This customer then contracts with one of the production ministries' design bureaus to provide a full-scale development proposal. The process includes these considerations:

- The customer (the military service) specifies resource and cost constraints along with initial technical requirements in soliciting proposals from the production ministry design bureau.

- The design bureau, in selecting among alternative designs, components, and materials, must stay within the resource and cost cap specified by the customer.

- Draft design plans must include not only the system cost but the cost for implementing serial production.

- Finally, since the mid-1970s, cost analysis has been an inherent part of production ministry project development, and so must also be a part of design bureau management.[31]

Level 3 decision-making for procurement is discussed in revealing detail in select Soviet military and economic materials.[32] Most significant, the problems associated with attaining a given level of effectiveness within an earmarked allotment of "costs" are discussed. Within those bounds, the armed services have the authority to select the system design alternative that they deem best to deliver the promised effectiveness and armed-service requirements. Soviet military-economic discussions clearly point to resources and costs as the disciplining criteria under which effectiveness is maximized.

The use of the term "costs" in the weapons design process deserves some attention. A generally applicable cost metric—a common defense ruble—must exist across the defense sector in order for Level 2 (the General Staff) to impose meaningful cost constraints on missions and programs, and to provide a framework in which it can examine the tradeoffs and opportunity costs among alternative weapons programs within a given mission. At Level 3, military specialists and weapons designers report that they compare resources and designs on an equivalency basis, trading off innovation against cost. Again, this ruble cost metric is not value based per se, but a compilation of fixed prices based on administrative fiat. Price estimates used in the planning stages are based on estimating norms and price books. Since the prices of "old" technologies are well established and stable compared with the uncertain and inevitably higher prices of new technologies, the risks of weapons system cost overruns are minimized by extensive use of design inheritance.[33] The triple constraints of aggregate resource limitations on defense resource allocations (Level 1), mission resource caps (Level 2), and program resource caps (Level 3) have made quality/quantity and cost/performance tradeoffs major procurement considerations at Level 3.

The armed services also procure myriad minor pieces of equipment that are transparent to Level 2 mission priorities in the sense that they form part of aggregate categories—small-caliber weapons, tactical communications gear, and trucks, for example. Here armed-service priorities can come into play—though again they are constrained by the procurement allotment imposed by the overall Level 2 disbursement decision. It appears that this is where the armed services run into trouble. In some instances they have reportedly failed to fill out their organization and equipment tables for the non-big-ticket hardware.[34] The problem may be poor quality control, cost overruns, diversion of resources to other procurement programs, waste, corruption, or all of the above. In any case, it seems that Level 2 oversight is poor with other than big-ticket procurement items. As a consequence, readiness levels may be greatly affected.

Operations, maintenance, and construction. Though operations, maintenance, and construction represent the largest area of Soviet military spending, they have never received anything close to the analytic attention given to procurement, or even R&D, by Western specialists.[35] Yet these three areas most certainly have a greater day-to-day impact on Soviet military power than R&D and procurement combined. After all, it is the readiness and preparation of Soviet forces for war, and their sustainability, that pose the greatest strategic threat to the West.

It is therefore especially significant that military O&M and construction have been the special targets of economic constraints over the past decade.[36] These resource-saving measures have certainly not been the result of self-imposed cuts by the armed services. Since resource categories are not fungible, there are no direct incentives for a military service to economize O&M resources on its own.[37] Where the U.S. Army might intentionally cut back on training in order to shift funds to procurement, this is not an option for the Soviet Ground Forces. Moreover, since planning for the next allotment of these resources is undoubtedly tied to prior use, there are actually incentives to use O&M and construction resources liberally.

One must look instead to either Level 1 or Level 2 decisions for the source of these constraints. In support of Level 1 intervention is the fact that "economizing and thriftiness" in O&M became a major campaign in the defense sector following Dmitrii Ustinov's appointment as minister of defense. Ustinov himself introduced the topic by emphasizing that economizing military O&M resources could save the economy hundreds of millions—if not billions—of rubles.[38] Not surprisingly, this occurred at the same time that economizing became a major slogan in Soviet industry as a whole. The military sector was not exempt from the larger effort.

However, where to implement military O&M savings seems to be a Level 2 decision. This setup allows the General Staff to ensure that its priority missions and forces are kept at highest readiness. In this respect, there is some interesting evidence that the air defense forces have been under special pressure to cut back on O&M since the end of the 1970s.[39] The navy also seems to have come under recent pressures to economize.[40] The armed services do appear to have some authority regarding how to implement Level 2–mandated O&M constraints, but Level 2 approval is most likely required.

Conclusion

The three-tiered structure of Soviet defense-budget decision-making outlined here suggests that explicit, as well as the more generally acknowledged implicit, economic constraints have played "disciplining" roles in Soviet defense policy for at least two decades. These constraints are imposed in cascading fashion, springing from the macro-level allocation decisions imposed by the political leadership. Those decisions are, in turn, implemented via distribution decisions within the Ministry of Defense that divide allotted resources according to mission priorities. Caps on resources within missions ultimately constrain program decisions.

Level 1 decisions. Based on our understanding of Level 1 decision-making, it appears that national economic requirements are given earlier and more balanced consideration vis-à-vis national security requirements than is often assumed by Western specialists. As mentioned, many Western officials believe that the Soviet defense constituency (some might prefer "military- industrial complex") receives virtually all the resources it demands, irrespective of the requirements of the national (and civilian) economy. While this is most certainly caricature rather than description, to assume that the Soviet political leadership accepts without question the economic tradeoffs and opportunity costs of defense does belie objectivity. It also reinforces the impression of a politically powerful defense "lobby" in Soviet politics.

Neither of these assumptions seems warranted, however; indeed they are historically inaccurate. Challenges to, and changes in, the makeup of the Soviet political leadership have been intimately intertwined with disputes over defense resource allocation. Consider the politics of defense spending immediately following the death of Stalin, the gyrations in defense spending plans during the Khrushchev years, and the consistency of the Brezhnev years capped by his "no new resources for defense" speech less than a month before his death. The last example supports William Odom's thesis that high levels of Soviet defense spending during the 1960s and 1970s can be better explained by the presence of a political leadership that shared the values and priorities of the military leadership than by significant independent political clout on the part of the military.[41] In contrast, past events under Khrushchev and current events under Gorbachev are inconsistent with Odom's thesis.[42] Similarly, the easy removals of popular General Staff chiefs such as Sokolovskii and Ogarkov over resource issues clearly show that

Soviet political leaders do not instinctively agree with the priorities of the military establishment, and give strong testimony to the relative political weakness of the military establishment.

A second, and closely related, implication of decision-making originating from Level 1 is that discussions and disputes over Soviet military doctrine—such as those currently taking place in the Soviet Union—play an important role in defense policy formulation.[43] While most students of Soviet military affairs have always assumed that Soviet defense spending was changed to fit doctrine, the structure of Level 1 decision-making also implies that Soviet military doctrine can be changed to fit economic assumptions. In essence: if you can't afford the requirements, change the threat. This is a well-known practice in the West, but one that is rarely considered for the Soviet Union.[44] There is good evidence, however, that this is precisely what happened during the late years of the Khrushchev era, and there can be little doubt that it is happening now under Gorbachev.[45]

A third implication concerns how the military burden is seen by the Soviet leadership. While Soviet leaders certainly know how various defense plans are projected to affect economic growth, they do not appear to have a ruble-based Soviet defense budget that can be related to Soviet national income in a meaningful way. In other words, the Politburo/Defense Council may not have precise knowledge about the size and scope of the defense burden as a share of national income (or GNP). For all the heat generated by Western debates over the share of Soviet GNP devoted to defense and its implications, such figures may not play any role in Soviet defense policy decisions or the leadership's perception of that burden. Feelings of pressure or constraint may be quite independent of such artificial reconstructions of the Soviet defense burden.

A fourth implication of Level 1 decision-making relates to the nature and scope of Level 2 decisions. The Ministry of Defense has little ability to shift resources among R&D, procurement, O&M, and construction once Level 1 decisions authorizing the defense plan have been made. This is in part a direct result of Gosplan's need to devise convergent forecasts of supply and demand, and of the incompatibility of the mix of indexes used in specifying defense allocations and constraints. Thus, when cutbacks appear in a resource category at Level 2, it is because there is a shortage in the general economy. Cutbacks within a specific service at Level 3 suggest either a general cutback or a redistribution among other missions and programs.

The fifth, and perhaps most important, implication associated with this level of decision-making concerns civil-military relations. The nature and timing of Level 1 decisions accentuate the importance of agenda-setting and option formulation in establishing the first-cut correlation between national economic requirements and defense requirements. Civil-civil and civil-military differences over "how much is enough" would be played out based on interpretations of the scale, scope, and immediacy of the national security threat to the Soviet Union—the strategic intent behind adversary military programs and the likelihood of a military confrontation or war. This level is also the place for debates over specific force-structure issues, weapon systems and programs, and deployments such as I believe we are seeing with the emergence of Gorbachev's new political thinking on security.[46]

Level 2 decisions. The distribution of Ministry of Defense resource allotments to the armed services as separate R&D, procurement, O&M, and construction "entitlements" allows the General Staff to enforce its own mission priorities across these categories. For example, if there was special concern for Strategic Defense Initiative–related countermeasures, the structure of Level 2 decision-making would enable the General Staff to earmark a certain portion of R&D resources to the strategic rocket forces and air defense forces for new program initiatives. These services would, in turn, be required to reflect this emphasis in their own R&D agendas. In other words, the General Staff's control of Level 2 decision-making enables it to enforce conformity among the armed services to the tenets of military strategy. Thus, economics plays an important role in the internal politics of the Ministry of Defense.

If we focus on changing priorities within the four major allotment categories—R&D, procurement, O&M, and construction—and assume that resources allotted to the categories are not fungible, then increased distributions to one armed service would require either an increase in resources to that allotment category or a corresponding decrease in resource distributions to other armed services. Without additional R&D allotments, increases in the air defense forces' R&D authorization would affect other service R&D resources rather than air defense procurement or O&M. Similarly, savings by the ground forces in O&M cannot be used to buy more tanks than specified by the plan. Thus, tradeoffs and opportunity costs operate within, not across, categories.[47]

Nowhere in the Soviet military-economic literature is there any suggestion that missions are compared on a cost- (or resource-) effectiveness basis. Level 2 strategic decisions on mission priorities do not appear to be influenced by relative resource requirements. If cost effectiveness is used at all, it is only to calibrate alternatives within individual programs. Thus, even if some future manifestation of SDI proved to be cost effective at the margin, there is no evidence that this would be an important consideration in the Soviet assessment of the priorities of missions associated with ballistic missiles. Indeed, one can only explain continued heavy Soviet investment in air defense by inattention to cost effectiveness considerations among missions.

Level 3 decisions. The main implication of the Level 3 decision-making process is that the armed services do not have much room to structure their forces or operations outside the framework established by the General Staff. Moreover, resource distribution is the tool the General Staff uses to control armed-service behavior; allowing it to create considerable synergy among the Soviet armed forces. The Soviet air forces, for example, are structured and trained to support the ground forces in ways that the United States will probably never see in its own forces.

A second major implication at Level 3 is that system capabilities are constrained not only by technology, but also by explicitly imposed resource and cost considerations. Thus the services must confront imposed quantity/quality tradeoffs from the very beginning of the design process. While it has always been assumed that the level of technology is frozen early in the Soviet design process to ensure producibility, it is probably required also to ensure conformity to imposed resource and cost ceilings.

Likewise, force readiness is strongly affected by imposed procurement and O&M constraints that cascade from Level 1 and 2 decisions. The armed services appear to buy the big-ticket items that are most closely tied to Level 2 decisions, and then skimp on procurement of the much-larger number of general procurement items. As a result, while combat power may not be affected by resource and cost constraints, force readiness and sustainability are significantly affected.

Gregory G. Hildebrandt

Models of the Military Sector in the Soviet Economy

T HE TRADITIONAL VIEW of the relationship between Soviet defense spending and the Soviet economy is that military activity is the priority good, and that the resource-allocation system is geared toward maintaining both high rates of military production and wartime mobilization potential. Historically, this relationship has repressed consumption and economic growth. It is important to remember that the basis for Soviet military activity is the Soviet economy itself, and that if it is unable to generate the technologies needed to produce the latest weapons, the country's superpower status may conceivably be placed at risk.[1]

However, many observers of the Gorbachev modernization program are now questioning whether defense activity continues to be the Soviet economy's priority good. It remains unclear to what extent *perestroika* is mainly concerned with long-run defense capability rather than general economic performance; indeed, this may never be fully understood. Just as it is unclear whether Stalin's "forced-draft" industrialization was motivated principally by a desire to support the Red Army or to build Soviet socialism, so too may the full rationale for the current modernization program remain a mystery.

Gregory G. Hildebrandt is a senior economist at the RAND Corporation.

To better understand the precise interaction between the defense sector and the Soviet economy, it is useful to employ both case studies and economy-wide models that contain defense activity as a key element. Detailed case studies provide both the institutional structure and qualitative dimensions of the defense-economic interaction. Economy-wide models, on the other hand, impose checks for consistency on the specified economic relations and associated data. Since these models are necessarily aggregate pictures of the Soviet economy, they may describe how members of the Soviet ruling elite view the tradeoffs between defense and economic performance.

Several large-scale, economy-wide models of the Soviet Union have been developed in the West. The first, SOVMOD, has been operated by SRI International and Wharton Econometric Forecasting Associates (WEFA); an outgrowth of this model, SOVECON, is now being used by PlanEcon. A third model, SOVSIM, was constructed by the U.S. Central Intelligence Agency (CIA). These three econometric-trend models of the Soviet economy can be viewed as sophisticated extrapolations from historical experience. Two large-scale, optimal-control models have also been developed, by the RAND Corporation and Decision-Science Applications (DSA); these models allocate resources to achieve a specified objective.[2]

Before discussing these large-scale, economy-wide models, it is helpful to begin with a simplified aggregate model. Besides its practical uses, this model highlights several general modeling uses—for example, to forecast Soviet economic performance through the year 2010 and to estimate the tradeoffs between the growth of defense spending and per capita consumption. I then discuss the econometric-trend models employed by WEFA, PlanEcon, and the CIA. These models maintain general consistency between production and final demand, but do not contain a detailed structure of the economy's input-output relationships. Particular attention is paid to the machinery sector because of its central role in producing military equipment, machinery investment, and consumer durables.

Because the econometric-trend models do not maintain consistency between the production of specific gross outputs and the fulfillment of a final demand vector, they are not effective in assessing the effect of bottlenecks. This is an important drawback, since the taut Soviet planning system is a planned disequilibrium system that generates pervasive bottleneck constraints. It is one of the considerations that led to the development of optimal-control models by DSA and RAND. Although these models meet the necessary consistency condition and have certain advantages over the econometric-trend models, as dynamic models that employ marginalist optimization methods they also minimize the impact of bottlenecks, and may not accurately portray the waste induced by taut central planning.

Instead of working around bottlenecks using optimization methods, the Soviets deal with these constraints using a priority allocation system. Work is underway at RAND to capture the nature of the Soviet priority system and shed light on the interplay between priority and bottlenecks. I provide some preliminary results of this analysis below. I also discuss the Soviet economy as a system in which the planners' priorities conflict with those of the managers within various sectors, which can generate a surplus of one or more material inputs in a nonpriority sector at the same time as shortages exist elsewhere. As a result, the defense sector may be motivated to support its priority status by vertically integrating the production processes that affect its output.

Aggregate Economic Model

The simplest model that can shed light on the broad nature of the interaction between defense and the Soviet economy consists of a single technological relationship in which GNP is produced with inputs of labor and capital combined at some level of total factor productivity. Final output is then distributed to consumption, defense, and investment, and the resulting investment is used to augment the remaining capital stock.

Figure 9.1 depicts such a model, and the next several figures portray some of the forecasts obtained using this model for the period 1990–2010. The two dashed lines in Figure 9.1 represent relationships not normally incorporated in economic models, but frequently mentioned in qualitative discussions. One of these lines represents a hypothesized relationship in which the Soviet defense sector's use of a significant proportion of high-technology resources impedes the growth and development of the more sophisticated manufacturing technologies that would otherwise increase total factor productivity. For example, each year's increment of high-quality research and development (R&D) engineers assigned to the defense sector might be more productively employed in the civilian sector. Not only might these engineers make the technologies of civilian enterprises more productive, but the increased openness of

FIGURE 9.1   Soviet Aggregate Economic Model

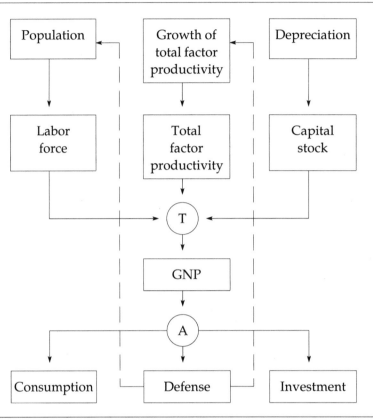

T=Technical relationship; A=Accounting relationship.
SOURCE: Author.

the civilian sector could result in a greater diffusion of the improved technologies than would be the case for the more specialized defense technologies. The potential civilian activities of these key technologies would, in fact, represent a type of public good, conferring benefits to the economy as a whole that would exceed either their defense or civilian cost.

The other dashed line in Figure 9.1 connects the defense sector to the Soviet population to suggest the interaction between the size of the military manpower pool and the civilian labor force, although this is not included in the present model. More difficult to assess quantitatively, but frequently mentioned, is the effect of military conscription on the socialization process and, in turn, on the effectiveness of the labor force.

FIGURE 9.2   Forecast Growth in Soviet GNP, 1990–2010 (at 4% annual
              growth in investment, 2% annual growth in defense)

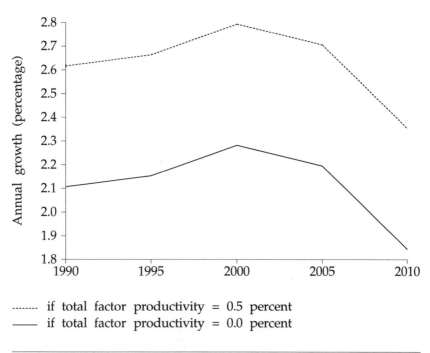

------- if total factor productivity = 0.5 percent
——— if total factor productivity = 0.0 percent

SOURCE: Author.

Quantitative estimates of this relationship and their effect on the model
would be worth further consideration.

We can now consider some of the empirical results obtained with
this model, ignoring the effects that might ensue from the links between
defense and both total factor productivity and labor effectiveness. To
illustrate the results for the time period 1990–2010, investment growth
is assumed to be 4 percent annually, which is consistent with the Twelfth
Five-Year Plan and might be a reasonable investment rate to assume for
the forecast period if the modernization program succeeds.[3] An annual
growth rate of 2 percent in defense spending is also assumed, which is
roughly consistent with a stable military-force structure and routine
force modernization.

In Figure 9.2, forecasts of GNP growth are provided for two alternative growth rates of total factor productivity. Recent historical experi-

FIGURE 9.3   Forecast Growth in Soviet per Capita Consumption,
              1990–2010 (at 4% annual growth in investment, 2%
              annual growth in defense)

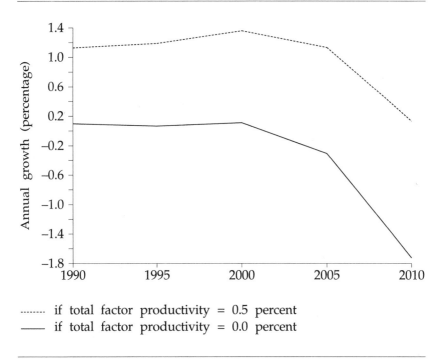

```
------- if total factor productivity = 0.5 percent
——— if total factor productivity = 0.0 percent
```

SOURCE: Author.

ence suggests negligible or possibly even negative growth in total factor
productivity in the Soviet economy. In other words, output has grown
no faster than the combined growth of labor and capital, and thus the
production process that combines these inputs has become no more
efficient. The bottom curve in Figure 9.2 can be viewed as a simple
extrapolation of historical experience on the premise of static efficiency
conditions rather than declining ones. The upper curve assumes that the
modernization program is reasonably successful and the growth of total
factor productivity amounts to 0.5 percent per year. Such a rate would
have approximately the same effect as a one-third increase in the marginal productivity of capital in the initial forecast year, and is slightly
lower than the growth productivity experienced by the United Kingdom
during the first half of the 1980s.

Note that the growth rate begins to decline in the twenty-first century as the Soviets encounter their third demographic shock since World War II. Such long-range forecasts should be treated with special caution, but it is important to be alert to impending demographic problems. The most important uncertainty, though, concerns the assumed growth of total factor productivity. Unfortunately, there is no systematic way of projecting the future value of this key variable, and each analyst must decide how much weight to give recent performance and other factors that may affect Soviet economic prospects.

Figure 9.3 contains forecasts of the growth in per capita consumption under the same two scenarios of factor productivity. Per capita consumption will remain flat and negligible if there is no growth in total factor productivity, but it can increase by 1 percent annually for the remainder of this century if total factor productivity increases by 0.5 percent annually. Again, Soviet economic performance is seen to decline during the twenty-first century as a result of the demographic shock.

This aggregate model can be used to illustrate the effect of any given growth rate of defense spending on the behavior of any other variable determined in the model. Figure 9.4 describes the tradeoff relationship between growth in defense spending and in per capita consumption. Based on the underlying assumption that investment continues to grow at 4 percent per year, GNP growth would remain constant under the two alternative assumptions about the growth of total factor productivity.

Figure 9.5 provides a hypothetical linear production-possibility curve (PPC) for consumption versus defense that applies to this model. Even if one is willing to assume that the prices used in the model reflect the initial rate of productive transformation, a more conventional view of the actual tradeoff relationship would be that depicted by the curved line tangent to the linear PPC at the current output level. This curve depicts an increasing marginal cost of defense in terms of consumption foregone as the defense sector is expanded. In many cases, however, one is not interested in analyzing major increases or decreases in the level of defense activity over a short period of time, but rather in assessing the effect of marginal changes in growth rates. Provided the underlying increments of labor and capital are reasonably transferable between defense and consumption, the linear PPC assumption of the aggregate model may not be very misleading.

On the other hand, it may not be realistic to expect the prices used to measure Soviet economic activity to reflect the true tradeoff relationship. Figure 9.5 also contains a tradeoff based on the assumption that

FIGURE 9.4   Soviet Growth Alternatives, 1990–2010 (at 4% annual
               growth in investment)

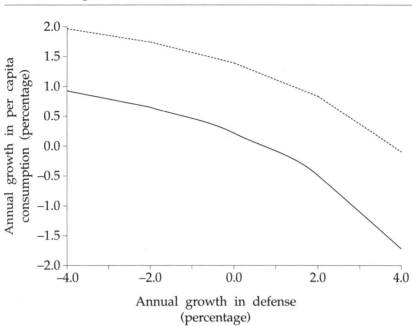

Annual growth in defense
(percentage)

------- if total factor productivity = 0.5 percent
——— if total factor productivity = 0.0 percent

SOURCE: Author.

defense goods are underpriced. The effect of such underpricing would
be to understate the burden of defense spending. Although there is a
belief within the intelligence community that defense prices are a reasonable measure of opportunity cost in the base year, the tradeoff
between defense and nondefense goods may change over time. In fact,
the intelligence community has recently concluded that the Soviet defense burden is higher in 1982 rubles than when measured in 1970 rubles.
So the two tradeoff curves in Figure 9.5 may depict the change in slope
that occurred between 1970 and 1982.

       The role of defense priority on the tradeoffs also has a bearing on
the slope and position of the PPC. The priority system has smoothed the
flow of resources to the defense sector. As all final demands that are
produced cannot receive priority treatment, this special attention is itself

FIGURE 9.5   Production-Possibility Curves of Aggregate Economic
              Model

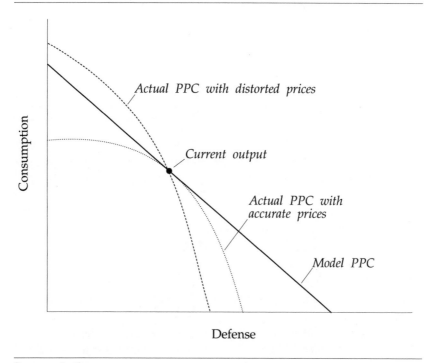

Defense

SOURCE: Author.

a scarce resource that would have an implicit shadow price that would
not, however, be adequately reflected in the cost of defense goods. The
result would be a further underpricing of defense activity.[4]

Econometric-Trend Models

To understand the common structure of the econometric-trend models,
it is helpful to abstract from the separate sectors, such as agriculture,
energy, and trade. A stylized version of the econometric-trend models
can be described using only two sectors, machinery and "other." Machinery is emphasized because consumer durables, machinery investment, and most defense procurement are assumed to be produced in this
sector. Figure 9.6 contains our simplified representation of the econometric-trend models. In this model, labor and investment are allocated

to the machinery and other sectors based on historical trends. Each sector's resulting capital stock and employment produces the added values that compose GNP. Given the investment determined by the model and defense spending, consumption is the residual.

Focusing on the left side of Figure 9.6, which depicts the machinery sector, the model links the value added produced in this sector to final demand using a historical factor. This final demand is divided among civilian machinery investment, consumer durables, and military machinery.[5] Military machinery consists mainly of weapons and supporting military equipment, associated spare parts, and capital repair. This category is nearly identical to military procurement, except that it may include some R&D prototypes built within the machinery sector, and exclude military ordnance, which is part of procurement but would not be contained within the machinery sector. The econometric-trend models assume that the three types of final machinery demand can be exchanged for each other on a ruble-for-ruble basis. My earlier comments about the linear versus curved PPC apply to machinery final demand as well, as do those about the arguable accuracy of defense prices. If the prices employed are reasonably accurate and the analysis is conducted in terms of growth tradeoffs, the forecasts are not likely to be seriously in error.

For example, all of the final demand elements of the machinery sector are produced with the aid of machine tools that are also produced within this sector. In fact, additions to the machinery sector's capital stock consist, in significant part, of the output of the machine-tool branch. In growth-tradeoff analysis, the new machine tools produced must be transferable, and it is probably not unreasonable to assume that there is sufficient flexibility within the machine-tool branch to reorient new output during an extended planning period. To the extent that this is not possible, however, one might obtain somewhat distorted results. A detailed analysis of the Soviet machine-tool branch might shed some light on this important question.

In operating the econometric-trend models, one would initially specify the levels of output over time for consumer durables and military machinery; the remainder of machinery final demand would then equal machinery investment, which would augment the civilian capital stock and contribute to economic growth. By changing the military-machinery trend to a different growth path, one can calculate the effect of such a reallocation of resources on economic performance. In a given period, a one-ruble reduction in military machinery would increase machinery

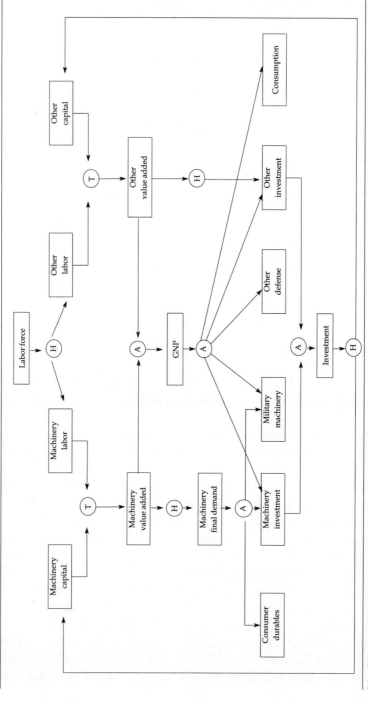

FIGURE 9.6 Simplified Soviet Econometric–Trend Model

H = Historical relationship; T = Technological relationship; A = Accounting relationship. SOURCE: Author; see also note 6 in text.

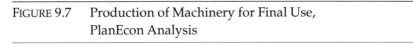

FIGURE 9.7   Production of Machinery for Final Use,
              PlanEcon Analysis

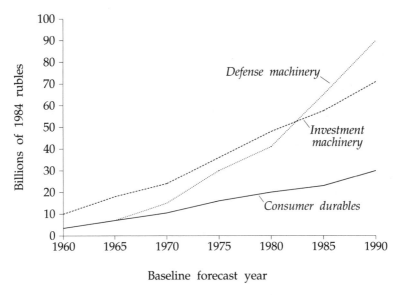

Baseline forecast year

SOURCE: Author; see also note 6 in text.

investment by one ruble. The increased civilian investment would, in turn, increase the civilian capital stock by one ruble. GNP would then rise by the marginal productivity of civilian capital. Alternatively, one could shift the defense ruble into consumer durables and obtain a ruble of extra consumption. In this case GNP would not change, because there has been no change in capital formation. All of this seems reasonably straightforward; the problem is that the Soviets do not publish data on military machinery. The CIA uses a building-block methodology to estimate this variable, and then incorporates the resulting series into the estimated final demand of the machinery sector. PlanEcon, on the other hand, employs a residual method that maintains consistency between final demand and its three components.[6]

It turns out there that there is sufficient uncertainty associated with the structure of machine-building final demand that there may be some interplay between the data available and the structure of the model selected. To illustrate this phenomenon, let us consider Figure 9.7, which was recently published by PlanEcon. The graph includes defense machinery, investment machinery, and consumer durables for the histori-

FIGURE 9.8   Comparison of CIA Estimate of Soviet Defense
Procurement with PlanEcon Estimate of Soviet Defense
Machinery

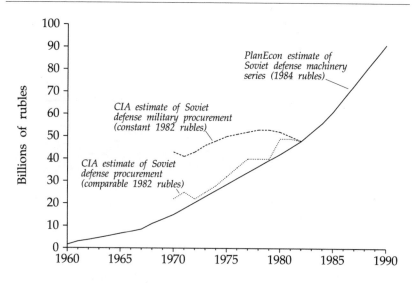

SOURCE: Author; see also note 6 in text.

cal period 1960–1985 and the forecast period 1986–1990. The defense
machinery series in this graph is estimated as a residual, given estimates
of the machinery sector's final demand total and of consumer durables
and machinery investment. The estimates are provided in 1984 rubles.

It is important to note that the defense machinery series experienced
sustained growth during the period 1974–1984, when the intelligence
community was reporting that procurement expenditures were flat. It is
therefore interesting to plot the PlanEcon defense machinery series on
the same graph as the CIA's military procurement estimates in both
comparable and constant 1982 rubles (Figure 9.8). The comparable ruble
measure is developed using the Soviet price deflator, whereas the constant 1982 series is developed using the CIA's price deflator. The PlanE-
con series and the CIA comparable ruble series are actually quite similar
over the relevant time periods. As expected, the CIA series in 1982
constant-resource rubles is fairly flat from 1974 to 1982. Indeed, it is the
agency's view that the difference between the comparable and constant
ruble series can be accounted for by the 5 percent inflation rate that has
affected military procurement.

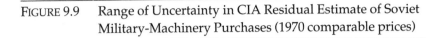

FIGURE 9.9   Range of Uncertainty in CIA Residual Estimate of Soviet
              Military-Machinery Purchases (1970 comparable prices)

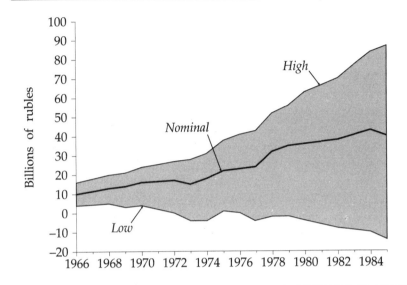

NOTE: Comparable prices represent the Soviet method of converting industrial
output from current prices to constant prices. These prices, however, reflect
considerable inflation.
SOURCE: Bonnie K. Matosich; see note 7 in text.

Although the issue seems at first to concern the difference between
comparable and constant rubles, the CIA has recently argued that there
is substantial uncertainty associated with the residual estimation technique. Figure 9.9 describes the range of uncertainty associated with the
residual estimate as seen by the CIA. In comparable prices, the growth in
military machinery can range from a negative figure to 9 percent. Presumably this increases confidence in the building-block estimates that the
CIA develops relative to those obtained using a residual method.[7]
    The other side of the coin, however, is that there is also uncertainty
associated with the estimates of civilian machinery. Figure 9.10 displays
CIA's calculations of the uncertainty associated with both military and
civilian machinery when these totals are estimated in current rubles.
Careful analysis would be required to determine how much of the
uncertainty about civilian machinery would remain if one accepted the
CIA's building-block estimate of procurement as a given. Some analysts,
whose estimates of the military-machinery residual are significantly

FIGURE 9.10 Range of Uncertainty in CIA Residual Estimate of Soviet
Military and Civilian Machinery Purchases (constant
1985 rubles)

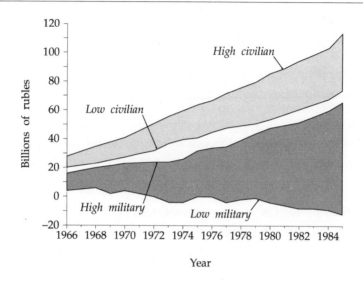

SOURCE: Bonnie K. Matosich; see also note 7 in text.

lower than the comparable-ruble building-block estimate, argue that the
model structure for the machinery sector depicted in Figure 9.6 is incor-
rect. They conclude that there is a defense final-assembly sector outside
the identified productive sphere of the economy that has been ignored
in much of the existing analysis. Interestingly, these analysts end up with
a total military-machinery estimate that, with final assembly included,
is roughly comparable to that obtained using the CIA building-block
approach.[8] None of these data uncertainties inspires confidence that the
model structure shown in Figure 9.6 is necessarily valid, but resolution
of the issue awaits further analysis.

Another issue associated with the econometric-trend models is that
there is only a partial connection between the production of gross
outputs and the achievement of final demands. Note in Figure 9.6 the
factor linking value added in the machinery sector to final demand,
based on historical data. Though frequently ignored in discussions of
Soviet models, this factor is quite important, and represents the simplified method used in the econometric-trend models to maintain consistency between gross outputs and final demand. While this factor is

frequently assumed to be constant, one might expect it to depend on the final-demand structure of the economy. For example, if nondurable consumption were to be significantly increased, one would expect a larger share of the machinery sector's intermediate output to be delivered to other sectors. This would reduce the ratio of final demand to value added in the machinery sector. However, only a relatively small portion of the machinery sector's intermediate output is used elsewhere; hence the approach taken by the model is a reasonable approximation.

A similar question concerns the allocation of investment and labor to different sectors of the economy. As indicated in Figure 9.6, labor and investment are allocated to sectors of the economy based on historical trends. Forecasting based on historical trends may be reasonable if one assumes that the final shares of GNP allocated to consumption, investment, and defense will continue in line with historical trends. But if these end-use shares change, or if one wants to explore the feasibility and implications of such a change, the model's historical allocations of investment and labor may no longer be relevant.

Optimal-Control Models

These considerations led to the development of optimal-control models by RAND and DSA. If there were a significant increase in defense at the expense of consumption, one would be interested in reallocating investment and labor to those sectors that directly and indirectly support defense and away from those that support consumption. Historical allocations of labor and investment might not be relevant. Furthermore, if bottlenecks emerged during the reallocation, perhaps because it became more costly to produce one of the supporting material inputs, this constraint should be taken into account.

Figure 9.11 shows a stylized representation of the optimal-control models. These models operate with between twenty-one and thirty-five sectors, but for exposition purposes the model is formulated in terms of machinery and "other" output. Outputs of these two sectors are produced with the labor and capital assigned to them. The model also contains the input-output relationships that tie the production of gross outputs to achievement of consumption, investment, and defense final demands. Rather than allocating investment and labor based on historical trends, the model bases the allocation on a choice of how best to achieve some objective, such as maximizing the growth rate of consump-

FIGURE 9.11   Simplified Soviet Optimal-Control Model

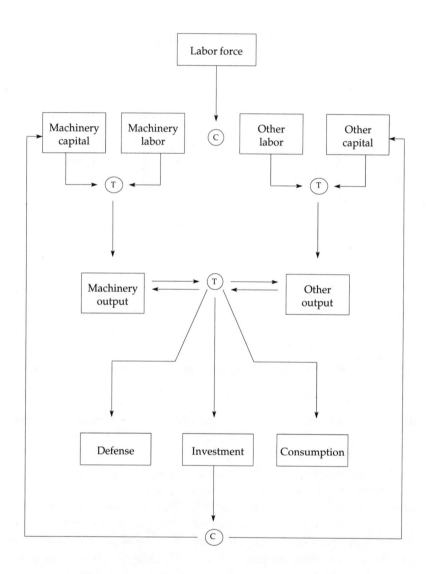

C = Choice relationship; T = Technological relationship.

SOURCE: Author, based on Gregory G. Hildebrandt, ed., *RAND Conference on Models of the Soviet Economy, October 11–12, 1984*, R-3322 (Santa Monica, Calif.: RAND, 1985).

FIGURE 9.12   RAND Analysis of the Effect of Imported Western
Machinery on Soviet Economic Performance, 1980–1990

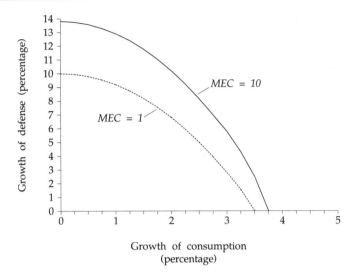

Growth of consumption
(percentage)

MEC = 1: Imported machinery as efficient as domestic machinery.
MEC = 10: Imported machinery ten times as efficient as domestic
machinery

NOTE: MEC=1: Imported machinery as efficient as domestic machinery.
MEC=10: Imported machinery ten times as efficient as domestic machinery.
SOURCE: Same as Figure 9.11.

tion subject to a specified growth rate for defense production. As the defense
growth rate is varied, allocations of investment and labor are changed, and
a different growth rate of consumption results.[9]

The optimal-control models have been used productively to evaluate
alternatives facing the Soviet leadership. Figure 9.12 presents one of the
RAND results.[10] Shown is the effect of Western machinery on Soviet
economic performance under alternative assumptions about the marginal
efficiency of imported capital. The tradeoff curve between consumption
and defense growth for the period 1980–1990 is depicted for two situations:
one in which the imported machinery is no more efficient than that produced domestically, and another in which the imported machinery is
assumed to be ten times as productive as that produced domestically. The
PPC expands more toward defense growth as the marginal efficiency of
imported capital increases, because when defense is emphasized, the mix

of imports favors machinery, which affects economic growth; when consumption is emphasized, the import mix favors agricultural goods, which do not influence economic growth in this model.

It is quite interesting that the curvature displayed in Figure 9.12 is similar to that presented in Figure 9.4, which we obtained using the aggregate model. For the marginal growth rates considered, there are no bottlenecks created that the optimal-control model cannot work around. The result is that total consumption and total defense can be exchanged on a ruble-for-ruble basis over the ten-year forecast period, as in the case of the aggregate model. This may happen because there is never a need to assign significant amounts of additional labor to fixed capital stocks and thereby induce significant diminishing marginal returns to labor and reductions in labor productivity. Rather, in this growth-tradeoff analysis, the underlying labor and capital increments can be allocated to different sectors over time. Although the capital/labor ratios in the two sectors would change as a result of the reallocations, the production functions that produce the defense and consumption final demands are sufficiently similar so that increasing costs do not ensue.

Thus the PPC for the ten-year period is close to linear, and if any bottleneck constraints are associated with the reallocation of resources, this model does not reflect them. Because the effect of such constraints on production is an important issue in the Soviet economy, it is necessary to know whether large changes in defense activity over several years can result in a measurable reduction in GNP. That effect would indicate a significant curvature in the PPC, as would be expected from bottleneck constraints.

DSA constructed an experiment using a thirty-five-sector optimal-control model in which there was a significant increase in defense activity over a five-year period. Table 9.1 presents a synopsis of the economic situation after three years relative to historical-trend levels.[11] Besides modest reductions in public and private consumption, significant reductions in investment occur. With labor/leisure choice incorporated in the DSA model, a 4 percent increase in the work week results. I calculated the change in GNP for this example and obtained a reduction of 4.4 percent from the historical-trend pattern. Whether this is a significant bottleneck effect can be inferred by comparing this result with that which would be obtained using an aggregate model, like that described in Figure 9.1, when investment is reduced and labor hours per week are increased: the trend pattern of GNP remains nearly unchanged. I therefore conclude that the effect of rising resource costs reduces GNP by less than 5 percent in this defense-surge situation. While the effect may be

TABLE 9.1   Percentage Change in Activity after Three Years of a
              Five-Year Surge in Soviet Defense Spending

	Percentage change
Government defense spending	+60
Government education and health spending	−10
Private consumption	−10
Capital investment	−33
New housing	−64
Labor hours per week	+4

SOURCE: Gregory G. Hildebrandt, ed., *RAND Conference on Models of The Soviet Economy, October 11–12, 1984*, R–3322 (Santa Monica, Calif.: RAND, 1985), p. 96.

slightly greater than that obtained from a marginal-growth-tradeoff analysis, it seems quite small considering the political environment that would induce such a defense-spending surge. We would expect the contraction in GNP to increase somewhat as the number of sectors in the model increased, but it is never quite clear how many sectors should be incorporated in a model in this type of analysis. Aggregate models may ignore the rising cost constraints, while very detailed models may fail to take account of the ability to make substitutions among material inputs and to shift capital capacities in the short run.

Priority Models

The reason the change in GNP obtained was so small is that optimal-control models minimize the effect of bottleneck constraints. If there is a shock to one of the economic sectors, optimal-control models assume that it is possible to increase output in any sector with appropriate additional amounts of labor and intermediate inputs. Labor and material inputs are reallocated to the appropriate sectors to minimize the cost of the shock.

In practice, the Soviets have historically reacted to shortages with a priority allocation system rather than with a system-wide optimization strategy. And when the Soviets specify an economic plan, the targets are set on the basis of "taut planning," so it seems reasonable to view them as reflecting capacity limits and assume that, during normal short-run operations of the economy, it is not possible to increase output significantly beyond the capacity level by simply using more labor and material inputs than specified in the plan.

As a result of these considerations and criticisms of existing models made at the RAND Conference on Models of the Soviet Economy, RAND has been developing alternative models.[12] Conference participants stated that existing models were based too extensively on Western economic concepts and constructs, and that it might be inappropriate to view Soviet decision-making as being based on marginalist principles when in fact there was a priority system in operation. This issue is dealt with by assuming that during the implementation phase of planning, the allocation of resources following a shock occurs sequentially according to priorities. First the number-one priority plan is fulfilled, and when its "needs" have been met, the second-priority plan is fulfilled, and so forth. This is a type of exogenous priority system in which the allocation of shortages is determined outside each sector's decision-making activities.

This formulation of the Soviet economy can be contrasted with several alternatives. In the marginalist model, resource allocation following a shock is based on plan prices. This is equivalent to maximizing GNP—or total final demand—following the shock, where GNP is valued using the prices contained in the economic plan. This criterion may not seem a realistic one to ascribe to the Soviet leadership; after all, part of the reason there is a priority system in the first place is that prices do not adjust following a shock, as would occur in a market economy, and the plan prices may no longer be useful guides to fulfilling the leaderships' objectives. Nevertheless, there is a type of endogenous priority system that operates in the Soviet economy that may tend to maximize GNP at plan prices. To understand how this system works in the marginalist model, recall that each enterprise employs *tolkachi*, whose task is to expedite the production process by obtaining shortage inputs. A *tolkach* can garner the most surplus during his transactions by first acquiring the material input of which a ruble results in the greatest increase in gross output; that is, by acquiring the input with the smallest input/output ratio. After having obtained this input, the attention of the *tolkach* would shift to the input with the second-lowest input/output coefficient. If each *tolkach* were successful in his endeavors, GNP at plan prices would be maximized.

Another alternative is a proportional-reduction model, in which the plan proportions are maintained during adjustment to the bottleneck. Although the Soviets apparently consider the principle of proportional growth in setting plans, adjustment to a shortage may not occur on this

TABLE 9.2   Four-Sector Planned Input-Output Values Used in
             Calculations of Prototype Model

From	To Light industry	To Infra-structure	To Heavy industry	To Defense
Light industry	0	0	10	0
Infrastructure	5	0	5	5
Heavy industry	15	0	0	5
Defense	0	0	0	0
Labor	30	5	20	5
Capital	10	10	15	5
Gross output	60	15	50	20

	Consumer	Investment	Defense	Final demand
Light industry	50	0	0	50
Infrastructure	0	0	0	0
Heavy industry	0	30	0	30
Defense	0	0	0	20
Total final demand				100
Labor				60
Capital				40

SOURCE: Author.

basis. It is nevertheless interesting to compare results obtained using the proportional-reduction model with the others, because they serve as a useful benchmark. This type of model can be illustrated using a proto-type four-sector input-output table that is assumed to be based on the economic plan. The model's sectors are light industry, infrastructure, heavy industry, and defense. Table 9.2 contains the input-output table used in the calculations. In this model, the defense sector is construed broadly to reflect not only the production and operation of weapons plus research, development, testing, and evaluation, but also the penetration of this sector into civil activities. Defense thus includes the design, construction, and location of industrial plant and infrastructure as well as expenditures on various types of mobilization preparation. Heavy industry produces many of the economy's material inputs, and the economy's investment goods are a final output of this sector. Light industry includes some intermediate inputs supporting other sectors, but this sector primarily produces the economy's consumer goods, including the agricultural commodities and consumer services produced for final demand. Infrastructure is a broad sector that includes not only such conventional categories as transportation and communications, but also those inputs that support much of the "civil" costs of military preparations. It also includes planning infrastructure that controls the priority allocation system. Infrastructure is a pure intermediate-input sector in which there are no deliveries to final demand.[13]

How should the sectoral priorities be ranked? Although the Soviets have not been explicit about this issue recently, a clear summary of Soviet supply priorities was made in 1967, only a few years after the start of the Brezhnev defense buildup:

1. military production and activities

2. current industrial production

3. consumption

4. material stocks and working capital

5. investment in repair activities, repair equipment, and technological change

6. capital construction[14]

The priority ranking used in this analysis is roughly consistent with the historical situation. Defense is assured first priority, heavy industry second, and consumption the lowest priority. The problems solved in the alternative models are represented in Table 9.3.

While many cases can be evaluated, we focus on the effect of a shock to the infrastructure sector in which the productivity of capital allocated to the sector declines by as much as 15 percent. For example, the shock might result from a transportation bottleneck. Figure 9.13 shows that, as the shock increases in size, defense output is maintained at plan (or target) values under the priority model. But reductions in defense do occur in the proportional-reduction model, and even more substantial reductions occur in the marginalist model. Figure 9.14 shows the impact

TABLE 9.3   Prototype Input-Output Optimization Problems
                Addressed by Alternative Models of the Soviet Economy

Marginalist and proportional-growth models	Priority model
Maximize	*Minimize*
defense + consumption + investment	deviation of defense from target deviation of heavy industry from target deviation of light industry from target
Subject to	*Subject to*
input-output relationships relevant labor and capital constraints relevant final demand constraints	input-output relationships relevant labor and capital constraints

SOURCE: Author.

of the capacity constraint on consumer-goods output. Target levels are met in the marginalist model; proportional cuts occur in the proportional-reduction model; and significant reductions occur in the priority model. A reduction in infrastructure capacity leads to more-than-proportional reduction in consumer goods. There is a supply-side consumption multiplier in operation in the priority model, and the consumer absorbs most of the shock associated with the infrastructure capacity shortage.

Figure 9.15 shows that a shock to the infrastructure sector can increase investment in the priority model: in this case, after fulfilling its deliveries to defense and to the lower-priority consumer-goods sector, the heavy-industry sector has capacity left over for investment. There is a slight increase in investment under the marginalist model, and the expected proportional reduction in the proportional-reduction model. Figure 9.16 shows that the greatest reduction of final demand (GNP) occurs in the priority model. Of course, the marginalist model, which maximizes GNP, achieves the greatest level of GNP for any level of capacity shortage, while the proportional-reduction model results in an expected reduction of GNP.

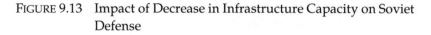

FIGURE 9.13   Impact of Decrease in Infrastructure Capacity on Soviet
Defense

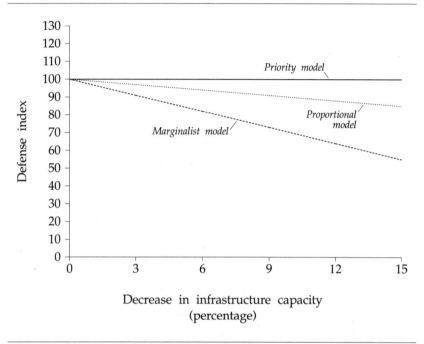

SOURCE: Author.

These models allow labor to flow across the sectors, but the capacity
constraints eliminate any advantages from short-run labor mobility that
result from a shock to infrastructure capacity. Figure 9.17 shows that
significant unemployment ensues in the priority model, in both the
infrastructure and consumer-goods sectors. The lowest level of unemployment occurs in the marginalist model, with the proportional-growth
model an intermediate case.

To summarize: in the priority model, under a shock to infrastructure
capacity, the defense target output level is achieved; such a shock can
have a multiplier effect on low-priority consumption; heavy-industry
priority can lift investment above target; there can be a multiplier
reduction in GNP; and significant underutilization of labor can occur.

The priority model portrays a basic tendency of the Soviet economy
to fulfill planners' objectives in what is called the exogenous priority
system. A countervailing tendency is for each sector, as a result of the
motivations of its managers as expressed through the behavior of the

FIGURE 9.14   Impact of Decrease in Infrastructure Capacity on Soviet
               Consumer Goods

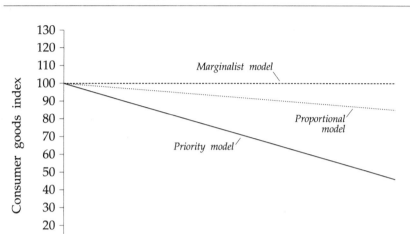

SOURCE: Author.

tolkachi, to fulfill its specified targets, which forms the endogenous priority system. With both systems in operation in the Soviet economy, there is clearly room for conflict. One force moves the system in the direction of leadership objectives; the other moves it toward the largest GNP. It is not surprising that this inconsistency can result in economic waste.

To explore the issue further, we consider a mixed shock to the economic system in which the capacity levels of both heavy industry and infrastructure are lower than the planned values. We then pass this shock through a pure (exogenous) priority model, a marginalist (endogenous) priority model, and a third, conflicting priority model. In this last model, we assume that the *tolkachi* of the light-industry sector are able to obtain the infrastructure services needed to fulfill their sector's plan; all other material inputs are allocated on the basis of exogenous priorities.

FIGURE 9.15   Impact of Decrease in Infrastructure Capacity on Soviet
Investment Goods

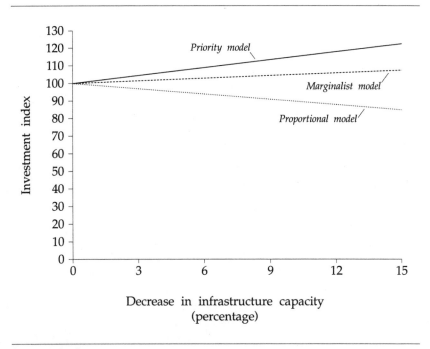

SOURCE: Author.

Figure 9.18 shows the final demand obtained as the size of the shock is increased. As expected, total final demand, or GNP, is highest in the endogenous priority model and lowest in the exogenous priority model. The conflicting priority model predicts a level of GNP somewhere between the two, and thus captures one of the important stylized facts of the Soviet economy: the existence of surplus material inputs in a sector while a general shortage exists. Figure 9.19 portrays the value of unused infrastructure that results from shocks of increasing size to the economy.

In the optimal-control models developed by RAND and DSA, all intermediate materials delivered to a sector are employed in the production of the gross outputs. We obtain the same result in the (exogenous) priority, marginalist (endogenous) priority, or proportional-reduction models. While these last three models do yield excess capacities and underemployed labor, each sector uses all of the delivered material inputs.

FIGURE 9.16   Impact of Decrease in Infrastructure Capacity on Soviet
               Final Demand

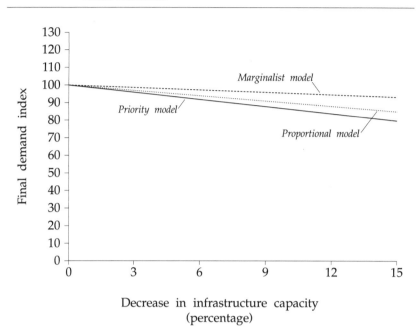

SOURCE: Author.

As shown in Figure 9.20, the defense sector's target output level is not achieved in either the conflicting priority model or the endogenous priority model. As in Figure 9.13, the defense target is achieved in the exogenous priority model. One should note that both the conflicting priority and endogenous priority models result in the same defense output level. Although the Soviets obtain additional total final demand in the conflicting priority model, the cost of this increase relative to that obtained in the exogenous priority model amounts to a reduction in defense output.

In conclusion, the conflict that exists from the two operating priority systems may hinder the Soviet leadership from achieving its defense goals. Clearly, this inconsistency between leadership objectives and economic outcome can be expected to have an effect on the organization of production in the Soviet economy. As David Holloway has argued, in the Soviet Union "demand and supply emanate from the same source": not only does demand call forth a supply of goods, as in a

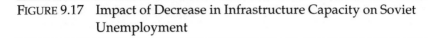

FIGURE 9.17   Impact of Decrease in Infrastructure Capacity on Soviet
Unemployment

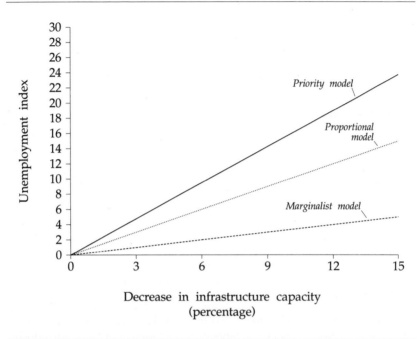

Decrease in infrastructure capacity
(percentage)

SOURCE: Author.

market economy, but the leadership also affects the nature of the supply institutions.[15]

One would therefore predict that the high-priority sector would have a vertically integrated production process in order to ensure that leadership objectives were achieved. This is precisely what has happened in the defense-machinery ministries, where production is "vertically integrated from basic industry to end product." This picture of the Soviet Union as a dual economy was also identified at the RAND conference as being inadequately captured by existing models.[16]

Embedded in this vertical integration is a significant amount of civilian production. The historical role of this civilian production capacity has been to act as a buffer should the defense sector need a surge in production. However, the leadership has made recent attempts to employ defense capabilities in the production of civilian goods in a clear effort to get the defense sector to provide assistance to the modernization program.[17] Indeed, several careful observers of the Gorbachev modern-

FIGURE 9.18   Impact of a Mixed Shock on Soviet Final Demand

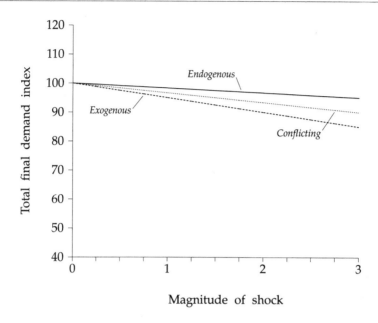

Magnitude of shock

NOTE: Capacity of heavy industry and infrastructure are lower than planned values. A magnitude 1 shock corresponds to a 1% reduction in heavy industry and a 3.33% reduction in infrastructure. Higher magnitude shocks are correspondingly greater.
SOURCE: Author.

ization program have argued that Soviet priorities have changed under Gorbachev. As Abraham Becker says of the General Secretary, "In the tens of thousands of words issued from his mouth during the first two years, and in the actions of the regime accompanying them, it was apparent that his top priority was economic growth, followed by consumer welfare; the defense budget appeared to be a distant third."[18] To support a new priority system, Gorbachev must contend with the priority institutions that have already been established to effectuate production in the defense sector. For example, he would certainly have to deal with the status of the Military Industrial Commission (VPK), which has effectively operated the military priority system.

To monitor developments in this area, it might be advisable to follow the activities of the Bureau of Machine Building to determine whether it becomes a competitor to the Military Industrial Commission. One

FIGURE 9.19   Value of Unused Infrastructure Inputs Resulting from
Mixed Shock to the Soviet Economy

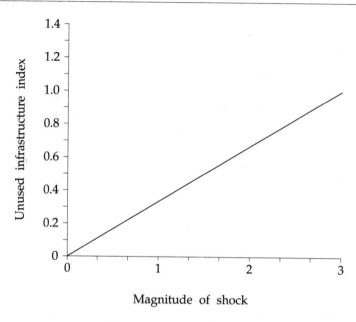

Magnitude of shock

NOTE: A magnitude 1 shock corresponds to a 1% reduction in heavy industry and a 3.33% reduction in infrastructure. Higher magnitude shocks are correspondingly greater.
SOURCE: Author.

should also look for tendencies toward vertical disintegration of the defense-machinery ministries.

Conclusion

In this examination of econometric-trend and optimal-control models against the background of an aggregate model and the foreground of priority models, I have attempted to clarify the role of these models in analysis of the defense sector and the Soviet economy. As one moves from the aggregate model to the econometric-trend models, the structure of the machinery sector is elaborated. This forces the analyst to be sensitive to potentially direct competition between machinery investment and military machinery. In light of the Gorbachev modernization

FIGURE 9.20   Impact of a Mixed Shock on Soviet Defense

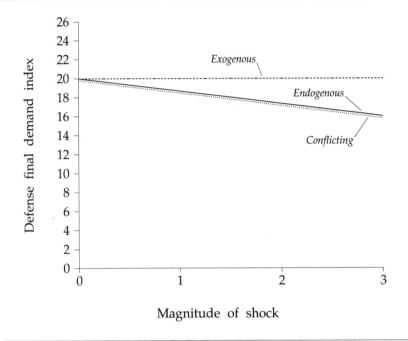

NOTE: A magnitude 1 shock corresponds to a 1% reduction in heavy industry and a 3.33% reduction in infrastructure. Higher magnitude shocks are correspondingly greater.
SOURCE: Author.

program, it is helpful to keep these two types of machinery closely linked. The machinery sector also involves dual-use technologies that support both the defense and civilian sectors, as an outgrowth of the modernization program. The simple structure of the machinery balance has also stimulated much of the recent data analysis, which may ultimately call for a redefinition of this sector.

Analysis of the econometric-trend models also helps in understanding the link between gross outputs and final demand. The models' simple method of dealing with this link may be satisfactory if economic changes are not so pronounced as to induce dramatic shifts in the ratio of value added to final demand. A related question is how relevant historical allocations of labor and investment are to the different sectors when either forecasting or scenario analyses are conducted. While we would expect bottlenecks to result from dramatic shifts in labor and investment allocations, the optimal-control models, which pay close attention to the links between final demand and gross output, do not seem adept at capturing these effects. By minimizing the effect of bottlenecks on the economy, these models yield tradeoff relationships that are similar to those obtained with either the aggregate or econometric-trend models.

The search continues, then, for methods of addressing bottlenecks, and particularly for the Soviet priority planning response to this common feature of taut central planning. As the discussion of the prototype priority models suggested, a priority planning system can exercise leverage on the output of a low-priority sector; reductions in capacity that generate a bottleneck can result in more-than-proportional reductions in both consumption and GNP. The next step is to build a dynamic version of a priority model.

Our priority model, based on a historical set of priorities, can also serve as a benchmark should the priority system change. We will attempt to use the dynamic model under development to test whether such a change has occurred. We need to recognize, however, that a change in priorities will not be easy for the Soviets. The conflict between the exogenous and endogenous priority systems has led the Soviets to put in place organizational forms that help achieve the leadership's objectives. Although the waste in the system indicates that they have not been completely successful, but due to the existing organizational forms, significant costs would probably be associated with any change in priority.

The Long-Run Decline in Soviet R&D Productivity

I N THE 1980s the Soviet Union suffered a setback in an area in which it had previously been spectacularly successful: military competition with the West. A revolution in military technology, American rearmament, and the announcement of the Strategic Defense Initiative (SDI) threatened the only Soviet achievement of the 1970s, military parity.[1] The boastful official cliché of "a new correlation of forces in the world" gave way to the alarmist "threat of becoming a second-rate power." It was this external challenge, rather than domestic crisis, that spurred Soviet leadership into the current cycle of reforms.[2]

In the past the Soviet Union managed to match all Western revolutions in military technology: tanks and aviation in the prewar period, nuclear weapons in the 1940s, missiles in the 1950s, and the numerous improvements of the 1960s and 1970s. The gap between the technological levels of weapons deployed by the USSR and by the United States was narrowing, even though the technological capabilities of the Soviet economy continued to lag considerably behind those of the United States.[3] The Soviet system was thought to be uniquely suited to the task of building up military power in a relatively poor economy. Why did

Vladimir Kontorovich is assistant professor of economics at Haverford College.

the Soviet leadership decide that the current military challenge could not be met without radical changes in the system?[4]

Responding to the military-technological challenge requires money and knowledge. Historically, resources for the buildup of new military plants were generated by economic growth, together with (in the 1930s and 1940s) holding consumption in check. Gaps in knowledge were compensated by additional resource allocations. But today, resources are lacking, and there is a crisis in the production of knowledge. If we viewed the economic situation as the Soviets themselves do, matching the external challenge would seem to lead to an economic catastrophe. (The standard, relatively optimistic, Western view of the Soviet economy would lead to a much less stark conclusion.[5]) The economy has been stagnant since the late 1970s;[6] living standards have been stagnant through the 1970s; and investment in the economy stopped growing in the mid-1970s and declined in the early 1980s.[7] Investment needs to be increased to offset the aging of capital stock and future economic contraction. Similarly, increases are needed in investment in infrastructure and public consumption to reverse the environmental and health crises. Cutting investment in favor of military buildup would precipitate an economic decline and undermine the very base of the buildup. Cuts in consumption, besides further undermining economic incentives, would generate the sort of political repercussions that all leaders after Stalin have tried to avoid.

Another factor that has made a strong response to the Western challenge impossible (short of a war-type mobilization) and alarmed the Soviet leadership into unprecedented reforms is a crisis in technological advances in research and development (R&D). But unlike other aspects of the current crisis (political, economic, and health), R&D has not been much noted by Western observers.[8] During 1951–1985, R&D employment increased more than sixfold, and expenditures by a factor of twenty-eight. The R&D sector grew much faster than the rest of the economy, swallowing up an ever-greater share of Soviet resources (Table 10.1). This emphasis continued even as economic growth slowed down.

Nonetheless, the world's largest R&D effort is doing poorly. Basic science is lagging increasingly behind world standards.[9] R&D establishments in production ministries, which receive 90 percent of the total funding for science, are largely unable to conduct applied research. They engage in trivial development projects, unrelated tasks, or even outright fraud.[10] Indicators of R&D output have been declining[11] or growing more slowly than those of inputs.[12] The number of registered discoveries

TABLE 10.1   Soviet Inputs into R&D as a Percentage of National
              Resources, Selected Years

	Employment (nonprivate)	National income
1950	1.05	1.35
1960	2.09	2.73
1965	2.74	3.62
1970	3.02	4.10
1975	3.44	4.79
1980	3.49	4.91
1985	3.50	5.04

SOURCE: *Narodnoe khoziaistvo SSSR* (Moscow: Finansy i statistika), various years
(abbreviated *Narkhoz*).

(the highest achievements of basic research in the natural sciences) has
been declining since the 1960s.[13] The number of prototypes of machines,
equipment, instruments, and computers created each year—the main
output of R&D in the machine-building sector[14]—has been declining
since the mid-1960s (Table 10.2). The ratio of all prototypes to total R&D
employment declined 67 percent from 1961 to 1985. Finally, the number
of patents granted is an indication—one that admittedly must be used
with care—of the results of applied R&D across all fields judged to be
practically useful and novel.[15] The number of patented inventions grew
over the long run, but declined in the early 1980s, and the number of
patents granted to Soviets abroad declined by 10.8 percent between 1981
and 1985.[16] There were fewer inventions per researcher in 1985 than in
1950 (Table 10.3).

R&D Productivity

Both inputs and outputs of R&D elude precise measurement. While
R&D expenditures or employment are customarily used as measures of
input, the choice of output measures is more problematic. Existing
quantitative characteristics of output (patent counts, number of innovations, bibliometric data) have two common shortcomings: incomplete
coverage of R&D activity, and the variable importance of particular
results.[17] These shortcomings do not preclude the use of the existing data
as indicators of true output, however.[18] An indicator is a function of the

TABLE 10.2   Growth in the Number of Prototypes Created, Absolute
and per Unit of Input, 1956–1985 (percentage)

	Machines	Instruments
1956–1960	167.1	502.6
1961–1965	57.2	181.7
1966–1970	−6.4	−12.8
1971–1975	−2.4	−15.7
1976–1980	−8.0	−5.5
1981–1985	−5.1	9.5
Prototypes per R&D employee, 1965–1984[a]		
Instruments	−74	
Chemical	−55	
Electrotechnical	−60	
Light and food	−53	
Automobile	56	
Machine tools	−29	

a. Selected machine-building ministries.
SOURCES: *Narkhoz,* various years; V. M. Logachev, et al., *Finansy i khozraschet v NII KB* (Moscow: Finansy i statistika, 1987), p. 186.

true output measure *and* a random disturbance. In order to separate the change in output from "noise," several different indicators need to be used.[19] In this section, I consider the biases likely for two output indicators of Soviet R&D—patents granted and prototypes of new equipment—to establish the reliability of conclusions about productivity based on these indicators and other information available about R&D since the 1950s.

Prototypes created in the 1980s are more valuable to society than those created in the 1950s. Machines built according to later prototypes will be more productive and perform new functions, as well as having other advantages. This improvement can be attributed only in small part, however, to currently employed scientists and engineers. Today's engineers design better computers than their colleagues thirty years ago, not because they are more productive, but because they have access to a greater stock of knowledge. Because we cannot quantify this stock of knowledge, it is an input into R&D that we are forced to omit. Scientists and engineers constantly produce prototypes, however, and each adds

TABLE 10.3   Soviet Patents Granted per Thousand Researchers, 1950–1985.

	R&D employees	Science workers	With two-year lag	
			R&D employees	Science workers
1950	16.25	71.38	—	—
1955	3.33	14.74	3.84	17.20
1958	6.05	28.52	7.40	33.77
1960	5.95	29.61	7.84	36.91
1965	5.26	20.76	5.82	24.38
1970	11.74	40.96	12.71	46.18
1975	8.18	27.06	8.86	29.86
1980	23.52	75.00	25.31	78.39
1985	18.88	57.67	19.24	60.07

SOURCE: V. Kontorovich, *Research and Development Productivity in the USSR: Causes of Decline since the 1960s and the Prospects for the 1980s* (Princeton, N.J.: Command Economic Research, 1987), p.110.

slightly to the total stock of knowledge. One can approximate their output by the number of prototypes produced.

Moreover, in the case of the Soviet Union, many of the prototypes produced represent only slight improvements on old models. Less than a third of applied R&D projects in industrial R&D has been based on new domestic inventions, and this share has been declining. The dominant development strategy has been to copy existing foreign models.[20] The share of prototypes "exceeding the domestic and world technological level"—that is, really new—is low and has been declining, from 18 percent in 1976–1980 to 14 percent in 1986.[21] This indicator is blatantly biased upward, so its decline is more likely to reflect a reality than its increase.[22] There is no evidence that increases in the average importance or value of a prototype explain their decline in number.

Similarly, there is no evidence that inventions have become increasingly important; in fact, the opposite is the case. Expert opinion is virtually unanimous in the belief that inventions became more trivial in the 1970s. Savings per implemented invention declined between 1964 and 1974, and also apparently in the early 1980s. This indicator is admittedly an indirect one. One could imagine a situation in which the average advance of inventions increased, but enterprises increasingly chose smaller ones for implementation. In such a situation, savings per implemented invention would be a misleading indicator of inventiveness. But such a situation is hypothetical. Soviet enterprises do prefer less-significant inventions because they are less disruptive to the production process. Moreover, the savings from implementation are greatly exaggerated; the actual decline in the number of truly new products and processes was probably larger than the data show. Finally, the number of inventions is a planning indicator, one that has been increasing in importance over time. Such an incentive mechanism from the planning authorities is bound to produce greater numbers of inventions at the expense of quality.[23]

A related phenomenon concerns increasing complexity. Soviet experts state that the increasing complexity of machines accounts for some—but by no means all—of the decline in the prototype/researcher ratio.[24] To the extent that larger and more-complex machines are more valuable, the decline in the ratio of prototypes to researchers should not be interpreted as a decline in productivity of R&D. Yet successive generations of machines need not be more complex. Progression from mechanical to electrical to electronic principles actually simplifies machines and instruments. When machines do become more complex, they need not necessarily become harder to design. Standard assemblies, parts, and subsystems used in different machines make development simpler; a standard microprocessor, for example, is used in hundreds of different designs. Standard elements introduce economies of scope into the development of new machines. Finally, designers are now better equipped with mathematical modeling, computers, and testing equipment, all of which increase their productivity. There is no obvious reason for more valuable machines to require more resources for their development.

Productivity data in Tables 10.2 and 10.3 might be misleading if inputs were shifted to R&D activities that produced outputs other than patents and prototypes. But the opposite has been the case. Resource shifts have favored technical disciplines and applied research and development. This is where prototypes and most inventions are produced.[25] There have been increases in the educational level of R&D employees and in the importation of knowledge from abroad (an input to R&D that is hard to quantify).[26] If data allowed us to take these changes into account, the ratios of prototypes and patents per researcher would have declined even more.

R&D Productivity Decline, 1950–1985

In most developed countries, the number of patents granted to citizens, as well as the number of patents per scientist and engineer and per dollar of R&D expenditures, declined in 1967–1980.[27] These world trends cannot explain developments in Soviet R&D, however, since its productivity lags behind that of the developed countries, and because measures of R&D output in the USSR generally represent advances in national, rather than world, knowledge.[28] Even if world R&D froze, Soviet R&D could still move ahead until it caught up. The decline in Soviet R&D productivity must be explained in terms specific to that country. This section explores the decline and its specific causes.

Commands and R&D resources.[29] In order to secure military might and economic advancement, the Soviet leadership generously allocated resources to the sector producing technological advances. The main recipients of this largesse were production ministries. Their research and design facilities expanded faster than R&D as a whole, and grew to absorb about 80 percent of the total resources of this sector.[30] Ministries attempted to guide their growing R&D empires by the same command methods used in production, but they could not determine the exact uses of these resources; this had to be decided at lower levels of the hierarchy. Such methods proved ineffective for R&D, with its inherent uncertainty.[31] Moreover, ministry and enterprise managers, who are oriented toward short-run production targets, were largely uninterested in innovation, and neither did customer demand guide R&D.[32] Without incentives for productive use, R&D resources were directed to the internal goals of the ministries and enterprises themselves.

Table 10.4 lists the specific causes of the R&D slowdown; the numbers in parentheses correspond to those in the following discussion. (1) Research institutes were founded, and existing institutes expanded for the sake of fashion and prestige, without regard for the scientific basis for research or the availability of qualified personnel, equipment, or facilities. Expansion became institutionalized, with planning procedures encouraging steady growth of inputs irrespective of need. (2) Ministries and enterprises diverted R&D resources to non-R&D uses, such as current production, planning and management, clerical support, and agricultural, construction, and sanitation work. (3) Resources were directed toward minor, routine, or trivial projects. (4) R&D organizations were often left without effective guidance, spinning their wheels, slum-

TABLE 10.4   Causes of Decline in R&D Productivity

	Civilian R&D	Military R&D
(1) Unwarranted expansion of inputs	yes	yes
(2) Diversion of inputs to non-R&D uses	yes	?
(3) Trivialization of R&D	yes	no
(4) Ineffective and fraudulent uses	yes	no
(5) Monopolization	yes	no
(6) Changes in design standards	yes	yes
(7) Coordination burden on designers	yes	yes
(8) Increasing share of resources in management and information systems	yes	yes
(9) Aging of research portfolio	yes	yes
(10) Aging of researchers	yes	yes
(11) Increasing use of researchers in support roles	yes	?
(12) Decline in the quality and motivation of employees	yes	no

SOURCE: V. Kontorovich, *Research and Development Productivity in the USSR: Causes of Decline since the 1960s and the Prospects for the 1980s* (Princeton, N.J.: Command Economic Research, 1987).

bering, or engaging in outright fraud. (5) Ministries, themselves monopolistic suppliers, supported the monopoly of their head R&D institutes in corresponding fields, hampering the work of outsiders.[33]

Alternative guidance mechanisms. "Scientific methods of planning and managing" were introduced in the late 1960s. Consisting of a complex set of rules and procedures, the new methods and mounting problems of operating in a command economy added to the management load, diverting time and energy from actual R&D. (6) Mandatory standards regulating the appearance of drawings have grown increasingly demanding and changed frequently. Altering drawings to conform to the latest revision has become a major drain on designers' time. (7) Designers need an increasing number of approvals, including the approval of supply organs or producers for parts included in design, an extremely time-consuming process. (8) New planning and management procedures implemented in the 1970s have increased the burden on R&D personnel of reporting and record-keeping. R&D organizations have also been burdened with "economic methods of management," including management information systems. Increasingly formal requirements for patent applications and the growing bias of the patent office in favor of "planned inventions" have squeezed out individual inventors, who usually generate the most radical ideas. The number of simple projects with a short payoff period has increased at the expense of radical innovations.[34] The introduction of bonuses tied to the implementation of innovations has had the same effect.

The ballooning of the R&D sector prompted a set of administrative restrictions on inputs into R&D. Arbitrary quotas for different kinds of personnel were imposed as a way of enforcing labor savings, eliminating technicians, blue-collar workers, and administrative and clerical staff from R&D organizations. (11) As a result, scientists and engineers have been involved in more support work at the expense of their direct duties. As the R&D sector grew larger, new restrictions were introduced. Hiring was frozen in the early 1980s, and the establishment of new R&D organizations was subject to approval by the Council of Ministers.

These restrictions interact with the organization of R&D in a perverse way. Soviet R&D is characterized by a rigid organizational structure, security of tenure, and wide discretion exercised by researchers in the choice of projects without adequate peer review, which perpetuates obsolete or fruitless projects and research. (9) Founding an institute or department is a good way to start a new direction of research, but restrictions on expansion result in the aging of the national portfolio of research projects, and an increasing share of exhausted topics. Similarly, the hiring freeze, coupled with secure tenure, leads to an increase in the average age of researchers.[35] (10) The single largest group of researchers, hired during the height of expansion in the late 1950s and early 1960s, is entering a period of declining individual productivity. Without an influx of new blood, this group will dominate R&D manpower in the years to come. (12) The decline in relative pay in the R&D sector and the parallel decline in the prestige of science and engineering as occupations is another major cause of deterioration in productivity.[36]

As Soviet R&D, subordinated to the production ministries, became less able to produce results, the leadership and production ministries turned to the academies for the solution of (often trivial) technological problems. Receiving less than 10 percent of total R&D resources, academics are charged with basic research. The Union Academy and some republican academies maintain high research productivity through tradition, professional ethics, and selectivity. Their increasing involvement in the direct service of production diverts their limited resources away from their mission of basic research and subjects them to the same influences that have trivialized applied R&D.[37]

Summary. The debasement of applied R&D and the ongoing corruption of academic science are not the results of a policy mistake; they reflect a genuine dilemma of a command economy in an age of rapid technological progress. To benefit production, R&D must be in close contact with it. But the incentives of production-sector managers are inimical to innovation, and therefore to productive R&D. Aligning R&D closer to production would hurt R&D, and in the long run benefit production little; keeping the two separate would not be any better. More broadly, the decline in productivity reflects the command economy's inability to apply R&D resources in the fashion required by a modern economy. R&D cannot be handled effectively by command methods. Successful R&D projects require either the direct intervention of the highest leadership—which is necessarily limited to a small number of projects—or tradition, ethics, and selectivity that can only survive in a relatively independent, small-scale institution—that is, the academy.

Military R&D Trends

All the evidence on productivity decline in R&D relates either to the sector as a whole or to its civilian component; no data are available on military R&D inputs and outputs. There are reasons to believe, however, that the causes of productivity decline in civilian R&D also exist in the military sector and have produced similar effects. The character of military R&D is usually described as being quite different from that of civilian R&D. It is guided by the demands of an interested and powerful customer, the central political leadership, or the Ministry of Defense. In many cases, designers dominate production plants so that the interests of production cannot subvert or redirect R&D.[38] The main structural causes of productivity decline in the civilian sector are thus absent.

Yet the Soviet military R&D effort may be as large, in terms of employment, as total American R&D.[39] It is too large for the political leadership to exercise effective control over all of it. Stratification of the military sector into elite and run-of-the-mill institutions becomes inevitable.[40] The mechanism for resource allocation described above therefore applies only to the part of military R&D with lower-priority institutions under less-stringent controls. The Ministry of Defense is represented there by officers concerned mainly with avoiding any risks to their careers. If for some reason the ministry has trouble formulating its demands, these institutions are unlikely to direct resources productively on their own.[41]

Table 10.4, which summarizes the causes of productivity decline for civilian R&D, also applies to military R&D. Once again, numbers in the text correspond to those in the table. While there is no evidence of automatic expansion of inputs in military R&D, (1) it is known that this sector has easier access to resources, and that some of its institutions operate with a virtual blank check ("open budget").[42] The easy availability of resources is bound to produce hoarding similar to that in civilian R&D. There are also instances of diversion of military R&D resources to non-R&D uses, such as agricultural work, but it is not known whether such diversion has been increasing over time.[43] There is no evidence concerning causes (3), (4), and (5), so we assume they do not apply to military R&D.

Designers of military hardware work under the same state standards as do civilian designers.[44] (6) They, too, have been burdened with revising drawings. (7) The military industry is also tied into the same supply system as the civilian one, so the increasing burden on designers to obtain permits from producers and supply organizations must operate there, too. (8) Military R&D shared in the expansion of "scientific methods of management," and was burdened with developing "economic methods of management."[45] (9), (10) Military R&D has less discretion in the choice of projects than civilian R&D, but the degree is still substantial.[46] The rigidity of organizational structure, security of tenure, and feudal relations between the boss and underlings are comparable to those of civilian institutions.[47] This means that slowing growth leads to an aging research portfolio and aging staff, increasing the share of exhausted topics and people and lowering productivity in the military sector just as it does in the civilian sector.[48] (11) Military R&D also has arbitrary restrictions on staffing and on the ratio of researchers to support personnel, but it is not known whether this leads to increasing use of scientists and engineers in support positions.[49] (12) In this sector, however, high salaries and generous benefits must have softened—and possibly neutralized—the effects of the declining salary and prestige of scientific and engineering jobs.

Of the twelve specific causes of decline in R&D productivity listed in Table 10.4, six also operate in military R&D. The four causes that were not detected may be assumed to be absent. Two more causes are uncertain. Of course, such a comparison does not take into account possible differences in the intensity of particular processes; still, it suggests that military R&D, especially design activities, has suffered from causes (6), (7), and (8). Moreover, much military R&D is performed in civilian institutions.[50] The involvement of universities and the academies of science in military work has been well established.[51] A wide variety of the R&D organizations of civilian ministries also participate in military R&D.[52] In appropriating the personnel of civilian institutions for its own needs, military R&D also imports the ills suffered by these institutions.

It might be argued that military ministries oversee more technologically progressive sectors than do civilian ones, and that the development of young technologies might produce increasing yields despite the negative factors discussed above. The same reasoning should then apply to productivity in new civilian sectors. Since new sectors, as well as old, receive an increasing share of total inputs, their output should at least decline less than that of traditional sectors. The data do not support this conclusion. For example, the field of instruments, controls, and computers is very technologically progressive, yet it experienced a somewhat deeper decline in the number of prototypes created in 1981–1985 relative to 1961–1965 than did civilian machinery, which is a more traditional technology. Among other technologically progressive categories, chemical equipment prototypes declined by more than the total, while those of electrotechnical equipment and casting machines peaked later (in 1966–1970) and declined by less than the total. The only technologically progressive civilian sector that did not show a decline is forges and presses. Variations in the mix of new and old technologies in military and civilian sectors seems to have played a minimal role, then, in determining R&D productivity. The direction of change in the productivity of military R&D must have been similar to that of civilian R&D—downward—though the extent of decline might have been smaller.

TABLE 10.5   Growth Rates of Soviet Machine and Equipment
Prototypes, 1956–1985, Relative to the Previous
Five-Year Period (percentage)

	All prototypes	Civilian ministries	Military ministries
1956–1960	167.14	150.78	—
1961–1965	57.20	44.23	198.20
1966–1970	−6.41	−15.18	39.71
1971–1975	−2.38	−1.81	−4.20
1976–1980	−8.03	−14.96	−0.06
1981–1985	−5.14	−10.99	12.01

SOURCE: *Narkhoz*, various years.

Output trends of military and civilian R&D. The trend in the number of machine prototypes created in military ministries is markedly different from that in the civilian sector (Table 10.5).[53] From 1961 to 1965, the number of military-ministry prototypes grew much faster than that of civilian prototypes.[54] Since then, the number of prototypes created in civilian ministries has been declining, while that in military machine-building has been increasing. Fifteen out of seventeen classes of civilian-sector prototypes declined; by contrast, prototypes of radio and communications equipment, the only military-ministry class reported separately, grew steadily through 1976 (when reporting stopped). In sum, between 1966 and 1985 the output of R&D in military machine-building ministries expanded, while that in civilian ministries fell.[55]

This divergence can be explained by a relatively smaller decline in productivity, or relatively faster growth of inputs, in military R&D. While there is no proof, the gap between the growth rates of civilian and military R&D outputs appears too large to be explained by different rates of productivity decline alone. It suggests that resources were shifted from civilian to military R&D in 1965–1985, exacerbating the effects of productivity decline in civilian R&D and mitigating them in the military.

R&D and procurement of new weapons. The impact of R&D on innovation can be traced through the share of prototypes that were put into production—in other words, the rate of implementation. This sheds light on the relationship between supply and demand for innovations. In 1966–1970, less than a third of all prototypes were put into production

TABLE 10.6   Soviet Prototypes Put into Production as a Percentage of
              Prototypes Created, 1966–1986

	Total	All machines	Civilian ministries	Military ministries	Instru- ments
1966–1970	31.97[a]				
1971–1975	55.10	60.11	59.14	62.82	39.33
1976–1980	65.20	66.80	55.70	92.34	60.31
1981–1985	75.75	70.78	62.06	88.82	91.75
1980	71.63	70.75	58.37	96.70	74.33
1981	77.25	82.07	57.83	132.05	62.00
1982	63.69	52.85	57.06	43.85	98.30
1983	73.83	58.73	55.69	65.07	127.25
1984	80.33	75.97	71.09	85.67	93.23
1985	83.69	85.64	68.80	120.23	77.26
1986	83.86	86.21	74.05	108.71	75.58

a. This share is likely to be biased upward; the number of prototypes put into
production may include items other than machines and instruments.
SOURCE: *Narkhoz*, various years.

(Table 10.6). Between 1971 and 1986, implementation rates increased,
though for different reasons in different sectors. For military machinery,
the number of prototypes increased, but more slowly than the industry's
appetite for innovations, which may be represented by the number of
new models put into production (Table 10.7). For instruments, the
number of prototypes declined, but more went into production. For
civilian machines, the rate of prototype creation declined more slowly
than the industry's demand for them. Between 1976 and 1985, ninety out
of a hundred military-sector prototypes were put into production (Table
10.7). Only one out of seventeen classes of civilian-sector machines had
such a high implementation rate, and only for a five-year period.[56] This
suggests a much higher demand for innovations by producers of military machinery than by those of civilian machinery. R&D in military
machine-building does not keep up with the demand.

Uncertainty in technological progress is fundamental and cannot be
eliminated by better planning and management.[57] Some prototypes that
are created will never be put into production. The share of machine
prototypes that are rejected varies from 15 to 30 percent.[58] Even current
rates of implementation of civilian machinery seem too high to allow for
this inevitable attrition.

TABLE 10.7   Growth in the Number of New Soviet Models Put into
Production, 1971–1986 (percentage)

	Total	Machines	Civilian ministries	Military ministries	Instruments
1971–1975	62.12[a]	—	—	—	—
1976–1980	9.54	2.21	−18.11	55.99	44.88
1981–1985	8.98	0.53	2.17	−1.77	37.72
1981	−3.09	5.20	−10.61	25.21	−27.15
1982	−12.29	−31.34	6.46	−65.48	67.49
1983	21.93	19.65	4.31	62.40	25.83
1984	8.66	23.83	20.17	30.37	16.11
1985	−1.65	9.28	−5.15	33.08	−27.99
1986	−8.94	−7.16	−4.20	−10.64	−15.45

a. This rate may be biased downward; see note to Table 10.3.
SOURCE: *Narkhoz*, various years.

An increase in the number of machine prototypes (sometimes by several orders of magnitude) is considered necessary for improvement, both in particular sectors and in machine-building as a whole.[59] But the rate of implementation in military machine-building is, *a fortiori*, too high. Such a high rate can be maintained only by relaxing standards of acceptance, and by debugging designs in the process of implementation.

Despite its expansion, R&D in military machine-building ministries in the late 1970s became a constraint on the introduction of new models of hardware. The stabilization in the number of new models introduced in 1981–1985 relative to 1976–1980 was likely caused by this constraint. Insufficient output of R&D may have been one of the causes of the slowdown in weapons procurement in the late 1970s.[60]

Conclusion

By the measure of the production of prototypes, productivity in the Soviet R&D sector has been falling since the 1960s, hurting Soviet military potential both directly and indirectly. Decline in R&D productivity contributed to the slowdown in economic growth by slowing technological progress.[61] Productivity also declined in military R&D— though probably by less than in civilian R&D—and offset the effect of a massive influx of resources into the sector. R&D in military machine-building ministries did not keep pace with the industry's demand for new models, and became the bottleneck in the weapons-acquisition process.

Boris Z. Rumer

What Happened to Soviet Investment?

THE SUCCESS of Mikhail Gorbachev's economic program depends upon dynamic Soviet investment activity. The new leadership inherited from its predecessors an investment sector that had experienced a decline unprecedented in Soviet history. In the years preceding *perestroika*, numerous party and government decrees that were intended to rejuvenate Soviet investment instead remained on paper. Have the architects of Gorbachev's economic program succeeded in bringing about fundamental changes in investment policy? Have they devised a new investment strategy? What positive shifts in the investment process have occurred in the first half of the Twelfth Five-Year Plan?

That plan, which went into effect in 1985, calls for an acceleration of investment growth at the expense of current consumption, with investment in production, especially heavy industry, given top priority. This is essentially the traditional Soviet approach; the only difference is that investment is now being applied to reindustrialization. There is nothing new in preferential treatment to upgrade old production capacities and reduce the share of investment in new projects; Gorbachev's predecessors tried to follow the same path in the hopes of accelerating capital

Boris Rumer is a research associate at the Harvard University Russian Research Center.

turnover and reducing the capital coefficient. Nor is the planned concentration of investment and cutbacks in a smaller number of simultaneously funded projects a new idea: for many decades every decree on investment contained this requirement. Increasing the share of decentralized investment was initiated in the 1960s reform, but cut back when that reform lost steam in the 1970s. The issue of restructuring industrial investment—cutting back the share of extractive and smokestack industries and increasing that of manufacturing branches—has also been raised before. The need for this measure has long been obvious.

In short, all the key parts of the investment program of the Twelfth Five-Year Plan (FYP) have been borrowed from the past, when strengthening of the defense sector was the dominant national goal. The architects of the Twelfth FYP—Zaikov, Ryzhkov, Talyzin—came from defense industries, and have shown no signs of departing from old recipes. Is it possible that Gorbachev intended a different investment program, but could not turn away from the old methods? This explanation is highly unlikely. Consider his statement in May 1985, when the Twelfth FYP was in preparation, comparing the goals of the contemporary Soviet economy with those on the eve of World War II, when "it was felt that the threat to the socialist state was increasing" and preparations for war were under way.[1] The same logic underlies the investment program for the Twelfth FYP. Let us examine its implementation.

The Growth of Investment

According to the Soviet statistical yearbook *Narodnoe khoziaistvo*, the average annual growth rate of investment in "comparable prices"—that is, accounting for inflation—was 7 percent in the 1960s, 5 percent in the 1970s, and 3.7 percent in 1981–1986.[2] However, in this period of greater candor, Soviet statistics have been subjected to severe criticism for distorting the true picture of economic growth, including the growth of investment. There is apparently not a single Soviet investment expert who doubts the presence of concealed inflation, or that the growth rate of investment is reported in statistical yearbooks without necessary adjustments. One such specialist, Vladimir Fal'tsman, speaks of "a decline in the purchasing power of the investment ruble."[3] Although he is obviously referring to the problem of inflation, he does not call it by name, for until recently there was a strict taboo on using the word, reserved solely for market economies. This ban has now been lifted. As Anatolii Komin, deputy chairman of the State Price Committee (Goskomtsen), wrote in the June 1987 issue of *Kommunist*, ignoring inflation would "simply reinforce the inflationary tendencies. However, we stubbornly do not want to come to grips with it. . . . The dynamics in prices are often ignored in analysis economic problems, and hence the root causes lying at the foundation are also not being addressed."[4] The current chairman of Goskomtsen, V. Pavlov, recently wrote in *Pravda*: "A distortion of the picture of the real volume of gross national product and national income, and the rate of their respective growth, makes it impossible to measure objectively the expenditures and returns in all sectors of the national economy."[5] The subject of inflation has finally come into the open.

The problem had not been neglected in the economic literature. Although one could not speak openly of inflation or cast doubt on official statistics, it was possible to replace the word with various euphemisms. These ersatz phrases included such circumlocutions as "unjustified rise in the cost of capital construction" or "blown-up prices" for machinery and equipment, "the unjustified rise in prices," and the like. In certain publications one encounters criticism, though in an extremely cautious form, of investment indexes based on unaltered prices of both equipment and construction. There have even been blunt warnings that one should not trust investment indexes that are calculated on the basis of so-called comparable prices. Thus Vladimir Shtanskii, one of the more serious researchers of investment problems, conducted an extensive study of the capital coefficient in ferrous metallurgy, and concluded: "There is a substantial distortion in the dynamics of the actual costs of production as a consequence of the value indexes for recalculation of capital investments and fixed capital in comparable prices, which do not correspond to the real change in value."[6]

In a recent study, Vladimir Kontorovich and I analyzed a number of authoritative quantitative assessments of inflation in construction projects and investment goods.[7] Such direct assessments of inflation are not available in Soviet economic literature; they were obtained from several surrogate and indirect sources, including the estimates of respected Soviet experts, surveys conducted by the investment bank of the USSR (Stroibank), and studies of institutes involved in economic research and the development of technology. Table 11.1 summarizes our estimates of inflation in Soviet investment. If accounts of investment dynamics published in official statistical yearbooks are adjusted for inflation, the real

TABLE 11.1   Estimates of the Average Annual Growth in Soviet
              Investment Inflation, 1961–1985 (percentage)

Period	Range of estimates
1961–1965	0.5–2.0
1966–1970	—
1971–1975	1.7–3.0
1976–1980	2.0–4.2
1981–1985	3.0–3.8

SOURCE: Boris Rumer, "Soviet Estimates of the Rate of Inflation," *Soviet Studies*, vol. XLI, no. 2, April 1989.

average annual growth rate of investment must have been 1 to 3 percent in the 1970s and sunk to zero in the first half of the 1980s (or possibly in the late 1970s), perhaps even turning negative. Incidentally, Soviet economist Konstantin Val'tukh came to the same conclusion in 1982.[8]

Perhaps Soviet leaders are aware of the nation's actual investment dynamics, and understand the implications of the negative investment trend for the economy as a whole and for its defense sector in particular. If so, the Twelfth FYP architects' determination to overcome the investment slump at any price is understandable.

Investment versus Consumption

According to the current plan, the annual rate of growth in investment should rise to 4.6 percent, a considerable increase over the 3.2 percent recorded for the previous FYP.[9] It is well known that the main source of investments is the accumulation fund, which in 1985 comprised 26.4 percent of the share of national income allocated to consumption and savings.[10] Some Soviet economists have long held the view, which I share, that the accumulation would constitute a much larger share of national income than indicated by current calculations if the national income were freed from the distortions inherent in the existing system of price formation. Vasilii Seliunin recently published the results of his own calculations, which show that the accumulation—corrected for the distortions caused by using data based on prices—comprises 40 percent of national income, leaving just 60 percent for consumption. He observed that "such a high share of accumulation, in essence, is a norm for a wartime period."[11]

Nevertheless, even this extraordinarily high investment quota did not seem sufficient to the authors of the Twelfth FYP, who provided for the first significant increase in the share of accumulation in a very long time. Premier Ryzhkov addressed this point at the Twenty-Seventh Party Congress: "Based upon the basic policy of acceleration, the Central Committee of the CPSU has deemed it expedient to increase the rate of increase of productive capital investments in the Twelfth Five-Year Plan by 25 percent, compared to 16 percent in the previous plan."[12] Naturally, this entails a change in the distribution of national income—an increase in the share of savings. Seliunin based his calculations on the official, published norms of accumulation for the first half of the 1980s. If one gives credence to his methods, then correcting his data for the previous plan accordingly, one arrives at accumulation funds (of which investments constitute the lion's share) that will—however strange this may sound—come close to making up nearly half the national income. The consumption fund would thus shrink to slightly more than half the national income. Such are the proportions built into the Twelfth FYP.

For the sake of higher rates of growth in investment, the authors of the plan have opted to further tighten the belt on consumption. According to official statistics, consumer goods made up 39.0 percent of industrial output in 1940, 27.5 percent in 1960, 26.6 percent in 1980, and finally reached a record low in 1986 (the first year of the current FYP) of 24.7 percent.[13] In his assessment of this allocation, Seliunin emphasizes that the dwindling share of consumption "is completely unacceptable for peacetime."[14] It is worth noting that the defense sector accounts for a major portion of accumulation. A leading Soviet statistician explains the distribution of defense expenditures between consumption and accumulation: "Everything connected with consumption by the army—food, uniforms—enters into consumption, whereas the increment of arms, military equipment, etc. [*"prirost voennykh sredstv i tak dalee"*] can only be attributed to accumulation."[15]

Thus, Seliunin, one of the most perspicacious critics of the economic system, has stressed the similarity of the present FYP with that of a wartime economy in two important respects: the rate of growth in investment and the exceptionally high share of producer goods in industrial output. Of course, this flatly contravenes the view (which has gained wide currency among observers) that the goal of the new Soviet leadership's economic policy is to redirect resources from the defense to the civil sector.

Investment in Producer versus Consumer Goods

The Twelfth FYP mandated an increase in investment in the productive spheres at the expense of the nonproductive spheres. In the passage quoted above, Ryzhkov speaks unequivocally of "an increase in the rate of growth of productive capital investments." The share of the producer sphere in investments has risen in the last twenty-five years (1960–1985) from 64.7 to 72.3 percent, bringing with it a corresponding decrease in investments in the consumption sphere of the economy (including housing). It is true that 1986 witnessed a decrease in the producer sphere's share of investment, but only by half a percentage point (from 72.3 to 71.8 percent).[16]

Another macro indicator of investment policy is the distribution of industrial investments between the production of "the means of production" (industrial goods) and consumer goods—that is, between the so-called A and B groups. In the Soviet Union this distribution has reflected the clear predominance accorded to group A: for 1970–1985 the share of group B declined from 5.2 to 4.4 percent, and fell in 1986 to 4.1 percent.[17] (There are not yet any data for 1987.) Here one must note with regret that in 1986, for the first time in many years, the statistical yearbook omitted data on investments in food-processing and light industries, which produce the bulk of consumer goods. Data on investments within industry are given as aggregate figures for large industrial sectors (energy and fuels, metallurgy, machine-building, chemicals, forestry, and construction), but food-processing and light industries have been silently dropped from this structure. The yearbook does give investments for the so-called social/cultural complex, which includes housing construction, public health care, education, and trade, but light and food-processing industries are not included in this sector.[18]

It is therefore quite clear that the investment strategy of the Twelfth FYP, which is aimed at the modernization of industry, intends to divert investment from consumption to production. When Ryzhkov, in his report to the Twenty-Seventh Party Congress, outlined the Communist Party's plan for dealing with social problems in the second half of the 1980s, he emphasized that priority would be given "to the resolution of social problems in the labor sphere," that is, in the sphere of production.[19]

The Extractive Sector versus Manufacturing

In June 1985, in his first programmatic statement on economic problems, Gorbachev noted that one of the main causes of the economy's grave condition was that "we did not demonstrate, at the right time, resoluteness in changing our structural policy." In speaking further of "problems in modifying the policy on investments and structure," Gorbachev declared: "The most acute problem is the relationship between capital investments in resource-extractive, processing, and manufacturing sectors."[20] One might expect the new Soviet leadership to "demonstrate resoluteness" at last and set about optimizing the distribution of resources among the sectors of industry.

But Gorbachev's declaration did not find its way into the FYP that was finally adopted. There was an obvious intention to rein in the escalating growth of investments in the mineral and raw-material sector, but it has not been fulfilled. Despite the impressive verbiage, the new leadership is exhibiting the same indecisiveness as its predecessors. Characterizing this situation, Aleksandr Arbatov wrote in January 1987:

> Although a series of steps have been outlined to deal with the situation, the real state of affairs has for the time being changed but little. Apparently, the main cause of the slow restructuring is an inappropriate investment policy. To a significant degree, it continues to follow the existing structure of production, directing means proportionately to previous expenditure and thereby sustaining the existing structural proportions. Evidence of this, for example, is found in the increase of capital investments in the fuel sector.[21]

However clearly Soviet leaders might recognize the ruinous consequences of continuous expansion of the fuel and raw material sectors at the expense of consumption and other investment, they cannot reduce investments in those sectors, given the country's energy crisis and the fact that export of those materials saves the country from starvation and permits the acquisition of much-needed Western technology. Hence Gorbachev's good intentions to balance the industrial sector have come to nought.

The Priority of the Machine-Building Sector

The main goal of Gorbachev's investment program is to achieve a leap forward in the machine-building sector. The key to understanding how and at what price this goal is sought is found in a November 1986 statement by Lev Zaikov, the Politburo member responsible for machine-building and defense industries:

> The machine-building complex has been given everything that is at the disposal of our economy. For a year or two, construction and development of a series of enterprises in other sectors have been halted. In a word, the absolute maximum has been given to ensure rapid progress in that one sector. In terms of the rate of growth of production, machine-building is supposed to surpass the rest of industry in the USSR by 1.7 times: the rate of growth for machine-building is to be 43.2 percent, compared to 25 percent for industry as a whole.[22]

Moreover, this investment capital will not flood evenly into all branches of machine-building, first priority goes to machine-tool branches and those producing advanced technology and computers. Investments in the machine-tool branch were thus increased by 42 percent in 1986 over the previous year.[23] Evidently, a group of top-priority branches for computers and highly sensitive equipment received a similar infusion of investment capital.[24] At the same time, the plan fixed the total investment increase for the entire machine-building sector at just 15 percent for 1986.[25]

Throughout Soviet history, increases in investment activity in the machine-building sector coincided with the development of new armament programs, notwithstanding other explanations. In the prewar years, the share of machine-building in industrial investment jumped from 29 to 33 percent; after the war it fell by half, to 16 percent, and remained at 13 to 16 percent for four FYPs, from 1946 until 1965. In the first Brezhnev FYP, 1966–1970, the share of machine-building jumped by 5 percentage points, to 22.5 percent, and remained below 25 percent. A new, 5 percent jump is taking place in the current FYP, in which the share of machine-building is supposed to reach approximately 30 percent.[26]

This increase could be explained by the needs of the civilian economy: several highly respected U.S. specialists believe that a transfusion of resources from the military to the civilian sector of machine-building is taking place. But I have serious doubts. The influx of investment is reaching neither the automobile industry nor machine-building for food and light industry. Indeed, the ministry for food machine-building was recently abolished. We do not know the defense sector's share of machine-building, but the allocation of resources to machine-tooling and other high-technology branches has increased dramatically. Of course, one could argue that these are basic branches of the economy, and that their rapid development creates a base for modernization of the automobile industry and machine-building for food and light industry. But defense machine-building needs this base just as much.

By 1987, one could observe a more sober attitude toward the plan's approach; it had become clear that the machine-building sector was unprepared to absorb such an intensive investment program, and that neither industry as a whole nor the construction sector were capable of fulfilling its demands. New capital stock in machine-building had risen by only 3 percent in 1986 amid an investment increase of 15 percent. A similar situation emerged in 1987.[27]

Although statistical data are not yet available for actual performance in 1987, some dismal evidence can be derived from a statement by the minister of instrument manufacturing, the most fundamental sector of machine-building for computer technology and other important high-tech sectors. Responding to a question in November 1987 about whether priorities are really sustained in his domain, the minister explained that such key sectors as his own had not been supplied with the requisite equipment, materials, and artifact complexes, and that the allocated investments were not accompanied by sufficient construction.[28] In other words, a significant part of the vast investments that had been allocated were left hanging in mid-air.

Reconsideration of the Investment Program

The growing recognition that the investment policy was unrealistic and that the leadership contemplated a change in course was indicated in a November 1987 article in *Planovoe khoziaistvo*, the journal of the State Planning Committee (Gosplan), by one of Gosplan's leading experts in investment planning, Evgenii Ivanov, who criticized the plan's priorities as well as the principles underlying them.[29] But what could a relatively unimportant official do in the face of pressure from Zaikov, Ryzhkov, Talyzin, and other technocrats tied to the defense industries who were determined to demonstrate what they could achieve, and who brought with them their customary methods of authoritarian rule but had no experience directing the immense scale of a national economy?

Noting that the choice of priorities was the most important function of central planning, Ivanov opposed extreme changes in the distribution of resources and spoke out against the deeply rooted policy of handling shortages of material and financial resources by diverting them to one sector at the expense of others. Although the lower-priority sectors are deemed to be of lesser significance, he said, they are nevertheless important for the balanced development of the economy. Ivanov was also critical of the tendency to ignore the real capacity of the economy to supply various resources. He offered examples from postwar history of sharp reallocations leading to dramatic results. Even "when implementing the most obvious and most indubitable priority," he argued, "it is essential that this be carefully linked to the general proportions of the national economy." Clearly he had in mind what had happened in machine-building when he concluded that the correct method for implementing priority

> must be the undeviating observance of proportionality. This means that recognition of one or another sector's priority and problems does not give the slightest grounds for directing resources to it and pursuing its accelerated development at the expense of proportionality in the national economy.[30]

Ivanov's thesis contradicted unequivocally the stance taken by Zaikov on the concentration of resources in machine-building at the expense of other industrial sectors.

That Ivanov publicly made such a statement, and that *Planovoe khoziaistvo* published his article, suggest to me that some members of the party bureaucratic elite have become disenchanted with the plan adopted at the Twenty-Seventh Party Congress, and especially with its investment foundations. This is quite natural: failure to fulfill plan targets amid massive investment in the machine-building sector has been widely observed. The growth rate of production in machine-building declined from 6.4 percent in 1986 to 4.6 percent in 1987 (without adjustment for "hidden inflation," which is not reported in official statistics).[31] In 1987 the machine-building sector failed to fulfill the plan to produce more than two-thirds of the most important forms of machine and tool output.[32] In February 1988 Egor Gaidar, the economic editor of *Kommunist* (the leading theoretical journal of the Central Committee), admitted, in effect, that the investment program for machine-building had failed because of the gap between investments and the real possibilities for supplying equipment given the capacities of the construction industry.[33]

Thus, it finally became clear that the strategy of the Twelfth FYP had been mistaken and naive, and that it had led to an intensification of the imbalances and disproportions that beset the Soviet economy. The planned investment boom not only failed to achieve its goal but also aggravated the crisis in consumption. Food supply conditions have worsened; shortages of basic necessities (such as footwear, clothing, and toothpaste) have become more acute; in 1987, the growth of retail trade shrank more than twofold from the previous year; because of falling prices for the main categories of Soviet export goods (oil and natural gas), the import of consumer goods has been sharply reduced; the consumer sphere has fallen victim to galloping inflation, which is not admitted by official statistics but is obvious to all and even openly discussed in the press; and the housing problem has grown still more dramatic.[34] Beyond all this, the mounting discontent of the populace, which has grown increasingly apprehensive about a future (and apparently inevitable) rise in food prices, together with the deterioration in living conditions, have begun to break through in the era of *glasnost* even to the pages of *Pravda*.[35]

Gaidar's article in *Kommunist* trumpeted the call for retreat. It candidly declared the plan to upgrade machine-building "unrealistic," noting the disproportion between its expectations and available resources. Gaidar recognized that increased savings through reduced consumption had not produced the expected results, and that a continuation of forced growth in expenditures without the corresponding planned returns could have serious social consequences. He further noted that efforts "to increase sharply the rate of growth of capital investments have not succeeded," and that it was impossible to implement the planned maneuver and still support necessary rates of growth for an adequate standard of living. As a result, "in 1988 the rate of growth of capital investments has been reduced in comparison with 1986–87."[36]

Kommunist did not limit its attack to the investment parameters of the five-year plan. The main mouthpiece of the Central Committee virtually condemned the plan as a whole for "exceeding the real possibilities of the economy" and making it "ungovernable." To achieve the reform, he said, "one must be ready to repudiate wrong decisions taken at a different time and in a different situation." Moreover, rejection of the planned tempos and proportions would make economic maneuvering possible, currenly seen as necessary if the reforms were to be successfully implemented.[37] Such is the main conclusion drawn in the *Kommunist* article. "Wrong decisions" were taken by the Twenty-Seventh Party Congress—a mere two years earlier. What does the phrase "in a different situation" imply? Leonid Abalkin, director of the Institute of Economics of the Academy of Sciences, admitted in a seminar at Harvard University in March 1988 that when the plan was being adopted at the beginning of the Gorbachev leadership, its architects underestimated the depth and complexity of the economy's problems.

The beginning of a reconsideration of investment policy is reflected in the significant reallocation of investment in the plan for 1988 in favor of the nonproductive sphere, where investment has grown by 8.4 billion rubles, or 18 percent, over the level specified by the five-year plan.[38] Most of this additional investment has been directed toward housing. The decision has also wrought "serious changes in the branch and technological structure of investments and construction work": the share of the nonproductive sphere in the construction plan has leaped to an unprecedented high level of 46 percent. Moreover, it has violated all the planned proportions in the distribution of resources, and created insurmountable difficulties for the remaining years of the plan in the supply of construction materials and in the capacities of the construction industry.[39]

Improvements in the Investment Process?

Hopes that the investment process would improve in the Twelfth FYP have not been realized. The plan's calculations were based on an increase in the return on capital investment by reducing construction time, by concentrating investments in the most important projects while suspending allocations to those with lower priority (to judge from Zaikov's declaration, investment was to be concentrated above all on expanding machine-building capacities); and by rechaneling investment from the creation of new capacities to upgrading old ones. It was further expected that overall savings would result from the smaller outlays to reconstruct and upgrade buildings and infrastructure than would be needed for entirely new projects.

Mothballing of construction projects. As it would be tedious to review the inordinately protracted construction times—the familiar, so-called long-drawn-out construction (*dolgostroi*) and its underlying causes about which so much has been written—we might ask, What is the current state of affairs?

In October 1987 there were some 300 unfinished big industrial projects that had been under construction for more than ten years, of which about 200 were in the machine-building sector. If one analyzes all the projects under construction, on average their completion time is about double what it should be.[40] To complete them in the prescribed period on the scale that is currently planned, the scope of the effort needs to be limited—that is, investment needs to be increased by about 40 percent.[41] No significant steps were taken in this direction, however, in either 1986 or 1987. In the opinion of Gosplan experts, the absence of increased concentration should also serve as a warning signal: they contend that the main cause, once again, is the imbalance between construction programs and available resources.[42]

The number of frozen projects increased slightly in 1987, but their value amounted to only 3.2 percent of the total cost of construction under way.[43] A "freezing" of lower-priority projects is thus proving no more successful in the current five-year plan than in previous ones. Freezing projects is not a new idea—yet Soviet authorities have never been successful in carrying it out. On paper it appears to make eminently good sense. But in practice, what does it mean to put thousands of projects on hold? As elsewhere, the approach itself reveals the naiveté of the new leaders, their bureaucratic vision, and their comprehension of the investment process. As Gosplan's own experts have pointed out:

> The complexity and real contradictions consist precisely in the fact that one must choose [for shutdown] from among those objects necessary to the national economy and included in the plan after the appropriate directives of the superior organs [that is, government]. But this goal simply cannot be reached satisfactorily in actual operation of the plan.[44]

The problem of "choosing objects for shutdown" is further complicated by the fact that such closings do not simply mean abandoning projects that are partly built. To prevent total waste of the expended sums, Gosplan and the State Committee on Construction (Gosstroi) must determine how to use unfinished structures. In most cases this proves impossible. For example, in the mid-1970s a decision was made to build a gigantic plant in the Ukraine to produce locomotives. It was to cost 700 million rubles. After eleven years, an enormous building had been completed (along with a number of other components of the infrastructure), when it was decided that the project would be shut down for an indefinite time. Many millions of rubles were frozen. Apart from the direct losses, an enormous economic blow was dealt to the city of Kirovograd (a large industrial center in the Ukraine), since the project was supposed to have become the basis for a large industrial network, the construction of which had already begun. The enterprises of this industrial center had been created on the basis of a transportation, energy, and sewage system that were to be built by the locomotive plant. All construction of this complex also came to a standstill. According to the first secretary of the Kirovograd *Obkom*, losses caused by the shutdown "are growing like a snowball." The entire development of the city—improvement of its ecological system, its water supply, housing, electricity supply, and other communal needs—had been based on the locomotive plant.

The local party leadership and state officials have proven powerless in their attempts to make some use of the finished buildings and to ameliorate the serious consequences of the shutdown. An enormous, vacant structure thus towers over the steppes like a huge ship run aground. The building gradually deteriorates, and the chances that the project will ever come alive again are negligible.[45] In the final analysis, the development of an important economic region will suffer, and this will have an impact on the living standards of the population. That is how plant shutdowns work in reality.

It is perfectly understandable why local authorities and ministries adamantly resist this policy. Recently their resistance has proven successful. *Kommunist* concedes that in 1987 authorities "failed to overcome the ministerial and local resistance to measures for a concentration of capital investments—which is absolutely necessary for the country."[46] In 1987 the introduction of fixed capital was to be increased by 13 percent; in reality the increase was only 5 percent. Operation of 1,109 of the most important productive objects was also planned; in fact there were start-ups in only 749 objects.[47]

Reconstruction versus construction of new capacities. The diversion of resources from the creation of new capacities to the upgrading of old ones carried greater hopes. But this strategy of the investment program has also failed.[48] As the plan for 1988 was reformulated, many enterprises reduced substantially the scale of reconstruction and upgrading that had been originally foreseen in the five-year plan.[49] There are several reasons for this. One is the obsolescence, low quality, and economic inefficiency of the technological and construction designs used in modernization projects. Several ministries conducted an analysis of approximately one thousand projects, of which a quarter were pronounced unsuitable. Spot checks of the technological level and quality of projects conducted by Gosstroi and the State Committee on Science and Technology showed that approximately half failed to measure up to contemporary standards. A second factor is the shortage of machinery and equipment, their obsolescence, and their inferior quality. Thus, in 1987 the value of equipment rejected because of inferior quality in the most important area of the machine-building sector—the production of high technology and computers—amounted to 140 million rubles.[50] A third factor was the illusory calculation that, in reconstructing and upgrading existing enterprises, investment resources would go primarily toward equipment and machinery, while outlays for infrastructure and construction would be minimized. A study by the State Committee for Statistics (Goskomstat) demonstrated, however, that in many cases of renovation and upgrading the share of expenditures for equipment was no greater than for new construction.[51]

Conclusion

Such are the realities of Soviet investment practice: they plainly confound the ideas of the new leadership, whose strategy was for intensive investment over a short period to reindustrialize the economy. That strategy, designed in Moscow offices and without a firm grasp of reality, simply failed to work. The idea of an industrial blitzkrieg has always had strong appeal to Soviet leaders—the current ones included. It is no accident that Gorbachev exuded such enthusiasm when he spoke on the seventieth anniversary of the October Revolution: "Industrialization in one burst has raised the country to a qualitatively new level."[52] He had in mind the industrialization of the 1930s, which had also been achieved at the expense of restricted consumption. We now know what sacrifices were made and what that industrialization cost the populace. Now there is a different regime, a different population, a different economy; there will be no great surge now like that of the 1930s. The investment policy of the Twelfth Five-Year Plan, so divorced from reality, has manifestly failed fully three years before its end. Its strategy, which counted on rapid steps to modernize machine-building and force the development of high technology and advanced machinery and equipment (important for both defense and civilian industries), has proven ineffectual. One can declare in all certainty that this program will not be fulfilled in the foreseeable future.

The Soviet Union's attempt to launch a great investment surge has miscarried because there is too much inertia in the investment sphere and too little prior preparation of the economy as a whole to allow such a violation of the investment rhythm. Ill-advised tampering with that system is fraught with serious consequences, including chaos in the investment sphere of the economy.

Notes

Introduction. Henry S. Rowen and Charles Wolf, Jr.

1. Mikhail Gorbachev, *Perestroika: New Thinking for Our Country and the World* (New York: Harper & Row, 1987), pp. 4–5.

2. Abel G. Aganbegyan, *The Economic Challenge of Perestroika* (Bloomington: Indiana University Press, 1988).

3. Vasilii Seliunin and Grigorii Khanin, "Lukavaia tsifra" ["Cunning Figures"], *Novy mir* 63 (February 1987).

4. Imogene Edwards and Gertrude Schroeder, *Consumption in the USSR: An International Comparison,* paper prepared for the U.S. Congress, Joint Economic Committee (Washington, D.C.: Government Printing Office, August 1981), pp. 5–19.

5. U.S. Congress, Joint Economic Committee, *Gorbachev's Economic Plans* (Washington, D.C.: GPO, November 1987), pp. viii, 136.

6. Cited in Paul Marer, *Dollar GNPs of the USSR and Eastern Europe* (Baltimore: Johns Hopkins University Press, 1985).

7. Charles Wolf, Jr., and Benjamin Zycher, *Military Dimensions of Communist Systems: Findings and Implications,* R-3629-USDP (Santa Monica, Calif.: RAND, January 1989).

8. Gregory Grossman and Vladimir G. Treml, "Measuring Hidden Incomes in the USSR" in Sergio Alessandrini and Bruno Dallango, eds., *The Unofficial Economy* (Brookfield, Vt.: Gower, 1987).

1. Anders Åslund

The writing of this chapter was facilitated by a generous grant from the Kennan Institute for Advanced Studies of the Woodrow Wilson International Center for Scholars. I am greatly indebted to a large number of economists, including numerous Soviet economists who have helped me to understand their statistics and presumably prefer to remain anonymous. Igor Birman, Wlodzimierz Brus, Richard Ericson, Gregory Grossman, John P. Hardt, Alec Nove, Henry Rowen, Vladimir G. Treml, and Peter Wiles have offered criticism of previous drafts. I am grateful for the many comments offered at the Conference on the Defense Sector in the Soviet Economy at Stanford University, March 23–24, 1988, especially those by Abraham S. Becker; they have helped me to improve this paper. I would also like to acknowledge conversations with Christopher Davis, Sergei Freidzon, Ed A. Hewett, and Jan Vanous. Sarah Klaus traced much of the material and helped improve my English. The views and any mistakes, however, are my own.

1. Vasilii Seliunin and Grigorii Khanin, "Lukavaia tsifra," *Novy mir* 63 (February 1987): 181–201.

2. *O korennoi perestroike upravleniia ekonomikoi, Sbornik dokumentov* (Moscow: Politizdat, 1987), pp. 178–90.

3. Igor Birman, *Ekonomika nedostach* [*The Economy of Shortages*] (New York: Chalidze Publications, 1983; idem, "The Soviet Economy: Alternative Views," *Survey* 29, no. 2 (1985): 102–15; idem, "The Soviet Economy: Alternative Views," *Russia*, no. 12 (1986): 60–75; Alec Nove, "A Note on Growth, Investment and Price Indices," *Soviet Studies* 33, no. 1 (January): 142–45; idem, "A Reply to Stanley Cohn," *Soviet Studies* 33, no. 2 (April 1981): 300–301; idem, "Has Soviet Growth Ceased?," Manchester Statistical Society lecture, November 15, 1983; idem, "A Note on Errors and Their Causes," *Soviet Studies* 37, no. 2 (April 1981): 276–79; idem, "Soviet Real Investment Growth: Are Investment Volume Statistics Overstated? A Reply to Bergson," *Soviet Studies* 39, no. 3 (July 1987): 431–33; Peter J. D. Wiles, "The Worsening of Soviet Economic Performance" in *Crisis in the East European Economy*, ed. J. Drewnowski (London: St. Martin's Press, 1982); idem, "Soviet Consumption and Investment Prices and the Meaningfulness of Real Investment," *Soviet Studies* 34, no. 2 (April 1982): 289–95; idem, "Soviet Inflation, 1982," *Jahrbuch für Wirtschaft Osteuropas*, vol. 10, pp. 132–56, 1983; Philip Hanson, "The CIA, the TsSU and the Real Growth of Soviet Investment," *Soviet Studies* 34, no. 4 (October

1984): 571–81; idem, "Soviet Real Investment Growth: A Reply to Bergson," *Soviet Studies* 39, no 3 (July 1987): 425–30; Michael Ellman, "Did Soviet Economic Growth End in 1978?" in Drewnowski; idem, *Collectivisation, Convergence and Capitalism: Political Economy in a Divided World* (London, 1984); idem, "The Macroeconomic Situation in the USSR, Retrospect and Prospect," *Soviet Studies* 38, no. 4 (October 1986): 530–42.

Probably their most important argument has been that "physical counts on which the CIA relies heavily can rarely make allowance for quality improvements, technological or other, which may and normally do occur over time in many industries of all industrialized countries" (Michael Boretsky, "The Tenability of the CIA Estimates of Soviet Economic Growth," *Journal of Comparative Economics* 11, no. 4 (December 1987): 517–42. This is a typical faulty analogy. Such a statement seems true only of industrialized market economies. Our complaint is that the CIA methodology does not take account of the quality deterioration that is characteristic of shortage economies. We also object to the agency's heavy reliance on raw material production in physical terms, but for other reasons.

4. Paul Marer, *Dollar GNPs of the USSR and Eastern Europe* (Baltimore and London: Johns Hopkins University Press, 1985); Robert W. Campbell, *The Conversion of National Income Data of the USSR to Concepts of the System of National Accounts in Dollars and Estimation of Growth Rate,* World Bank Staff Working Papers No. 777 (1985).

5. Gertrude Schroeder and Imogene Edwards, *Consumption in the USSR: An International Comparison,* paper prepared for U.S. Congress, Joint Economic Committee (Washington, D.C.: GPO, August 1981), p. vi.

6. U.S. Central Intelligence Agency (CIA), *Handbook of Economic Statistics, 1987* (Washington, D.C.: GPO, 1987), pp. 24–25.

7. Abel G. Aganbegyan, "Programma korennoi Perestroiki," *EKO* 18, no. 11 (November 1987): 3–19.

8. Aganbegyan, *The Economic Challenge of Perestroika* (Bloomington: Indiana University Press, 1988), p. 2.

9. Admittedly, Aganbegyan cites official statistics to the contrary just after this statement. *Literaturnaia gazeta,* February 18, 1987.

10. *Ogonek,* no. 2 (1988).

11. Marshall I. Goldman, *USSR in Crisis: The Failure of an Economic System* (New York and London: Norton, 1983), backcover; Harry G. Schaffer, "The Conventional Wisdom vs. Soviet Economic Reality," *Osteuropa Wirtschaft* 31, no. 2 (1986): 132–42.

12. Letter by Ralph Chernoff, *New York Times,* January 20, 1988.

13. It is impossible to acknowledge all insights that have been published in the West.

14. Nove "Errors and Their Causes," p. 279.

15. *Izvestiia*, October 12, 1986. Moscow evening edition of *Izvestiia* is used up to August 1987, for later dates the national morning edition, dated one day later.

16. I attempt to use the correct term for the respective periods, when discussing TsSU/Goskomstat.

17. See statements by the chairman of Goskomstat, Mikhail A. Korolev, in *Pravda*, August 11, 1987, and his deputy, Nikolai Belov, "Zadachi statistiki v usloviiakh reformy khoziaistvennogo upravleniia," *Vestnik statistiki* 69, no. 7 (July 1987): 16–18.

18. Foreign Broadcast Information Service (Daily Report: Soviet Union), January 29, 1987, pp. 59–60.

19. Ibid., p. 62.

20. *Izvestiia*, January 26, 1988.

21. Stephen Shenfield, "State Statistical Work in the USSR: Findings from Interviews with Former Soviet Statistical Personnel," *Soviet Interview Project*, working paper no. 23, (Champaign-Urbana: University of Illinois, June 1986), p. 9.

22. Seliunin and Khanin, "Lukavaia tsifra"; idem, "Statistika znaet vse?" *Novy mir* 63, no. 2 (December 1987): 255–57; V. Kniazevskii, "Po povodu lukavoi stat'i o tsifrakh," *Vestnik statistiki* 69, no. 6 (June 1987): 53–55; T. Kozlov, ibid., 55–58; N. Sheremet, ibid., no. 7 (July 1987): 8–19.

23. Shenfield, "State Statistical Work," p. 4.

24. Belov, "Zadachi statistiki," p. 13.

25. Author interview with a senior Soviet economist and price expert in March 1987.

26. Shenfield, "State Statistical Work," p. 4.

27. Mikhail Korolev in *Pravda*, August 11, 1987.

28. Alec Nove, *The Soviet Economic System* (London: Allen and Unwin, 1977); D. Mario Nuti, "Hidden and Repressed Inflation in Soviet-Type Economies: Definitions, Measurements and Stabilization," *Contributions to Political Economy* 5 (1986): 37–82.

29. G. A. Kulagin, "Nomenklatura, tsena, pribyl'," *EKO* 16, no. 11 (November 1985): 89–106, 94–95.

30. Nikolai P. Fedorenko, "Planirovanie i upravlenie: kakimi im byt'?," *EKO* 15, no. 12 (1984): 3–20, 13; N. Ia. Petrakov, V. Volkonskii, and A. Vavilov, "Tsena: Nuzhny krutye izmeneniia," *Sotsialisticheskaia industriia*, April 3, 1987.

31. Fedorenko, "Planirovanie i upravlenie," pp. 13–14.

32. Nikolai T. Glushkov, "Planovoe tsenoobrazovanie i upravlenie ekonomikoi," *Voprosy ekonomiki* 54, no. 8 (August 1982): 9; Anatolii A. Deriabin and Iniatulla K. Salimzhanov, *Tsena: Instrument upravleniia ekonomikoi* (Moscow: Znanie, 1985), pp. 91–92; Hanson, "Real Growth of Soviet Investment," p. 573.

33. To arrive at this figure, we simply take the means, assuming that price proposals are inflated by 40 percent on average. Two-thirds pass undetected, while one-third is reduced by 25 percent on average. Thus, average unjustified price rises among new commodities = $40 \times 2/3 + (140 \times 3/4 - 100) \div 3 = 28$.

34. On a visit to ministries and enterprises in Soviet Georgia in September 1986, I was surprised to hear that control of price calculations for new products were not perceived as a problem, since the Georgian Goskomtsen cooperated closely with the branch ministries and did not cause mischief. See Deriabin and Salimzhanov, *Instrument upravleniia*, pp. 55–56.

35. Petrakov, et al., "Tsena."

36. *O korennoi perestroike*, pp. 162–63.

37. Abram Bergson, *The Real National Income of Soviet Russia since 1928* (Cambridge: Harvard University, 1961).

38. Separate interviews with three senior Soviet economists in the spring of 1987. The retail trade index they mentioned may be a relatively recent innovation.

39. Grigorii I. Khanin, "V poiskakh bolee tochnykh ekonomicheskikh otsenok (iz istorii sovetskoi ekonomicheskoi nauki vtoroi poloviny 30-kh i 40-kh godov)," *Izvestiia Sibirskogo Otdeleniia Akademii Nauk SSSR, Seriia ekonomiki i prikladnoi sotsiologii* 4, no. 1 (January 1987): 21–28.

40. See Shenfield, "State Statistical Work."

41. A. A. Sergeev is a Doctor of Economics working at the Institute of Economics. Unlike most of the economists mentioned here, he is a conservative (*antitovarnik*) in the Soviet economic debate. Aleksei A. Sergeev, "Prestizh chestnogo rublia" (interview), *Sovetskaia Rossiia*, March 18, 1987.

42. Iurii Chernichenko, "Svoi khleb," *Novy mir* 61, no. 8 (August 1985): 6–48, 35; see Birman, "The Soviet Economy," p. 103.

43. Nove, *The Soviet Economic System*, p. 352.

44. Ellman, *Collectivisation, Convergence and Capitalism*, p. 138; Aganbegyan, *Economic Challenge of Perestroika*, p. 2.

45. Leonid Ivanov, "Khitrye tsifry agroproma," *Literaturnaia gazeta,* May 11, 1988.

46. Boris Milner, "Stil' protiv antistilia," *Literaturnaia gazeta,* May 14, 1987.

47. E. Zhbanov, "Delo o khlobke," *Izvestiya,* September 4, 1986. Calculated from *Narodnoe khoziaistvo SSSR, 1979* (Moscow: Finansy i statistika, 1980), p. 250, abbreviated as *Narkhoz 1979*; *Narkhoz 1980*, p. 232; *Narkhoz 1983*, p. 232. Although the exaggeration was revealed in 1984, cotton statistics were not revised until the autumn of 1987, when *Narkhoz 1987* (p. 228) was published.

48. Milner, "Stil' protiv antistilia."

49. Campbell, *Conversion of National Income Data of the USSR,* table 1.

50. Mikhail Ia. Lemeshev, "Podnimaetsia nad vedomstvennymi interesami," *Nash sovremennik* 53, no. 7 (July 1985): 134–35.

51. Mikhail S. Gorbachev, *Korennoi vopros ekonomicheskoi politiki partii* (Moscow: Politizdat, 1985), p. 13.

52. Fyodor I. Kushnirsky, "The Role of Industrial Modernization in Soviet Economic Planning" in *Gorbachev's Economic Plans,* U.S. Congress, Joint Economic Committee (Washington, D.C.: GPO, 1987), p. 258.

53. *Moscow News,* no. 34, 1987, p. 8.

54. *Ekonomicheskaia gazeta,* no. 40 (1987): 14.

55. *Narkhoz 1987,* pp. 122, 627.

56. *Pravda,* March 23, 1987.

57. Vasilii Seliunin, "Eksperiment," *Novy mir* 61, no. 8 (August 1985): 173–94, 175.

58. Nikolai P. Fedorenko, "XXVI s'ezd KPSS i intensifikatsiia sotsialisticheskoi ekonomiki," *Voprosy filosofii,* no. 10 (October 1981): 3–13, 9.

59. *Ekonomicheskaia gazeta,* no. 48 (1986): 7.

60. E. Vasil'kova, "Kachestvu—garantiiu zakona," *Sotsialisticheskaia industriia,* March 29, 1987.

61. Fedorenko, "XXVI s'ezd KPSS," p. 12; see I. Pashko, "Paradoksy lishnego metalla," *Sotsialisticheskaia industriia,* December 5, 1986; and Seliunin, "Eksperiment," p. 187.

62. Evgenii Primakov, "Vzgliad v proshloe i budushchee," *Pravda,* January 8, 1988; Seliunin, "Eksperiment," p. 187.

63. Gavriil Kh. Popov, *Effektivnoe upravlenie* (Moscow: Ekonomika, 1985), p. 225.

64. D. Murzin, "V plenu nepogreshimosti," *Sotsialisticheskaia industriia,* April 24, 1987.

65. United Nations Economic Commission for Europe (ECE), Energy Data Bank (*Nota bene*, ECE estimates of the Soviet GNP are also exaggerated, as the commission is conservative in its estimates). Jan Winiecki, "Are Soviet-Type Economies Entering an Era of Long-Term Decline?" *Soviet Studies* 38, no. 3 (July 1986): 325–48, 327, presents an earlier, not quite as pessimistic, estimate.

66. Winiecki, "Are Soviet-Type Economies . . . ?" p. 327.

67. Vasilii Parfenov, "Nachinat' s sebia," *Pravda*, January 31, 1987.

68. Henry Norr, "Shchekino: Another Look," *Soviet Studies* 38, no. 2 (April 1986): 141–69, 142.

69. Seliunin, "Eksperiment," p. 182.

70. Abel G. Aganbegyan, "Chelovek i ekonomika," part 1 (interview), *Ogonek*, no. 29 (July 1987): 2.

71. In June 1985, I went on a U.N. tour to the steelworks in Stary Oskol, a modern West German turnkey project in the southern portion of the Russian Soviet Federated Socialist Republic. The accompanying Western specialists listening to input and output data, could not comprehend how the Soviets managed to use twice as much gas in various stages of production as was consumed by identical equipment in the West. *Narkhoz 1987*, p. 688.

72. The growth of national income is grossly exaggerated, but so is the growth of working capital and material costs, though presumably not that of labor resources. Fedorenko "XXVI syezd KPSS," p. 6.

73. Gavrliil Kh. Popov and V. Novikov, "Reshaetsia na meste," *Pravda*, July 1, 1986.

74. Nuti, "Hidden and Repressed Inflation," p. 77.

75. Grigorii I. Khanin, "Puti sovershenstvovaniia informatsionnogo obespecheniia svodnykh planovykh narodnokhoziaistvennykh raschetov," *Izvestiia Akademii Nauk SSSR, Seriia ekonomicheskaia* 15, no. 3 (May/June 1984): 58–67, 59.

76. This majority view has been disputed by Richard Portes and others, but their arguments have been rejected in so many places that I see no need to discuss them further here (see, for example, Janos Kornai, *Economics of Shortage* (Amsterdam: North-Holland, 1980). Holzman's indicator of repressed inflation vacillates from 1966 until 1971, after which it rises firmly (Franklyn D. Holzman, "Soviet Inflationary Pressures, 1928–1957: Causes and Cures," *Quarterly Journal of Economics* 74, no. 2 [May 1960]: 167–88; G. Garvey, *Money, Financial Flows and Credit in the Soviet Union* (Cambridge, Mass.: Ballinger, 1977); E. Dirkens, "The Control of Inflation? Errors in the Interpretation of CPE Data," *Economica* 48 [August 1981]: 305–8.) Seliunin

and Khanin, "Lukavaia tsifra," p. 194, as well as Kulagin, argue that the 1965 reforms gave rise to a hidden increase in prices at the enterprise level spurred by the financial targets of the reform.

77. Gregory Grossman, "Inflationary, Political, and Social Implications of the Current Economic Slowdown," in *Economics and Politics in the USSR: Problems of Interdependence,* ed. H. Hohmann et al. (Boulder and London: Westview Press, 1986).

78. Konstantin G. Kagalovskii, "Podzhatsia!" *Kommunist* 65, no. 11 (July 1988): 66–73, 70.

79. *Narkhoz 1987,* pp. 122, 635.

80. *Narkhoz 1985,* p. 554.

81. Abel G. Aganbegyan, "Na putiakh obnovleniia" (interview), *Literaturnaia gazeta,* February 18, 1987; Seliunin, "Eksperiment," p. 191.

82. *Pravda,* December 25, 1987; Grossman "Current Economic Slowdown," p. 185.

83. Nikolai Ia. Petrakov, "Ukreplenie denezhnogo obrashcheniia i strategiia uskoreniia," *Voprosy ekonomiki* 59, no. 8 (August 1987): 3–11.

84. Stanislav S. Shatalin, "Kak izmerit' ekonomicheskii rost (How To Measure Economic Growth)," *Ekonomicheskaia gazeta,* no. 31 (July 1987).

85. R. Khasbulatov, "Chto vidno v zerkale tseny," *Pravda,* June 15, 1986.

86. *Pravda,* June 17, 1986.

87. *Pravda,* July 13, 1985.

88. *Literaturnaia gazeta,* April 15, 1987.

89. V. Tolstov, "Kto isportil appetit," *Izvestiia,* March 27, 1987.

90. Igor Birman, *Ekonomika nedostach* (New York: Chalidze Publications, 1983), pp. 198–99.

91. Fyodor I. Kushnirsky, "Inflation Soviet Style," *Problems of Communism* 33, no. 1 (January–February 1984): 48–53, 51.

92. Deriabin and Salimzhanov, *Instrument upravleniia,* p. 76.

93. Nove "Growth, Investment, and Price Indices," p. 145.

94. Aleksandr Bim and Aleksandr Shokhin, "Sistema raspredeleniia: na putiakh perestroiki," *Kommunist* 63, no. 15 (October 1985): 64–73, 69.

95. Nuti, "Hidden and Repressed Inflation," p. 76.

96. For example, Birman, *Ekonomika nedostach,* p. 178.

97. Tolstov, "Kto isportil appetit."

98. Tolstov, "Tovary i defitsit (Commodities and Shortage)," *Izvestiia,* January 2, 1987; idem, "'Import' ne zavozili?" *Izvestiia,* January 16, 1987; idem, "Po tsenam kooptorga," *Izvestiia,* March 6, 1987; idem,

"Kto isportil appetit"; idem, "Bliudechko s zolotoi kaemochkoi," *Izvestiia*, April 24, 1987.

99. Tolstov, "Kto isportil appetit."

100. Aganbegyan, "Chelovek i ekonomika," p. 5.

101. *Izvestiia*, January 23, 1988.

102. Nikolai Shmelev, "Avansy i dolgi," *Novy mir* 63, no. 6 (June 1987): 142–58, 154.

103. Benedykt Askanas and Kazimierz Laski, "Consumer Prices and Private Consumption in Poland and Austria," *Journal of Comparative Economics* 9, no. 2 (1985): 164–77.

104. U.S. Congress, Joint Economic Committee, *USSR: Measures of Economic Growth and Development, 1950–80* (Washington, D.C., GPO, 1982), p. 44.

105. Askanas and Laski, "Private Consumption in Poland and Austria."

106. *Narkhoz 1987*, p. 468.

107. *Narkhoz 1987*, pp. 192, 641.

108. See *Narkhoz 1987*, p. 726. Vladimir Treml identified this problem a decade ago (*Radio Liberty Research*, RL 177/77, July 26, 1977). For the first quarter of 1988, Goskomstat has amended this shortcoming by introducing a new figure for sales of cars "out of current production," which is at a much lower level (*Pravda*, April 26, 1988).

109. Thomas A. Wolf and Ed A. Hewett, "A Puzzle in Soviet Foreign Trade Statistics and Possible Implications for Estimates of Soviet Arms Exports to Developing Countries," in *The Soviet Economy in the 1980s: Problems and Prospects*, U.S. Congress, Joint Economic Committee (Washington, D.C.: GPO, 1983), pp. 575–81.

110. Aganbegyan, "Na putiakh obnovleniia."

111. Seliunin and Khanin, "Lukavaia tsifra," p. 181.

112. *Narkhoz 1987*, p. 455.

113. Admittedly, *Narkhoz 1987* included a new table on meat sales by weight (p. 466), but its value is dubious, for the reasons mentioned above.

114. *Narkhoz 1987*, p. 711.

115. Albert Vainshtein, *Narodnyi dokhod Rossii i SSSR* (Moscow: Nauka, 1969), p. 113.

116. Philip Hanson, "USSR: Puzzles in the 1985 Statistics," *Radio Liberty Research*, RL 439/86, November 20, 1986; idem, "The Plan Fulfillment Report of 1986: A Sideways Look at the Statistics," *Radio Liberty Research*, RL 76/87, February 26, 1987; Jan Vanous, "The Dark Side of

'Glasnost': Unbelievable National Income Statistics in the Gorbachev Era," *PlanEcon* 3, no. 6 (February 13, 1987).

117. As Hanson and Vanous based their calculations on preliminary data, I refrain from using their exact figures and take the most recent official Soviet estimates.

118. M. Siuniaev, "Ekonomicheskomu rostu—novye izmeriteli," *Ekonomicheskaia gazeta*, no. 3 (January 1988): 14.

119. Aleksandr I. Anchishkin, "Novoe kachestvo ekonomicheskogo rosta," *Voprosy ekonomiki* 68, no. 9 (September 1986): 3–14, 4. Turnover tax revenues peaked at 102.9 billion rubles in 1983 (*Narkhoz 1984*, p. 562; *Narkhoz 1987*, p. 628).

120. The effects Siuniaev discusses had similar impacts in both 1985 and 1986 (see Table 2 and alcohol sales in both years), so our criticism of the discrepancy in CIA estimates of Soviet GNP growth in 1985 and 1986 stands. Abraham S. Becker, "National Income Accounting in the USSR" in *Soviet Economic Statistics*, ed. Vladimir G. Treml and John P. Hardt (Durham, N.C.: Duke University Press, 1972), p. 109.

121. Hanson, "USSR: Puzzles in the 1985 Statistics"; *Narkhoz* 1985, p. 572.

122. Vladimir G. Treml, "Foreign Trade and the Soviet Economy: Changing Parameters and Interrelations" in *The Impact of International Economic Disturbances on the Soviet Union and Eastern Europe*, ed. Egon Neuberger and Laura D'Andrea Tyson (New York: Pergamon, 1980), pp. 184–207, Campbell, *Conversion of National Income Data*; Alec Nove, "Some Statistical Puzzles Examined," *Soviet Studies* 38, no. 1 (January 1986): 98–102; Igor Birman, "A Note on Soviet Trade Gains," *Soviet Studies* 38, no. 4 (October 1986).

123. Treml, "Foreign Trade and the Soviet Economy," pp. 187–88; Shmul' B. Sverdlik, *Obshchestvennyi produkt i denezhnyi oborot* (Novosibirsk: Nauka, 1981), p. 63.

124. Birman, "A Note on Soviet Trade Gains," p. 588.

125. Thomas A. Wolf, "Foreign Trade and National Income Statistics in the Soviet Union: A Comment," *Soviet Studies* 39, no. 1 (January 1987): 122–28.

126. Siuniaev, "Ekonomicheskomu rostu"; *Pravda*, February 19, 1988; Alec Nove, "A Reply to Wolf and Birman," *Soviet Studies* 39, no. 1 (January 1987): 131–37; Birman, "A Note on Soviet Trade Gains."

127. Abram Bergson, "Comment," in *The Impact of International Economic Distrubances*, ed. Neuberger and Tyson (New York: Pergamon Press, 1989), pp. 207–11.

128. *Narkhoz 1987*.

129. N. V. Talyzin in *Pravda*, November 18, 1986, p. 2; Hanson (1987), p. 3.

130. See *Pravda*, January 24, 1988.

131. Nove, "Growth, Investment, and Price Indices"; Vladimir K. Fal'tsman, "Moshchnostnoi ekvivalent osnovnykh fondov," *Voprosy ekonomiki* 52, no. 8 (August 1980): 117–28; and Viktor P. Krasnovskii, "Ekonomicheskie problemy fondootdachi," *Voprosy ekonomiki* 52 (January 1, 1980).

132. Nove, "Growth, Investment, and Price Indices," p. 145.

133. Peter J. D. Wiles, "Soviet Consumption and Investment Prices and the Meaningfulness of Real Investment," *Soviet Studies* 34, vol. 2 (April 1982), pp. 289–95.

134. Hanson, "Real Growth of Soviet Investment"; K. K. Val'tukh, "Investitsionnyi kompleks i intensifikatsiia proizvodstva," *EKO* 13, no. 3 (March 1982): 4–31; Grigorii I. Khanin, "Alternativnye otsenki rezul'tatov khoziaistvennoi deiatel'nosti proizvodstvennykh iacheek promyshlennosti," *Izvestiia Akademii Nauk SSSR, Seriia ekonomicheskaia* 12, no. 6 (November/December 1981): 62–73; Vladimir K. Fal'tsman and Aleksandr K. Kornev, "Rezervy snizheniia kapitaloemkosti moshchnostei promyshlennosti," *Voprosy ekonomiki* 56, no. 6 (June 1984): 36–45.

135. Stanley H. Cohn, "A Comment on Alec Nove, 'A Note on Growth, Investment and Price Indices,'" *Soviet Studies* 33, no. 2 (April 1981): 296–99; and Abram Bergson, "On Soviet Real Investment Growth," *Soviet Studies* 39, no. 3 (July 1987): 406–24.

136. Nove, "Growth, Investment, and Price Indices," pp. 143–44.

137. Cohn, "Comment on Alec Nove," p. 296.

138. Bergson, "On Soviet Real Investment Growth," p. 412.

139. See ibid., p. 410.

140. Ibid.

141. Ibid., p. 421. He writes, for instance, "I assume, as Hanson does, that in the calculation of investment in comparable prices, machinery imports are simply included at current prices. That could be so, though it is troubling that Fal'tsman and Kornev nowhere expressly say it is" (p. 418).

142. Cohn, "Comment on Alec Nove," p. 297.

143. Bergson, "On Soviet Real Investment Growth," p. 416, 417.

144. Ibid., p. 410.

145. Nove, "Reply to Bergson."

146. Bergson, "On Soviet Real Investment Growth," p. 406.

147. Schroeder and Edwards, *Consumption in the USSR.*

148. Irving B. Kravis, Alan Heston, and Robert Summers, *World Product and Income: International Comparisons of Real Gross Product* (Baltimore and London: Johns Hopkins University Press, 1982).

149. Schroeder and Edwards, *Consumption in the USSR,* p. 4.

150. Birman, *Ekonomika nedostach,* p. 377; Peter J. D. Wiles, *The Political Economy of Communism* (Oxford: Blackwell, 1962).

151. Schroeder and Edwards, *Consumption in the USSR,* and Birman, *Ekonomika nedostach.*

152. Schroeder and Edwards, *Consumption in the USSR,* p. v.

153. Ibid., pp. 26–29.

154. The bias in their estimates of various components of consumption is likely to be similar, so the structure of consumption is presumably depicted correctly.

155. Kravis et al., *World Product and Income,* pp. 22, 372.

156. Ibid., p. 372.

157. The ICP matching methods are very conservative (ibid., pp. 39–40). Marer, *Dollar GNPs of the USSR and Eastern Europe,* pp. 35–37.

158. Ibid.

159. Birman, *Ekonomika nedostach,* pp. 215–470; Schroeder and Edwards, *Consumption in the USSR,* especially p. 4.

160. Birman, *Ekonomika nedostach,* pp. 382, 377.

161. Murray Feshbach, "Soviet Military Health Issues," in *Gorbachev's Economic Plan,* pp. 462–80; and Christopher M. Davis, "Developments in the Health Sector of the Soviet Economy, 1970–90" in *JEL* (1987), pp. 312–35.

162. Alexander Zaichenko, "On Our Daily Bread," *Moscow News,* no. 34 (1988).

163. *Narkhoz 1987,* p. 12.

164. Genadii Zoteev is a Ph.D. candidate of economics. He was a disciple of Anchishkin at TsEMI and must have been brought to Gosplan by him. An early official Soviet estimate of the Soviet GNP was about 825 billion rubles in actual prices in 1987 (*SSSR v tsifrakh v 1987 godu,* [Moscow: Finansy i statistika, 1988], p. 14), close to Zoteev's figures. Genadii Zoteev, "Ob otsenke natsional'nogo produkta," *Ekonomicheskaia gazeta,* no. 42 (October 1987).

165. Data from the Vienna Institute for Comparative Economic Studies.

166. *Narkhoz 1960,* p. 168.

167. *Narkhoz 1922–1972*, p. 64.

168. *Narkhoz 1922–1972*, p. 168.

169. *Narkhoz 1987*, p. 13.

170. U.S. CIA, *Handbook of Economic Statistics, 1986* (Washington, D.C.: GPO, 1986), p. 34.

171. Boris Bolotin, "Sovetskii Soiuz v mirovoi ekonomike (1917–1987 gg.)," *MEMO*, no. 11 (November 1987): 145–57, 150.

172. 1929, 1938, 1950, 1986, and 1987, with a gap of 36 years between 1950 and 1986, although 1980 is his base year. He covers the whole world and presents 18 extensive tables. Both these factors indicate that he relies on some other statistical work, which he conceals (as is common when Soviet scholars use Western materials). U.S. CIA and DIA, "Gorbachev's Modernization Program: A Status Report," paper presented to U.S. Congress, Joint Economic Committee, Subcommittee on National Security Economics (Washington, D.C.: GPO, 1987), pp. 24–25.

173. Marer, *Dollar GNPs of the USSR*, p. 7.

174. Ibid., p. 41.

175. Ibid., p. 8.

176. Kravis et al., *World Product and Income*, p. 22.

177. Marer, *Dollar GNPs of the USSR*, p. 7.

178. Wharton Econometric Forecasting Associates, "Comparison of Absolute and per Capita National Income in CMEA Countries" in *Centrally Planned Economies: Current Analysis*, July 13, 1984, p. 9.

179. The ratios of NMP to GNP are rather similar in Hungary and the Soviet Union. According to Zoteev, "Ob otsenke nationalnogo produkta," Hungary has more nonproductive services, while the Soviet Union more amortizations.

180. In this and the comparisons that follow, we try to concentrate on reasonably populous countries and avoid one-sided economies, such as major oil producers, as well as countries without market-oriented exchange rates. In order to give some idea of GNP ranking, I have included the World Bank figures for 1985, which are based simply on exchange-rate conversion.

181. Schroeder and Edwards, *Consumption in the USSR*, p. vi.

182. Zaichenko, "On Our Daily Bread."

183. *Pravda*, June 30, 1988.

184. *Pravda*, April 24, 1986.

185. Abel G. Aganbegyan, "Chelovek i ekonomika," part 2 (interview), *Ogonek*, no. 30 (1987): 12.

186. *Sotsialisticheskaia industriia*, March 26, 1987.

187. *Pravda*, February 4, 1987.

188. Boris Bolotin, "A More Complete Picture: New Findings from the USSR State Committee for Statistics," *Moscow News*, no. 11 (1988).

189. *Narkhoz 1985*, p. 446.

190. *Vestnik statistiki*, no. 8 (1986): 42.

191. The figure for imports in domestic prices is taken from Campbell, *Conversion of National Income Data of the USSR*, table 8, and we use Zoteev's calculation of GNP (Zoteev, "Ob otenke nationalnogo produkta.") Treml, "Foreign Trade and the Soviet Economy."

192. Vladimir K. Fal'tsman, "Mashinostroenie: puti peremen," *EKO* 16, no. 12 (December 1985): 3–20, 5.

193. *Vneshtorg 1985*, p. 32.

194. *Narkhoz 1987*, p. 209.

195. *Foreign Trade by Commodities* (Paris: Organization for Economic Cooperation and Development, 1985); idem, *National Accounts, 1960–1986, Main Aggregates*, vol. 1 (Paris: 1988), p. 18.

196. *Vneshtorg 1985*, pp. 8, 61.

197. *Economic Bulletin for Europe* (New York: UN Economic Commission for Europe, 1985), pp. 3, 27.

198. *Economic Bulletin for Europe*, 1983, Table 3.7.

199. U.S. GNP per capita grew by 12.7 percent from 1980 to 1986 (OECD, *National Accounts*, p. 131); with a Soviet population growth of 5.7 percent from January 1, 1981, to January 1, 1987 (*Narkhoz 1987*, p. 373), an NMP growth estimated by Khanin at 3 percent from 1980 to 1985 (Table 9), and poor economic results in 1986, the Soviet GNP per capita has stagnated at best.

200. The World Bank, *World Development Report 1987* (New York: Oxford University Press, 1987), p. 211; *Narkhoz 1985*, p. 411.

201. Vasilii Seliunin, "Tempy rosta na vesakh potrebleniia," *Sotsialisticheskaia industriia*, January 5, 1988.

202. David F. Epstein, "The Economic Cost of Soviet Security and Empire," this volume.

203. Andrew W. Marshall, "Commentary," in *Gorbachev's Economic Plans*, p. 484, has similarly guessed at 20 to 30 percent of Soviet GNP. The popular perception among Moscow intellectuals is that defense absorbs more than half of NMP, but this perception is likely to be exaggerated, as people wonder where all the produced wealth disappears but do not realize the full extent of waste.

204. Gur Ofer and Aaron Vinokur, "Inequality of Earnings, Household Income, and Wealth in the Soviet Union in the 1970s" in *Politics,*

Work, and Daily Life in the USSR: A Survey of Former Soviet Citizens, ed., James R. Millar (Cambridge: Cambridge University Press, 1987), p. 70.

205. The Grossman-Treml definition of private income was broader; it included agriculture and a wider geographic area and was undertaken later, when the second economy had probably grown. Gregory Grossman and Vladimir G. Treml, "Measuring Hidden Personal Incomes in the USSR" in *The Unofficial Economy,* ed. Sergio Alessandrini and Bruno Dallago (Aldershot, England: Gower, 1986), pp. 285–296, p. 219.

206. Wiles "Soviet Consumption and Investment Price," p. 291.

207. Seliunin and Khanin, "Lukavaia tsifra."

208. Richard E. Ericson has elaborated Khanin's ideas in his contribution to this volume. Khanin, "Alternativnye otsenki rezul'tatov," "Puti sovershenstrovaniia informatsionnogo."

209. Khanin, "Puti sovershenstrovaniia informatsionnogo."

210. Seliunin and Khanin, "Lukavaia tsifra," p. 192.

211. See *Narkhoz 1987,* p. 7.

212. V. Adamov, "Chto stoit za indeksami," *Ekonomicheskaia gazeta,* no. 29 (July 1987).

213. Bolotin, "Sovetskii soiuz v mirovoi ekonomike," p. 153.

214. Ibid., p. 150; calculated from Richard E. Ericson, "The Soviet Statistical Debate: Khanin vs. TsSU," Table 1, in this volume.

215. Seliunin and Khanin, "Lukavaia tsifra," p. 193.

216. Vainshtein, *Narodnyi dokhod Rossii i SSSR,* p. 106.

217. Ibid., p. 107.

218. Ericson, "Soviet Statistical Debate."

219. Zoteev, "Ob otsenke nationalnogo produkta."

220. Grossman, "Current Economic Slowdown."

221. Seliunin and Khanin, "Lukavaia tsifra," p. 193.

222. *Narkhov 1922–1972,* p. 216.

223. Ibid., p. 256.

224. Ibid., p. 9.

225. J. G. Chapman, *Real Wages in Soviet Russia since 1928* (Cambridge, Mass.: Harvard University Press, 1963).

226. Vainshtein, *Narodnyi dokhod Rossii i SSSR,* pp. 103–6.

227. *Pravda,* January 26, 1986, and January 18, 1987.

228. *Narkhoz 1987,* p. 58; U.S. CIA and DIA, "Gorbachev's Modernization Program."

229. Ibid., Appendix, Table 1.

230. The CIA and DIA have begun to present common estimates, but they have not explained how the change has affected CIA methodology.

Presumably they have departed from documented CIA methodology into the sphere of negotiation.

231. Otto Lacis, "Kak shagaet uskorenie?" *Kommunist* 64, no. 4 (1987): 53–63, 58.

232. See *USSR: Measures of Economic Growth and Development, 1950–1980,* U.S. Congress, Joint Economic Committee (Washington, D.C.: GPO, 1982).

233. *Pravda,* January 24, 1988.

234. Having traveled extensively in the countrysides of both nations, I may assert that it is far more easy to find a sufficiently clean eating place in India than in the Soviet Union, where food poisoning is almost inevitable outside the biggest cities. However, restaurants are not representative of the culture of either country; Tolstov, "'Import' ne zavozili?"

235. Lacis, "Kak shagaet uskorenie?"

236. *Pravda,* January 24, 1988.

237. Interview with a Western importer of Soviet textiles.

238. In the West, the production of a ship that was financed entirely by state subsidies and scrapped immediately after its completion would still contribute to the GNP as it is defined. Such a situation is absurd if we are to use GNP as a measurement of national income and an indication of national wealth, but might pass by, because it is an exception. In the Soviet Union, on the other hand, production that is a waste and degradation of good raw materials is the rule. If the system were not to change, the most rational economic solution would probably be to phase out most of Soviet manufacturing, export the raw materials and import better manufactured goods.

239. Aganbegyan, "Chelovek i ekonomika 1," p. 5.

240. For example, Winiecki, "Are Soviet-Type Economics . . . ?"

241. *Narkhoz 1985,* p. 240.

242. Ibid., p. 445.

243. Aleksei Ochkin, "'Naguliaet' li tsena pribyl'?" *Nash Sovremennik* 55, no. 12 (1987): 158.

244. The sizable sales of meat through factory canteens and the direct distribution of meat at enterprises are supposed to be included in the retail sales statistics (*Narkhoz 1987,* pp. 466–67, 726).

245. *Narkhoz 1987,* p. 455.

246. On the basis of their interview survey of Soviet émigrés, Gregory Grossman and Vladimir G. Treml estimated that sales on urban *kolkhoz* markets amounted to 33.8 billion rubles in 1977, while the official

estimate was only 7.3 billion rubles. Grossman and Treml, "Measuring Hidden Personal Incomes in the USSR" in *The Unofficial Economy*.

247. However, a large and growing share of private agricultural production is being credited as public-sector output (Karl-Eugen Wadekin, "Soviet Agriculture in 1987 and the Private Sector," *Radio Liberty Research,* RL 110/88, March 15, 1988; see Ivanov, "Khitrye tsifry agroproma").

248. *Narkhoz 1987,* pp. 464, 466.

249. *Literaturnaia gazeta,* December 16, 1987.

250. The lowest price I observed—3.50 rubles per kilogram—was in Vilnius in Lithuania in February 1987. Many factors contribute to uncommonly low market prices in Lithuania. Its private animal husbandry is probably the best developed in the Soviet Union; its trade is comparatively well organized; incomes are not very high, and few wealthy travelers come to Lithuania. Official statistics on sales by *kolkhozy* and *sovkhozy* at *kolkhoz* markets in 264 towns state their average price on October 1, 1987, at 3.45 rubles per kilogram for beef and 3.23 rubles per kilogram for pork (*Planovoe khoziaistvo,* no. 3 (1988): 125), but these form only part of cooperative sales, and the prices seem too low to be taken seriously. The corresponding private prices given are 4.70 rubles for beef and 4.50 rubles for pork, which seem more plausible.

251. See *Narkhoz 1987,* p. 455.

252. *Izvestiia,* November 19, 1987.

253. *Narkhoz 1987,* p. 726.

254. *Narkhoz 1987,* p. 455.

255. After having related the results of a recent family budget survey (*Izvestiia,* October 10, 1987), Iurii Rytov wrote, "Never before have I received so many angry, irritated and indignant letters" (*Izvestiia,* December 19, 1987) about the State's exaggerations of the standard of living; Vanous "The Dark Side of 'Glasnost,'" p. 1.

256. The CIA reacted to Vanous's report with a brief memorandum, concluding: "While agreeing with most of what Vanous has to say about the discrepancies in Soviet statistics, we disagree with the alternative estimates that he makes of Soviet economic performance in 1986. Mr. Vanous's figures are derived by manipulating Soviet data for statistical aggregates—retail trade and national income—and are therefore distorted when Soviet data are inconsistent. CIA estimates, which are based on disaggregated Soviet data, offer a different picture. Rather than believing that Soviet economic performance in 1986 was as bad as

Vanous portrays it, we believe 1986 was a fairly good year for the Soviet economy" (U.S. CIA, *Handbook of Economic Statistics*, pp. 6–7). Laurie Kurtzweg, "Trends in Soviet Gross National Product," in *Gorbachev's Economic Plans*, p. 165, reiterates this view. These statements reflect the CIA's inability to relate its figures to alternative data and to check their plausibility.

257. Vanous, "The Dark Side of 'Glasnost,'" p. 6.

258. Ibid., pp. 7, 9.

259. Siuniaev, "Ekonomicheskomu rostu."

260. Nove, "A Reply to Wolf and Birman."

261. *Pravda*, February 19, 1988.

262. I owe this information to Igor Birman and a senior Soviet economist.

263. One of the foremost Soviet price experts explained this to me in the spring of 1987.

264. Seliunin, "Tempy rosta."

265. Deriabin and Salimzhanov, *Instrument upravleniia*, p. 55.

266. Rem A. Belousov, and A. Z. Seleznev, eds., *Upravlenie ekonomikoi: Slovar', Osnovnye poniatiia i kategorii* (Moscow: Ekonomika, 1986), p. 290.

267. *Narkhoz 1987*, p. 723.

268. I have not managed to find any good Soviet explanation of this, but it is a rather obvious interpretation of Soviet practices. Igor Birman, who is well-acquainted with these pricing practices from previous work in Moscow, assures me that it is correct.

269. *Narkhoz 1987*, p. 723.

270. This remark was brought to my attention by Peter Wiles. Sverdlik, *Obshchestvennyi produkt*, p. 91.

271. *Ekonomicheskaia gazeta*, no. 35, 1986, p. 14; *Sotsialisticheskaia industriia*, August 14, 1985.

272. *O korennoi perestroike*, p. 157.

273. Delez M. Palterovich, "Problemy ispol'zovaniia strategicheskikh i takticheskich rezervov mashinostroeniia," *Ekonomika i matematicheskie metody* 23, no. 4 (July/August 1987): 589–601.

274. Khanin, "Al'ternativnye otsenki rezul'tatov," "Puti sovershenstvovaniia informatsionnogo."

275. Oleg T. Bogomolov, "Skol'ko stoiat den'gi," *Literaturnaia gazeta*, September 16, 1987.

276. Ochkin, "'Naguliaet' li tsena pribyl'?" p. 155.

277. *Narkhoz 1987*, p. 456.

278. Seliunin, "Eksperiment," p. 186.

279. D. S. L'vov and Nikolai Ya. Petrakov, "Mekhanizm upravleniia ekonomikoi i nauchno-tekhnicheskii progress," *Kommunist* 64, no. 4 (1987): 86–92, 88.

280. Fal'tsman "Mashinostroenie," p. 4–5; see Seliunin and Khanin "Lukavaia tsifra," p. 191.

281. Seliunin and Khanin, "Lukavaia tsifra," p. 187.

282. K. K. Val'tukh and B. L. Lavrovskii, "Proizvodstvennyi apparat strany: ispol'zovanie i rekonstruktsiia," *EKO* 17, no. 2 (February 1986): 17–32.

283. Ibid., p. 30.

284. Vadim N. Kirichenko, "Piatiletka kachestvennykh peremen v ekonomike," *Voprosy ekonomiki* 58, no. 11 (November 1986): 3–12, 7.

285. *Literaturnaia gazeta,* April 1, 1987.

286. Wiles, "Soviet Inflation, 1982," p. 136.

287. Wiles, "Soviet Consumption and Investment Prices," p. 291.

288. Ibid., p. 293.

289. Wiles, "Soviet Inflation, 1982," p. 291.

2. Richard E. Ericson

This paper is based partially on research supported by IREX and a Fulbright-Hays grant during a visit to the Soviet Union, January–June 1987.

1. Aside from the article under discussion, the most notable of these was Nikolai Shmelev, "Avansy i dolgi," in the July issue. Also of interest were Vasilii Seliunin, "Eksperiment," in August 1985; L. Popkova, "Gde pirogi pyshnee," in May 1987; and N. Petrakov, "Zolotoi chervonets vchera i zavtra," in August 1987. All caused excited responses in letters to the editors of the central papers.

2. This impression is based on several visits to the Soviet Union in the late 1970s and early 1980s, discussions with Soviet colleagues, and articles in the Soviet press.

3. Among these writings are V. Krasovskii, "Ekonomicheskie problemy fondootdachi," *Voprosy ekonomiki,* no. 1 (1980); V. K. Fal'tsman, "Moshchnostnyi ekvivalent osnovnykh fondov," *Voprosy Ekonomiki,* no. 8 (1980); K. K. Val'tukh, "Investitsionnyi kompleks i intensifikatsiia proizvodstva," *EKO,* no. 3 (1982); and Fal'tsman, "Zakaz na novuiu

tekhniku," *EKO*, no. 7 (1983). See also Alec Nove, "A Note on Growth, Investment, and Price Indices," *Soviet Studies* 23, no. 1 (January 1981): 142–45; and P. Hanson, "The CIA, the TsSU, and the Real Growth of Soviet Investment," *Soviet Studies* 26, no. 4 (October 1984): 571–81. Nove, "Has Soviet Growth Ceased?" Manchester Statistical Society lecture, November 15, 1983, contains a good summary and explanation.

4. Of this series I attended two, on February 25 at Moscow State University (MGU) and on May 7 at the Central Economic-Mathematical Institute of the USSR Academy of Sciences (CEMI AN SSSR). The presentations and the data presented were essentially identical, though the discussion and questions raised naturally differed. Khanin's numbers were published, in slightly revised form, as "Ekonomicheskii rost: al'ternativnaia, 1988, pp. 83–90 in *Kommunist*. Khanin's earlier methodological pieces were "Al'ternativnye otsenki rezul'tatov khoziaistvennoi deiatel'nosti proizvodstvennykh iacheek promyshlennosti," *Izvestiia akademii nauk*, Seriia ekonomicheskaia, no. 6 (1981); and "Puti sovershenstvovaniia informatsionnogo obespecheniia svodnykh planovykh narodnokhoziaistvennykh raschetov," *Izvestiia akademii nauk*, Seriia ekonomicheskaia, no. 3 (1984).

5. This was noted by Khanin in response to questions, and by Seliunin in a separate seminar at MGU on March 11.

6. Defense of TsSU methodology coupled with direct attack on Khanin can be found in three articles in *Vestnik statistiki*, no. 6 (1987), and in a piece by V. Adamov, "Chto stoit za indeksami," *Ekonomicheskaia gazeta*, no. 29 (1987). Less substantial, more *ad hominem*, criticism appeared in press interviews, for example, of M. Korolev in *Izvestiia*, April 22, 1987, and in press conferences, such as that of N. Belov on April 30, 1987, at the information center of the Ministry of Foreign Affairs.

7. Among the numerous articles reflecting this criticism, see A. Rubinov, "Chto pochem, ili o poezii zhizni i proze tsen," *Literaturnaia gazeta* 15 (April 1987); almost any 1987 "Kommercheskoe obozrenie" column appearing on Saturdays in *Izvestiia* (for example, April 11 and 24 and May 8); and S. Senina, "Taina indeksa 'N'," *Leninskoe znamia*, April 12, 1987.

8. These points are made in the articles cited in note 7. This was something of a favorite topic for *Izvestiia*, with frequent articles such as "Besstyzhnaia dynia" on May 9, 1987, and "Ukorochennyi udav" on June 6, 1987.

9. Typical of this discussion, although it appeared after the Khanin-Seliunin piece, is a series of articles in *Ekonomicheskaia gazeta* in 1987: N. Petrakov and D. L'vov, "Kachestvo tempov," no. 3; S.S. Shatalin, "Kak izmerit' ekonomicheskii rost," no. 31; and in 1988, "Strukturnye sootnosheniia ekonomicheskogo rosta," no. 32; I. Pogosov, "Kriterii kachestva tempov," no. 33; G. Zoteev, "Ob otsenke valovogo natsional'nogo produkta," no. 42; M. Siuniaev, "Ekonomicheskomu rostu—novye izmeriteli," no. 3.

10. Another alternative, though less complete, internal reconstruction of Soviet national income accounts was recently carried out by a group at the Institute of World Economy and International Relations (IMEMO). Some of their results were published in the institute's journal, *Mirovaia ekonomika i mezhdunarodnye otnosheniia,* under the title "Sovetskii soiuz v mirovoi ekonomike (1917–1987 gg)" [The Soviet Union in the World Economy (1917–1987)], no. 11 (1987): 145–57; and no. 12 (1987): 141–48. I discuss this alternative further in the section "Khanin's Statistics: An Alternative."

11. For a clear summary of the Western consensus, see G. Ofer, "Soviet Economic Growth: 1928–1985," *Journal of Economic Literature* 25, no. 4 (December 1987): 1767–1833.

12. The list is based on Khanin's discussions. For a more detailed evaluation of the sectors believed to be reliable in their reporting, see J. Noren, "The New Look at Soviet Statistics: Implications for CIA Measures of the USSR's Economic Growth," paper presented at a CIA conference on December 11, 1987, and revised December 22, 1987.

13. This debate has pitted the "British school" of A. Nove, P. Wiles, and P. Hanson against A. Bergson and S. H. Cohn, the supporters of the CIA methodology for reconstruction of Soviet national income accounts. The latest round in this discussion is presented in *Soviet Studies* 39, no. 3 (July 1987): 406–31, in which Bergson's major paper, "On Soviet Real Investment Growth," is followed by comments by Hanson and by Nove.

14. A discussion of these distortions can be found in J. Hardt and V. Treml, *Soviet Economic Statistics* (Durham, N.C.: Duke University Press, 1972).

15. The case for the consensus view has been summarized most recently in A. Bergson, "On Soviet Real Investment Growth," *Soviet Studies* 39, no. 3, (July 1987): 406–24. The methodology of CIA reconstructions is explained in J. Pitzer, "Gross National Product of the USSR,

1950–80" in U.S. Congress, Joint Economic Committee, *USSR: Measures of Economic Growth and Development, 1950–80* (Washington, D.C.: Government Printing Office, 1982).

16. Some recent Soviet work is indicated in Nove's response to Bergson in *Soviet Studies* (note 13). The methodological study is an unpublished paper by V. Kontorovich and B. Rumer, "Inflation in the Soviet Investment Complex," December 1987.

17. Khanin and Seliunin make this point (p. 192) and gave it particular importance in their seminars. The impact of excess, easy "money" in the system on this process is also emphasized, for example, in articles by V. Perlamutrov in *Stroitel'naia gazeta*, February 27 and March 3; and in "Gruz 'legkikh' deneg," April 5, 1987.

18. See, for example, G. A. Kulagin, "Nomenklatura, tsena, pribyl'," *EKO* 14, no. 11 (1983); N. P. Fedorenko, "Planirovanie i upravlenie: Kakimi im byt'," *EKO* 15, no. 12 (1984); and N. Petrakov, V. Volkonskii, and A. Vavilov, "Tsena: nuzhnyi krutie izmeneniia," *Sotsialisticheskaia industriia*, April 3, 1987. The point is also made indirectly in Khanin and Seliunin, pp. 182, 192.

19. The quality-change issue is directly addressed in, among other places, N. Ia. Petrakov and D. L'vov, "Kachestvo tempov," *Ekonomicheskaia gazeta*, no. 3 (1987): 14.

20. Literally thousands of articles in the Soviet central economic press have pointed this out. A particularly striking one was V. Mel'nikov, "Byl' o zolotom ekskavatore," *Sotsialisticheskaia industriia*, April 2–3, 1987. It gave examples of extractive-equipment prices rising 10 to 15 percent per year without noticeable quality change, and indeed some possible deterioration in productivity of the equipment.

21. See, for example, A. Rubinov in *Literaturnaia gazeta*, April 15, 1987; *Pravda*, June 19, 1986; or the section "Kommercheskoe obozrenie" on any Saturday in *Izvestiia*. This perception is also apparent in the reporter's questioning of A. N. Komin, deputy chairman of Goskomtsen, in *Izvestiia*, May 19, 1987. Also see Khanin and Seliunin's response to their critics in a letter to the editor of *Novy mir*, "Statistika znaet vse," no. 12 (December 1987): 255–57.

22. See, for example, "Kauchukovye tsfiry," *Moskovskaia pravda*, April 11, 1987, and "Strannaia slepota," *Leninskoe znamia*, May 14, 1987.

23. A. Sergeev, "Prestizh chestnogo rublia," *Sovetskaia Rossiia*, March 18, 1987.

24. Among many possible references are "Pripiski na kolesakh," *Izvestiia*, April 14, 1987; Iu. Chernichenko, "Svoi khleb," *Novy mir* 51,

no. 8 (1985); M. Lemeshev, "Podnimaettsia nad vedomstvennymi interesami," *Nash sovremmenik,* no. 7 (1985); and Mikhail S. Gorbachev's June 11, 1985 speech, *Korennoi vopros ekonomicheskoi politiki partii: Doklad na soveshchanii v TsK KPSS po voprosam uskoreniia nauchnotekhnicheskogo progressa 11 iiunia 1985 goda* (Moscow: Politizdat, 1985).

25. These are repeated themes in *Stroitel'naia gazeta.* See, for example, "Spor o zavode, kotorogo net," October 25, 1986; "A byl li zavod?," April 2, 1987; "Avtograf besprintsipnosti—kak sdavali zavod, kotorogo eshche net," March 20, 1987; "Ne pozvat li prokurora?" May 29, 1987; "Dogovor—ne sgovor," May 31, 1987.

26. This point was made particularly strongly by Soviet economists in private discussions. It is also a recurrent theme in discussions of *perestroika* and the *zatratnyi mekhanizm.* See, for example, the *Ekonomicheskaia gazeta* round table *"Ekonomika na pereput'e"* in no. 23 (June 3, 1987). When it is not further used this "product" becomes final output, if only as an addition to inventory, and hence adds to industrial production, national income, and productivity, as well as plan fulfillment of the individual producer.

27. The IMEMO reconstruction, somewhat less ambitious, aimed at allowing international comparisons of Soviet aggregate economic performance. See note 10.

28. See note 4.

29. The story of their cooperation is told in a Japanese correspondent's interview with Seliunin in Moscow on February 10, 1987, just after the *Novy mir* piece appeared. Other aspects of Khanin's career related here are based on his seminar comments.

30. See P.R. Gregory and R.C. Stuart, *Soviet Economic Structure and Performance, 3rd ed.* (New York: McGraw-Hill, 1983), chap. 11.

31. In the words of his seminar, *"zolotoi vek sovetskoi ekonomiki,"* when people finally began to be rewarded and to work as they should. It was an age of more realistic plans, growing decentralization of responsibility, minimal cheating, no hidden inflation—and hence relatively reliable statistics.

32. This was explicitly repeated in the seminars. Seliunin spoke at MGU on "The Sharp Corners of *Perestroika*" ("Ostrye ugly perestroiki") on March 11, 1987.

33. This basic position appears in many of the writings of both authors, if only indirectly. See the articles cited in *Pravda,* December 30, 1985; *Novy mir,* August 1986; and *Sotsialisticheskaia industriia,* August 27, 1986; as well as Seliunin's articles in *Sotsialisticheskaia industriia,* January

1987, March 24, 1987, and January 5, 1988. They also took this position at their respective seminars at Moscow State University.

34. The Western view can be seen in comments by Noren (note 12) and Kushnirsky, "New Challenges to Soviet Official Statistics: A Methodological Survey," presented to a CIA conference December 11, 1987. The Soviet critique is cited in notes 6 and 51.

35. D. S. L'vov, N. Ia. Petrakov, "Mekhanizm upravleniia ekonomikoi i nauchno-tekhnicheskii progress," *Kommunist*, no. 4 (1987); V. K. Fal'tsman, "Mashinostroenie: puti peremen," *EKO* 16, no. 12 (1985); V. Kirichenko, "Piatiletka kachestvennykh peremen v ekonomike," *Voprosy ekonomiki* 58, no. 11 (1986); V. Seliunin, "Eksperiment," *Novy mir* no. 7 (1986) gives additional inflation estimates of Doronin; inflation in housing construction is discussed in S. Korneev, V. Loginov, "Otdel'naia kvartira," *Literaturnaia gazeta*, April 1, 1987. Also see Mel'nikov (note 20) on machine-building prices and quality change.

36. See note 34 and K. K. Val'tukh and B. L. Lavrovskii, "Proizvodstvennyi apparat strany: ispol'zovanie i rekonstruktsiia," *EKO*, no. 2 (1986): 17–32.

37. This can be seen in his capital series, and is explicitly stated in his article "Sochtem fondy. . .," *Sotsialisticheskaia industriia*, August 27, 1986.

38. A. G. Aganbegyan, "Programma korennoi perestroiki," *EKO*, no. 11 (1987): 3–19.

39. Aganbegyan, *The Economic Challenge of Perestroika* (Bloomington: Indiana University Press, 1988), chapter 1, pp. 2–3.

40. I am indebted to Anders Åslund and particularly to Vlad Treml for bringing this work to my attention.

41. IMEMO, p. 148 (note 10).

42. See note 4.

43. Khanin lists these in his 1984 article, pp. 60–61 (note 4).

44. See Kushnirsky (note 34). In response to a question at MGU, Khanin asserted that he and Seliunin had access to unpublished ministerial data, including defense industry data.

45. This method is given fifth in the methodology papers (note 4).

46. In his seminar, Khanin gave the following example: Reported fulfillment in physical terms was 80 percent, in value terms 150 percent, making the "real" growth in value terms 120 percent (0.8 x 150). Hidden inflation, then, was 30 percent.

47. If real material inputs per unit of output were actually to decline by 0.25 percent per year, this assumption would reduce the estimate of

real output by 1.26 percent every five years, or by 15 percent over the whole Soviet period 1928–1985.

48. There is a problem with the formula Khanin provides on p. 66 of his 1981 paper (note 4). Kushnirsky, p. 7 (note 34) provides a correct version under a reasonable interpretation of Khanin's intentions, but is unable, either with this or other indexes, to generate significant differences from Soviet official indexes.

49. This paragraph and the next summarize Khanin's 1981 paper, pp. 69–72. The methodological discussion below is taken from his 1984 paper.

50. This procedure essentially assumes aggregate linear homogeneity of real, quality-adjusted ouput.

51. See note 6. The "hired guns" in *Vestnik statistiki*, no. 6 (1987): 53–60, were V. Kniazevskii, T. Kozlov, and N. Sheremet, who wrote indignant letters published under the heading "Po povodu lukavoi stat'i o tsifrakh" ("About a 'Tricky' Article on Numbers"). I also refer to the speech by M. Korolev, "Zadachi perestroiki statistiki," *Vestnik statistiki,* no. 4 (April 1987): 3–12. Khanin and Seliunin have published a censored, but still sharp response to these critics in a letter to the editor of *Novy mir* (note 21).

52. The methodology pieces were published before any sort of serious discussion was possible, and even the *Novy mir* article was limited by space considerations, as Seliunin indicated in his Japanese press interview (note 29).

53. Adamov is somewhat disingenuous in his discussion of chaining, failing to note that recalculations for proper normalization are only done for "comparable" (*sopostavimye*) products, and so does not address the problems of hidden inflation and assortment change. He also provides some questionable numerical examples challenging the K-S estimates. See Kushnirsky (note 34).

54. Quality must be related to use value, while, as Soviet critics note, the changes and improvements in products and assortment have little relation to user needs or desires. Further, Khanin does incorporate changes in quality and assortment in determining the labor input coefficients that he uses as physical index weights at the beginning of each five- to ten-year period for which he develops an index. While his methods may result in some understatement of real quality change, and hence overstatement of hidden inflation, which he recognizes, the impact on his indexes should be minimal in the slowly changing, standardized, planned environment of the Soviet economy.

55. For example, Kozlov, p. 57.

56. This is done in Kushnirsky (note 34).

57. Abram Bergson, *Real National Income of Soviet Russia since 1928* (Cambridge: Harvard University Press, 1961): 261, 266. Bergson has pointed out to me that his estimate of the size of the Soviet economy in 1928 was determined by calculating backward from Western estimates of Soviet real national income in 1955, using Western indexes of growth. The direction of any induced bias is, however, unclear.

58. This figure has common currency among the *intelligentsiia*, including most economists, in the Soviet Union. It is consistent with the CIA figures for direct Soviet military expenditures, given the general belief in intellectual circles that the Soviet defense effort absorbs 35 to 45 percent of national income.

59. This is not to deny its effectiveness in short-run emergency situations, such as war. When the objectives are clear, and economic costs no object, results can clearly be commanded.

60. This was stated at their respective seminars, February 25 and March 11, 1987, at MGU.

61. This is the thrust of much of his writing, especially "Sochtem fondy . . . ."

62. This argument is presented in Seliunin, "Tempy rosta na vesakh potrebleniia," *Sotsialisticheskaia industriia*, January 5, 1988. On the new enterprise law, see R. Ericson, "The New Enterprise Law," *The Harriman Forum* 1, no. 2 (February 1988).

63. See note 4.

64. "My eschche mozhem nauchit'sia," *Nauka urala*, no. 14, April 5, 1989, pp. 1, 4–6.

65. For example, N. Illarionov, "Gde my nakhodimsia" *EKO*, no 12, 1988, pp. 39–55; and N. Shmelev and V. Popov, *Na perelome: Ekonomicheskaia perestroika v SSSR* (Moscow: APN, 1989), in particular chapter 2.

3. D. Derk Swain

1. See U.S. Central Intelligence Agency, *A Guide to Monetary Measures of Soviet Defense Activities*, Reference Aid SOV 87-10069 (unclassified), November 1987, for a detailed discussion of major monetary measures and their applicability to particular issues.

2. See U.S. CIA, *The Impact of Gorbachev's Policies on Soviet Economic Statistics,* Conference Report SOV 88-10049 (unclassified), July 1988, for discussions of the accuracy of our estimates of Soviet GNP.

4. Norbert D. Michaud

The opinions in this chapter are those of the author and not necessarily those of the Defense Intelligence Agency.

1. Mikhail S. Gorbachev, *Pravda,* September 18, 1987, pp. 1–2.

2. V. Zhurkin, *Kommunist,* no. 1, (January 1988):1.

3. V. F. Petrovskii, *Izvestiia,* August 27, 1987, p. 4.

4. W. T. Lee, *The Estimation of Soviet Defense Expenditures, 1955–75* (New York: Praeger, 1977), pp. 298–340.

5. U.S. Defense Intelligence Agency (DIA), *Soviet Professional, Scientific, and Technical Manpower, Executive Summary,* DST-1830E-049-85 OUO (Washington, D.C.: GPO, April 1985), p. 1.

6. See volumes of *Narodnoe khoziaistvo* for 1984, 1985, and 1986 (Moscow: Finansy i statistika).

7. V. Kontorovich, *Research and Development Productivity in the USSR: Causes of Decline since the 1960s and Prospects for the 1980s* (Princeton, N.J.: Command Economic Research, 1987), p. 300.

8. Ibid., p. 272.

9. L. Osipovich, "State Budget and Union Budget" translated in Joint Publication Research Service from *Ekonomicheskie nauki,* no. 6 (1976):125–28.

10. U.S. DIA, *Gorbachev's Modernization Program: A Status Report,* DDB-1900-140-87 (Washington, D.C.: GPO, August 1987).

5. David F. Epstein

The views, opinions, and findings in this chapter are those of the author and should not be construed as an official position, policy, or decision of the Department of Defense unless so designated by other official documentation.

1. U.S. Central Intelligence Agency (CIA), Directorate of Intelligence, *A Guide to Monetary Measures of Soviet Defense Activities: A Reference Aid* (Washington, D.C.: Government Printing Office, November 1987), p. 8.

2. Robert Gates, in U.S. Congress, Joint Economic Committee, *Allocation of Resources in the Soviet Union and China, 1984*, hearings before the Subcommittee on International Trade, Finance, and Security Economics (Washington, D.C.: GPO, 1985), part 10, p. 51.

3. In its 1978 paper on Soviet defense spending, the CIA notes that, "To the extent that these measures [of the economic impact of Soviet defense efforts] fail to take qualitative considerations into account, they tend to understate the impact of defense programs on the Soviet economy." U.S. CIA, *Estimated Soviet Defense Spending: Trends and Prospects* (Washington, D.C.: National Foreign Assessment Center, June 1978), p. 2.

4. Daniel L. Bond and Herbert S. Levine, "An Overview," in *The Soviet Economy: Towards the Year 2000*, ed. Abram Bergson and Herbert S. Levine (London: George Allen & Unwin, 1983), p. 21.

5. Daniel Bond, in U.S. Congress, *Soviet Military Economic Relations*, proceedings of a workshop sponsored jointly by the Joint Economic Committee, Subcommittee on International Trade, Finance, and Security Economics and the Library of Congress Congressional Research Service, July 7–8, 1982 (Washington, D.C.: GPO, 1982), p. 189.

6. Gates, *Soviet Union and China, 1984*, p. 52.

7. Even numbers derived fairly directly from sources cited should be understood as rough approximations, as I have in some cases had to read from graphs, extrapolate from information that may be dated, and interpret summary statements.

8. U.S. CIA and Defense Intelligence Agency (DIA), *Gorbachev's Modernization Program: A Status Report*, paper presented to the U.S. Congress Joint Economic Committee (Washington, D.C.: GPO, August 1987), p. 31.

9. My approximation of the factor-cost adjustment is based on the statement that it "has little practical effect on total procurement" but does "change the relative shares of the different resource categories within defense, primarily increasing the shares of military pay and research, development, testing, and evaluation (RDT&E) and lowering the share of procurement" (U.S. CIA, *Monetary Measures*, p. 18n). Assuming that the factor-cost adjustment raises the shares of personnel and RDT&E one percentage point each, the procurement share falls two percentage points while its ruble value is unchanged, implying that the

total rises by 4.4 billion rubles (0.6 percent of GNP), making the total defense share at factor cost 15.3 percent of GNP. This is consistent with statements that defense at factor cost was 15 percent of GNP in 1982 (ibid., p. 8), and that "CIA and DIA agree that defense's share of Soviet GNP rose from about 12–14 percent in 1970 to about 15–17 percent in 1982" (U.S. CIA and DIA, *Gorbachev's Modernization Program,* p. 8).

10. Marshal Sokolovskii, quoted by Michael Checinski, "The Soviet Military Elite in Economic Decision-Making," paper prepared for the annual conference of the American Association for the Advancement of Slavic Studies, September 20–23, 1981, p. 3.

11. Michael Checinski, "The Soviet War-Economic Doctrine in the Years of Military-Technological Challenge (1946–1983): An Overview," *Crossroads* no. 12 (1984): 42.

12. Of these three categories, peacetime services might, in principle, be included in the CIA's estimate of Soviet operations and maintenance (O&M) costs, but it is unclear whether the military pays the full cost of these services, or how the CIA estimates that cost.

13. Ralph Ostrich, "Aeroflot," *Armed Forces Journal* (May 1981).

14. Ibid.

15. See also Lev Chaiko, *Helicopter Construction in the USSR*, Monograph Series on Soviet Union (Falls Church, Va.: Delphic Associates, 1985), p. 15: "In the Soviet Union, the military is the sole customer for new helicopters. For this reason, helicopters are usually custom-designed for specific military missions. Furthermore, existing helicopters in civilian and technical use in peacetime are listed in the inventory of military units, and in the event of war, would immediately revert to the military."

16. Ostrich, "Aeroflot." While I lack data on the respective carrying capacities of U.S. and Soviet civilian air fleets, a simple comparison of passenger miles and ton miles with numbers of aircraft shows that in 1982 the average U.S. aircraft carried three times the passenger miles and four times the ton miles of freight of the average Soviet aircraft (calculated from U.S. CIA, *Handbook of Economic Statistics, 1987: A Reference Aid* [Washington, D.C.: GPO, September 1987], pp. 218–19). Even if this comparison is not distorted by aircraft sizes, it surely reflects general Soviet economic inefficiencies as well as military priorities.

17. Andrew W. Marshall, "Commentary," in U.S. Congress, Joint Economic Committee, *Gorbachev's Economic Plans,* vol. 1 (Washington, D.C.: GPO, November 1987), p. 483.

18. Ibid.

19. Because most Soviet economic activities appear relatively less productive than their foreign counterparts, this fact is far from conclusive regarding the fishing fleet's military role. The following figures represent metric tons of fish caught in 1980 per gross registered ton of fishing fleet inventory: Norway, 10; Japan, 9.4; United States, 6.9; European Community, 4.7; Eastern Europe, 1.8; Soviet Union, 1.4. Calculated from U.S. CIA, *Handbook of Economic Statistics*, pp. 195, 223.

20. "Aganbegyan Assesses Reform Problems," *Izvestiia*, August 25, 1987, Foreign Broadcast Information Service Daily Report (Soviet Union), September 1, 1987, p. 35.

21. James T. Reitz, "The Military Readiness of the Soviet Economy," *East Europe*, May 1972.

22. The 3 million ruble figure is from *Washington Post*, August 19, 1987; the 4300 kilometer figure is from *Jane's Defence Weekly*, March 16, 1985.

23. This suggestion does not assume that all production is optimized for the military, or that military and civilian preferences always differ. One observer has noted that the Soviets produce too few diesel engines and trucks for civilian needs, even though diesels would be more militarily advantageous.

24. Calculations were made as follows. In 1982, the transportation sector of origin produced 74.4 billion rubles (U.S. CIA and DIA, *Gorbachev's Modernization Program*, p. 31). Of that, I assume 30 billion rubles is sea, truck, and air (based on weights calculated from 1970 ruble price and quantity data in U.S. Congress, Joint Economic Committee, *USSR: Measures of Economic Growth and Development, 1950–80* [Washington, D.C.: GPO, December 1982], pp. 92, 94). I add 13 billion rubles for vehicle production (5 percent of the CIA's calculation of 1982 industry sector of origin in *Gorbachev's Modernization Program*, p. 31; the 5 percent factor is based on 1972 data from *USSR: Measures of Economic Growth*, p. 242, for transport machinery and equipment plus automobiles—minus the automobiles delivered to final demand—as a share of total 1972 industrial production). And for fishing fleet operations, I add 2 billion rubles (35 percent of the figure for sea transportation sector of origin calculated above, a share based on relative tonnage of fishing and merchant fleets in 1980 taken from the CIA's *Handbook of Economic Statistics*, pp. 223, 225). I omit the internal waterway fleet and railroads, where military costs are probably much less.

25. Although the CIA's estimate of defense spending in 1978 included "certain civil defense activities," with no further definition (CIA,

Soviet Defense Spending, p. 1), in 1984 Gates referred to "civil defense programs" as among the items that "we do not even consider in our estimates" (*Soviet Union and China, 1984,* p. 52).

26. Checinski, "Soviet War-Economic Doctrine," p. 39.

27. Michael Checinski, "The Mobilization Aspect of the Soviet Economy as a Factor in Preparedness for War," in *The U.S. Defense Mobilization Infrastructure: Problems and Priorities,* ed. Robert L. Pfaltzgraff, Jr., and Uri Ra'anan (Medford, Mass.: Archon Books, 1983), pp. 152–53.

28. U.S. Department of Defense, *Soviet Military Power 1987* (Washington, D.C.: GPO, March 1987), p. 52.

29. U.S. Department of Defense, *Soviet Military Power 1988* (Washington, D.C.: GPO, April 1988), p. 59.

30. Gates, *Soviet Union and China, 1984,* p. 52.

31. William Odom, "The 'Militarization' of Soviet Society," *Problems in Communism* (September/October 1976): 44.

32. U.S. Department of Defense, *Soviet Military Power 1985* (Washington, D.C.: GPO, April 1985), pp. 52–53.

33. U.S. Department of Defense, *Soviet Military Power 1988,* p. 60; and Seymour Weiss, "Labyrinth under Moscow," *Washington Post,* May 25, 1988, p. 19. Procurement for Soviet strategic offensive forces for the years 1965–1981 amounted to 135 billion 1983 dollars, according to *The FY 1983 Department of Defense Program for Research, Development, and Acquisition* (Washington, D.C.: GPO, March 1982), p. II-9. Converted to 1986 dollars, this amounts to an average of $8.8 billion per year; the DOD's 1988 comparison might mean operating costs should be added to that. If Weiss's "several hundred billions" means $200 billion to $300 billion, that would be an average of $5 billion to $7.5 billion per year over 40 years. Was the program, like the Soviet economy, bigger in 1982 than in 1950? Using the CIA's dollar valuation of Soviet GNP for 1982 (*Handbook of Economic Statistics,* p. 35), 5 billion to 10 billion 1986 dollars equals 0.2 to 0.5 percent of GNP (1.7 billion to 3.4 billion rubles). Adding these figures to the 1.5 billion ruble total from *Soviet Military Power 1985* gives a range of 3.2 billion to 4.9 billion rubles (0.4 to 0.7 percent of GNP).

34. Eitan Berglas, *Defense and the Economy: The Israeli Experience,* Discussion Paper No. 83.01 (Jerusalem: Maurice Falk Institute for Economic Research, January 1983), undated draft, p. 298.

35. Shelley Deutch, "The Soviet Weapons Industry: An Overview," in *Gorbachev's Economic Plans,* vol. 1, p. 407.

36. The increase is through 1986, based on the change read from graphs, *Soviet Union and China, 1984,* p. 89 (for 1965–1970); and U.S. CIA,

Monetary Measures, p. 11 (for 1970–1982); 1983 and 1984 figures are based on the "steady rate of growth of about 1 percent" noted by Douglas McEachin in U.S. Congress, Joint Economic Committee, *Allocation of Resources in the Soviet Union and China, 1985*, hearings before the Subcommittee on Economic Resources, Competitiveness, and Security Economics (Washington, D.C.: GPO, 1986), part 11, p. 7; 1985 and 1986 growth was "about 3 percent per year," according to U.S. CIA and DIA, *Gorbachev's Modernization Program*, p. 8.

37. William Odom, "The Riddle of Soviet Military Spending," *Russia* 2 (1981): 55.

38. Checinski, "Mobilization Aspect of the Soviet Economy," p. 147.

39. Checinski, "Soviet War-Economic Doctrine," p. 42.

40. Aron Katsenelinboigen, "Interaction of Foreign and Economic Policy in the Soviet Union," in *Papers of the Peace Science Society (International)* 28 (1978): 29.

41. Berglas, "Israeli Experience," p. 298.

42. Katsenelinboigen, "Foreign and Economic Policy," p. 31.

43. Ibid., pp. 32–33.

44. Ibid., pp. 33–34.

45. Aron Katsenelinboigen, *Studies in Soviet Economic Planning* (White Plains, N.Y.: M.E. Sharpe, 1978), p. 191.

46. If we assume that 20 percent of the weapons price is for capital services, that would be 9.8 billion rubles (of the 49 billion ruble CIA estimate for 1982 procurement). If there was no excess capacity in 1965, in 1982 there was 23 percent (based on the 1986 comparison—at notes 35 and 36 above—adjusted to 1982 by assuming a constant rate of growth in defense production capacity, 1965–1986). The annual investment cost for excess weapons production capacity would be 23 percent of the 9.8 billion ruble cost attributed to the capacity that is not excess. My estimate is an understatement if there was any excess capacity in 1965 or if there was qualitative improvement in capacity in addition to the "doubling" noted. It is an overstatement if the prices applied to weapons actually produced include capital charges to cover the excess capacity.

47. The figure represents total investment for industry (57 billion rubles in 1984 prices, according to *Soviet Union and China, 1985*, p. 82), minus investment attributed to defense industries (12 billion rubles, total from previous note), times 2 to 4 percent (a wild guess as to the relative cost imposed on civil-sector investment by the policies described). Checinski's example of the dairy equipped for mobilization would fall

outside the industrial investment category, but most examples probably would not.

48. One half the share of GNP used by Israel for stockpiles as estimated by Berglas.

49. Charles Wolf, Jr., et al., *The Costs and Benefits of the Soviet Empire, 1981–1983,* R-3419-NA (Santa Monica, Calif.: RAND, August 1986), pp. 3, 13.

50. Current operating costs should be included in the O&M figure; equipment losses would show up in procurement figures only when the equipment was replaced.

51. A calculation of Soviet military costs and GNP in world market prices would reflect this kind of opportunity cost to the Soviets. See Aganbegyan, quoted by Hedrick Smith, *New York Times Magazine,* April 10, 1988: "You have no idea what our military budget is because our prices are totally out of line with world market prices. Our price on oil for military purposes is several times lower than world prices. . . ."

52. This raises the broader question of whether the economic effects of Soviet policies intended to promote relative autarky should themselves be considered military-imperial costs.

53. My figure is based on the assumption that this category would be closer to the pre-1979 totals shown by RAND (Wolf et al., *Costs and Benefits of the Soviet Empire,* p. 13) if the world oil-price effect were removed. In either case, I raise Soviet GNP by the amount of the trade subsidies, as these represent income foregone rather than actual expenditures.

54. Odom, "Riddle of Soviet Military Spending," pp. 54–55.

55. Lt. Gen. Samuel Wilson, in U.S. Congress, Joint Economic Committee, *Allocation of Resources in the Soviet Union and China, 1977,* hearings before the Subcommittee on Priorities and Economy in Government (Washington, D.C.: GPO, 1977), part 3, p. 79.

56. U.S. Congress, Joint Economic Committee, *Allocation of Resources in the Soviet Union and China, 1976,* hearings before the Subcommittee on Priorities and Economy in Government (Washington, D.C.: GPO, 1976), part 2, p. 17.

57. Gates, *Soviet Union and China, 1984,* p. 52.

58. The communications sector is 1.1 percent of Soviet GNP (U.S. CIA, DIA, *The Soviet Economy under a New Leader* [Washington, D.C.: GPO, July 1986], p. 19). Attributing, say, 3 percent of this sector's output to the military would give a cost of 0.2 billion rubles.

59. Philip Taubman, "Lemons Make Soviet Arctic Life a Little Sweeter," *New York Times,* October 26, 1985.

60. Even 2 billion rubles, divided equally among either the 405,000 residents of Murmansk or the million residents of the entire *oblast'* (or "administrative region"), would come to 4,900 or 1,900 rubles for each one, respectively, while average Soviet per capita consumption is only 1,300 rubles (based on U.S. CIA *Handbook of Economic Statistics*, pp. 53, 66). Even assuming a high cost of providing goods and services in that inhospitable climate, this number seems high. I will assume that 1 billion to 2 billion rubles covers the cost of subsidizing Murmansk and its analogues.

61. Odom, "Riddle of Soviet Military Spending," p. 56.

62. There is some dispute, however, about how the military's educational contribution to the civilian economy should be assessed. In one view, the disruptive and unpleasant experience of conscripts makes the net effect of military service on Soviet "human capital" a negative one.

63. Robert Huffstutler, in U.S. Congress, House of Representatives, *CIA Estimates of Soviet Defense Spending,* hearings before the Subcommittee on Oversight of the Permanent Select Committee on Intelligence (Washington, D.C.: GPO, 1980), pp. 5, 6.

64. U.S. Congress, Joint Economic Committee, *Allocation of Resources in the Soviet Union and China, 1983,* hearings before the Subcommittee on International Trade, Finance, and Security Economics (Washington, D.C.: GPO, 1983), part 9, p. 349.

65. But compare Robert Foelber, *Estimates of Soviet Defense Expenditures: Methodological Issues and Policy Implications* (Washington, D.C.: Congressional Research Service, July 1985), p. 26.

66. Donald F. Burton, "Estimating Soviet Defense Spending," *Problems in Communism* 32, no. 2. (March/April 1983): 86.

67. Abram Bergson, "On the Measurement of Soviet Real Defense Outlays," in *Marxism, Central Planning, and the Soviet Economy: Economic Essays in Honor of Alexander Erlich,* ed. Padma Desai (Cambridge, Mass.: MIT Press, 1983), p. 86.

68. U.S. Congress, House of Representatives, *CIA Estimates,* pp. 41–42.

69. Burton, "Estimating Soviet Defense Spending," pp. 86–87.

70. U.S. Congress, Joint Economic Committee, *USSR: Measures of Economic Growth and Development,* p. 167.

71. U.S. CIA, *Monetary Measures,* p. 18n.

72. Jim Barry, in U.S. Congress, House of Representatives, *CIA Estimates,* p. 78.

73. Dmitri Steinberg, "Estimating Total Soviet Military Expenditures: An Alternative Approach Based on Reconstructed Soviet National Accounts," in *The Soviet Defence Enigma: Estimating Costs and Burden,* ed. Carl G. Jacobsen (Oxford: Stockholm International Peace Research Institute, Oxford University Press, 1987), p. 42.

74. Assuming profit is earned on goods other than weapons that are procured by the military (e.g., trucks, typewriters, etc.), I apply a 12 percent profit markup to the four-fifths of procurement that I assume to be made up of weapons. According to Steven Rosefielde, "Correspondence," *Problems of Communism* 34, no. 2 (March/April 1985): 128, 12 percent is the profit that weapons prices supposedly already include, according to the source (P. Sokolov) cited by Donald Burton. As a low estimate, I will assume that Soviet weapons prices already include profit.

75. Abraham Becker, *The Burden of Soviet Defense: A Political-Economic Essay,* R-2752-AF (Santa Monica, Calif.: RAND, October 1981), p. 5.

76. Paul Cockle, "Analyzing Soviet Defence Spending: The Debate in Perspective," *Survival* 20, no. 5 (September/October 1979): 217.

77. Igor Birman, "Professor Holzman, the CIA, Soviet Military Expenditures and American Security," *Russia* 10 (1984): 48.

78. Michael Checinski, *The Costs of Armament Production and the Profitability of Armament Exports in Comecon Countries,* Research Paper No. 10 (Jerusalem: Hebrew University Soviet and East European Research Centre, November 1974), pp. 14ff.

79. Checinski, *The Military-Industrial Complex in the USSR: Its Influence on R&D and Industrial Planning and on International Trade,* SWP-AZ 2302 (Ebenhausen: Stiftung Wissenschaft und Politik, September 1981), p. 57.

80. Checinski, *Costs of Armament Production,* p. 22.

81. R. Jeffrey Smith, "Soviet Arms Budget Said To Be Falling," *Washington Post,* July 27, 1988. Another Soviet source makes the same point: "Vadim Kuznetsov, deputy director of the U.S.A. desk at the Soviet Foreign Ministry, said in a recent Moscow interview that his nation would make good on its pledge to publish a detailed defense budget by the early 1990s. That will take a new system of accounting. . . . 'Under the old system, a truck could cost many times less for the military than for a collective farm' because of price manipulation, Mr. Kuznetsov said" ("In Surprise, Soviets Promise to Reveal 'Secret' Defense Budget," *Washington Times,* August 1, 1988). For "dual-use" goods such as trucks, the CIA presumably uses civilian prices for its military costing, but the manipulation referred to calls into question all military prices. See also

Aganbegyan's statement on military prices quoted by Hedrick Smith, *New York Times Magazine*, April 10, 1988.

82. For the higher figure, I assume that 30 percent of the CIA's weapons prices are for overhead and capital services, and that the military is getting 15 percent more of these items than it pays for.

83. U.S. CIA, *Monetary Measures*, p. 4.

84. Deutch, "Soviet Weapons Industry," p. 407.

85. Odom, "Riddle of Soviet Military Spending," p. 55; see also Checinski, *Costs of Armament Production*, p. 3.

86. Gur Ofer, *The Opportunity Cost of the Nonmonetary Advantages of the Soviet Military R&D Effort*, R-1741-DDRE (Santa Monica, Calif.: RAND, August 1975). Mikhail Agursky and Hannes Adomeit ("The Soviet Military-Industrial Complex," *Survey* 24, no. 2 [Spring 1979]) dispute Ofer's view that the best people work in the military sector, arguing that because military industry is isolated and closely watched, the best-qualified people would rather work in laxer civilian conditions where they can, for example, moonlight by teaching or produce for the black market while on the job. They say there is a "salary advantage of 20 to 25 percent for work in the military-industrial complex." For both researchers and laborers, "it is the less dynamic and those possessing on average lower skills who prefer to work in military industry." But Agursky and Adomeit agree with Ofer and others that "materials destined for use in the military industry are superior to those used in civilian industry."

87. Harley Balzer, "Soviet Research and Development: Information and Insights from the Third Emigration," report to the National Council for Soviet and East European Research, July 1986, pp. 128–29.

88. David Wechsler, *The Range of Human Capacities* (Baltimore: Johns Hopkins University Press, 1952), cites the results of typing, radio tube assembly, and card punching tests of samples of adults, in which the 70th to 75th percentiles of the population outperformed the mean by 9 to 12 percent, 9 to 12 percent, and 7 to 9 percent, respectively.

89. Excluded are military personnel and a third of O&M that is assumed to be for "standard" goods such as oil and food. My procedure assumes that goods produced with lower-quality inputs deserve a corresponding reduction in price, keeping total GNP the same.

90. Birman, "Professor Holzman," p. 48.

91. Igor Birman, "The Imbalance of the Soviet Economy," *Soviet Studies* 40, no. 2 (April 1988): 215.

92. To quantify this effect, I assume that in the military production sector (i.e., producers of weapons, RDT&E, and military construction) timely supply permits labor and capital to be used 90 percent of the time, whereas in the civilian sector untimely supply allows labor and capital to work only 80 percent of the time. So if the apparent value added to a good in the military sector is 100 rubles, the real value added is 90 rubles; if the apparent value added to a good in the civilian sector is 100 rubles, the real value added is 80 rubles (to repeat, in both cases I subtract the amount paid for idle labor and capital). Now the final military product will include not only the value added within the privileged military production sector, but also the raw and intermediate goods produced outside that sector (if this were not the case, and the military were autarkical, there would be nothing for the military to have privileged access to). Further supposing that one-half the price of military goods is due to value added within the sector, the average 200 ruble military good will include 170 rubles of real factor activity (and a 30 ruble charge for idle factors); whereas for the civilian sector the average 200 ruble good will include 160 rubles of real factor activity. If we assume for the moment that military production is between 10 and 30 percent of the economy's total production, the average 200 ruble good for the whole economy will include 161 to 163 rubles of real factor activity; so a 200 ruble military good, priced like an "average" good in the economy, would cost 200 times 170 divided by 161 or 163, i.e., about 210 rubles. Applying this 5 percent markup to the CIA figures for military procurement, construction, and RDT&E adds 3.7 billion rubles (0.5 percent of GNP) to the Soviet defense burden.

93. Earl R. Brubaker, "The Opportunity Costs of Soviet Military Conscripts," in U.S. Congress, Joint Economic Committee, *Soviet Economic Prospects for the Seventies* (Washington, D.C.: GPO, 1973), p. 174.

94. A Brubaker-style estimate would seem to require second-guessing Soviet wage rates; I do not know if the factor-cost adjustment attempts to do this.

95. U.S. CIA, DIA, *Soviet Economy under a New Leader*, p. 19.

96. Brubaker's 1973 opportunity-cost adjustment of 34 percent is excessive for this calculation because he is concerned with conscripts only, not careerists, and because it is based on Soviet pay rates and not the CIA adjusted figure. It is an understatement if he is correct that the trend continued upward. A 34 percent markup on 13 billion rubles would give a total of 17.4 billion rubles. If one attributed an opportunity

cost in simple proportion to the share of uniformed personnel in the Soviet labor force, the total would be 20.4 billion rubles (based on numbers for 1982 in Stephen Rapawy, "Labor Force and Employment in the USSR," in *Gorbachev's Economic Plans*, vol. 1, p. 194). If one assumed that labor's "weight" in production were 56.5 percent (the figure used by the CIA in making productivity calculations, based on Soviet data for 1982 in the CIA's *Handbook of Economic Statistics*, p. 70), then that figure would drop to 11.5 billion rubles (below the CIA's factor-cost estimate). But Brubaker suggests that "civilian wages understate the contribution of the Soviet labor force to output" ("Soviet Military Conscripts," p. 174).

97. Steinberg, "Soviet Military Expenditures," p. 32.

98. See Vasilii Seliunin and Grigorii Khanin, "Lukavaia tsifra" ["Cunning Figures"] *Novy mir* 63 (February 1987) and Richard Ericson's contribution to this volume.

99. Based on the statement that "in the Ninth Five-Year Plan income increased 17 percent, in the 10th, 5 percent, and in the first years of the 11th there was an absolute decline therein. . . ." ("Cunning Figures") I interpret this last statement to mean –1 percent annual growth in 1981 and 1982.

100. Increasing GNP by 10 to 13 percent reduces the CIA defense share by about 1.5 percentage points; it reduces my estimate of the security-imperial share by 2 to 3 percentage points.

101. He would therefore add 20.4 billion rubles to the GNP estimate for 1982 (Steinberg, "Soviet Military Expenditures," p. 32).

102. According to Ericson (in this volume), "There is a claim that even the central organs estimate that 1.5 percent to 3 percent of reported physical output is fictitious, though the author believes it to be much greater." Wasted and worthless output should be added to that. Some worthless output may be related to the issue of quality advantages, discussed and adjusted for earlier. But to reflect the lack of managerial care that leads to worthless, wasted, and fictitious output, I suggest reducing GNP by 3 to 6 percent.

103. If any of the ruble prices applied to Soviet activities are derived not from "actual ruble prices" concerning military activities but from ruble/dollar ratios for civilian goods, a different view of the relative size of GNP, implying a different ruble/dollar ratio for (some) civilian goods, would affect the computation. Foelber, "Soviet Defense Expenditures," p. 26, speaks of weapons prices being derived from "a sample of Soviet civilian and military items for which ruble prices are known"; but compare "Missing Prices" section of my chapter.

104. "Dollar/ruble ratios" throughout this section will be ratios of 1985 dollars to 1982 rubles, the price bases of CIA's most recent published defense estimates (in its *Monetary Measures*).

105. See Imogene Edwards, Margaret Hughes, James Noren, "U.S. and U.S.S.R.: Comparisons of GNP" in *Soviet Economy in a Time of Change*, a compendium of papers submitted to the Joint Economic Committee (Washington, D.C.: GPO, October 10, 1979), vol. 1, p. 380.

106. As a crude variant estimate, I will assume that the ruble/dollar ratio for one-fourth of Soviet procurement and half of RDT&E (the highest-technology portions) is the same as for 1980 imports, and that the ruble/dollar ratio for the rest of Soviet procurement and RDT&E corresponds to Birman's lower estimate of the size of the Soviet economy in dollars. (This alternative approach to valuing Soviet defense activities subsumes most of the price and GNP adjustments suggested earlier, and so should not be considered as an addition to them.) The result adds 23.5 billion rubles to the CIA's defense estimate. Using Birman's implied ruble/dollar ratio (rather than the CIA's) would also raise the ruble estimate of Soviet sheltering programs (see "Hardening, protection, and civil defense" in text) by 1.7 billion to 3.3 billion rubles.

6. Christopher M. Davis

Research for this paper was supported by grants from the Volkswagen Foundation, Ford Foundation, Economic and Social Research Council, and PEW Charitable Trusts, as well as by CREES, the University of Birmingham, and the Hoover Institution. I would like to thank Peter Almquist, Robert Campbell, David Holloway, and Henry Rowen for comments on the outline and first draft.

This chapter is an abbreviated version of a paper prepared for the Hoover-RAND Conference on the Defense Sector in the Soviet Economy, Stanford, Calif., March 23–24, 1987. The paper contained mathematical formulations of the ten sectoral priority indicators and a section on the shortage model of the Soviet defense enterprise. A revised version of that section is presented in C. Davis, "The Shortage Model of the Soviet Defense Industry Enterprise: An Empirical Assessment," discussion paper, University of Birmingham, forthcoming.

1. Three recent studies of priority in the socialist economy are: Richard C. Ericson, "Priority, Duality and Penetration in the Soviet

Command Economy," N-2643-NA (Santa Monica, Calif.: RAND, December 1988); L. D. Badgett, "Defeated by a Maze: Historical and Structural Aspects of Modeling the Soviet Economy and Its Defense-Industrial Sector," N-2644-NA (Santa Monica, Calif.: RAND, October 1988); and C. Davis, "Priority and the Shortage Model: The Medical System in the Socialist Economy," in *Models of Disequilibrium and Shortage in Centrally Planned Economies,* ed. C. Davis and W. Charemza (London: Chapman and Hall, 1989).

2. G. G. Hildebrandt, ed., *RAND Conference on Models of the Soviet Economy, October 11–12, 1984,* R-3322 (Santa Monica, Calif.: RAND, October 1985).

3. For a survey of disequilibrium and shortage models of socialist economies, see Davis and Charemza, *Centrally Planned Economies.*

4. Soviet writings on the relationship between economic and military power include: S. Bartenev, "Sovremennaia voina i ekonomika," *Kommunist vooruzhennykh sil,* no. 22 (1965); A. Lagovskii, "Ekonomika i voennaia moshch' gosudarstva," *Krasnaia zvezda,* September 25, 1969; M. Cherednichenko, "Sovremennaia voina i ekonomika," *Kommunist vooruzhennykh sil,* no. 18 (September 1981); S. Bartenev, "Ekonomika i voennaia moshch'," *Kommunist vooruzhennykh sil,* no. 14 (1980); A. Gurov, "Ekonomicheskaia osnova mogushchestva rodiny," *Kommunist vooruzhennykh sil,* no. 7 (1981); A. I. Pozharov, *Ekonomicheskie osnovy oboronnogo mogushchestva sotsialisticheskogo gosudarstva* (Moscow: Voennoe Izdatel'stvo, 1981); and V. Serebriannikov, "Osnova osnov ukrepleniia oborony strany," *Kommunist vooruzhennykh sil,* no. 4 (1986).

5. Pozharov, *Ekonomicheskie osnovy,* pp. 91–104.

6. Ibid, pp. 116–17.

7. I have used a similar approach to define the Soviet health sector. There, the common activity is the production of health, and its institutions include consumers, the medical system, medical supply network, medical industry, biomedical R&D, medical foreign trade, and the central health bureaucracy. See C. Davis, "The Economics of the Soviet Health System," in U.S. Congress, Joint Economic Committee, *Soviet Economy in the 1980s: Problems and Prospects* (Washington, D.C.: Government Printing Office, 1983); and C. Davis, "Developments in the Health Sector of the Soviet Economy, 1970–90," in U.S. Congress, Joint Economic Committee, *Gorbachev's Economic Plans* (Washington, D.C.: GPO, 1987).

8. J. Kornai argues that the concept of the market can be interpreted in a "broad" sense to include "transaction processes based on direct

horizontal relations between supplier and recipient of the goods, even if price and money play little or no role in these processes." See J. Kornai, *Economics of Shortage* (Amsterdam: North-Holland, 1980), p. 127.

9. It should be noted that several analysts use an extended definition of the Soviet security sector that they believe facilitates comprehensive measurement of the defense burden; see H. Rowen, "Biting the Bullet and Other Hard Choices for Moscow," paper presented at the National Defense University Conference on the Soviet Economy, Washington, D.C., 1984; and, in this volume, David F. Epstein, "The Economic Cost of Soviet Security and Empire," and D. Derk Swain, "The Soviet Military Sector: How It Is Defined and Measured."

10. The defense-sector production process has a similar structure to the health production process described in Davis, "Health Sector of the Soviet Economy."

11. In reality the central authorities exercise only imperfect control over subordinate institutions, even in the defense sector. Considerable evidence indicates that informal processes and illegal activities play important roles in the socialist economy. See C. Davis, "The Second Economy in Disequilibrium and Shortage Models of the Centrally Planned Economy," *Berkeley-Duke Occasional Papers on the Second Economy in the USSR*, no. 12 (1988).

12. For information about the central defense bureaucracy, see S. A. Tiushkevich et al., *Sovetskie vooruzhennye sily* (Moscow: Voennoe Izdatel'stvo, 1978); M. Checinski, *A Comparison of the Polish and Soviet Armaments Decisionmaking Systems*, R-2662-AF (Santa Monica, Calif.: RAND, January 1981); H. F. Scott and W. F. Scott, *The Armed Forces of the USSR*, 3rd. ed. (Boulder, Colo.: Westview, 1984); U. S. Department of Defense, *Soviet Military Power 1987* (Washington, D.C.: GPO, 1987); P. Almquist, *The Organization and Influence of Soviet Military Industry*, Ph.D. dissertation, M.I.T., Cambridge, Mass., 1987.

13. Information about the institutional features of the Soviet armed forces can be found in A. A. Grechko, *Vooruzhennye sily sovetskogo gosudarstva* (Moscow: Voennoe Izdatel'stvo, 1974); Tiushkevich et al., *Sovetskie vooruzhennye*; A. Cockburn, *The Threat: Inside the Soviet Military Machine* (New York: Vintage, 1984); Scott and Scott, *Armed Forces of the USSR*; W. T. Lee and R. F. Staar, *Soviet Military Policy since World War II* (Stanford, Calif.: Hoover Press, 1986); C. Davis, "The Production of Military Power by the Soviet Defense Sector, 1975–85," University of Birmingham, August 1986; U. S. Department of Defense, *Soviet Military Power*; A. A. Babakov, *Vooruzhennye sily SSSR posle voiny (1945–1986 gg)*

(Moscow: Voennoe Izdatel'stvo, 1987); C. Davis, "Military and Civilian Economic Activities of the Soviet Armed Forces, 1975–85," in *Der Sowjetunion als Militärmacht* [*The Soviet Union as a Military Power*], ed. H. Adomeit et al. (Stuttgart: Kohlhammer, 1987).

14. Among the sources containing information about the supply network are I. V. Safonov, ed., *Spravochnik ofitsera po voiskovomu khoziaistvu* (Moscow: Voennoe Izdatel'stvo, 1968); Scott and Scott, *Armed Forces of the USSR*, U.S. Central Intelligence Agency (CIA), *The Soviet Weapons Industry: An Overview*, DI86-10016 (Washington, D.C.: GPO, September 1986); and L. Despres, "The Economic Planning and Management of the Tyl in the Soviet Armed Forces," discussion paper, University of Nantes, June 1987.

15. Pozharov, *Ekonomicheskie osnovy*, p. 147.

16. The operations of the Soviet pharmacy system are described in C. Davis, *The Health and Pharmaceutical Sectors of the Soviet Economy* (Washington, D.C.: Wharton Econometric Forecasting Associates, March 1984).

17. The structure and operations of the Soviet defense industry are described in D. Holloway, *The Soviet Union and the Arms Race* (London: Yale University, 1983); idem, "The Soviet Union," in *The Structure of the Defense Industry: An International Survey*, ed. N. Ball and M. Leitenberg (London: Croom Helm, 1983); U.S. CIA, *Soviet Weapons Industry*; Almquist, *Soviet Military Industry*; and S. Deutch, "The Soviet Weapons Industry: An Overview" in *Gorbachev's Economic Plans*.

18. The military R&D institution is described in V. M. Bondarenko, *Sovremennaia nauka i razvitie voennogo dela* (Moscow: Voennoe Izdatel'stvo, 1976); A. Alexander, *Decision-Making in Soviet Weapons Procurement*, no. 147/8 (London: IISS Adelphi, 1979); D. Holloway, "Innovation in the Defense Sector," in *Industrial Innovation in the Soviet Union*, ed. R. Amann and J. M. Cooper (London: Yale University, 1982); Holloway, *Soviet Union and the Arms Race*; J. R. Thomas, "Militarization of the Soviet Academy of Sciences," *Survey* 29, no. 1 (Spring, 1985); U.S. CIA, *Soviet Weapons Industry*; and Almquist, *Soviet Military Industry*.

19. See Checinski, *Polish and Soviet Armaments*; and idem, "Warsaw Pact/CEMA Military-Economic Trends," *Problems of Communism* (March-April 1987).

20. Holloway, *Soviet Union and the Arms Race*; R. E. Kanet, "The Politics and Economics of Soviet Arms Exports," in *Economics and Politics in the USSR: Problems of Interdependence*, ed. H. H. Hohmann, A. Nove,

and H. Vogel (London: Westview, 1986); and M. N. Kramer, "Soviet Arms Transfers to the Third World," *Problems of Communism* (September/October 1987).

21. The Soviet *spetsinformatsiia* system is described in P. Audigier, "Les implications stratégiques du commerce Est-Ouest," *Défense national* (February 1984); D. Buchan, *Western Security and Economic Strategy towards the East*, no. 192 (London: IISS Adelphi, 1984); U.S. Department of Defense, *Soviet Acquisition of Militarily Significant Western Technology: An Update* (Washington, D.C.: GPO, September 1985); idem, *Soviet Military Power 1987*; C. Lamoureux, "L'enjeu technologique," in *La drôle de crise: De Kaboul à Genève 1979–1985*, ed. G. Sokoloff (Paris: Fayard, 1986); T. Wolton, *Le KGB en France* (Paris: Bernard Grasset, 1986); P. Hanson, *Soviet Industrial Espionage: Some New Information*, RIIA Discussion Papers (London: RIIA, 1987); and C. Lamoureux, "Western Technologies and the Soviet Defense Sector," paper presented at the Hoover-RAND Conference on the Defense Sector in the Soviet Economy, Stanford, Calif., March 23–24, 1988.

22. Numerous authors have examined general aspects of military-civilian economic relationships and tradeoffs in the USSR, such as A. Becker, *The Burden of Soviet Defense: A Political-Economic Essay*, R-2752-AF (Santa Monica, Calif.: RAND, October 1981); M. M. Hopkins and M. Kennedy, *The Tradeoff between Consumption and Military Expenditures for the Soviet Union during the 1980s*, R-2927-NA (Santa Monica, Calif.: November 1982); A. Becker, "Gorbachev's Defense-Economic Dilemma," in *Gorbachev's Economic Plans*; and C. Davis, "Interdependence of the Defense and Civilian Sectors in the Contemporary Soviet Economy: Concepts, Problems, and Reform," in *Defense, Modernization, and Reform: The Military Sector of the Soviet Economy in the Perestroika Period*, ed. C. Davis et al., in German, forthcoming.

23. Davis, "Defense and Civilian Sectors" and idem, "Soviet Armed Forces."

24. Holloway, "Innovation in the Defence Sector"; U.S. CIA, *Soviet Weapons Industry*; J. M. Cooper, "The Civilian Production of the Soviet Defense Industry," in *Technical Progress and Soviet Economic Development*, D. R. Amann and J. Cooper (Oxford: Blackwell, 1986); idem, "Technology Transfer between Military and Civilian Ministries," in *Gorbachev's Economic Plans*; Almquist, *Soviet Military Industry*; and J. M. Cooper, "The Scales of Output of Civilian Products by Enterprises of the Soviet Defence Industry,"*CREES SITS No. 3*(Birmingham: CREES, August 1988).

25. Cooper, "Soviet Defence Industry."

26. R. W. Campbell, "Management Spillovers from Soviet Space and Military Programmes," *Soviet Studies* 23, no. 4 (1972): 586–607; and Holloway, "Innovation in the Defence Sector."

27. Hanson, *Soviet Industrial Espionage*.

28. M. Agursky and H. Adomeit, "The Soviet Military-Industrial Complex," *Survey* 24, no. 2 (1979): 123.

29. Davis, "Priority and the Shortage Model."

30. Ericson, "Soviet Command Economy"; and Davis, "Priority and the Shortage Model."

31. Kornai, *Economics of Shortage,* chapters 10 and 12.

32. Ericson, "Soviet Command Economy."

33. J. Kornai, "The Soft Budget Constraint," *Kyklos* 39 (1986), Fasc. 1, pp. 3–30.

34. Kornai, *Economics of Shortage*.

35. Ericson, "Soviet Command Economy."

36. K. Crane, *Military Spending in Eastern Europe,* R-3444-USDP (Santa Monica, Calif.: RAND, 1987), p. 43. His estimates were adjusted upward to include R&D in accordance with the methodology of T. Alton et al., "East European Defense Expenditures, 1965–82," in U.S. Congress, Joint Economic Committee, *East European Economies: Slow Growth in the 1980s* (Washington, D.C.: GPO, 1985).

37. Becker, *Burden of Soviet Defense,* pp. 15–17.

38. See Ia. E. Chadaev, *Ekonomika SSSR v gody velikoi otechestvennoi voiny* (Moscow: Mysl', 1985); and M. Harrison, *Soviet Planning in Peace and War, 1938–1945* (Cambridge: Cambridge University Press, 1985).

39. U.S. Congress, Joint Economic Committee, *Allocation of Resources in the Soviet Union and China, 1983* (Washington, D.C.: GPO, 1984); and idem, *Allocation of Resources in the Soviet Union and China, 1984* (Washington, D.C.: GPO, 1985).

40. L. Kurtzweg, "Trends in Soviet Gross National Product," in *Gorbachev's Economic Plans,* p. 136.

41. See my comments in the section entitled "Responsiveness to Tolerance-Limit Violations" concerning an alternative interpretation of trends in defense spending when measured in current rubles. Also see Becker, "Gorbachev's Defense-Economic Dilemma," pp. 379, 384; and Davis, "Defense and Civilian Sectors."

42. Kornai, *Economics of Shortage,* chapter 10.

43. Davis, "Priority and the Shortage Model."

44. B. Parrott, *Politics and Technology in the Soviet Union* (Cambridge, Mass.: MIT Press, 1985), pp. 183–85.

45. C. Davis, "Economic and Political Aspects of the Military-Industrial Complex in the USSR," in *Economics and Politics in the USSR.*

46. C. Davis, "Perestroika in the Soviet Defense Sector, 1985–87: National Security Elite Participation and Turnover," paper presented at the Conference on Elites and Political Power in the USSR, Birmingham, England, July 1–2, 1987; and Davis, "Defense and Civilian Sectors."

47. U.S. Congress, Joint Economic Committee, *Soviet Union and China, 1983,* p. 94.

48. Cockburn, *Soviet Military Machine,* p. 141.

49. M. Voslensky, *Nomenklatura: The Soviet Ruling Class* (Garden City, N.Y.: Doubleday, 1984); and D. K. Willis, *Klass: How Russians Really Live* (New York: St. Martin's Press, 1985).

50. USSR Central Statistical Administration, *Narodnoe khoziaistvo SSSR v 1985 g.* (Moscow: Finansy i statistika, 1986), p. 397.

51. Agursky and Adomeit, "Soviet Military-Industrial Complex," p. 115.

52. Ibid.

53. Ibid.

54. Almquist, *Soviet Military Industry.*

55. Cockburn, *Soviet Military Machine,* p. 141.

56. Almquist, *Soviet Military Industry,* pp. 187–89.

57. Holloway, "Innovation in the Defence Sector," p. 302.

58. U.S. CIA, *Estimated Soviet Defense Spending: Trends and Prospects,* SR 78-10121 (Washington, D.C.: GPO, 1978).

59. Almquist, *Soviet Military Industry,* p. 120.

60. Ibid., pp. 122–24.

61. For information about military representatives, see U.S. CIA, *Soviet Weapons Industry;* "Voenpredy," *Krasnaia zvezda,* January 27, 1987; and Almquist, *Soviet Military Industry,* pp. 128–30.

62. Cockburn, *Soviet Military Machine,* p. 140.

63. Davis, "Soviet Armed Forces, 1975–85," pp. 54–55.

64. U.S. Congress, Joint Economic Committee, *Soviet Union and China, 1984,* pp. 7–8.

65. R. F. Kaufman, "Causes of the Slowdown in Soviet Defense," *Soviet Economy,* no. 1 (1985).

66. Ibid.

67. Ibid., p. 16.

68. Kornai, *Economics of Shortage.*

69. J. Kornai, "Adjustment to Price and Quantity Signals in a Socialist Economy," *Economie appliquee* 15, no. 3 (1982): 508.

70. Davis, "Priority and the Shortage Model."

71. Kornai, *Economics of Shortage;* and idem, "Soft Budget Constraint."

72. Almquist, *Soviet Military Industry*, p. 163.

73. Ibid, p. 175.

74. U.S. CIA, *Soviet Weapons Industry*, p. 15.

75. Ibid., p. 5.

76. Cockburn, *Soviet Military Machine*, p. 133.

77. Almquist, *Soviet Military Industry*, p. 198.

78. J. McDonnell, "The Soviet Defense Industry as a Pressure Group," in *Soviet Naval Policy: Objectives and Constraints*, ed. M. McGwire, K. Booth, and J. McDonnell (New York: Praeger, 1975); and U.S. CIA, *Soviet Weapons Industry.*

79. Cockburn, *Soviet Military Machine*, pp. 133–39; and U.S. CIA, *Soviet Weapons Industry*, p. 20.

80. Cockburn, *Soviet Military Machine*, p. 132.

81. Ibid., pp. 132–37; and Almquist, *Soviet Military Industry*, p. 174.

82. Almquist, *Soviet Military Industry*, pp. 161, 163.

83. Ibid., p. 268.

84. U.S. Congress, Joint Economic Committee, *Soviet Union and China, 1984* and *1985;* and U.S. CIA, *Soviet Weapons Industry.*

85. Kaufman, "Slowdown in Soviet Defense," p. 14.

86. P. R. Gregory and R. C. Stuart, *Soviet Economic Structure and Performance*, 2d. ed. (New York: Harper & Row, 1981), p. 180.

87. U.S. CIA, *Soviet Weapons Industry*, p. 3.

88. Agursky and Adomeit, "Soviet Military-Industrial Complex," pp. 109, 123.

89. Cockburn, *Soviet Military Machine*, p. 123; and Almquist, *Soviet Military Industry*, p. 141.

90. U.S. CIA, *Soviet Weapons Industry*, p. 135.

91. Iu. Frolov, "Gosudarstvennyi zakaz," *Ekonomicheskaia gazeta*, no. 38 (1987); M. S. Gorbachev, "O zadachakh partii po korennoi perestroike upravleniia ekonomikoi," *Ekonomicheskaia gazeta*, no. 27 (July 1987); "Zakon S.S.S.R. o gosudarstvennom predpriiatii (ob'edinenii)," *Ekonomicheskaia gazeta*, no. 28 (July 1987).

92. Kornai, *Economics of Shortage.*

93. Davis, "Priority and the Shortage Model."

94. U.S. CIA, *Soviet Weapons Industry,* pp. 3–4.

95. Agursky and Adomeit, "Soviet Military-Industrial Complex," p. 109.

96. Kornai, *Economics of Shortage;* and idem, *Growth, Shortage and Efficiency* (Oxford: Basil Blackwell, 1982).

97. Davis, "Priority and the Shortage Model."

98. See various sections in Almquist, *Soviet Military Industry.*

99. Hanson, *Soviet Industrial Espionage;* and Lamoureux, "Western Technologies."

100. Kanet, "Soviet Arms Exports"; and Kramer, "Soviet Arms Transfers."

101. Almquist, *Soviet Military Industry.*

102. Ibid., p. 284.

103. Davis, "Defense and Civilian Sectors."

104. Davis, "*Perestroika.*"

105. Davis, "Defense and Civilian Sectors."

106. U.S. CIA, *Soviet Defense Spending,* pp. 7–9.

107. Cockburn, *Soviet Military Machine,* p. 12.

108. Almquist, *Soviet Military Industry,* p. 302.

109. U.S. CIA, *Soviet Defense Spending,* pp. 3–5.

110. Davis, "Defense and Civilian Sectors"; and Almquist, *Soviet Military Industry.*

111. Kaufman, "Slowdown in Soviet Defense"; and Davis, "Defense and Civilian Sectors."

112. Almquist, *Soviet Military Industry,* p. 84.

113. Davis, "*Perestroika.*"

114. U.S. CIA, *Soviet Weapons Industry,* p. 2.

115. A. Gorokhov, "Liudi. Rakety. Kontrol'," *Pravda,* January 27, 1988; and C. Walker, "Soviet Rocket-Makers Afraid for Jobs," *The Times* (London) January 28, 1988.

116. U.S. CIA, *Soviet Weapons Industry,* p. 38.

117. Ibid., p. 8.

118. Almquist, *Soviet Military Industry,* pp. 156–79.

119. Holloway, "Innovation in the Defence Sector"; Cockburn, *Soviet Military Machine;* and U.S. CIA, *Soviet Weapons Industry.*

7. Arthur J. Alexander

1. Joseph S. Berliner, *The Innovation Decision in Soviet Industry* (Cambridge, Mass.: MIT Press, 1976), chapter 1.

2. These points are taken from Berliner, ibid., pp. 70–72.

3. This point is made by Gur Ofer, "Soviet Economic Growth: 1928–1985," *Journal of Economic Literature* (December 1987):1802.

4. Berliner, *Soviet Industry*, p. 33.

5. The development of NPOs is described by Julian Cooper, "Innovation for Innovation in Soviet Industry," in *Industrial Innovation in the Soviet Union*, ed. R. Amann and J. Cooper (New Haven, Conn.: Yale University Press, 1982), pp. 456–63.

6. Ibid., pp. 478–80.

7. Ibid., p. 479.

8. Berliner, *Soviet Industry*, p. 78.

9. A. S. Becker, *Soviet Central Decisionmaking and Economic Growth: A Summing*, R-3349-AF (Santa Monica, Calif.: RAND Corporation, January 1986), pp. 9, 19–21.

10. It is not clear when the VPK was established in its present form, but from the 1930s chief designers in aviation performed functions similar to those now established by VPK decisions, although they did not have authority beyond their own ministry.

11. Ofer, "Soviet Economic Growth," p. 1799.

12. Ibid., p. 1800.

13. Paul Cocks, "Soviet Science and Technology Strategy: Borrowing from the Defense Sector," in U.S. Congress, Joint Economic Committee, *Gorbachev's Economic Plans*, vol. 2 (Washington, D.C.: Government Printing Office, November 1987).

14. Ibid., p. 154.

15. Gertrude E. Schroeder, "Anatomy of Gorbachev's Economic Reform," in *Gorbachev's Economic Plans*, p. 234.

16. Ibid., p. 235.

8. Stephen M. Meyer

Research for this paper was supported by the U.S. Department of Defense Office of Net Assessment. The views expressed are those of the author. I would like to thank Judyth Twigg for her comments on an earlier draft.

1. See, for example, William T. Lee, *The Estimation of Soviet Defense Expenditures, 1955–1975: An Unconventional Approach* (New York: Praeger, 1977); Paul Cockle, "Analyzing Soviet Defense Spending: The Debate in Perspective," *Survival* 20, no. 5 (September/October 1978): 66–70; Franklyn D. Holzman, "Soviet Military Spending: Assessing the Numbers Game," *International Security* 6, no. 4: 78–101; Steven Rosefielde, *False Science* (New Brunswick, N.J.: Transaction, 1982); U.S. Central Intelligence Agency (CIA), Directorate of Intelligence, *A Guide to Monetary Measures of Soviet Defense Activities* (Springfield, Virginia: National Technical Information Service, 1987).

2. There are some notable exceptions. An especially insightful piece that was the stimulus for my own work is Abraham Becker, *Soviet Central Decisionmaking and Economic Growth*, R-3349-AF (Santa Monica, Calif.: RAND, 1986). Some uniquely valuable work has been done by Arthur Alexander on lower levels of defense acquisition decision-making. See, for example, Arthur Alexander, "Decision-Making in Soviet Weapons Procurement," *Adelphi Papers*, nos. 147 and 148 (Winter 1978–79).

3. Among the more revealing references are A. Parkamenko, "Analysis of Armament Systems," *Military Thought*, no. 1, pp. 33–42; B. Makeev, "Nekotorye vzgliady na teoriiu vooruzheniia VMF," *Morskoi sbornik*, no. 4 (1982): 27–31; V. M. Raev, *Za ekonomiiu i berezhlivost' v voiskovom khoziaistve* (Moscow: Voenizdat, 1985); O. A. Vestman and Iu. N. Shvarev, "Voenno-ekonomicheskii analiz, ego zadachi i osnovnye printsipi," *Morskoi sbornik*, no. 5 (1966): 28–32; Iu. Solnyshkov, *Optimizatsiia vybora vooruzheniia, 1965: ekonomicheskie faktory i vooruzhenie* (Moscow: Voenizdat, 1973). A detailed examination of the defense-economic decision-making process is found in Stephen M. Meyer, *Defending the USSR* (forthcoming).

4. The exact boundaries between Politburo and Defense Council authority remain vague. For our purposes it is sufficient to recognize that the top political leadership of the USSR heads Level 1 decision-making, irrespective of the particular forum.

5. I will use the term "defense budgeting" as shorthand for decision-making on defense resource allocation. I do not impart any fiscal or budgetary meaning to the term.

6. See the discussion by A. Gurov, "Rezhim ekonomii," *Krasnaia zvezda*, October 15, 1985, pp. 2–3; "27-oi s'ezd KRPP o dal'neishem ukreplenii oboronosposobnosti strany i povyshenii boevoi gotovnosti vooruzhennykh sil," *Voenno-istoricheskii zhurnal*, no. 4 (1986): 3–12; M.

Iazykov, "Vo glave voennogo stroitel'stva," *Krasnaia zvezda*, December 3, 1986, pp. 2–3.

7. See N. Karasev, "Sledovat' logike permen," *Krasnaia zvezda*, June 5, 1988, p. 2, on the requirement that the Ministry of Defense submit annual plans to Gosplan. By definition, coordination of five-year plans would be even more important, since annual plans attempt to adjust expectations to actual performance. Even after the Gorbachev economic reforms take effect, state orders will still play an important role in economic planning and will remain the basis of defense-sector activity. In fact, one can imagine how coordination between the defense plan and the general economic plan might become even tighter as state orders decrease in relative size over time.

8. Lincoln Bloomfield, Walter C. Clemens, and Franklyn Griffiths, *Krushchev and the Arms Race* (Cambridge, Mass.: MIT, 1966); Michael Deane, *Political Control of the Soviet Armed Forces* (New York: Crane, Russak, 1977); Timothy Colton, *Commissars, Commanders and Civilian Authority* (Cambridge: Harvard, 1979); Stephen M. Meyer, "The Sources and Prospects of Gorbachev's New Political Thinking on Security," *International Security* 13, no. 2 (Fall 1988); idem, "The Near-Term Impact of SDI on Soviet Strategic Program: An Institutional Perspective," in *The Future of SDI*, ed. Joseph S. Nye, Jr. and James A. Schear (Lanham, Md.: University Press of America, 1988).

9. See Raymond Garthoff, "New Thinking in Soviet Military Doctrine," *Washington Quarterly* (Summer 1988): 131–58; Meyer, "Gorbachev's New Political Thinking on Security," pp. 124–63.

10. Undoubtedly, many first-order disagreements appeared between these two Level 2 institutions during initial planning stages. In such instances the Ministry of Defense first wrangles with Gosplan on an institution-to-institution basis, working through Gosplan's military department. In most cases, disputes were resolved at this level. It is, to be sure, in these institutions' interest to resolve disputes at Level 2, rather than engage the top political leadership. However, when problems were not resolved "quietly," the dispute was ultimately moved to the Politburo/Defense Council for resolution.

11. I am making a crucial distinction between allocative mechanisms and accounting mechanisms. The former are the basis upon which resources are apportioned among claimants; the latter are *ex post facto* tools for implementing the distribution of resources. The author has had the opportunity to conduct interviews with numerous high-level Soviet defense officials over the past two years. While many expressed no

concern about being quoted directly, others did. Consequently, in place of naming specific individuals, I have simply designated these sources "Interviews." I am open to requests for further information from those with recognized scholarly interests.

12. It was explained during interviews that the canonical 20 billion ruble figure represents "out-of-pocket expenses for the Ministry of Defense," explicitly excluding weapons procurement. It is likely that this figure also includes direct fiscal allocations to the Ministry of Defense to finance those parts of R&D and operations and maintenance that are contracted outside its own network.

13. Interviews. This does not mean that the Ministry of Defense does not have a ruble-based budget; it certainly does. But this budget is for all intents and purposes an accounting tool, not a decision-making tool.

14. Interviews with high-level Soviet defense officials clearly support the "materials balance" approach. They emphasize that it is done on a program correlation basis.

15. A. Fedoseev, *Zapadnaia* (Frankfurt: Posev, 1979), pp. 161–73. There does appear to be a Ministry of Defense R&D budget, some of which is "spent" by the ministry itself and some of which is spent by the armed services. See E. Zhuravlev, "Upravleniia poiskom," *Krasnaia zvezda,* May 8, 1987. E. Zhuravlev, the chief of a scientific research department at the Timoshenko Military Academy of Chemical Defense, suggests that the chief customers of R&D products also become the chief distributors of material technical and financial means, freeing the Ministry of Defense budget of R&D. This implies that the ministries, rather than the Ministry of Defense, should pick up the tab.

16. A. Plotnikov, "Den'gi est', a platit' nechem," *Krasnaia zvezda,* April 21, 1988, p. 2.

17. "General'nyi shtab," *Voennyi entsikolopedicheskii solvar'* (Moscow: Voenizdat, 1986), pp. 185–86. In fact, there are some hints—albeit presented in historical allegory—that the armed-service chiefs have come to resent this development. M. A. Gareev, *M. V. Frunze—voennyi teoretik* (Moscow: Voenizdat, 1984), p. 189.

18. Eugene Rumer, *Military History and Strategic Assessment in Soviet Military Thought,* doctoral dissertation, Department of Political Science, Massachusetts Institute of Technology, 1988.

19. The existence of these *a priori* Level 2 resource ceilings is confirmed in Iu. Solnyshkov, *Optimizatsiia vybora vooruzheniia* (Moscow: Voenizdat, 1968), pp. 84–86; Makeev, "Nekotorye vzgliady na teoriiu

vooruzheniia VMF," pp. 28–29; Parkamenko, "Analysis of Armament Systems," pp. 35, 39.

20. Even though the armed services would not know what their share of the defense pie was going to be, they, like corresponding units of industrial ministries, are able to estimate resource needs on the basis of past and current projects, norms and models, and plain guesswork. The approximate first-order ruble costs are based on defense-sector ruble prices and are not comparable to civil-sector prices. Interviews indicate that prices are not comparable even within the defense sector.

21. U.S. CIA, Directorate of Intelligence, *Monetary Measures of Soviet Defense Activities*, pp. 2–7.

22. Interviews.

23. Makeev, "Nekotorye vzgliady na teoriiu vooruzheniia VMF," pp. 28–29.

24. Ibid.

25. Interviews.

26. The collegium also gives final approval to the draft defense plan, though this is largely pro forma [Interviews]. If the Ministry of Defense operates as other ministries do, then actual decision authority within the collegium resides with the minister of defense. Nevertheless, if for no other reason than institutional harmony, he almost certainly makes his decision with the advice of the collegium.

27. This sequence of events is suggested in P. T. Ablamonov, *O dvazhdy geroe sovetskogo soiuza S. G. Gorshkove* (Moscow: Politizdat, 1986): 32–33. Once the Brezhnev Politburo was swept aside, so was Gorshkov, and, it appears, any further expansion of the Soviet surface fleet. The new chief of the Soviet Navy, Admiral Chernavin, has reaffirmed the navy's more traditional emphasis on submarines and land-based air-power. He has also said that further quantitative enlargement of segments of the fleet is not expected. See the interview with Chernavin in V. Shmyganovskii, "V dal'nem pokhode," *Izvestiia*, July 26, 1987, pp. 2–3.

28. Interviews. While armed-service chiefs theoretically have the authority to use allotted resources as they desire, in fact they are prohibited from shifting resources around by strict compartmentalization within program categories.

29. Interviews.

30. Victor Yevsikov, *Re-entry Technology and the Soviet Space Program* (Falls Church, Va.: Delphic Associates, 1982).

31. There is some ambiguity as to whether cost effectiveness was well established at the time. Although there are numerous references to

cost analysis in Soviet works, interviews strongly suggest that it is still not a serious decision-making tool.

32. V. Burov and L. Khudiakov, "Razvitie metodov issled-ovatel'skogo proektirovaniia korablei," *Morskoi sbornik,* no. 10 (1985): 66–70; Makeev, "Nekotorye vzgliady na teoriiu vooruzheniia VMF."

33. Weapons designers are acutely aware of the severe penalties of cost overruns on weapons projects. They stay strictly within agreed-upon contract price. [Personal communication with Arthur Alexander, based on his interviews.]

34. See O. Falichev, "Tonkaia Nit'," *Krasnaia zvezda,* October 1, 1987, p. 2, for an incredible discussion of the total absence of radio communications between battalion level antiair defense (PVO) units and subordinate units because authorized equipment was never provided.

35. One of the few researchers to pay any attention to this issue has been Rebecca Strode, "The Soviet Armed Forces: Adaptation to Resource Scarcity," *The Washington Quarterly* (Spring 1986): 55–69.

36. "Economizing" of O&M and construction materials has been a major campaign among the armed forces since the early 1980s. It is an ever-present theme throughout the military press. See Stephen M. Meyer, *The Soviet Economy and the Demands of Military Preparedness* (Cambridge, Mass.: MIT Center for International Studies, 1983), pp. 83–85.

37. There is a link between economizing on O&M and cuts in procurement allotments. If a service knows that its procurement allotment is going to be reduced, it may impose a reduction on operations in order to increase the service life of its major weapons systems as a hedge against a decline in its forces. The Soviet navy in particular seems to have adopted this approach with its surface fleet in the last several years.

38. His kick-off speech on this subject was delivered to an all-army conference in 1977. See D. F. Ustinov, "V interesakh povysheniia boevoi gotovnosti," in *Izbrannye rechi i stat'i* (Moscow: Politizdat, 1979), pp. 402–12.

39. Stephen M. Meyer, *"Economizing" in the Soviet Military Literature: Patterns among Service Journals,* Soviet Security Studies Working Paper (Cambridge, Mass.: MIT Center for International Studies, 1989).

40. *Jane's Defence Weekly,* "Economics Force Cut-Back in Naval Power," March 26, 1988, p. 600.

41. William Odom, "Who Controls Whom in Moscow?," *Foreign Policy,* no. 25 (Winter 1975): 195–210.

42. Meyer, "Gorbachev's New Political Thinking on Security," pp. 124–63.

43. Formal definitions aside, Soviet military doctrine addresses the following questions:

- What are the greatest external dangers facing the Soviet Union?

- What are Soviet options for coping with those dangers?

- What kinds of military capabilities are required?

- How much is enough?

- How should it be allocated?

44. That the Soviet Union does follow this practice is implicitly acknowledged in S. A. Bartenev, *Ekonomicheskoe protivoborstvo v voine* (Moscow: Voenizdat, 1986), p. 9.

45. Meyer, "Gorbachev's New Political Thinking on Security," discusses how Gorbachev is attempting explicitly to change the definition of the threat.

46. Ibid.

47. Interview. Priority conflicts are discussed for the particular case of Soviet responses to SDI in Stephen M. Meyer, "The Near-Term Impact of SDI on Soviet Strategic Programs."

9. Gregory G. Hildebrandt

1. For a discussion of the concerns of the Soviet General Staff and of Marshall Nikolai Ogarkov in particular about the emergent "scientific-technical revolution in military affairs," see Jeremy R. Azrael, *The Soviet Civilian Leadership and the Military High Command, 1976–1986*, R-3521-AF (Santa Monica, Calif.: RAND Corporation, June 1987).

2. For a discussion of these models, see Gregory G. Hildebrandt, ed., *RAND Conference on Models of the Soviet Economy, October 11-12, 1984*, R-3322 (Santa Monica, Calif.: RAND, October 1985).

3. The model is operated with 1985 as the base year. Soviet GNP and defense burden data for that year are contained in U.S. Central Intelligence Agency (CIA) and Defense Intelligence Agency (DIA), *Gorbachev's Modernization Program: A Status Report*, paper presented to U.S. Con-

gress, Joint Economic Committee, Subcommittee on National Security Economics (Washington, D.C.: Government Printing Office, March 1987). The investment and consumption shares of GNP and the value of civilian capital stock in 1985 are contained in U.S. CIA, *Handbook of Economic Statistics, 1987: A Reference Aid*, CPAS 87-10001 (Washington, D.C.: GPO, September 1987). The labor-force data to 2010 were obtained from the Bureau of the Census. For a discussion of capital formation, see James Noren, *Soviet Investment Strategy under Gorbachev*, paper prepared for the Eighteenth National Convention of the American Association for the Advancement of Slavic Studies, New Orleans, November 20–23, 1986.

4. If resources, but not priority, are transferred to consumption, a measured ruble's worth of defense may generate less than a ruble's worth of consumption. On the other hand, transfer of a ruble of defense to consumption, with the transfer of priority at the margin, might yield more than a ruble of consumption. If the defense sector were to lose its priority status, the point depicted as the current output level might no longer be feasible, and the entire production-possibility curve would shift.

5. Figure 9.6 most closely approximates the CIA model, SOVSIM. For a discussion of a recent application of this model, see Robert L. Kellogg, "Modeling Soviet Modernization: An Economy in Transition," *Soviet Economy* (January–March 1988): 36–57. A description of the current version of SOVECON is contained in Ed. A. Hewett et al., "On the Feasibility of Key Targets in the Soviet Twelfth Five-Year Plan (1986–90)," in U.S. Congress, Joint Economic Committee, *Gorbachev's Economic Plans*, vol. 1 (Washington, D.C.: GPO, November 1987), pp. 27–53.

In its current version, SOVECON does not contain labor-force inputs to the model's production functions as described by Figure 9.6. Rather, output in each sector depends only on the sector's capital stock and is determined by specifying a value for capital productivity in each sector. Furthermore, total gross investment is determined in SOVECON by dividing the calculated level of machinery and equipment investment by this investment category's exogenously specified share of total gross investment.

6. The CIA building-block estimates of military procurement are reported in U.S. CIA, *A Guide to Monetary Measures of Soviet Defense Activities*, SOV 87-10069 (Washington, D.C.: GPO, November 1987). PlanEcon reports its residual estimate in Jan Vanous and Bryan Roberts, "Time to Choose between Tanks and Tractors: Why Gorbachev Must

Come to the Negotiating Table or Face a Collapse of His Ambitious Modernization Program," *PlanEcon Report* 2, nos. 25 and 26 (June 27, 1986).

7. See Bonnie K. Matosich, "Estimating Soviet Military Hardware Purchases: The 'Residual' Approach" in *Gorbachev's Economic Plans*, pp. 431–61.

8. See Michael Zelina and George Pugh, *Reconstruction of the Unified Soviet National Economic Balance Tables, 1970–1983: A Replication and Evaluation of Steinberg's Reconstruction Methodology*, vol. 1: Technical, DSA Report #790 (Arlington, Va.: DSA, March 1987). Also see Dmitri Steinberg, *Estimating Total Soviet Military Expenditures: An Alternative Approach Based on Reconstructed Soviet National Accounts*, January 1987.

9. RAND solves this type of problem, while DSA maximizes a utility function that contains defense and consumption as arguments. Because these models do not run over an infinitely long planning horizon, it is necessary to impose a restriction on the terminal values of the capital stocks. This insures that the model continues to take a long-sighted view as the end of the planning horizon is approached. The cost of this restriction, however, is that the models must be used carefully if one is interested in assessing the effects of various modernization programs on GNP. With terminal capital specified, and the size of the labor force exogenously specified, the value of GNP at the end of the planning horizon is essentially determined in the model. To assess GNP development issues in the near term, it may be necessary to operate the model for extended periods of time. But it is still difficult to specify long-run terminal capital values (or shadow prices) that reflect the preferences of Soviet leadership.

10. Reported in *RAND Conference on Models of the Soviet Economy*, pp. 63–64.

11. Ibid., pp. 95–98.

12. The research summarized here is being conducted with Peter Staugaard and is sponsored by OSD/Net Assessment. It will be published as *The Soviet Priority Economy: Modeling the Conflict between Gold and the Sword* (Santa Monica, Calif.: RAND, forthcoming). Other work on this project includes Lee D. Badgett, *Defeated by a Maze: Historical and Structural Aspects of Modeling the Soviet Economy and Its Defense-Industrial Sector*, N-2644-NA (Santa Monica, Calif.: RAND, October 1988); Richard E. Ericson, *Priority, Duality, and Penetration in the Soviet Command Economy*, N-2643 (Santa Monica, Calif.: RAND, December 1988); and Alvin

H. Bernstein, *Soviet Defense Spending: The Spartan Analogy* (Santa Monica, Calif.: RAND, forthcoming).

13. One could also interpret "infrastructure" as any potential bottleneck sector that does not directly produce some component of final demand.

14. *Materials Equipment Supply* (Journal of Gassnab), November 1967.

15. See David Holloway, "Economics and the Soviet Weapons Acquisition Process," in *Soviet Military Economic Relations,* proceedings of a workshop sponsored jointly by the Joint Economic Committee, Subcommittee on International Trading, Finance, and Security Economics and the Library of Congress Congressional Research Service (Washington, D.C.: GPO, 1983), p. 47.

16. U.S. DIA, *USSR: Military Economic Trends and Resource Allocations, 1983* (Washington, D.C.: GPO, August 1983), p. 1.

17. For a discussion of the military's support of civilian activities, see Julian Cooper, "Technology Transfer between Military and Civilian Ministries," *Gorbachev's Economic Plans,* pp. 388–404.

18. Abraham Becker, *Ogarkov's Complaint and Gorbachev's Dilemma: The Soviet Defense Budget and Party-Military Conflict,* R-3541-AF (Santa Monica, Calif.: RAND, December 1987).

10. Vladimir Kontorovich

This paper is based in part on research supported by a contract from the U.S. Secretary of Defense Director of Net Assessment.

1. Abraham S. Becker, *Soviet Central Decisionmaking and Economic Growth,* R-3349-AF (Santa Monica, Calif.: RAND Corporation, January 1986), pp. 50–51; idem, "Gorbachev's Defense-Economic Dilemma," in U.S. Congress, Joint Economic Committee, *Gorbachev's Economic Plans,* vol. 1 (Washington, D.C.: Government Printing Office, November 1987), p. 381; and idem, *Ogarkov's Complaint and Gorbachev's Dilemma,* R-3541-AF (Santa Monica, Calif.: RAND, December 1987), pp. 14–15.

2. See Becker, *Soviet Central Decisionmaking,* pp. 50–51; V. Kontorovich, "Reagan Is the Father of 'Glasnost'," *Chicago Tribune,* August 29, 1987; and Russel Bova, "The Soviet Military and Economic Reform," *Soviet Studies* (July 1988).

3. U.S. Congress, Joint Economic Committee, Subcommittee on Economic Resources, Competitiveness, and Security Economics, *Allocation*

of Resources in the Soviet Union and China, 1985 (Washington, D.C.: Government Printing Office, 1986), p. 117.

4. It has been suggested that the technology underlying the new weapon systems itself creates unusual difficulties for the Soviet economy (Shelly Deutch, "The Soviet Weapons Industry: An Overview," in U.S. Congress, Joint Economic Committee, *Gorbachev's Economic Plans,* p. 424). But the difficulties in mastering new technologies must have looked just as formidable in the past as they do now.

5. Becker, *Soviet Central Decisionmaking,* p. 51.

6. Abel G. Aganbegyan, "Programma korennoi perestroiki," *Ekonomika i organizatsiia promyshlennogo proizvodstva,* no. 11 (1987): 7; "Tezisy Tsentral'nogo Komiteta KPSS k XIX Vsesoiuznoi partiinoi konferentsii," *Pravda,* May 27, 1988, p. 1.

7. On consumption, see Aleksei Ochkin, "Naguliaet li tsena pribyl'?" *Nash sovremennik,* no. 12 (1987): 155. On investment, see the overview of Soviet estimates in V. Kontorovich and B. Rumer, *Inflation in the Soviet Investment Complex* (Princeton, N.J.: Command Economic Research, May 1988): 70–77.

8. Becker, pp. 19–21.

9. R. Sagdeev, "Gde my poteriali temp," *Izvestiia,* April 28, 1988; G. I. Marchuk, "Perestroika nauchnoi deiatel'nosti akademicheskikh uchrezhdenii v svete reshenii XXVII s'ezda KPSS," *Vestnik AN SSSR,* no. 1 (1987): 3–4.

10. See speeches at the last Party Congress by Solomentsev, Grishkiavichius, and many others; also, N. I. Ryzhkov, *O gosudarstvennom plane ekonomicheskogo i sotsial'nogo razvitiia SSSR na 1986–1990 gody* (Moscow: Politizdat, 1986); V. Shalgunov, "Peizazh s pripiskoi," *Pravda,* July 6, 1986.

11. See, for example, V. I. Belousov, "Pochemu novatsii ne vstrechaiut ovatsii?" *Ekonomika i organizatsiia promyshlennogo proizvodstva,* no. 8 (1980): 197; A. A. Bogaev and A. A. Savel'ev, "Voprosy regulirovaniia chislennosti personala i stimulirovaniia nauchnogo truda," *Naukovedenie i informatika,* no. 23 (1982): 57–58; Iu. Arakelian and V. Gubarev, "Povyshaia trebovatel'nost'," *Pravda,* January 27, 1986; V. Medvedev, "Rasshiriat' set' mezhotraslev ob'edinenii," *Ekonomicheskaia gazeta,* no. 7 (February 1986); V. Kushlin, "Sotsializm i nauchno-tekhnicheskii progress," *Ekonomicheskaia gazeta,* no. 41 (1987); Iu. Kaz'min, "Podenshchiki iz NII," *Pravda,* April 9, 1987.

12. V. I. Belousov, "Intensifikatsiia novatorskogo dvizheniia," *Ekonomika i organizatsiia promyshlennogo proizvodstva,* no. 11 (1986): 15; A.

Solov'ev, "Ekonomicheskie i organizatsionnye usloviia vnedreniia novoi tekhniki v proizvodstvo," *Planovoe khoziaistvo*, no. 12 (1987): 64–65; V. M. Logachev et al., *Finansy i khozraschet v NII i KB* (Moscow: Finansy i statistika, 1987), pp. 39–40; G. Nesvetailov, "Organizatsiia fundamental'nykh issledovanii," *Voprosy ekonomiki*, no. 12 (1987): 55–56.

13. Nesvetailov, "Organizatsiia fundamental'nykh," pp. 55–56.

14. See V. Kontorovich, "Prototype Statistics as Indicators of Soviet R&D Priorities in Civilian and Military Machinebuilding," *Comparative Economic Studies* 30, no. 3 (Fall 1988), for a description of the data.

15. *Patent* denotes the inventor's certificate.

16. Nesvetailov, "Organizatsiia fundamental'nykh," p. 56.

17. On the general problems of measurement of R&D input and output, see Charles E. Falk, "The Measurement of Productivity of Science and Technology" in *Understanding Research and Development Productivity*, ed. Fusfelf and Langlois (New York: Pergamon Press, 1982); and Roberta Balstad Miller, "Measurement Issues in Research and Development Productivity" in Fusefeld and Langlois.

18. See, for example, William S. Comanor and Frederick Michael Scherer, "Patent Statistics as a Measure of Technical Change," *Journal of Political Economy*, vol. 77, Dec. 1969; L. G. Soete and Sally M. E. Wyatt, "The Use of Foreign Patenting as an Internationally Comparable Science and Technology Indicator," *Scientometrics*, vol. 5, no. 1 (1983); Robert E. Evenson, "International Invention: Implications for Technology Market Analysis," in *R&D, Patents, and Productivity*, ed. Zvi Griliches (Chicago: University of Chicago, 1984), pp. 107–114, as well as other papers in the same collection.

19. On the methodology of using output indicators, see Ariel Pakes and Zvi Griliches, "Patents and Research and Developoment at the Firm Level: A First Look" in Griliches, ed., *R&D, Patents, and Productivity*, pp. 55–61. Also see Keith Pavitt, "R&D Patenting and Innovative Activities," *Research Policy*, vol. 11 (1982).

20. See, for example, Kaz'min, "Podenshchiki iz NII"; and references in V. Kontorovich, *Research and Development Productivity in the USSR: Causes of Decline since the 1960s and the Prospects for the 1980s* (Princeton, N.J.: Command Economic Research, 1987), pp. 2, 312.

21. However, the share of another category of prototypes, those considered "matching the domestic/world level," has increased. Solov'ev, "Ekonomicheskie i organizatsionnye," p. 65; *Narodnoe khoziaistvo SSSR za 70 let* (Moscow: Finansy i statistika, 1987), p. 82.

22. See, for example, Kaz'min, "Podenshchiki iz NII."

23. See references in Kontorovich, *Research and Development Productivity in the USSR,* pp. 112–117, and Belousov, "Intensificatsiia novatorskogo," p. 16. According to the chairman of the State Committee on Inventions, "the share of inventions with low efficiency is very high. Some of them save tens or hundreds of rubles." I. Naiashkov, "Izobretatel'stvo: problemy i perspektivy," *Ekonomika i organizatsiia promyshlennogo proizvodstva,* no. 8 (1987): 26.

24. R. Leshchiner, "Nauchno-tekhnicheskii potentsial SSSR," *Politicheskoe samoobrazovanie,* no. 5 (1979): 25; G. M. Grinchel', *Izmerenie effektivnosti nauchno-tekhnicheskogo progressa* (Moscow: Ekonomika, 1974), p. 79; D. M. Palterovich, "Ekonomiia orudii truda," *Kommunist* 10, 1984, p. 57.

25. See W. F. Yankevich, "Analysis of Publication and Invention Productivity in Some Soviet Academic Institutions," *Scientometrics,* vol. 4, no. 6 (1982), on the relative inventive productivity of different disciplines.

26. Also, non-R&D activities that statistics include in R&D (such as meteorological service and geological survey) were receiving a declining share of resources.

27. This has been attributed to a depletion of the pool of potential inventions (Evenson, "International Invention," pp. 116–117, 119), or, alternatively, to the change in the propensity to patent (Frederic M. Scherer, "Comment," in *R&D, Patents, and Productivity,* ed. Griliches, p. 124).

28. Kontorovich, *Research and Development Productivity in the USSR,* section 1.3.

29. This discussion is condensed, and most references omitted for considerations of space. For fuller analysis and documentation, see Kontorovich, *Research and Development Productivity in the USSR,* parts III and IV.

30. According to Marchuk, the figure is 90 percent (note 9).

31. See, for example, Solov'ev, "Ekonomicheskie i organizatsionnye," pp. 65–66. The absurdity of command methods of managing R&D is clearly seen in the attempts to make researchers spend a full working week in their offices (V. I. Nikitinskii and L. V. Nikitinskii, "Rabochii den' Arkhimeda," *Ekonomika i organizatsiia promyshlennogo proizvodstva,* no. 11 [1986]).

32. Solov'ev, "Ekonomicheskie i organizatsionnye," p. 65, also cites other causes of decline in R&D productivity that overlap with those given here.

33. "O vakhterakh v nauke i nauke bez vakhterov," *Ekonomika i organizatsiia promyshlennogo proizvodstva,* no. 9 (1987), pp. 42–44.

34. See, for example, "Shtab otrasli," *Pravda,* March 4, 1987.

35. See, for example, Nesvetailov, "Organizatsiia fundamental'nykh," pp. 54–55.

36. See Kontorovich, *Research and Development Productivity in the USSR,* chapter 11.

37. Marchuk, "Perestroika nauchnoi," pp. 3–11.

38. David Holloway, *The Soviet Union and the Arms Race,* 2d. ed. (New Haven, Conn.: Yale University Press, 1984), pp. 141–145; Arthur J. Alexander, *R&D in Soviet Aviation,* R-589-PR (Santa Monica, Calif.: RAND, November 1970), p. 14.

39. See Louvan E. Nolting and Murray Feschbach, "Statistics on Research and Development Employment in the USSR," U.S. Department of Commerce, Bureau of the Census International Population Reports Series P-95, no. 76 (Washington, D.C.: GPO, June 1981), p. 44; Robert W. Campbell, *Reference Source on Soviet R&D Statistics, 1950–1978* (Washington, D.C.: National Science Foundation, 1978), pp. 24, 38; *Soviet R&D Statistics 1977–1980* (Washington, D.C.: National Science Foundation, 1980), p. 24, on comparison of R&D employment and expenditures in the two countries.

40. On the variety of military R&D institutions, see Harry Balzer et al., "Soviet R&D: Information and Insights from the Third Emigration," report to the National Council for Soviet and East European Research, Washington, D.C., 1985. Michael Agursky, *The Research Institute of Machine-Building Technology,* Soviet Institutions Series Paper no. 8 (Jerusalem: Soviet and East European Research Centre, Hebrew University, September 1976), contains a description of a nonelite military R&D institute.

41. Lev Chaiko, *Helicopter Construction in the USSR* (Washington, D.C.: Delphic Associates, 1986), pp. 69–71.

42. Henry E. Firdman, *Decision-Making in the Soviet Microelectronics Industry* (Washington, D.C.: Delphic Associates, 1985), p. 95.

43. Balzer et al., "Soviet R&D," p. 106.

44. Arthur J. Alexander, *Soviet Science and Weapons Acquisition,* R-2942-NAS (Santa Monica, Calif.: RAND, 1982), p. 11.

45. Agursky, *Machine-Building Technology,* pp. 36–38, 43; Firdman, *Soviet Microelectronics Industry,* p. 97.

46. Balzer, et al., "Soviet R&D," p. 108.

47. Agursky, *Machine-Building Technology,* pp. 38–39, 42, 47.

48. See A. Steinhaus, *The Beginnings of Soviet Military Electronics, 1948–1961* (Washington, D.C.: Delphic Associates, 1986), p. 119, on aging of management in military electronics.

49. Firdman, *Soviet Microelectronics Industry,* p. 95.

50. See Balzer et al., "Soviet R&D," p. 88, for interconnection of military and civilian R&D.

51. See, for example, Simon Kassel, *The Relationship between Science and the Military in the Soviet Union,* R-1457-DDRE/ARPA (Santa Monica, Calif.: RAND, July 1974), pp. 38–39; David Holloway, "Innovation in the Defence Sector," in *Industrial Innovation in the Soviet Union,* ed. R. Amann and J. Cooper (New Haven: Yale University, 1982), p. 314.

52. Karl Greenberg, *Central Materials Research Institute of the Soviet Ministry of the Defense Industry* (Washington, D.C.: Delphic Associates, 1986), pp. 5–6.

53. See Kontorovich, "Prototype Statistics," on identification of military-sector prototypes.

54. *Prototype* refers both to a weapon system and to its subsystems, parts, etc., that are being developed as separate projects. See *Sovetskaia voennaia entsiklopediia,* vol. 3 (Moscow: Voenizdat, 1977), pp. 616–17; Firdman, *Soviet Microelectronics Industry,* p. 68.

55. There is no reason to believe that the quality of prototypes in civilian ministries improved more than in military ministries. Taking quality into account should therefore not change our conclusion about diverging trends in civilian and military R&D.

56. Namely, printing equipment in 1981–1985.

57. See, for example, Richard R. Nelson, "Assessing Private Enterprise: An Exegesis of a Tangled Doctrine," *Bell Journal of Economics* 12, no. 1 (Spring 1981): 105–106.

58. L. S. Bliakhman, *Ekonomika nauchno-tekhnicheskogo progressa* (Moscow: Vysshaia shkola, 1979), p. 228; A. G. Koriagin, V. I. Plaksia, and V. V. Tsatsunkov, eds., *Sotsialisticheskoe vosproizvodstvo: dinamizm i effektivnost'* (Moscow: Mysl', 1983), p. 88; L. G. Marin and R. V. Pavelko, "Statisticheskie izuchenie obnovleniia produktsii mashinostroeniia," in Adademiia nauk SSSR, Tsenitral'nyi ekonomiko-matematicheskii institut, *Statisticheskoe issledovaniia v otrasliakh narodnogo khoziaistva* (Moscow: Nauka, 1974), p. 35; S. D. Beshelev and F. G. Gurvich, *Nevospolnimyi resurs* (Moscow: Nauka, 1986), p. 41.

59. "Rech' tovarishcha Dinkova V. A.," *Pravda,* March 3, 1986; V. K. Fal'tsman, "Mashinostroenie: puti peremen," *Ekonomika i organizatsiia*

promyshlennogo proizvodstva, no. 12 (1985): 14; "V Politburo TsK KPSS," *Pravda,* January 23, 1987.

60. See Richard F. Kaufman, "Causes of the Slowdown in Soviet Defense," *Soviet Economy* 1, no. 1 (1985).

61. V. Kontorovich, "Soviet Growth Slowdown: Econometric vs. Direct Evidence," *American Economic Review Papers and Proceedings* 76, no. 2.

11. Boris Z. Rumer

1. *Kommunist,* no. 8 (1985): 26.

2. *Narodnoe khoziaistvo SSSR v 1987 godu* (Moscow: Finansy i statistika, 1988), p. 49.

3. V. Fal'tsman, "Metodologicheskie problemy planirovaniia i prognozirovaniia uskoreniia razvitiia mashinostroeniia," *Ekonomika i matematicheskie metody,* no. 4 (1987): 579.

4. A. Komin, "Finansy i tseny," *Kommunist,* no. 9 (June 1987): 60.

5. V. Pavlov, "Radikal'naia reforma tsenoobrazovaniia," *Pravda,* August 25, 1987, p. 2.

6. *Metody i praktika opredeleniia effektivnosti kapital'nykh vlozhenii i novoi tekhniki,* no. 26 (1976): 107.

7. Vladimir Kontorovich and Boris Rumer, *Inflation in the Soviet Investment Complex* (Princeton, N.J.: Command Economic Research, 1988).

8. Konstantin Val'tukh, "Investitsionnyi kompleks i intensifikatsiia proizvodstva," *EKO,* no. 3 (1982):19.

9. *Ekonomicheskaia gazeta,* no. 11 (1986): 23, 25.

10. *Narodnoe khoziaistvo SSSR v 1986 godu,* p. 430.

11. Vasilii Seliunin, "Tempy razvitiia na vesakh potrebleniia," *Sotsialisticheskaia industriia,* January 5, 1988.

12. *Ekonomicheskaia gazeta,* no. 11 (1986): 26.

13. *Narodnoe khoziaistvo SSSR v 1986 godu,* p. 128.

14. Seliunin, "Tempy razvitiia na vesakh potrebleniia."

15. Peter Wiles and Moshe Efrat, *The Economics of Soviet Arms,* occasional paper no. 7 (London: Suntory-Toyota International Center for Economics and Related Disciplines, London School of Economics and Political Science), p. 1.

16. *Narodnoe khoziaistvo SSSR v 1986 godu,* p. 327.

17. Ibid., pp. 328–29.

18. Ibid., p. 330.

19. *Ekonomicheskaia gazeta*, no. 11 (1986): 24.

20. *Pravda*, June 12, 1985, p. 1.

21. A. Arbatov, "Problemy obespecheniia ekonomiki SSSR mineral'nym syr'em," *Voprosy ekonomiki*, no. 1 (1987): 40.

22. "Korennye zadachi mashinostroitelei," *Ekonomicheskaia gazeta*, no. 47 (1986).

23. "Mashinostroeniiu—operezhaiushchee razvitie," *Stanki i instrument*, no. 2 (1986): 3.

24. "Uroki khozrashcheta," *Pravda*, December 4, 1987, p. 2.

25. E. Gaidar, "Kursom ozdorovleniia," *Kommunist*, no. 2 (1988): 45.

26. Boris Rumer, "The Problems of Industrial Modernization in the USSR," in *The Soviet Economy: A New Course?* (Brussels: NATO, 1987), p. 241.

27. Ibid.

28. "Uroki khozrashcheta," *Pravda*, December 4, 1987, p. 2.

29. E. Ivanov, "Problema prioritetov v sotsialisticheskom planirovanii," *Planovoe khoziaistvo*, no. 11 (1987).

30. Ibid.

31. *Sotsialisticheskaia industriia*, January 24, 1988, p. 2; *Narodnoe khoziaistvo SSSR v 1986 godu*.

32. E. Gaidar, "Kursom ozdorovleniia," p. 44.

33. Ibid., p. 45.

34. Ibid., p. 44.

35. See letters to the editor of *Pravda*.

36. E. Gaidar, "Kursom ozdorovleniia," p. 45.

37. Ibid., p. 50.

38. V. Kirichenko and Iu. Uvarov, "Plan 88-go goda," *Planovoe khoziaistvo*, no. 12 (1987): 6.

39. Ibid.; "A na dele vse po staromu," *Sotsialisticheskaia industriia*," February 10, 1988, p. 4.

40. "V stroitel'stve poka bez peremen," *Izvestiia*, October 13, 1987.

41. Gaidar, "Kursom ozdorovleniia," p. 46.

42. V. Pchelkin et al., "Plan i povyshenie kontsentratsii v kapital'nom stroitel'stve," *Planovoe khoziaistvo*, no. 12 (1986): 78.

43. Gaidar, "Kursom ozdorovleniia," p. 46.

44. Pchelkin et al., "Plan i povyshenie," p. 78.

45. "Izvlech' urok," *Ekonomicheskaia gazeta*, no. 49 (1987): 8.

46. Gaidar, "Kursom ozdorovleniia," p. 46.

47. Ibid.

48. See B. Rumer, "USSR Investment Policy," *Problems of Communism* (September/October 1982): 59–60; idem, "Realities of Gorbachev's Economic Program," *Problems of Communism* (May/June 1986): 26–27; idem, "Industrial Modernization in the USSR," pp. 230–33.

49. V. Serov, "Investitsionnaia samostoiatel'nost'," *Ekonomicheskaia gazeta*, no 2 (1988).

50. Ibid.

51. Gaidar, "Kursom ozdorovleniia," p. 45.

52. *Sotsialisticheskaia industriia*, November 3, 1987, p. 3.

Index